Robert Sihler

STUDENT MAP MANUAL

Historical Geography of the Bible Lands

History & Sources — H.T. Frank
J. Monson
General Archaeology — D. Urman
Jerusalem Archaeology — S. Margalit
Indexes: Transliteration — R. Reich
Roman Road System — I. Roll

Cartography — S. Duieb
Base Relief-Map — M. Karmon
Satellite Imagery — K. Estep
Design — T. Rigg

No titles, dates, legends.

B

1 — 6-6
2 — 8-8
3 — 42
4 — 48
5 — 44

Published as part of:
THE WIDE SCREEN PROJECT: Historical Geography of the Bible Lands

PICTORIAL ARCHIVE (Near Eastern History) Est.

Publishers:
Pictorial Archive (Near Eastern History) Est.
Printed in Israel by the Survey of Israel

Photon Type-setting:
Yanetz Ltd., Jerusalem

First Edition: November 1979
Reprinted: March 1983

East-Orientation

← East-West Axis →

↑ North-South Axis ↓

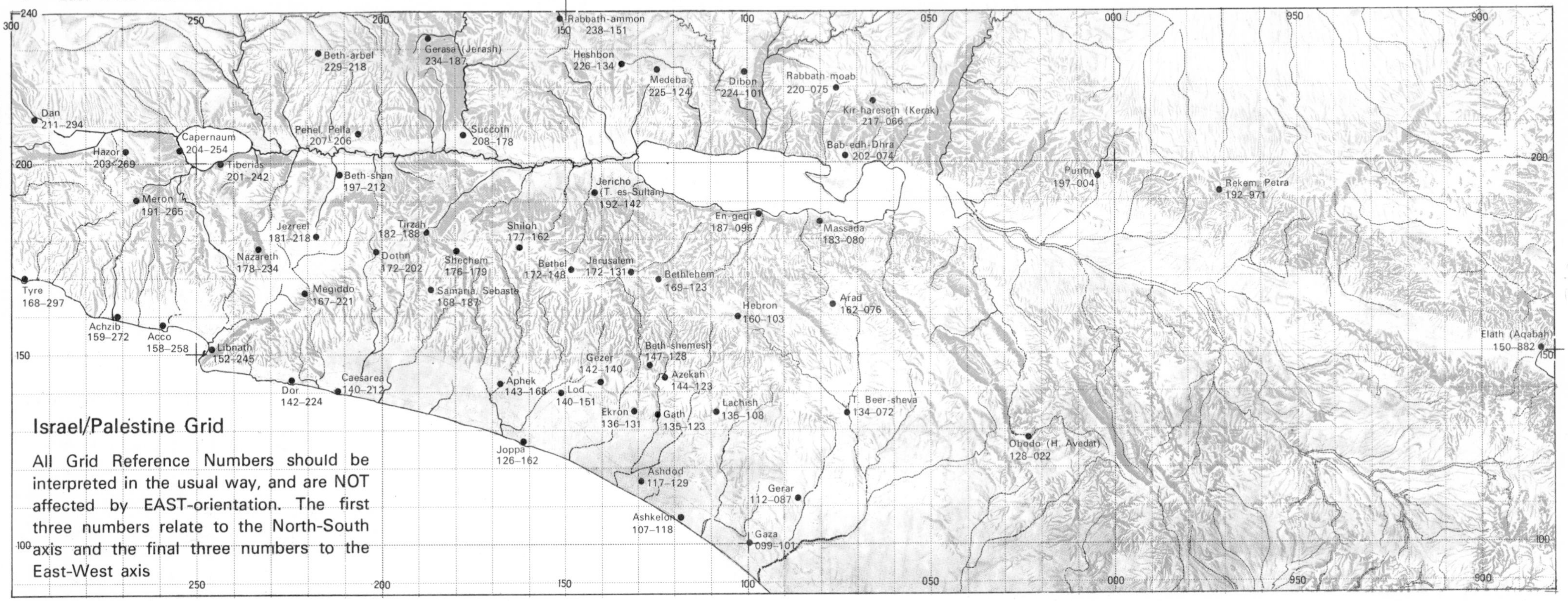
Israel/Palestine Grid
All Grid Reference Numbers should be interpreted in the usual way, and are NOT affected by EAST-orientation. The first three numbers relate to the North-South axis and the final three numbers to the East-West axis
Dan 211–294
Hazor 203–269
Capernaum 204–254
Tiberias 201–242
Meron 191–265
Beth-arbel 229–218
Pehel, Pella 207–206
Gerasa (Jerash) 234–187
Succoth 208–178
Beth-shan 197–212
Rabbath-ammon 238–151
Heshbon 226–134
Medeba 225–124
Dibon 224–101
Rabbath-moab 220–075
Kir-hareseth (Kerak) 217–066
Bab edh-Dhra 202–074
Punon 197–004
Rekem, Petra 192–971
Jericho (T. es-Sultan) 192–142
En-gedi 187–096
Massada 183–080
Jezreel 181–218
Tirzah 182–188
Dothn 172–202
Shechem 176–179
Shiloh 177–162
Bethel 172–148
Jerusalem 172–131
Bethlehem 169–123
Nazareth 178–234
Megiddo 167–221
Samaria, Sebaste 168–187
Tyre 168–297
Achzib 159–272
Acco 158–258
Libnath 152–245
Hebron 160–103
Arad 162–076
Beth-shemesh 147–128
Gezer 142–140
Azekah 144–123
Caesarea 140–212
Dor 142–224
Aphek 143–168
Lod 140–151
Ekron 136–131
Gath 135–123
Lachish 135–108
T. Beer-sheva 134–072
Joppa 126–162
Ashdod 117–129
Gerar 112–087
Ashkelon 107–118
Gaza 099–101
Obodo (H. Avedat) 128–022
Elath (Aqabah) 150–882

All Pictorial Archive mapping is EAST-oriented. This is not as heretical as it might at first appear. The Bible itself is East-oriented too, as the Hebrew words for the points of the compass indicate (Viz. Yamin, Semol, Qedem, Ahor & Yam: see Genesis 13.14; Isaiah 9.11 and Psalm 89.13 etc.). The Medeba Mosaic map is one of the most ancient available and it also is East-oriented, as are many other early and Mediaeval maps. However, the main reason for this RETURN to East-orientation was dictated by the WIDE SCREEN PROJECT in which the wide screen format necessitated a HORIZONTAL map for inclusion in the audio-visual presentations. Since the map of the Holy Land is elongated along its North-South axis, there was no alternative but to turn the map and East-orientation was chosen, rather than West-orientation, because of the Biblical precedent. However, this new orientation to the East conferred other important advantages, which might have justified this change on their own.

(1) It is possible to hang a MUCH LARGER map of the Holy Land, if it is horizontal, rather than vertical. Thus the DISPLAY Version of the Student Maps 'A' and 'B' became possible **solely because of the horizontal format.** Indeed, the teaching of historical geography of the Holy Land has been held back because of the absence of such a large and detailed map, for classroom use.

(2) With East orientation the Mediterranean Sea area, which covers 30% of the NORTH sheet, can be made available for an index or other related text. Since most of the history is concentrated in the North, this is an ideal position for any supporting text. With NORTH-oriented maps this area is usually wasted.

(3) Nearly all the geographical regions in the Holy Land are elongated along the North-South axis. With East-orientation this axis is horizontal and, as a result, these geographical regions fit very well into the wide screen format, since this too is horizontal. Since the history of the Holy Land reflects a strong regional element, wide-screen slides of GEOGRAPHICAL regions also emphasise HISTORICAL priorities.

Foreword From the Publisher

STUDENT MAP MANUAL: Satellite Edition

In this new 'Satellite' edition, two separate maps have been included:

The 'General' Map **The Satellite 'Key' Map**

The 'General' Map places the Holy Land in the broader geographical context of the Near and Middle East. It is divided into the same two historical periods as Student Maps 'A' & 'B'. The Satellite 'Key' Map provides the plan of subdivision for all the new satellite maps in the Student Map Manual (Section I: Regional Maps). The 'Key' Map covers the whole eastern seaboard from Cilicia and the Upper Euphrates, in the North, all the way to Sinai and Egypt, in the South. These two maps (plus Student Maps 'A' &'B') together with the Student Map Manual comprise a basic unit of Biblical mapping, designed specially for the student, which is termed the 'Student Package' in the context of the Wide Screen Project & Bonus System.

The 48 new pages in Section I (Regional Maps) provide systematic satellite coverage of the whole Levant, utilising the same scales as those used previously in the historical sections (Sections 3-13). These 'photo-maps' provide total over-views and details of the land bridges to Mesopotamia, Asia Minor, Arabia, Sinai and Egypt, depicting the surface terrain (and geology) with total objectivity. The earlier use of grid references in the first edition has greatly simplified the integration of this satellite imagery into the present Manual, since grid lines provide an accurate system of localisation which does not necessitate the over-printing of names, thus leaving the satellite image in tact and unspoiled.

Special acknowledgement is given here to Mr. Friedrich Hänssler, of Hänssler Verlag, Neuhausen-Stuttgart, for his support and cooperation in the co-publication of the German edition of the Student Map Manual, without which the present expanded English edition would not have been possible. Special acknowledgement is also given here to the National Aeronautics and Space Administration for making the original satellite data available; to Mr. Peter Powers and Dr. Farouk El-Baz of the Smithsonian Institution, for their initial help and advice; also to Dr. Charles Sheffield, Mr. Max Miller and Mrs. K. Estep of Earth Satellite Corporation, Washington, for all the computer enhancement and digital splicing needed to prepare such high-quality images; to Mr. Raymond Chazan of Spectra Scanner Graphics Ltd., Jerusalem, for the final scanning and colour matching; to Mr. Simon Crouch and Mr. Ken Robertson of Transart Ltd., Godmanchester, for their cooperation in printing these images onto film, for the overhead colour transparencies; and also to Mr. Emmanuel Polato and Fr. Augustino Corbanesi of Editice Libreria Dottrina Cristiana (L.D.C.), Torino, for their careful laboratory work in the preparation of the colour slides.

Pictorial Archive's special interest in satellite imagery has not resulted in any real increase in the cost of the new Student Map Manual and this despite a 38 per cent increase in content. The present price increase is the first since 1979 and is only a partial correction for inflation. Also, the Bonus System, on which an increasing number of smaller institutions now rely for the acquisition of Pictorial Archive materials at 'zero net cost' is unaffected.

This satellite imagery has also been published in the form of overhead colour transparencies and as sets of 35mm colour slides, for use with the standard map-slides in the Mini-Archive. We are also publishing two separate large format satellite maps: one in 2 sheets (scale 1:600,000), covering the whole Levant and another, in 4 sheets (scale 1:200,000) limited to the area from Damascus/Beirut to Aqaba/Eilat. These maps are the equivalent of the 'Display Versions' of the Student Maps 'A' & 'B', published previously.

The rest of the Student Map Manual remains unchanged.

BIBLE LANDS EXHIBIT

The Bible Lands Exhibit consists of 262 full-size posters (39" x 24", 66cm x 98cm), divided into 36 'Regional Units', in which the data from the Student Maps and Manual, and the new satellite imagery, are combined with aerial and ground-level panoramic pictures. These same pictures are then enlarged to considerable size, in sets of 'side posters', which provide the ultimate in detail. Indeed, one can probably learn more about the Holy Land, as far as the terrain is concerned, from careful study of these enlargements, than from the usual two or three week tour! Further information and samples can be supplied on request.

The Bible Lands Exhibit is made from exactly the same pictures as those used for the wide screen audio-visual presentations, to which it is, of course, totally complementary. The impact of the projected image is still paramount, but the Bible Lands Exhibit can provide a prolonged visual stimulus, due to continuous exposure, which can greatly facilitate actual memorisation of the visual content of the wide screen presentations. Also, because it requires absolutely no 'hardware', not even electricity, it can be used on its own wherever projection facilities are inadequate. It is already available in several languages.

The various Regional Units of the Exhibit can be displayed **singly** (in the school library or church hall/synagogue), on a regular rotational basis or as a **fixed display** in some shared facility within the community. The same Regional Units can also provide ideal preparation for any pilgrimmage to the Holy Land. The relevant Units can be selected in advance, to correspond with the planned itinerary. Videocassettes are being prepared on each Regional Unit which will be suitable for individual study at home, even without a teacher. These are purely descriptive in nature, to provide a knowledge of the Land before the visit.

The production of the Bible Lands Exhibit would not have been possible without the personal generosity of F. Howard and Mary D. Walsh, of Fort Worth, Texas; nor without the encouragement and participation of Mr. Truett Myers and Dr. George Kelm, both of Southwestern Baptist Theological Seminary. This does not imply any editorial control on their part, only that they shared our vision of what could be done and then helped to turn that vision into reality.

Southwestern Baptist Theological Seminary is now offering regular workshops involving the Bible Lands Exhibit and the Student Map Manual, as part of general refresher courses for alumni and missionaries on furlough. Participants in these workshops can then purchase the Exhibit (with special discounts), for subsequent use in their own communities. These courses of community Bible study can be coordinated so that interested individuals can join together for a 'consolidated' pilgrimmage to the Holy Land. Each participant will have been prepared on the same Regional Units, selected in advance to match the itinerary.

This system is open to all users of the Wide Screen Project. Of course, no attempt is made to structure Bible study and teachers are expected to determine their own priorities. Pictorial Archive seeks only to supply the relevant topographical teaching aids, within the narrow limits of historical geography.

Thus Pictorial Archive's own priorities remain the same: to bring the Holy Land to all those who can never visit the area themselves. This represents the majority of mankind and the new edition of the Student Map Manual is dedicated, as was the first, to this majority. It is a source of great satisfaction to see these materials increasingly used throughout the world, fulfilling this very purpose.

Contents

Foreword & Introduction

Section 1 Regional Maps (full colour)

1-1 to 1-16 Regional Maps
1-1S to 1-48S Satellite Maps

Section 2 Archaeology

Introduction
2-1 Chalcolithic Period
2-2 Early Bronze Period
2-3 Middle Bronze Period
2-4 Late Bronze Period
2-5 Iron Age I Period
2-6 Iron Age II Period
2-7 Persian Period
2-8 Hellenistic Period
2-9 Herodian/Early Roman Period
2-10 Late Roman and Byzantine Periods

Section 3 Canaanite (EB) Period

Summary of contents and sources
3-1 Early Bronze/Canaanite Period

Section 4 Canaanite (MB/LB) Period

Summary of contents and sources
4-1 Overview (north) and Egypt's operations in Canaan in the 19th Dynasty
4-2 Political Centres from the Execration texts
4-3 The Patriarchs: Abraham and Isaac
4-4 The Patriarchs: Jacob and Joseph
4-5 Egypt's expansion into Canaan in the 18th Dynasty
4-6 Detail: campaign of Thutmose III (southern)
4-7 Detail: campaign of Thutmose III (central)
4-8 The Amarna Age: kings of Canaan and inter-relations
4-9 Egypt's operations in Canaan in the 19th Dynasty

Section 5 Israelite Conquest

Summary of contents and sources
5-1 Overview (north) and kings of Transjordan and Canaan
5-2 Overview (south) and Wilderness Wanderings
5-3 Campaigns in Transjordan and entry into Canaan
5-4 Detail: entry into Canaan and initial campaign; Jericho and Ai
5-5 Campaigns in central Canaan: Gibeon and the Shephelah
5-6 Campaign in northern Canaan: Meron and Hazor

Section 6 Settlement and Judges

Summary of contents and sources
6-1 Overview (north), a preview of regional settlement problems and the book of Ruth
6-2 Tribal territories and city-lists in Canaan (Tribal territories in Transjordan taken from 5-3 b)
6-3 Early developments in and around Judah
6-4 Western confrontation: the tribe of Dan and Samson, the judge
6-5 Northern confrontation: Deborah and Barak
6-6 Eastern confrontation: Ehud, Gideon and Jephthah
6-7 Internal confrontation: Abimelech and the Benjaminite civil war

Secton 7 Samuel and the United Monarchy

Summary of contents and sources
7-1/2 Overviews, David's census and Solomon's reign
7-3 Samuel's ministry
7-4 Saul's beginning and end
7-5 David and Saul
7-6 David works for the Philistines at Ziklag
7-7 David's reign

Section 8 Divided Kingdom 'A'

Summary of contents and sources
8-1 Overview (north) and Elijah's ministry
8-2 Division of the kingdom and Shishak's campaign in Israel (northern kingdom)
8-3 Judah under Rehoboam and Shishak's campaign in Judah (southern kingdom)
8-4 Judah-Israel border disputes, Ethiopian threat to Judah and internal political strife in Israel

STUDENT MAP 'A'

Cross-reference to Historical Maps (Sections 3 to 13)

Genesis

	Map No.
12	4-3 a
13	4-3 b
14	4-3 c
18, 19	4-3 d
20, 21	4-3 e
22, 23	4-3 f
25, 26	4-3 g
28	4-4 a
31-33	4-4 a
34, 35	4-4 b
37	4-4 c
38	4-4 d
42-46	4-4 e

Numbers

13	5-2 c
14	5-2 d
20	5-2 e
21.1-3	5-2 d
21.4-15	5-2 e
21.13-22.1	5-3 a
32	5-3 b
33.34-44	5-2 e
33.40	5-2 d
33.45-49	5-3 a
34.1-5	5-2 b
34.6, 10-12	6-1 b
35.1-8	6-1 e
35.9-34	6-1 d

Deuteronomy

1.6-2.15	5-2 e
1.22-39,	5-2 c
1.41-45	5-2 d
2.16-3.11	5-3 a
3.12-17	5-3 b
3.18-29	5-3 a
4.41-43	6-1 d
11.26-32	5-3 d
27	5-3 d
34	5-3 a

Joshua

1.1-8.29	5-3 c
8.30-35	5-3 d
9	5-5 a
10.1-15	5-5 b
10.16-39	5-5 c
10.36-37	6-3 b
10.38-39	6-3 c
10.40	5-1 d
11.1-15	5-6
11.16-20	5-1 d
11.17	5-2 b
11.21	5-5 c
11.21	6-3 b, c
11.22	6-3 e
12.1-6	5-1 c
12.7-24	5-1 d
12.7	5-2 b
12.9, 16	5-3 c

	Map No.
23.8-39	7-5 e
27	7-6 a
28,29	7-4 h
29	7-6 b
30	7-6 c
31	7-4 h

2 Samuel

1	7-6 d
1.6-10	7-4 h
2.1-5.5a	7-7 a
2.46-7	7-7 f
5.5-16	7-7 b
5.17-25	7-7 c
6-7	7-7 d
8.1-18	7-7 a
9	7-7 f
10,11	7-7 e
11.1-12.25	7-7 f
12.26-31	7-7 e
13-19	7-7 f
19.24-30	7-7 f
20.1-22	7-7 f
20.23-26	7-7 e
21.1-14	7-7 f
21.15-22	7-7 e
23.1-7	7-7 f
24	7-1/2 b

1 Kings

1.1-2.12	7-7 f
2.12-11.43	7-1/2 c
4.7-21	7-1/2 c
9.15-28	7-1/2 c
11.15-18	7-7 e
11.26-12.24	8-2 a
12.25-14.20	8-2 b
13.1-3	9-6 i
14.21-24, 29-31	8-3 a
14.25-28, 30	8-2 b, c
15.1-8	8-4 b
15.9-15	8-4 c
15.16-24	8-4 e
15.16-21	8-5 a
15.25-34	8-4 d
16.1-23	8-4 f
16.24-28	8-5 b
16.29-34	8-5 c
16.34	8-6 a
17-19	8-1 b
19.15-21	8-7 a
19.15-17	8-7 c
20.1-21	8-5 e
20.22-43	8-5 f
21	8-1 b
	8-7 d
22.1	8-5 g
22.2-40	8-5 h
22.41-50	8-6 b
22.51-53	8-1 c

	Map No.
16.1-5	8-5 a
16.7-10	8-4 c
17	8-6 b
18	8-5 h
19	8-6 b
20.1-30	8-6 e
20.31-21.1	8-6 b
21	8-6 f
21.11-15	8-7 a
22.1-9	8-7 d
24.23-25	9-1 d
22.10-24.27	9-1/2 c
25	9-2 g
26, 27	9-1/2 i
28.1-19	9-1/2 j
28.18	9-3 a
28.20-27	9-4
29.1-32.8, 23-33	9-6 a
32.1, 9-22	9-6 b
33.1-20	9-6 d
33.21-25	9-6 h
34-35	9-6 i
36.1-4	9-7 a
36.5-8	9-7 b
36.9-10	9-7 c
36.11-21	9-7 d
36.22-23	10-1 b

Ezra

Ezra	10-1 b
2.1-35	10-2
3.1-7	10-2

Nehemiah

Nehemiah	10-1 b
2.9-4.23	10-2
7.6-38	10-2
11.20, 25-36	9-7 f
	10-1 b

Esther .... 10-1 b

Psalms

51	7-7 f
83.9-12	6-6 b
83.9-10	6-5 a
90	5-2 e
137.7	9-7 e

Isaiah

6	9-1/2 i
7-12	9-1/2 j
9.1-7	9-4
10.28-32	9-6 c
15-16	9-1/2 k
18-20	9-5 b
22.8-11	9-6 a
30.1-31.3	9-6 b

Habbakuk ..... 9-7 b

Zephaniah ..... 9-6 i

Haggai .... 10-1 b

Zechariah ...... 10-1 b

Malachi .... 10-1 b

Judith .... 11-9 d

1 Maccabees

1,2	11-4 a
1.1-9	11-2 a
3.1-4.35	11-4 b
4.36-61	11-4 c
5.1-54	11-5
5.55-68	11-6 a
6.1-27	11-6 b
6.28-54	11-6 c
6.55-63	11-6 d
7.1-32	11-6 e
7.33-50	11-7 a
8	11-7 b
9.1-22	11-7 c
9.23-33	11-7 d
9.33-49	11-8 a
9.50-53	11-7 f
9.54-73	11-7 g
10.1-66	11-8 b
10.67-11.19	11-8 c
11.20-37	11-8 d
11.38-12.38	11-8 e
12.39-13.30	11-8 f
13.31-16.24	11-9 a

2 Maccabees

1..11-17	11-6 b
4-7	11-4 a
8.1-29, 34-36	11-4 b
9	11-6 b
10.1-8	11-4 c
10.15-23	11-5
11.1-21, 27-33, 34-38	11-4 b
11.13-33	11-6 d
12.3-9, 32-45	11-6 a
12.10-31	11-5
13.1-17	11-6 c
13.18-23	11-6 d
14.1-22	11-6 e
15.25-28	11-7 a

under Ahab and Jezebel, Elijah's ministry
8-6 Israel and Judah's relations with Moab and Edom
8-7 Elisha, J(eh)oram, Jehu and Israel's relations with Syria and Assyria
8-8 Approaches to Samaria and regional settlement reflected in the Samaria ostraca

Section 9 Divided Kingdom 'B'
Summary of contents and sources
9-1/2 Internal politics and wars prior to major Assyrian invasions (Israel, Syria/Aram, Judah, Edom and Philistia)
9-3 Warnings in the Shephelah: Philistine conquests and Micah, the prophet
9-4 The campaigns and provincial organization of Tiglath-pileser III of Assyria
9-5 Fall of Samaria, Assyrian expansion under Shalmaneser V and Sargon II
9-6 Resistance of Hezekiah of Judah against Sennacherib of Assyria
9-7 The rise of Babylon, Judah's closing years and the fall of Jerusalem

Section 10 Persian Period
Summary of contents and sources
10-1 Overview, the 'Return' and Persian administration
10-2 The land of Judah and administrative districts during the 'Return'

Section 11 Hellenistic/Hasmonaean Period
Summary of contents and sources
11-1 Overview and the Hellenistic cities
11-2 Hellenistic rule in Palestine I
11-3 Hellenistic rule in Palestine II
11-4 Hasmonaean Revolt I: Mattathias and Judas Maccabaeus
11-5 Hasmonaean Revolt II: Judas Maccabaeus; rescue operations: Idumaea, Gilead and Galilee
11-6 Hasmonaean Revolt III: Judas Maccabaeus
11-7 Hasmonaean Revolt IV: Judas Maccabaeaus and Jonathan
11-8 Hasmonaean Revolt V: Jonathan
11-9 Hasmonaean Independence I: Simon, John Hyrcanus and Aristobulus I
11-10 (north) and 11-11 (south) Hasmonaean Independence II: Alexander Jannaeus, Alexandra, Hyrcanus II and Aristobulus II
11-12 Hasmonaean internal strife and Decline I
11-13 Hasmonaean internal strife and Decline II

Section 12 Herodian Period
Summary of contents and sources
12-1 Overview and administration in Jewish territory
12-2 Reign of king Herod: selected passages
12-3 Sons of Herod and direct rule by Rome in Judaea
12-4 The four Gospels
12-5 Detail: central Judaea, southern Peraea (Across-the-Jordan)
12-6 Detail: Samaria, northern Peraea, Bethshan/Scythopolis valley
12-7 Detail: Upper and Lower Galilee
12-8 Detail: sea of Galilee and environs
12-9 Detail: central and western Judaea (Shephelah)
12-10 Agrippa I and II, later procurators and the Acts of the Apostles
12-11 The First Revolt against Rome (complete)
12-12 Detail of Galilee: Josephus' defence and Vespasian's campaigns
12-13 Detail of Judaea: defence and defeat of Judaea and Jerusalem

Section 13 Late Roman and Byzantine Periods
Summary of contents and sources
13-1 Overview and urbanization under Roman rule
13-2 Annexation of the Nabataean kingdom and establishment of the Roman province of Arabia
13-3 The Bar Kokhba Revolt I
13-4 The Bar Kokhba Revolt II
13-5 Centre of Jewish life moves to Galilee and the Golan

Section 14 Archaeology of Jerusalem
Introduction and Selected Bibliography
14-0 Key to visible remains (in 14-1 to 14-3)
14-1 First Temple Period
14-2 Second Temple Period
14-3 Byzantine Period

Section 15 Indexes
15-1 Index of Alternative Names
15-2 Index of Main Names
15-3 Index of Grid References

STUDENT MAP 'B'

12.14 .... 5-2 d
12.19-20 5-6
12.19-23 .... 6-5 a
13.1-33 .... 5-2 b
13.1-6 .... 6-1 b
14.1-5 .... 6-2 a
14.6-15 .... 6-3 b
15.1-4 .... 5-2 b
15.5-12 .... 6-2 a
15.13-14 .... 6-3 b
15.15-19 .... 6-3 c
15.20-63 .... 6-2 a
15.59a (LXX) .... 6-2 a
15.63 .... 6-1 c,f
16.1-10 .... 6-2 a
16.10 .... 6-1 c
17.1-13 .... 6-2 a
17.11-18 .... 6-1 c
17.14-18 .... 6-2 a
18.1-19.48 .... 6-2 b
19.47 .... 6-4 a
19.49-51 .... 6-2 b
20 .... 6-1 d
21 .... 6-1 e
24.1-28 .... 5-3 d
24.29-33 .... 6.2 b

Judges

1.1-7 .... 6-3 a
1.8-10, 20 .... 6-3 b
1.11-15 .... 6-3 c
1.16-17 .... 6-3 d
1.18 (cf LXX) .... 6-3 e
1.21, 27-35 .... 6-1 c
1.21 .... 6-3 f
1.22-26 .... 6-3 g
1.34-35 .... 6-4 a
2 .... 6-2 b
3.1-3 .... 6-1 b
3.7-11 .... 6-3 c
3.12-30 .... 6-7 a
3.31 .... 6-5 b
4,5 .... 6-5 a
5.6 .... 6-5 b
6-8 .... 6-6 b
8.30-9.57 .... 6-7 b
10.1-2 .... 6-7 d
10.3-5 .... 6-6 d
10.6-12.7 .... 6-6 c
12.8-10, 13-15 .... 6-7 d
12.11-12 .... 6-5 b
13-16 .... 6-4 b
17,18 .... 6-4 a
19-21 .... 6-7 c

Ruth .... 6-1 f

1 Samuel

1-3 .... 7-3 a
4 .... 7-3 b
5.1-7.2 .... 7-3 c
7.3-14 .... 7-3 d
7.15-17 .... 7-3 e
8 .... 7-4 a
9-10 .... 7-4 b
11-12 .... 7-4 c
13.1-14.46 .... 7-4 d
15 .... 7-5 a
16 .... 7-5 b
17 .... 7-5 c
18-26 .... 7-5 d
22.1-2 .... 7-5 e

2 Kings

1.1 .... 8-6 c
1.2-2.18 .... 8-1 c
2.1-9.10 .... 8-7 a
3.1-5 .... 8-6 c
3.6-27 .... 8-6 d
6-7 .... 8-7 b
8.7-15 .... 8-7 c
8.16-27 .... 8-6 f
8.28-10.31 .... 8-7 d
10.32-36 .... 9-1 d
11-12 .... 9-1/2 c
12.17-18 .... 9-1 d
13.1-9, 20-23 .... 9-1 d
13.10-25 .... 9-1 e
13.14-21 .... 8-7 a
14.1-22 .... 9-2 g
14.23-29 .... 9-1 e
15.1-7, 32-38 .... 9-1/2 i
15.8-12 .... 9-1 e
15.13-28 .... 9-1/2 h
15.29-31 9-4
15.37 .... 9-1/2 j
16.1-6 .... 9-1/2 j
16.7-20 9-4
17 .... 9-5 a
18.1-8 .... 9-6 a
18.9-12 .... 9-5 a
18.13-19.37 .... 9-6 b
20 .... 9-6 a
21.1-18 .... 9-6 d
21.19-26 .... 9-6 h
22.1-23.30 .... 9-6 i
23.31-37 .... 9-7 a
24.1-7 .... 9-7 b
24.8-17 .... 9-7 c
24.18-25.21 .... 9-7 d
25.22-26 .... 9-7 f
25.27-30 .... 9-7 c

1 Chronicles

3.1-4a .... 7-7 a
4.38-43 .... 9-6 a
5.6, 25-26 9-4
6.54-81 .... 6-1 e
10 .... 7-4 h
11.1-3 .... 7-7 a
11.4-9 .... 7-7 b
11.10-12.22 .... 7-5 e
12.23-40 .... 7-7 a
13 .... 7-7 d
14.1-7 .... 7-7 b
14.8-16 .... 7-7 c
15-17 .... 7-7 d
18.1-20.8 .... 7-7 e
21.1-27 .... 7-1/2 b
21.28-22.19 .... 7-7 f
23-26 .... 7-7 f
27 .... 7-7 e
28-29 .... 7-7 f

2 Chronicles

1-9 .... 7-1/2 c
8.1-6, 17-18 .... 7-1/2 c
10.1-11.4 .... 8-2 a
11.5-23 .... 8-3 a
11.5-23 .... 8-4 a
12.1,13-16 .... 8-3 a
12.2-12 .... 8-2 c
.... 8-3 b
13 .... 8-4 b
14-15 .... 8-4 c
16.1-14 .... 8-4 e

38, 39 .... 9-6 a

Jeremiah

1-20 .... 9-6 i
21 .... 9-7 d
22.1-23 .... 9-7 a
22.24-30 .... 9-7 c
23 .... 9-6 h
24 .... 9-7 c, d
25 .... 9-7 b
26 .... 9-7 a
27-34 .... 9-7 d
35 .... 9-7 a
36 .... 9-7 b
37.1-39.10 .... 9-7 d
39.11-44.30 .... 9-7 f
40 .... 10-1 b
45 .... 9-7 a
46 .... 9-7 b
47 .... 9-6 i
.... 9-7 b
47.1 .... 9-6 g
48.1-51.58 .... 9-7 b
48.1-49.6 .... 9-1/2 k
52.1-30 .... 9-7 d
52.31-34 .... 9-7 c

Lamentations

4.21-22 .... 9-7 e

Ezekiel

1-24 .... 9-7 d
47.17-18 9-4
47.18-20 .... 5-1 b
47.19 .... 5-2 b
48.28 .... 5-2 b

Daniel .... 10-1 b

Hosea .... 9-1 e

Amos

Amos .... 9-1 e
1.3-5 .... 9-1 d
6.1-3 .... 9-1 d
6.13 .... 9-1 e

Obadiah .... 9-7 e

Jonah .... 9-1 e

Micah

Micah .... 9-3 b
1.10-16 .... 9-6 b

Nahum .... 9-6 i

Matthew

Matthew 12.4-9
1.18-2.20 .... 12-2 h
2.19-23 .... 12-3 b
14.3-12 .... 12-3 e

Mark

Mark 12.4-9
6.17-29 .... 12-3 e

Luke

Luke 12.4-9
1.5-2.40 .... 12-2 h
3.1-3 .... 12-3 d
3.19-20 .... 12-3 e
24.50-52 .... 12-10 a

John 12.4-9

The Acts of the Apostles

1-11 .... 12-10 a
11.28 .... 12-10 b
12.1-25 .... 12-10 b
13.1-18.21 .... 12-10 c
18.22-24.27 .... 12-10 c
25-28 .... 12-10 c

2 Corinthians

11.30-33 .... 12-10 a

Galatians

1.11-20 .... 12-10 a
1.21-2.10 .... 12-10 c

Introduction

Innovative Features

(1) Absence of Illustrations

It is illogical to print illustrations, especially in colour, in a STUDENT textbook on Historical Geography. A picture in a book can only be seen by one student at a time, whereas the same picture when projected as a slide can be seen by the whole class. Also, in a book, it is impossible to print many pictures because of the cost, so no effective visualisation of the subject can be achieved. The pictures, because they are few, tend to be spectacular rather than informative and the motive for their inclusion is often more commercial than didactic. The only logical solution is to take the illustrations out of the book and to provide them *separately* as slides, preferably in colour, for projection. In this way it is possible to increase the total number of illustrations without increasing the cost of the book. This also takes the selection and use of pictures away from the editor and places them in the hands of the teacher, where they belong.

Pictorial Archive takes this argument to its logical conclusion by offering the 'BONUS SYSTEM'* whereby actual use of the Student Manual can generate the income for the slides. This provides maximal communication with minimal cost for both student and school. The 'REGIONAL TOUR' takes the process one step further replacing 'visualisation' with the ultimate reality of direct vision itself.

(2) Minimal Text

The Student Manual provides a comprehensive system of mapping which is directly relevant to the Bible and other related sources. It does not attempt to compete with the students' major textbooks, as far as the text is concerned. The 'Summary of Contents & Sources' at the beginning of each historical section (Sections 3 - 13) gives the major primary sources for each map, but leaves space for students to insert the relevant dates and cross-references to the secondary sources, subject to the teacher's recommendations.

(3) Maximal priority to Mapping

Because of the economies made possible by the elimination of illustrations and the reduction of text, it has been possible to produce highly professional mapping throughout the Student Manual. The single most important feature in all this mapping is the use of accurate contour-based relief-shading. This relief-shading was prepared by M. Karmon, of the Department of Geography at the Hebrew University of Jerusalem and is the basis of ALL Pictorial Archive Mapping.

Viz. Archaeology Series 1-12
Student Maps 'A' & 'B' (Student and Display Versions)
Student Map Manual
Map-Slides

(4) Maximal Cross-Indexing

a) TO THE BIBLE

In the List of CONTENTS, the entire Biblical cross-index is given, on one double page, next to the total contents of the Student Manual. This establishes the true priority of the Student Manual and enables the student to check its relevance at a glance, to any part of the Bible.

b) TO THE OTHER PRIMARY SOURCES

In the 'Summaries of Contents & Sources' at the beginning of each historical section (Sections 3 -.13) all the primary sources are cross-indexed to the individual maps in each section, indicating their major relevance.

c) TO ARCHAEOLOGY

In the Index of Main Names (Section 15-2, Column 4) is a cross-index to the Encyclopedia of Archaeological Excavations in the Holy Land (EAEHL), which in turn provides a succinct archaeological report on all the excavated sites listed. The EAEHL also provides an invaluable point of entry to the professional literature on this subject.

d) TO THE MINI-ARCHIVE*

In the Index of Main Names (Section 15-2, Column 1) is a cross-index to the 'Mini-Archive Reference Number', to which all the 2500 slides of the Mini-Archive are indexed. This Index also provides a useful resumé (in Columns 5 - 92) of the archaeological and historical relevance of all the sites listed. This, in combination with the 'Summaries of Contents & Sources', provides a potential caption for *any* slide of *any* site in the Mini-Archive.

(5) Direct Student Involvement

Ample space has been left throughout the Student Manual for students to insert their own notes and observations. Students are expected to annotate the Archaeology and History maps (Sections 2 - 13), adding whatever graphic information is deemed necessary (e.g. map-titles, dates, roadways, battlefields, lines of advance and/or retreat, political boundaries and areas of influence etc.). The absence of layer tints (= full colour) in these maps makes them ideal for colour-coding. Cross-reference is made in the 'Summaries of Contents & Sources' (Column 4) to the Macmillan Bible Atlas, which contains a wealth of information of this type. Teachers should evaluate these data before the students transfer them to their own Manuals.

Students should regard their Manuals as a permanent aid to Bible study, for the future and for any subsequent visit to the Holy Land.

* For further information on the 'WIDE SCREEN PROJECT', the 'BONUS SYSTEM' and the 'REGIONAL TOUR' see inside front cover.

Place-Names, Road Systems & Abbreviations

Place-Names

The Student Manual is derived from Student Maps 'A' and 'B' (Student and Display Versions) and these are described first.

STUDENT MAP 'A': Patriarchs through Ezra-Nehemiah

Student Version: Scale 1:275,000
Display Version: Scale 1:150,000

The historical names used in Student Map 'A' are based on Aharoni's 'Land of the Bible'. The archaeological names are based upon the official lists published by the appropriate Government Department of Antiquities (including the earlier Mandatory Government of Palestine, prior to 1948). Both historical and archaeological names are printed in small black letters, without distinction. Major modern towns are shown as grey built-up areas, with grey names. Major geographical regions, such as Samaria, Judaea etc., are shown in large grey letters.

Most of the historical names are BIBLICAL, taken from the REVISED STANDARD VERSION.

STUDENT MAP 'B': Ezra-Nehemiah through Justinian

Student Version: Scale 1:275,000
Display Version: Scale 1:150,000

This map follows the same system, for archaeological names; but historical names are based on Avi-Yonah's 'The Holy Land' and the 'Gazetteer of Roman Palestine'. Student Map 'B' reflects the impact made by the Greeks and Romans, especially with regard to place-names, many of which were changed. Thus Ashdod became Azotus and Aphek became Antipatris or Pegae. It is for this reason that the two Student Maps are divided at this point. Of course, many of the earlier names, as shown on Student Map 'A', continued in use together with the Graeco-Roman names and in the majority of cases finally survived them.

In the selection of 'MAIN NAMES' for the Index of Main Names, priority is given to the names in Student Map 'A' since these are earlier and more commonly BIBLICAL. Thus in the examples given above, Ashdod and Aphek are indexed as Main Names, whereas Azotus, Antipatris and Pegae are indexed as Alternative Names.

STUDENT (MAP) MANUAL

(1) REGIONAL MAPS (Section 1)
In these REGIONAL maps, the historical names are distinguished from the purely archaeological names:

Student Map 'A' (= 'A' names):	brown
Student map 'B' (= 'B' names):	purple
Archaeological names:	black
Geographical names:	grey

(21 ARCHAEOLOGY MAPS (Section 2)
For further details see Section 2: Introduction.

(3) HISTORICAL MAPS (Sections 3-13)
All the names derived from the primary (historical) sources, on which all the individual historical maps are based (= PRIMARY names/sites), are printed in RED. All the other names (= BACKGROUND names/sites), are printed in BLACK. These background names are derived from the relevant archaeology map in Section 2 and from the primary names of other maps in each Section.

In this way the main historical content of each map (in RED) is shown against a full contemporary background (in BLACK). Some geographical names are also included, usually in red, when these are mentioned in the primary sources and are especially important. However, as a general rule, students are referred to the Regional Maps (Section 1) for such geographical data, or to the Macmillan Bible Atlas. Students are recommended to add such geographical information onto their own maps where necessary.

Road Systems

Student Map 'A' - Student Version
- Display Version.
Student Map 'B' - Student Version
- Display Version
Student (Map) Manual

STUDENT MAP 'A'

The Student Version contains no roads of any kind. There is little archaeological evidence for roads in these early periods and certainly not enough to indicate continuous lines on a map, which students might interpret as ordinary roads. It was decided, therefore, to omit all such information from the Student Version, but to give a complete system of 'LINES OF COMMUNICATION', based upon primarily geographical considerations, on the DISPLAY Version. This enables the teacher to evaluate their relevance as 'roads', leaving the students the option of drawing their own 'lines' afterwards. International roads are shown in red.

STUDENT MAP 'B'

Both the Student and the Display Versions of this map carry a ROMAN ROAD SYSTEM. These are only the MAJOR Roman roads and no attempt has been made, either in the Student Map or in the relevant parts of the Student Manual, to separate these roads chronologically, according to the dates of their construction. Thus all the major Roman roads, for the duration of Roman rule, are shown in one colour as a SINGLE system.

NOTE: There are some minor discrepancies between the two versions of the Student Maps, the Student Manual and the Map-slides of the Mini-Archive, since these were not all published simultaneously and up-dating was continued during production. The DISPLAY VERSIONS of the Student Maps and the MAP-SLIDES take priority in all cases of ambiguity.

STUDENT (MAP) MANUAL

(a) Regional Maps (Section 1):	MODERN ROADS
(b) Historical Maps (Sections 3-11):	LINES OF COMMUNICATION
(c) Historical Maps (Sections 12-13):	ROMAN ROAD SYSTEM (without milestones)

Students should colour-code the roads relevant to the subject of each map, with the guidance of their teachers. It is understood that many of the roads indicated are largely irrelevant to the MAIN subject of the map. Nevertheless, the whole system has been reproduced for each map, to allow the use of the same map in other ways, on the basis that students can colour-code the roads appropriate to the subjects taught.

Abbreviations

Summaries of Contents & Sources: Bibliography (Sections 3-13)

ANET — Pritchard, J. B., ed.
1969 *Ancient Near Eastern Texts Relating to the Old Testament.* 3rd edition. Princeton: Princeton University.

ANEP — Pritchard, J. B., ed.
1969 *The Ancient Near East in Pictures Relating to the Old Testament.* 2nd edition. Princeton: Princeton University.

ANE I — Pritchard, J. B., ed.
1973 *The Ancient Near East, An Anthology of Texts and Pictures,* Vol. 1 (paperback). Princeton: Princeton University.

ANE II — Pritchard, J. B., ed.
1975 *The Ancient Near East, A New Anthology of Texts and Pictures,* Vol. 2 (paperback). Princeton: Princeton University.

EAEHL — Avi-Yonah, M., and Stern, E., ed.
1975-8 *Encyclopedia of Archaeological Excavations in the Holy Land.* Jerusalem: Massada.

GLAJJ — Stern, M.
1974 *Greek and Latin Authors on Jews and Judaism,* Vol. 1. Jerusalem :The Israel Academy of Sciences and Humanities. Vol. 2 in preparation.

MBA — Aharoni, Y., and Avi-Yonah, M.
1978 *The Macmillan Bible Atlas.* 2nd edition. New York: The Macmillian Company.

From the works of Flavius Josephus:

Ant. — *The Antiquities of the Jews*
Life — *The Life of Flavius Josephus*
Wars — *The Wars of the Jews*

The Loeb Classical Library.
Cambridge, Mass.: Harvard University.
Whiston, W.
1960 *Josephus, Complete Works.*
Grand Rapids: Kregel Publications.

Key to Regional Maps (1 to 16)

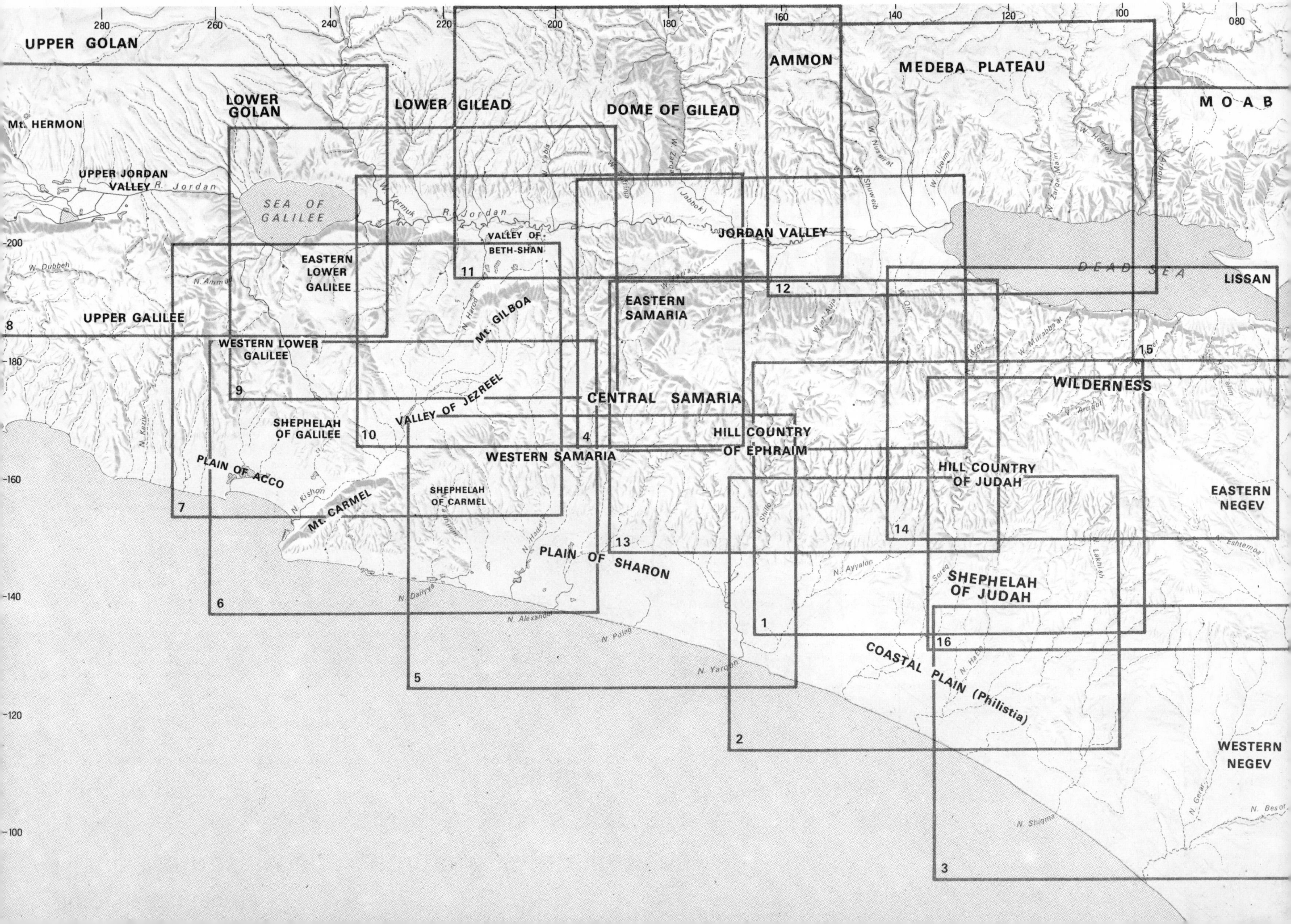
SCALE
10 Km
6 M
E
UPPER GOLAN
LOWER GOLAN
Mt. HERMON
UPPER JORDAN VALLEY
R. Jordan
SEA OF GALILEE
EASTERN LOWER GALILEE
UPPER GALILEE
WESTERN LOWER GALILEE
SHEPHELAH OF GALILEE
PLAIN OF ACCO
Mt. CARMEL
SHEPHELAH OF CARMEL
VALLEY OF JEZREEL
Mt. GILBOA
VALLEY OF BETH-SHAN
LOWER GILEAD
DOME OF GILEAD
AMMON
MEDEBA PLATEAU
M O A B
JORDAN VALLEY
DEAD SEA
LISSAN
EASTERN SAMARIA
CENTRAL SAMARIA
WESTERN SAMARIA
HILL COUNTRY OF EPHRAIM
HILL COUNTRY OF JUDAH
WILDERNESS
EASTERN NEGEV
PLAIN OF SHARON
SHEPHELAH OF JUDAH
COASTAL PLAIN (Philistia)
WESTERN NEGEV
W. Yarmuk
W. Yabis
W. Zarqa
(Jabbok)
W. Nusei'rat
W. Shuweib
W. Uzeimi
W. Zarqa Ma'in
W. Heidan
(Arnon)
W. Dubbeh
N. Ammud
N. Harod
N. Kishon
N. Keziv
N. Hadera
N. Daliyya
N. Alexander
N. Poleg
N. Yarqon
N. Shilo
N. Ayyalon
N. Soreq
N. Lakhish
N. Ha'ela
N. Eshtemoa
W. Murabba'at
W. Qilt
N. Arugot
N. Ze'elim
N. Gerar
N. Besor
N. Shiqma
1
2
3
4
5
6
7
8
9
10
11
12
13
14
15
16
280
260
240
220
200
180
160
140
120
100
080
-200
-180
-160
-140
-120
-100

Regional Map

SCALE 1:215,000

10 Km

6 M

ISRAEL GRID

LEGEND:
- Historical Sites in Student Map A — • Ashdod
- Historical Sites in Student Map B — • Azotus
- Name common to both Student Maps — *
- Archaeological Sites (see Section 2) — • H. Shurah
- Modern Roads

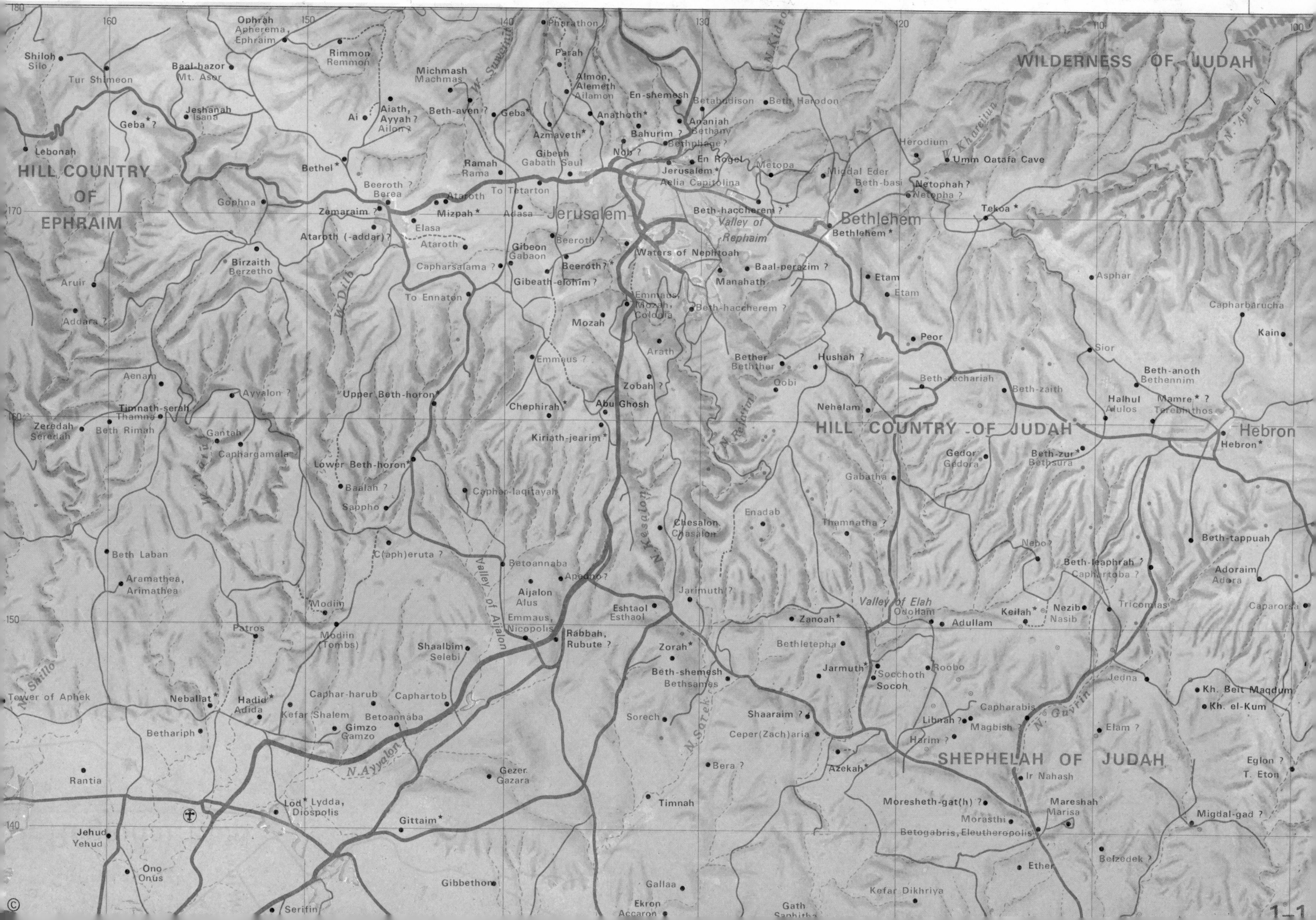

180
160
150
140
130
120
110
100
170
160
150
140
WILDERNESS OF JUDAH
HILL COUNTRY OF EPHRAIM
HILL COUNTRY OF JUDAH
SHEPHELAH OF JUDAH
Jerusalem
Bethlehem
Hebron
Shiloh
Silo
Tur Shimeon
Lebonah
Geba ?
Jeshanah
Isana
Baal-hazor
Mt. Asor
Ophrah
Apherema,
Ephraim
Rimmon
Remmon
Michmash
Machmas
W. Suweinit
Pherathon
Parah
Almon,
Alemeth
Ailamon
En-shemesh
N. Kidron
Betabudison
Beth Harodon
Ai
Aiath,
Ayyah ?
Ailon ?
Beth-aven ?
Geba*
Anathoth*
Ananiah
Bethany
Azmaveth*
Bahurim ?
Bethphage ?
Nob ?
En Rogel
Jerusalem*
Aelia Capitolina
Metopa
Migdal Eder
Beth-basi
Herodium
W. Khareitun
Umm Qatafa Cave
N. Arugot
Netophah ?
Netopha ?
Tekoa*
Bethel*
Beeroth ?
Berea
Ramah
Rama
Gibeah
Gabath Saul
To Tetarton
Ataroth
Mizpah*
Adasa
Gophna
Zemaraim ?
Elasa
Ataroth (-addar) ?
Ataroth
Gibeon
Gabaon
Beeroth ?
Beeroth ?*
Gibeath-elohim ?
Capharsalama ?
Beth-haccherem ?*
Valley of Rephaim
Bethlehem*
Waters of Nephtoah
Baal-perazim ?
Manahath
Etam
Etam
Asphar
Birzaith
Berzetho
Aruir
Addara ?
W. Dilb
To Ennaton
Emmaus,
Mozah,
Colonia
Beth-haccherem ?
Mozah
Arath
Peor
Capharbarucha
Kain
Sior
Bether
Bethther
Hushah ?
Oobi
Beth-zechariah
Beth-zaith
Beth-anoth
Bethennim
Emmaus ?
Aenam
Ayyalon ?
Upper Beth-horon*
Zobah ?
Chephirah*
Abu Ghosh
Kiriath-jearim*
N. Refaim
Nehelam
Halhul
Alulos
Mamre* ?
Terebinthos
Hebron*
Timnath-serah
Thamna
Zeredah
Seredah
Beth Rimah
Gantah
Caphargamala
W. Natif
Lower Beth-horon*
Baalah ?
Sappho
Caphar-laqitayah
Gedor
Gedora
Beth-zur*
Bethsura
Gabatha
Enadab
Chesalon
Chasalon
N. Kesalon
Thamnatha ?
Beth-tappuah
Beth Laban
Aramathea,
Arimathea
C(aph)eruta ?
Betoannaba
Apeiro ?
Aijalon
Alus
Valley of Aijalon
Nebo ?
Beth-leaphrah ?
Caphartoba ?
Adoraim
Adora
Modiim
Patros
Modiin
(Tombs)
Emmaus,
Nicopolis
Rabbah,
Rubute ?
Eshtaol
Esthaol
Jarimuth ?
Valley of Elah
Odollam
Adullam
Zanoah*
Keilah*
Nezib
Nasib
Tricomias
Caparorsa
Shaalbim
Selebi
Zorah*
Bethletepha
Jarmuth*
Socchoth
Socoh
Roobo
Jedna
N. Shillo
Tower of Aphek
Neballat*
Hadid*
Adida
Caphar-harub
Kefar Shalem
Caphartob
Betoannaba
Beth-shemesh
Bethsames
Sorech
N. Sorek
Shaaraim ?
Ceper(Zach)aria
Libnah ?
Capharabis
Magbish ?
N. Guvrin
Kh. Beit Maqdum
Kh. el-Kum
Elam ?
Bethariph
Gimzo
Gamzo
Harim ?
Rantia
N. Ayyalon
Gezer
Gazara
Bera ?
Azekah*
Ir Nahash
Eglon ?
T. Eton
Lod* Lydda,
Diospolis
Timnah
Moresheth-gat(h) ?
Mareshah
Marisa
Morasthi
Migdal-gad ?
Jehud
Yehud
Gittaim*
Betogabris, Eleutheropolis
Ono
Onus
Gibbethon
Gallaa
Ether
Belzedek ?
Kefar Dikhriya
Serifin
Ekron
Accaron
Gath
Saphitha
E

©

Section 1–2

Regional Map

SCALE 1:215,000

10 Km

6 M

ISRAEL GRID

LEGEND:

- Historical Sites in Student Map A — • **Ashdod**
- Historical Sites in Student Map B — • Azotus
- Name common to both Student Maps — *
- Archaeological Sites (see Section 2) — • **H. Shurah**
- Modern Roads

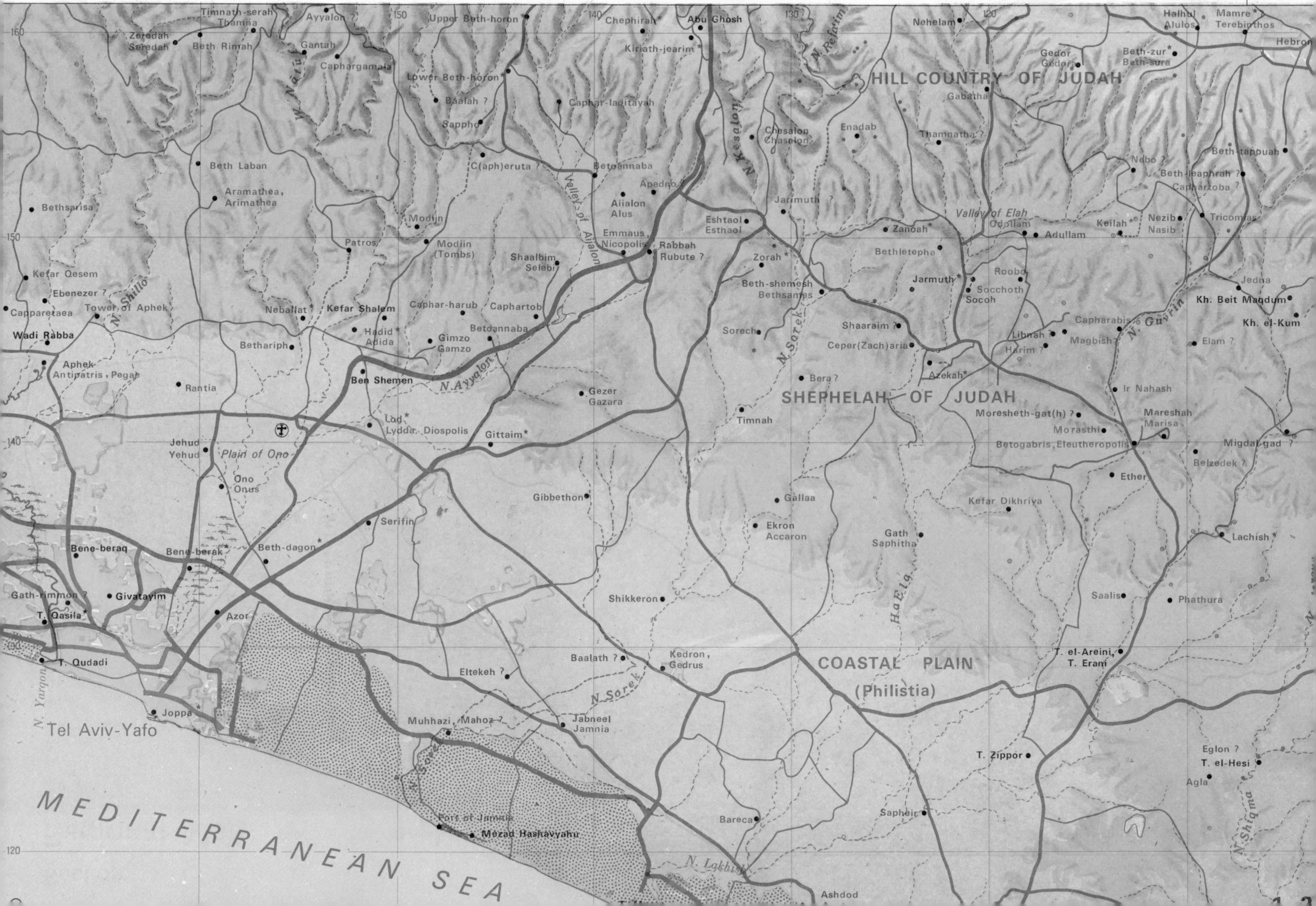

HILL COUNTRY OF JUDAH
SHEPHELAH OF JUDAH
COASTAL PLAIN
(Philistia)
MEDITERRANEAN SEA
Tel Aviv-Yafo
Timnath-serah
Thamna
Zeredah
Seredah
Beth Rimah
Ayyalon
Gantah
Caphargamala
Upper Beth-horon
Lower Beth-horon
Baalah ?
Sappho
Chephirah
Kiriath-jearim
Abu Ghosh
Caphar-laqitayah
Nehelam
Gedor
Gedor
Beth-zur
Beth-sura
Halhul
Alulos
Mamre
Terebinthos
Hebron
Gabatha
Chesalon
Chaselon
Enadab
Thamnatha ?
Beth-tappuah
Nebo ?
Beth-leaphrah ?
Caphartoba
Beth Laban
C(aph)eruta ?
Betoannaba
Apedno ?
Aijalon
Alus
Jarmuth ?
Eshtaol
Esthaol
Aramathea,
Arimathea
Bethsarisa
Modiin
Modiin
(Tombs)
Patros
Emmaus,
Nicopolis
Rabbah
Rubute ?
Shaalbim
Selebi
Zorah
Zanoah
Bethletepha
Valley of Elah
Odollam
Adullam
Keilah
Nezib
Nasib
Tricomias
Kefar Qesem
Ebenezer ?
Tower of Aphek
Capparetaea
Wadi Rabba
Neballat
Kefar Shalem
Hadid
Adida
Caphar-harub
Caphartob
Gimzo
Gamzo
Betoannaba
Beth-shemesh
Bethsames
Jarmuth
Socchoth
Socoh
Roobo
Jedna
Kh. Beit Maqdum
Kh. el-Kum
Bethariph
Aphek
Antipatris, Pegae
Ben Shemen
N. Ayyalon
Sorech
Shaaraim ?
Ceper(Zach)aria
Capharabis
Libnah
Harim ?
Magbish ?
Elam ?
Azekah
Bera ?
Rantia
Gezer
Gazara
Timnah
Ir Nahash
Lod
Lydda, Diospolis
Gittaim
Moresheth-gat(h) ?
Morasthi
Mareshah
Marisa
Betogabris, Eleutheropolis
Migdal-gad ?
Belzedek ?
Jehud
Yehud
Plain of Ono
Ono
Onus
Gibbethon
Gallaa
Ether
Kefar Dikhriya
Serifin
Ekron
Accaron
Gath
Saphitha
Lachish
Bene-beraq
Bene-berak
Beth-dagon
Gath-rimmon ?
Givatayim
T. Qasila
Azor
Shikkeron
Saalis
Phathura
T. Qudadi
Baalath ?
Kedron,
Gedrus
Eltekeh ?
T. el-Areini,
T. Erani
Joppa
Muhhazi, Mahoz ?
Jabneel
Jamnia
T. Zippor
Eglon ?
T. el-Hesi
Agla
Bareca
Saphei
Port of Jamnia
Mezad Hashavyahu
Ashdod
N. Yarqon
N. Shillo
W. Natuf
N. Refaim
N. Kesalon
Valley of Aijalon
N. Sorek
HaEla
N. Guvrin
N. Shiqma
N. Lakhish
160
150
140
130
120

Section 1–3

Regional Map

SCALE 1:215,000
10 Km
6 M
ISRAEL GRID

LEGEND:
- Historical Sites in Student Map A — • Ashdod
- Historical Sites in Student Map B — • Azotus
- Name common to both Student Maps — *
- Archaeological Sites (see Section 2) — • H. Shurah
- Modern Roads

E

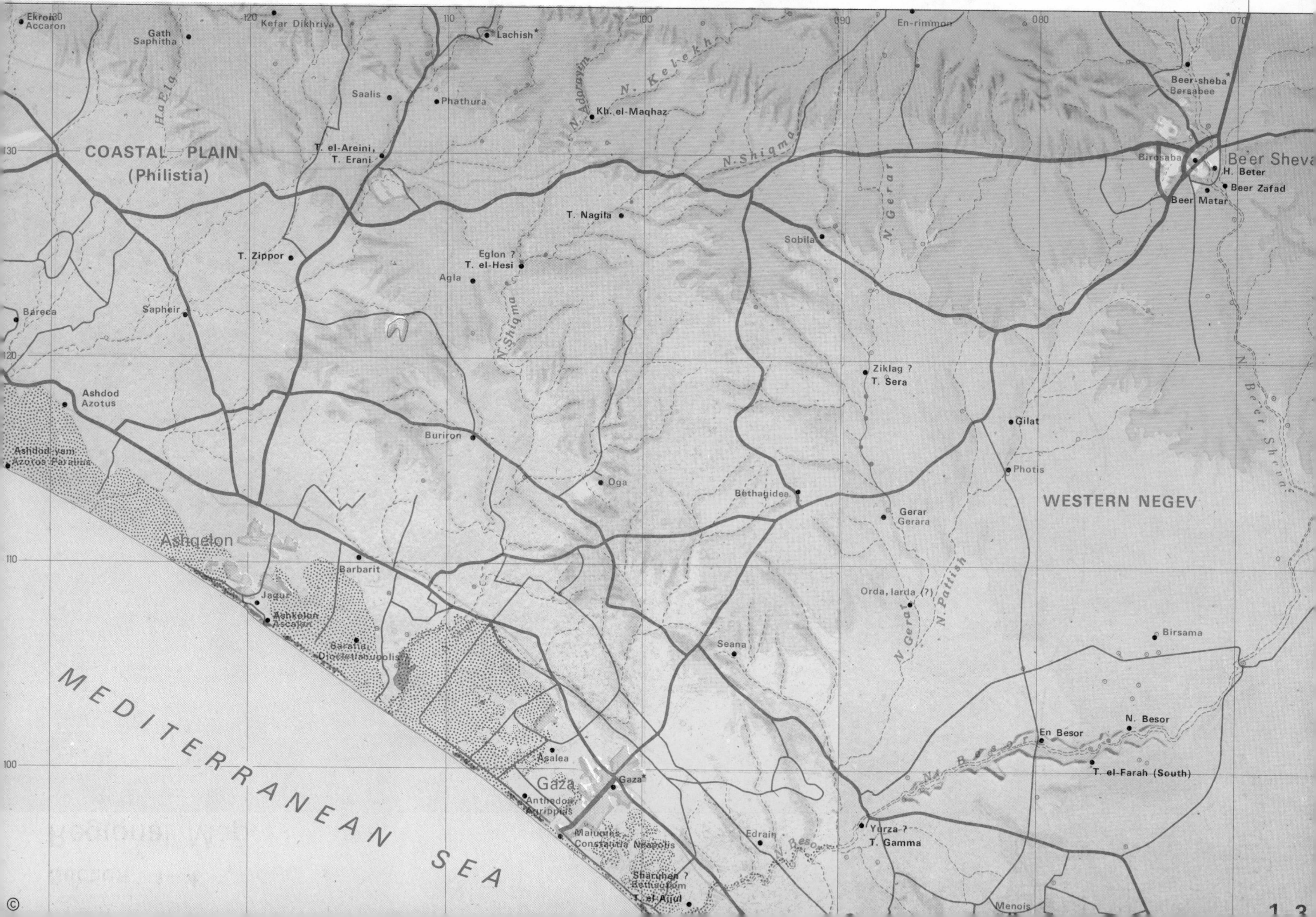

Ekron
Accaron
130
120
Kefar Dikhriya
110
100
090
080
070
Gath
Saphitha
Lachish*
En-rimmon
Beer-sheba*
Bersabee
Saalis
Phathura
Kh. el-Maqhaz
N. Adorayim
N. Kelekh
HaEla
COASTAL PLAIN
(Philistia)
T. el-Areini,
T. Erani
N. Shiqma
N. Gerar
Birosaba
Beer Sheva
H. Beter
Beer Zafad
Beer Matar
T. Nagila
Sobila
T. Zippor
Eglon ?
T. el-Hesi
Agla
Bareca
Sapheir
N. Shiqma
Ziklag ?
T. Sera
Ashdod
Azotus
Gilat
N. Beer Sheva
Buriron
Ashdod-yam
Azotos Paralius
Photis
Oga
Bethagidea
WESTERN NEGEV
Gerar
Gerara
Ashqelon
Barbarit
N. Pattish
Orda, Iarda (?)
Jagur
Ashkelon
Ascalon
N. Gerar
Birsama
Sarafia
Diocletianupolis (?)
Seana
MEDITERRANEAN SEA
N. Besor
En Besor
N. Besor
T. el-Farah (South)
Asalea
Gaza
Gaza*
Anthedon
Agrippias
Maiumas
Constantia Neapolis
Edrain
Yurza ?
T. Gamma
N. Besor
Sharuhen ?
Bethaglaim
T. el-Ajjul
Menois

Section 1–4

Regional Map

SCALE 1:215,000

10 Km

6 M

ISRAEL GRID

LEGEND:
- Historical Sites in Student Map A — ● Ashdod
- Historical Sites in Student Map B — ● Azotus
- Name common to both Student Maps — *
- Archaeological Sites (see Section 2) — ● H. Shurah
- Modern Roads

LOWER JORDAN VALLEY
EASTERN SAMARIA
CENTRAL SAMARIA
HILL COUNTRY OF EPHRAIM
WILDERNESS
Jericho
Jerusalem
Nablus
Beth-nimrah
Abila
Bethennabris
Beth-jeshimoth
T. el-Ghassul
Besimoth
Zaphon ? Amathus
Succoth Taralah T. Deir Alla
Zaphon ? Asophon
Zarethan ?
Aenon, Bethany (?)
Adam
Bethabara
Kh. el-Makhraq
Bethmaela
Choba
Beth-hoglah ? Bethagla
Beth-arabah
Jokmeam ? Coreae
Abelmea
Magdalsenna
Archelais
Alexandrium, Sartaba
Gilgal ?
Beth Hakkoz
Phasaelis
Jericho* T. es-Sultan
Jericho T. Abu el-Alayiq
Naaran Neara
Docus, Dok
Cypros, Threx (?)
Chozba
Aser
W. Faria
W. Samiya
W. Auja
W. Na'eima
W. Qilt
W. Mukallik (N. Og)
Beth Dagon
Taanath-shiloh Thena
Janoah
Jano
Acrabeta
Eduma
Thebez
Ascent of Adummim
Maledomnei
Salem, Salim (?)
Tirzah Aenon ?
Ein Samiya
St. Euthymious
Baddan
Arumah
Gerasa
Galod
Pharathon
Ophrah Apherema, Ephraim
Rimmon Remmon
Parah
Shiloh Silo
Tur Shimeon
Baal-hazor Mt. Asor
Michmash Machmas
Almon, Alemeth Ailamon
En-shemesh
Yazith
Tur Lozah
Sychar
Jacob's Well
Shechem
Tirathana ?
Mt. Gerizim Garizein
Mt. Ebal
Awartha
Anathoth*
Betabudison
Anamah
Bethany
Hazeroth ?
Luza
Neapolis
Michmethath Macher
Hivria
Kefar Yatma
Anuathu Borcaeus
Chusi
Lebonah
Jeshanah Isana
Geba* ?
Ai
Aiath, Ayyah ? Aiath ?
Beth-aven ?
Geba*
Azmaveth*
Bahurim ?
Bethphage ?
Nob ?
Gibeah Gabath Saul
En Rogel
Yashub ? Jeshub
Tappuah Tephon ?
Bethel*
Ramah Rama
Jerusalem*
Aelia Capitolina
Geba*
Azzah
Beeroth ? Berea
Gophna
Ataroth
To Tetarton
Mizpah*
Zemaraim ?
Adasa
Elasa
Samaria* Sebaste
En Naqura
Ataroth (-addar)?
Ataroth
Gibeon Gabaon
Beeroth ?
Beeroth ?
Waters of Nephtoah
Birzaith
Kefar Silah
1-4

Section 1–5

Regional Map

SCALE 1:215,000

10 Km

6 M

ISRAEL GRID

LEGEND:
- Historical Sites in Student Map A — • Ashdod
- Historical Sites in Student Map B — • Azotus
- Name common to both Student Maps — *
- Archaeological Sites (see Section 2) — • H. Shurah
- Modern Roads

E

70
220
210
200
190
180
170
160
Megiddo
Caparcotnei, Legio, Kefar Otnay
Batoaenea
Fahma
Kefar Silah
Samaria*
Sebaste
En Naqura
Kozoh
Pirathon
Elmattan
Ataroth
Aruir
Addara ?
Arus ?
N. Iron
WESTERN SAMARIA
Kiriath Haggah
Anabtah
Sepher
Apharaea
SHEPHELAH OF CARMEL
Beth Rimah
Zeredah
Seredah
Aruna
Siphtan ?
Zeitah
Mezer
Narbata, Arbatta
Gath (-padalla)
Borim
Yaham
Socoh
Socho
Jeshub
Birat Soreqah
Beth Laban
T. Esur
Tibetah
Bethsarisa
Sindenon
Zephath
N. Tanninim
N. Hadera
N. Shekhem
N. Alexander
N. Qana
50
Mearath Telimon
Migdal ?
T. Zeror*
Kefar Qesem
Calecaelea
Ebenezer ?
Capparetaea
Tower of Aphek
N. Shilo
Galgulis
Kefar Shuni
Burgatah
Theraspis
Betthar
W. Rabba
Dor
Dora
T. Mevorach*
Soran
Aphek
Antipatris,
Pegae
Hedera
Kefar Monash
Crocodilon
Polis
Capharsaba
Rantia
Caesarea,
Strato's Tower
Hepher ?
PLAIN OF SHARON
40
T. Poleg
Bene-beraq
Bene-berak*
MEDITERRANEAN SEA
Apollonia
Gath-rimmon ?
Givatayim
T. Mikhal
T. Qasila*
30
T. Qudadi
Yarqon
1–5
Joppa*

©

Section 1–6

Regional Map

SCALE 1:215,000

10 Km

6 M

ISRAEL GRID

LEGEND:

- Historical Sites in Student Map A — ● **Ashdod**
- Historical Sites in Student Map B — ● Azotus
- Name common to both Student Maps — *
- Archaeological Sites (see Section 2) — ● **H. Shurah**
- Modern Roads

WESTERN LOWER GALILEE
SHEPHELAH OF GALILEE
PLAIN OF ACCO
VALLEY OF JEZREEL
SHEPHELAH OF CARMEL
Mt. CARMEL
WESTERN SAMARIA
PLAIN OF SHARON
MEDITERRANEAN SEA
Nazareth
Akko
Haifa
Acco
Ptolemais
Aphek
Geuru
Achshaph ?
Beten ?
Bethbeten
Gaba ?
Geba-shemen
Helkath ?
Jokneam
Cimona
Deir Muhraqa
Husifah
Kh. Summaqa
Libnath ?
Calamon
T. Abu Huwam
Castra Samaritanorum
Sycaminum
T. es-Samak
T. Megadim
Certha
Athlit
Bucolon Polis
Migdal Malhah
Carmel Caves
Mearath Telimon
Geba
Dor
Dora
Crocodilon Polis
Caesarea
Strato's Tower
T. Mevorach
Kefar Shuni
Sindenon
Zephath
T. Esur
Narbata, Arbatta
Mezer
Borim
Gath (-padalla)
Yaham
Zeitah
Migdal ?
T. Zeror
Hedera
Hepher ?
Aruna
Betoaenea
Fahma
Capercotnei, Legio, Kefar Otnay
Megiddo
Taanach
Thaanach
Janua ?
Dothan
Dothaim
Sanur
Merrus
Ibleam
Belemoth
Bemeselis ?
Bethoma ?
Beth-haggan
Ginae
Jezreel
Esdraelon
Shunem
Sulem
Ophrah ?
Arbela ?
Tarbenet
Ginneigar
Sarid
Gabatha
Maralah ?
Dabbesheth ?
Ein el-Jarba
ha-Zorea, T. Qiri
Apharaea
Besara
Beth Shearim
Tibon
Ardasqus
Kefar Sasay
Ushah
Hali
Shefaram
Rehob ?
H. Uza
Mishal ?
T. Kison
Abelim
Kefar Tamartah
Kabul
Chabulon
Neiel
Saab
Cochaba ?
Beth-haccherem
Beth-anath ?
Hukkok ?
Jotbah
Jotapata
Mt. Asamon
Kefar Mandi
Hannathon
Asochis
Sogane
Kanah
Cana
Rimmon
Rumah
Ruma
Valley of Iphtahel
Sepphoris, Diocaesarea
Japhia
Aitalo
Mahalol
Shimron
Simonias
Bethlehem
Hivria
Apharatha ?
Gath-hepher
Rani ?
Abel ?
Chesulloth
Exaloth
Garis ?
(G)Araba, Gabara
Bet-haccerem Valley
N. Kishon
N. Iphtahel
N. Tanninim
N. Hadera
N. Iron
N. Meforot

Section 1–7

Regional Map

SCALE 1:215,000
10 Km
6 M
ISRAEL GRID

LEGEND:
- Historical Sites in Student Map A — • Ashdod
- Historical Sites in Student Map B — • Azotus
- Name common to both Student Maps — *
- Archaeological Sites (see Section 2) — • H. Shurah
- Modern Roads

E

260
240
210
190
Plain of Gennesaret
Rakkath
Tiberias
Taricheae
Magdala
Mt. Arbel
Caves
Arbela
Bethmaus
Sergunin
Sayydatah
Jabneel
Beth-shemesh ?
Kefar Yamma
Ullama
En-gannim ?
En-haddah
H. Sarona
Remeth ? Jarmuth ?
Cochaba ? Agrippina ?
Gebul ?
Beth-shan
Scythopolis
VALLEY OF BETH-SHAN
Salim ?
Rehob
Roob
Cola
Jamnith
Biri
Acchabare
Sepph
Zefat
N. Ammud
N. Zalmon
Huqoq
EASTERN LOWER GALILEE
Adamah ?
Adamah
Adami-nekeb
Kefar Hittaya
Kefar Shabtay
Anaharath ?
Hapharaim ?
N. Harod
Tekoa
H. Shema
Merom ?
Meron
Parod
Kefar Hananiya
Bersabe
Mamliah
Kefar Nimrah
Lubiya
Heleph ?
Bet Alfa
Harod Valley
UPPER GALILEE
H. Ammudim
Mashkanah
Mearaia
Mt. Hazon
Ailabo
Ramah
Beth Netofa
Mt. Tabor
Itabyrium
Kishion ?
Neoran
En-dor
Aendor
Mt. GILBOA
Gelbus
Beth-dagon
Selame
Mt. Tiran
Turan ?
Aznoth-tabor ?
Daberath
Dabaritta
Tubani
Araba
Rama
Kefar Yohannah
Mt. Netofa
Bet Netofa Valley
Turan Valley
En Teena
En Tab ?
Nain
Hill of Moreh
En Harod
Bethacath
Baca
Shezor
(G)Araba,
Gabara
Garis ?
Shunem
Sulem
Jezreel
Esdraelon
WESTERN LOWER GALILEE
Abel ?
Chesulloth
Exaloth
Rimmon
Gath-hepher
Rani ?
Beth-haggan
Ginae
(Ca)parasima
Kanah
Cana
Nazareth
Sogane
Rumah
Ruma
N. Iphtahel
Ophrah ?
Arbela ?
Ibleam
Belemoth
Bet-haccerem Valley
Jotbah
Jotapata
Valley of Iphtahel
Sepphoris,
Diocaesarea
Japhia
VALLEY OF JEZREEL
Beth-anath ?
Hukkok ?
Mt. Asamon
Kefar Mandi
Ginnegar
Janoah
Beth-haccherem
Hannathon
Asochis
Aitalo
Tarbenet
Merrus
Saab
Cochaba ?
Mahalol
Dothan
Dothaim
Gath
Sarid
Janua ?
Neiel
Kabul
Chabulon
Shimron
Simonias
Gabatha
Taanach
Thaanach
Beth Hobaya
Kefar Tamartah
Apharatha ?
Bethlehem
Abelim
Megiddo
SHEPHELAH OF GALILEE
Hivria
Kefar Amiqo
Shefaram
Maralah ?
Capercotnei,
Legio,
Kefar Otnay
Rehob ?
Betoaenea
Kefar Yasif
Beth-emek
H. Uza
Mishal ?,
T. Kison
Hali
Dabbesheth ?
Ardasqus
N. Kishon
N. Iron
PLAIN OF ACCO
Ushah
Tibon
Ein el-Jarba
Kefar Sasay
Besara,
Beth Shearim
Heikath ?
ha-Zorea (T. Qiri)
Evron
Aphek
Beten ?
Bethbeten
Gaba ?
Yokneam
Cimona
Apharaea
SHEPHELAH OF CARMEL
Gedru
Geba-shemen
Akko
Acco
Ptolemais
Achshaph ?
Deir Muhraqa
Mt. CARMEL
Husifah
Aruna

Section 1–8
Regional Map

SCALE 1:215,000
10 Km
6 M
ISRAEL GRID

LEGEND:
- Historical Sites in Student Map A — • Ashdod
- Historical Sites in Student Map B — • Azotus
- Name common to both Student Maps — *
- Archaeological Sites (see Section 2) — • H. Shurah
- Modern Roads

230
290
280
270
260
250
240
210
200
190
Quneitra
Farj
Chaspho
Caspein
Nob
Lake Phiale
Seleucia ?
UPPER GOLAN
Mt. HERMON
Kafr Nafakh
Gamala
Umm el-Qanatir
El Al
Yaarut
Dabiyya
LOWER GOLAN
Upper Aphek
Apheca
Amudiyya
Qisrin
Sogane
Deir Aziz
ed-Danqalle, Ghadriyya
Caesarea Philippi
Panias
Kanaf
Shuqayyif
Skoufiye
Ram Baraq
Kh. el-Asaliya
Hermon
Ayyanosh
Hippus
Ain ?
Iyyon
Emmatha
Hammath Gader
Kefar Harub
Dab(u)ra
Aduru
Bascama ?
Dan*
Antiochia
T. Anafa
Lower Aphek ?
En Gev
Gergesa
Kursi
Daphne
R. JORDAN
Julias,
Bethsaida (?)
Kh. er-Rafid
Kh. ed-Dikke
Thella
Bethsaida ?
SEA OF GALILEE
UPPER JORDAN VALLEY
(Huleh Basin)
N. Hazor
Kefar Semah
Abel-beth-maachah
Qiryat Shemona
H. Shurah
Rosh Pinna Sill
Capernaum
Beth-yerah
Philoteria
Kefar Agon
Kefar Giladi
Kh. Harrawi
Hazor
Chorazin
N. Korazim
Hammath
Ammathus
Kedesh
Sennabris ?
Yenoa
N. Dishon
Heptapegon
Tiberias
Lakkum ?
Cadasa
Rosh Pinna
Chinnereth
Gennesaret
Tiberias
Kefar Menori
Oak in Zaanannim
Kedesh
Qisyon
Jamnith
Plain of Gennesaret
Taricheae
Magdala
Rakkath
Beth-shemesh ?
Sayydatah
Jabneel
Kefar Neboraya
Zefat
Acchabare
Bethmaus
Kefar Yamma
Alma
Dalton
Biri
Sepph
N. Ammud
Mt. Arbel
Sergunin
En-gannim ?
N. Zalmon
Caves
W. Dubbeh
Huqoq
Arbela
H. Sarona
En-hadda
EASTERN LOWER GALILEE
Adamah
Kefar Hittaya
Adamah ?
Adami-nekeb
UPPER GALILEE
Safsofah
Meroth ?
Gischala
Mamliah
Kefar Shabtay
Beth-anath ?*
Merom ?
Tekoa ?
Merom ?
H. Shema
Meron
Parod
Kefar Nimrah
Lubiya
Bersabe
Kefar Hananiya
Heleph ?
Yiron
Mt. Meron
H. Ammudim
Taphnith
Kefar Baram
Abel
Ramah
Mt. Hazon
Mearaia
Ailabo
Mashkanah
Sasa
Beth Netofa
Aznoth-tabor ?
Mt. Tabor
Itabyrium
©

Regional Map

SCALE 1:215,000

10 Km

6 M

ISRAEL GRID

LEGEND:

- Historical Sites in Student Map A — Ashdod
- Historical Sites in Student Map B — Azotus
- Name common to both Student Maps — *
- Archaeological Sites (see Section 2) — H. Shurah
- Modern Roads

E

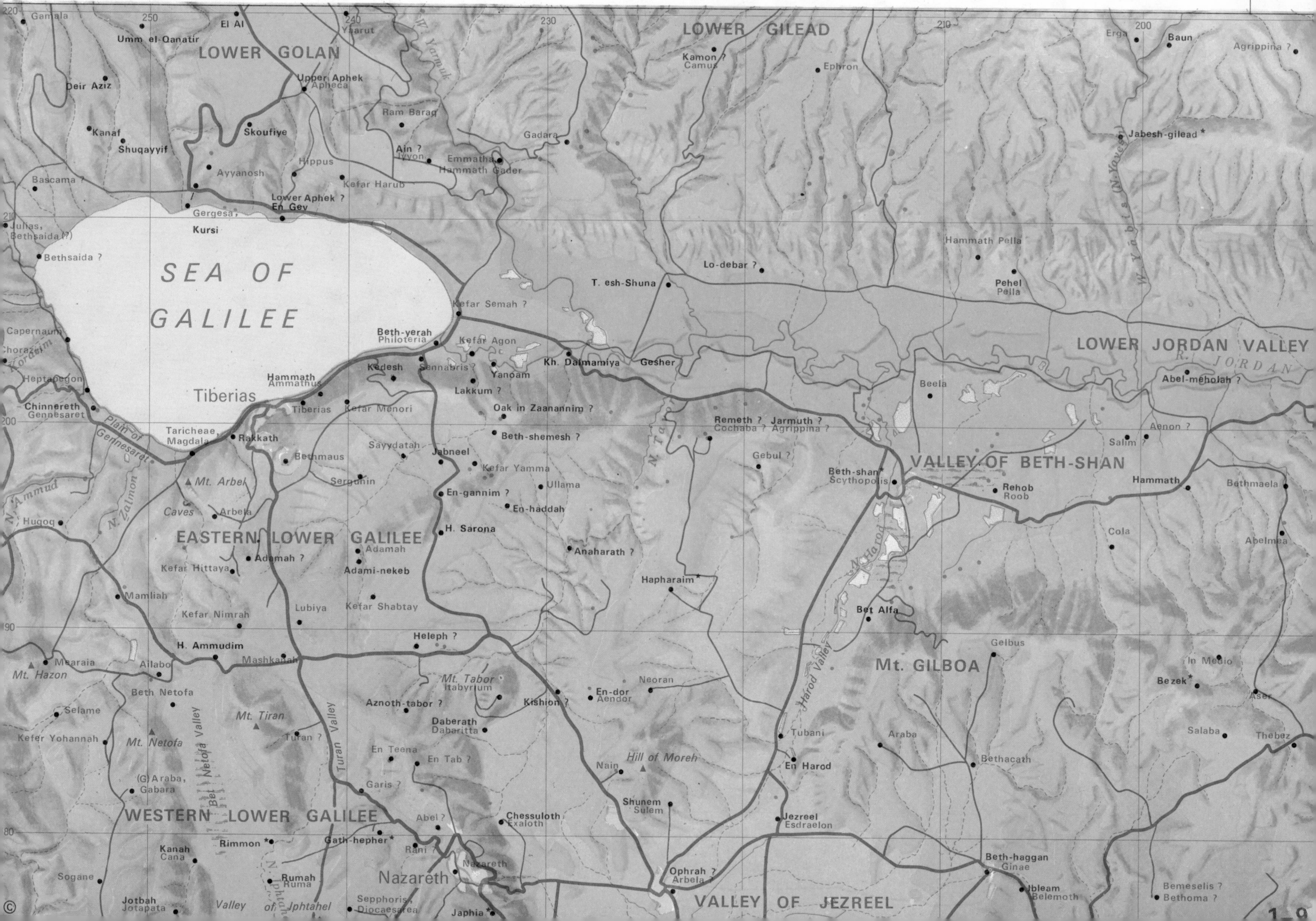
220
Gamala
250
El Al
240
Yaarut
230
LOWER GILEAD
210
Erga
200
Baun
Agrippina ?
Umm el-Qanatir
LOWER GOLAN
W. Yarmuk
Kamon ?
Camus
Ephron
Upper Aphek
Apheca
Deir Aziz
Ram Baraq
Kanaf
Skoufiye
Gadara
Jabesh-gilead *
Shuqayyif
Ain ?
Iyyon
Emmatha
Hammath Gader
Hippus
Ayyanosh
Kefar Harub
Bascama ?
Lower Aphek ?
En Gev
Gergesa
Kursi
210
Julias,
Bethsaida (?)
W. Yabis (N. Yavesh)
Bethsaida ?
SEA OF GALILEE
Hammath Pella
Lo-debar ?
T. esh-Shuna
Pehel
Pella
Kefar Semah ?
Capernaum
Chorazin
Korazim
Beth-yerah
Philoteria
Kefar Agon
LOWER JORDAN VALLEY
R. JORDAN
Heptapegon
Kedesh
Sennabris ?
Yanoam
Kh. Dalmamiya
Gesher
Hammath
Ammathus
Lakkum ?
Beela
Abel-meholah ?
Tiberias
Chinnereth
Gennesaret
Tiberias
Kefar Menori
Oak in Zaanannim ?
200
Plain of Gennesaret
Remeth ?
Cochaba ?
Jarmuth ?
Agrippina ?
Aenon ?
Taricheae
Magdala
Rakkath
Beth-shemesh ?
Salim ?
Sayydatah
Gebul ?
Bethmaus
Jabneel
VALLEY OF BETH-SHAN
Kefar Yamma
Beth-shan *
Scythopolis
Hammath
Mt. Arbel
Sergunin
Ullama
Rehob
Roob
Bethmaela
N. Ammud
N. Zalmon
En-gannim ?
Caves
Arbela
En-haddah
Huqoq
H. Sarona
Cola
EASTERN LOWER GALILEE
Adamah
Abelmea
Anaharath ?
Kefar Hittaya
Adamah ?
Adami-nekeb
Hapharaim *
N. Harod
Mamliah
Kefar Shabtay
Bet Alfa
Kefar Nimrah
Lubiya
90
Heleph ?
Harod Valley
H. Ammudim
Gelbus
Mearaia
Allabo
Mashkanah
Mt. GILBOA
In Medio
Mt. Hazon
Mt. Tabor
Itabyrium
Neoran
Bezek *
Beth Netofa
Kishion ?
En-dor
Aendor
Aser
Selame
Aznoth-tabor ?
Mt. Tiran
Bet Netofa Valley
Daberath
Dabaritta
Tubani
Salaba
Kefer Yohannah
Mt. Netofa
Turan ?
Turan Valley
Araba
Thebez
En Teena
En Tab ?
Hill of Moreh
Bethacath
Nain
En Harod
(G) Araba,
Gabara
Garis ?
Shunem
Sulem
WESTERN LOWER GALILEE
Abel ?
Chessuloth
Exaloth
Jezreel
Esdraelon
80
Rimmon *
Gath-hepher *
Rani ?
Kanah
Cana
Nazareth
Beth-haggan
Ginae
Sogane
Rumah
Ruma
Nazareth
Ophrah ?
Arbela
Bemeselis ?
Bethoma ?
Ibleam
Belemoth
Jotbah
Jotapata
Valley of Iphtahel
Sepphoris
Diocaesarea
Japhia *
VALLEY OF JEZREEL

Section 1–10

Regional Map

SCALE 1:215,000

10 Km

6 M

ISRAEL GRID

LEGEND:
- Historical Sites in Student Map A — ●Ashdod
- Historical Sites in Student Map B — ● Azotus
- Name common to both Student Maps — *
- Archaeological Sites (see Section 2) — ● H. Shurah
- Modern Roads

E
LOWER JORDAN VALLEY
R. JORDAN
VALLEY OF BETH-SHAN
EASTERN LOWER GALILEE
EASTERN SAMARIA
Mt. GILBOA
VALLEY OF JEZREEL
CENTRAL SAMARIA
T. esh-Shuna
Lo-debar ?
Hammath Pella
Pehel
Pella
W. Yabis
Zaphon ?
Amathus
Succoth
Taralah
T Deir Alla
Kefar Semah ?
Kefar Agon
Yeroam
Kh. Dalhamiya
Gesher
Lakkum ?
Zaphon ?
Asophon
Zarethan ?
Zarethan ?
Abel-meholah ?
Beela
Oak in Zaanannim ?
Remeth ?
Jarmuth ?
Cochaba ?
Agrippina ?
Beth-shemesh ?
Salim ?
Aenon ?
Kefar Yamma
Gebul ?
Beth-shan
Scythopolis
Rehob
Roob
Ullama
Hammath
Bethmaela
Kh. el-Makhruq
Jokmeam ?
Coreae
En-haddah
Cola
Abelmea
Anaharath ?
N. Harod
N. Tavor
Hapharaim
Bet Alfa
Harod Valley
Gelbus
In Medio
Bezek
Aser
Mt. Tabor
Itabyrium
Kishion ?
En-dor
Aendor
Neoran
Daberath
Dabaritta
Tubani
Araba
Salaba
Thebez
Beth Dagon
Taanath-shiloh
Thena
Janoah
Jano
W. Far'a
En Harod
Bethbaath
Hill of Moreh
Nain
Tirzah
Aenon ?
Acrabeta
Shunem
Sulem
Jezreel
Esdraelon
Chesulloth
Exaloth
Salem,
Salim (?)
Baddan
Arumah
Beth-haggan
Ginae
Nazareth
Ophrah ?
Arbela ?
Ibleam
Belemoth
Bemeselis,
Bethoma ?
Tur Lozah
Sychar
Shechem
Jacob's Well
Tirathana ?
Mt. Ebal
Mt. Gerizim
Garizein
Awartha
Japhia
Yazith
Nablus
Neapolis
Hazeroth ?
Luza
Michmethath
Macher
Kefar Yatma
Ginnegar
Tarbenet
Merrus
Hivria
Chusi
Mahalol
Sanur
Sarid
Dothan
Dothaim
Yashub ?
Jeshub
Janua ?
Azzah
Shimron
Simonias
Taanach
Thaanach
Geba
Gabatha
En Naqura
Capercotnei
Samaria
Sebaste
Kefar Silah
230
220
210
200
190
180
170
210
200
190
1 10

Section 1 – 11

Regional Map

SCALE 1:215,000

10 Km

6 M

ISRAEL GRID

LEGEND:
- Historical Sites in Student Map A — Ashdod
- Historical Sites in Student Map B — Azotus
- Name common to both Student Maps — *
- Archaeological Sites (see Section 2) — H. Shurah
- Modern Roads

E

210
200
190
180
170
160
240
220
210
200
LOWER GILEAD
Dathema ?
Gerasa
Rabbath-ammon
Philadelphia
Amman
AMMON
Jogbehah
Mahanaim ?
Jazer ? *
Ham
Rogelim ?
Enganna
Ramath-mizpeh ?
Ramoth ?
DOME OF GILEAD
Gedor
Gedora
Jazer ?
Erga
Baun
Agrippina ?
Ephron
Zia
Betonim
Ragaba
Penuel
Mahanaim ?
Jabesh-gilead *
W. Yabis (N. Yavesh)
W. Zarqa (N. Yabboq)
Hammath Pella
Pehel
Pella
Zaphon ?
Amathus
Succoth
Taralah
T. Deir Alla
Zaphon ?
Asophon
Zarethan ?
Zarethan ?
LOWER JORDAN VALLEY
R. JORDAN
Beela
Abel-meholah ?
Adam
Salim ?
Aenon ?
Beth-shan
Scythopolis
VALLEY OF BETH-SHAN
Rehob
Roob
Hammath
Bethmaela
Abelmea
Kh. el-Makhraq
Jokmeam ?
Coreae
Choba

Section 1–12

Regional Map

SCALE 1:215,000

10 Km

6 M

ISRAEL GRID

LEGEND:
- Historical Sites in Student Map A — Ashdod
- Historical Sites in Student Map B — Azotus
- Name common to both Student Maps — *
- Archaeological Sites (see Section 2) — H. Shurah
- Modern Roads

AMMON
Yaduda
Bezer ?
Jahaz(ah) ?
Maschana ?
Beth-gamul
Kedemoth ?
Jogbehah
Maanith
Samaga
Almon-diblathaim ?
Dabaloth
Aroer*
Jazer ?*
Abel-keramim ?
Abela ?
Elealeh*
MEDEBA PLATEAU
Heshbon
Esbus
Medeba*
Kh. el-Aqraba
Nadabath
Valtha
Kh. Iskandar
Dibon*(-gad)
Lemba, Libba
Tyre of Tobiah
Tyrus, Birtha
Mt. Nebo
Kiriathaim ?
Nebo ?
Gedor
Gedora
Nebo ?
Beth-baal-meon*
Jazer ?
Pisgah
Fasga
Betonim
Beth-Peor
Kerioth
Cariatha
Beth-haram
Abel-shittim
Ataroth
Abila
Livias, Julias,
Beth-ramatha
Beth-nimrah
Bethennabris
Machaerus
Beth-jeshimoth
Baaras
T. el-Ghassul
Besimoth
Aenon,
Bethany (?)
Zereth-shahar ?
Callirhoe
LOWER JORDAN VALLEY
Bethabara
Beth-hoglah
Bethagla
Beth-arabah
DEAD SEA
Magdalsenna
Archelais
Gilgal ?
Beth-hakkoz
Jericho
Jericho
City of Salt ?
Mezad Hasidim
Kh. Qumran
160
150
140
130
120
100
230
20
210
200

Regional Map

SCALE 1:215,000

10 Km

6 M

ISRAEL GRID

LEGEND: Historical Sites in Student Map A • Ashdod
Historical Sites in Student Map B • Azotus
Name common to both Student Maps *
Archaeological Sites (see Section 2) • H. Shurah
Modern Roads

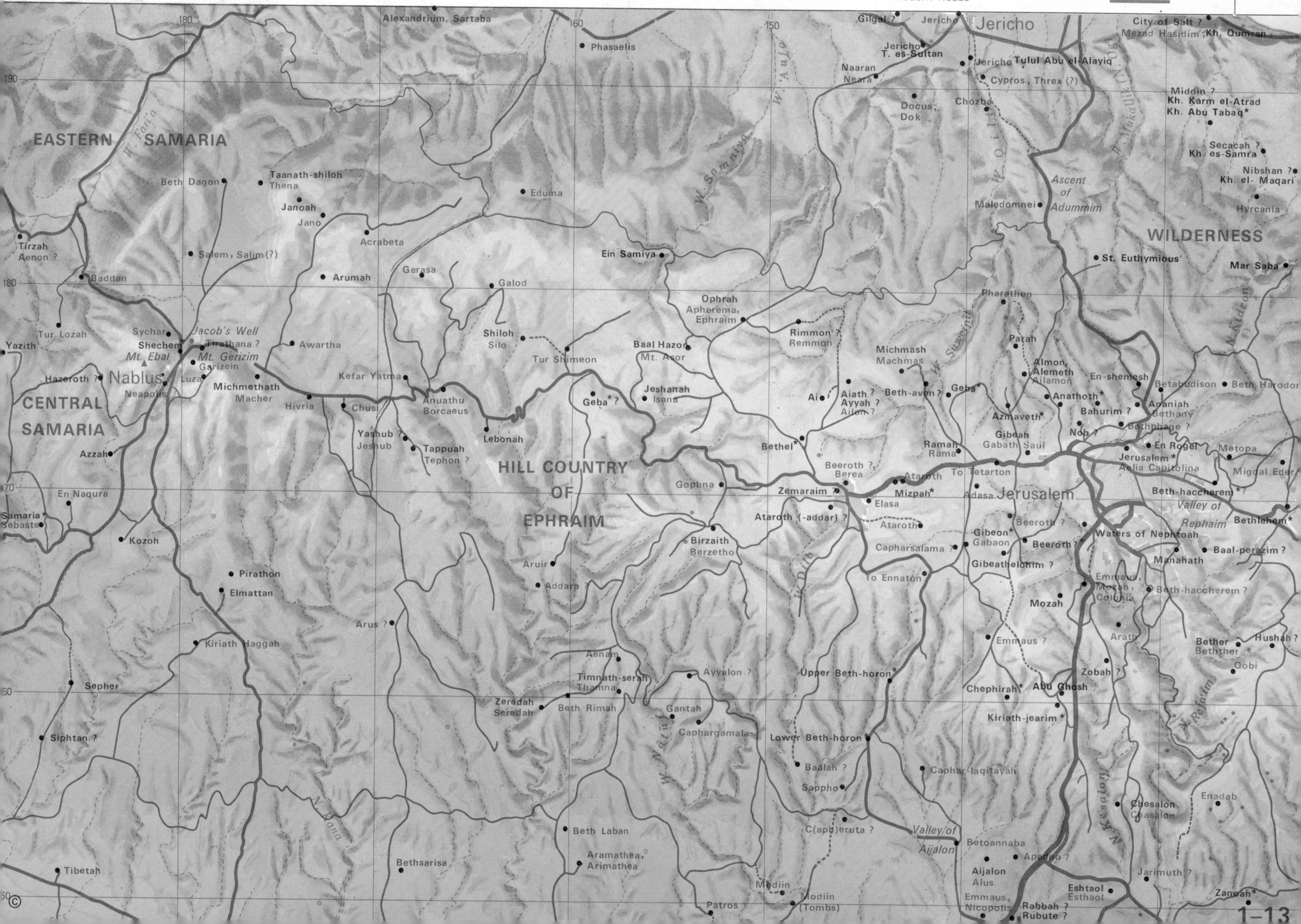

E
Alexandrium, Sartaba
Phasaelis
Gilgal ?
Jericho
Jericho
Jericho T. es-Sultan
Jericho
Tulul Abu el-Alayiq
City of Salt ?
Mezad Hasidim
Kh. Qumran
Naaran Neara
Cypros, Threx (?)
Docus, Dok
Chozba
Middin ?
Kh. Karm el-Atrad
Kh. Abu Tabaq*
Secacah ?
Kh. es-Samra
Nibshan ?
Kh. el- Maqari
Hyrcania
W. Auja
W. Samniya
W. Qilt
W. Mukallik
W. Far'a
EASTERN SAMARIA
Taanath-shiloh Thena
Beth Dagon
Janoah Jano
Acrabeta
Eduma
Ascent of Adummim
Maledomnei
WILDERNESS
Tirzah Aenon ?
Salem, Salim (?)
Ein Samiya
St. Euthymious
Mar Saba
Baddan
Arumah
Gerasa
Galod
Pharathon
Ophrah Apherema, Ephraim
Rimmon ? Remmon
N. Kidron
Tur Lozah
Sychar
Jacob's Well
Shechem
Tirathana ?
Mt. Ebal
Mt. Gerizim Garizein
Yazith
Awartha
Shiloh Silo
Tur Shimeon
Baal Hazor Mt. Asor
Michmash Machmas
W. Suweinit
Parah
Almon, Alemeth Ailamon
En-shemesh
Betabudison
Beth Harodon
Hazeroth ?
Nablus Neapolis
Luza
Michmethath Macher
Kefar Yatma
Anuathu Borcaeus
Hivria
Chusi
Geba* ?
Jeshanah Isana
Ai
Aiath ? Ayyah ? Ailon ?
Beth-aven ?
Geba*
Anathoth*
Ananiah Bethany
Bahurim ?
Azmaveth*
Nob ?
Bethphage ?
CENTRAL SAMARIA
Yashub ? Jeshub
Tappuah Tephon ?
Lebonah
Bethel*
Ramah Rama
Gibeah Gabath Saul
En Rogel
Metopa
Azzah
HILL COUNTRY OF EPHRAIM
Beeroth ? Berea
Ataroth
To Tetarton
Jerusalem* Aelia Capitolina
Migdal Eder
Gophna
Zemaraim ?
Mizpah*
Adasa
Jerusalem
Beth-haccherem* ?
En Naqura
Elasa
Valley of Rephaim
Bethlehem*
Samaria* Sebaste
Ataroth (-addar) ?
Ataroth
Beeroth ?
Waters of Nephtoah
Kozoh
Birzaith Berzetho
Gibeon* Gabaon
Beeroth ?
Capharsalama ?
Baal-perazim ?
Manahath
Gibeathelohim ?
Aruir
W. Dilb
Pirathon
Addara ?
To Ennaton
Emmaus, Mozah, Colonia
Beth-haccherem ?
Elmattan
Mozah
Arus ?
Arath
Kiriath Haggah
Emmaus ?
Bether Bethther
Hushah ?
Aenam
Qobi
Sepher
Timnath-serah Thamna
Ayyalon ?
Upper Beth-horon*
Zobah ?
Chephirah*
Abu Ghosh
N. Refaim
Zeredah Seredah
Beth Rimah
Gantah
Kiriath-jearim*
Siphtan ?
W. Natuf
Caphargamala
Lower Beth-horon
Baalah ?
Caphar-laqitayah
Sappho
N. Kesalon
Enadab
Chesalon Chasalon
N. Lidda
Beth Laban
C(aph)eruta ?
Valley of Aijalon
Betoannaba
Aramathea, Arimathea
Apedno ?
Tibetah
Bethsarisa
Aijalon Alus
Jarimuth ?
Modiin
Eshtaol Esthaol
Modiin (Tombs)
Patros
Emmaus, Nicopolis
Rabbah ? Rubute ?
Zanoah*
180
160
150
190
180
170
160
150
©

Section 1–14

Regional Map

SCALE 1:215,000

10 Km

6 M

ISRAEL GRID

LEGEND:
- Historical Sites in Student Map A — ● **Ashdod**
- Historical Sites in Student Map B — ● Azotus
- Name common to both Student Maps — *
- Archaeological Sites (see Section 2) — ● **H. Shurah**
- Modern Roads

DEAD SEA
LISSAN
WILDERNESS OF JUDAH
HILL COUNTRY OF JUDAH
Jericho
Jerusalem
Bethlehem
Hebron
Kh. Qumran
Mezad Hasidim
City of Salt ?
Tulul Abu el Alayiq
Cypros, Threx (?)
Chozba
Middin ?
Kh. Karm el-Atrad,
Kh. Abu Tabaq *
Secacah ?
Kh. es-Samra
Nibshan ?
Kh. el-Maqari
Hyrcania
Ascent of Adummim
Maledomnei
St. Euthymious
Mar Saba
W. el-Murabbaat Cave
Cave of the Pool
En-gedi
Cave of Letters
Cave of Horrors
Roman Camps
Cave of the Treasure
(N. Mishmar)
N. Zeelim Caves
Masada
'The Stronghold'
Pharathon
Parah
Michmash
Machmas
Almon, Alemeth
Ailamon
Beth-aven ?
Geba
Anathoth*
Azmaveth*
Bahurim ?
Nob ?
Bethphage
Ananiah
Bethany
En-shemesh
Betabudison
Beth Harodon
Herodium
Umm Qatafa Cave
Ramah
Rama
Gibeah
Gabath Saul
Jerusalem*
Aelia Capitolina
En Rogel
Metopa
Migdal Eder
Beth-basi
Netophah
Netopha
Tekoa *
Ataroth
To Tetarton
Adasa
Beth-haccherem* ?
Valley of Rephaim
Bethlehem*
Beeroth ?
Gibeon
Gabaon
Beeroth ?*
Waters of Nephtoah
Baal-perazim ?
Manahath
Etam
Gibeath-elohim ?
Emmaus,
Mozah,
Colonia
Mozah
Beth-haccherem ?
Asphar
Capharbarucha
Kain
Ziph
Aristobulias
Carmel
Chermela
Maon*
Kerioth ?
Arad
Oresa ?
Peor
Sior
Arath
Bether
Bethther
Hushah ?
Beth-zechariah
Beth-zaith
Beth-anoth
Bethennim
Emmaus ?
Zobah ?
Qobi
Chephirah*
Abu Ghosh
Nehelam
Halhul
Alulos
Mamre * ?
Terebinthos
Hebron*
Kh. Suseya
Kiriath-jearim*
Beth-zur*
Bethsura
Gedor
Gedora
Juttah*
Kefar Aziz
Anaea
Gabatha
Esthemoa
Esthemoa
Anim
Anaea
Enadab
Thamnatha ?
Aphekah
Chesalon
Chasalon
Beth-tappuah
Nebo?
Beth-leaphrah ?
Adoraim
Aijalon
N. Kidron
W. Murabbaat
N. Darga
N. Arugot
N. Hever
N. Mishmar
N. Ze'elim
N. Kesalon
N. Refaim
W. Khareitun
W. Mukallik
W. Qilt
N. Sorek
Beth Hakkoz
Jericho
es-Sultan
Docus,
Dok
Upper Beth-horon*
Caphar-laqitayah
Capharsalama
To Emmaton
Mizpah
140
130
120
110
100
090

Regional Map

SCALE 1:215,000

10 Km

6 M

ISRAEL GRID

LEGEND:
- Historical Sites in Student Map A — Ashdod
- Historical Sites in Student Map B — Azotus
- Name common to both Student Maps
- Archaeological Sites (see Section 2) — H. Shurah
- Modern Roads

090
080
070
060
050
040
220
210
200
190
MOAB
Ar ?
Adara
Adir, Ader
Dannaea
Rabbath-moab
Dhat Ras
Ainuatha
Ije-abarim ?
Thona ?
Agal(t)ain ?
Kir-hareseth
Charachmoba
Kerak
Madmen ?
Motha
Kh. et-Tannur
Ellebana
EDOM
Afra
Horonaim ?
Oronaim
Gabalis
Robotha
W. Mujib
N. Arnon
W. Shuqeiq
W. Kerak
W. Hasa
N. Zered
Naar Safrai
Bab edh-Dhra
Mazraa,
Agal(t)ain ?
Numeira
Bennamarim
LISSAN
DEAD SEA
Zoar
Zoara
Feifeh
Praesidium
Khanazir
ARABAH
En-gedi*
N. Arugot
N. Mishmar
N. Ze'elim
N. Hever
Masada
'The Stronghold'
En Boqeq
Mezad Zohar
Cave of Letters
Cave of Horrors
Cave of the Treasure
(N. Mishmar)
Roman Camps
©

Section 1–16

Regional Map

SCALE 1:215,000

10 Km

6 M

ISRAEL GRID

LEGEND:

Historical Sites in Student Map A	• Ashdod
Historical Sites in Student Map B	• Azotus
Name common to both Student Maps	*
Archaeological Sites (see Section 2)	• H. Shurah
Modern Roads	

WILDERNESS OF JUDAH
HILL COUNTRY OF JUDAH
SHEPHELAH OF JUDAH
EASTERN NEGEV
Valley of Rephaim
Valley of Elah
N. Arugot
N. Hever
N. Ze'elim
N. Malhata
N. Be'er Sheva'
N. Eshtemoa
N. Hebron
N. Guvrin
N. Sorek
N. Refaim
Hebron
Bethlehem
En-shemesh
Betabudison
Ananiah
Bethany
Beth Harodon
Herodium
Umm Qatafa Cave
En Rogel
Metopa
Migdal Eder
Jerusalem
Aelia Capitolina
Beth-basi
Netophah ?
Netopha ?
Tekoa
Beth-haccherem
Baal-perazim ?
Manahath
Etam
Asphar
Capharbarucha
Kain
Beth-haccherem ?
Peor
Sior
Ziph
Aristobulias
Carmel
Chermela
Maon
Oresa ?
Beth-anoth
Bethennim
Bether
Betther
Hushah ?
Beth-zechariah
Beth-zaith
Halhul
Alulos
Mamre ?
Terebinthos
Kerioth ?
Arad
T. Arad
Zobah ?
Obi
Nehelam
Kh. Suseya
Gedor
Gedora
Beth-zur
Bethsura
Juttah
Kefar Aziz
Anaea
Gabatha
Eshtemoa
Esthemoa
Anim
Aenea
Chesalon
Chasalon
Enadab
Thamnatha ?
Aphekah
Beth-tappuah
Nebo ?
Beth-leaphrah ?
Caphartoba ?
Adoraim
Adora
Jattir
Jethira
Arad
Malatha
T. Malhata
Debir
Jarimuth ?
Eshtaol
Esthaol
Keilah
Nezib
Nasib
Tricomias
Caparorsa
Socoh
Zanoah
Odollam
Adullam
Bethletepha
Dumah
Duma
Jeshua ?
Jekabzeel ?
Zorah
Jarmuth
Socchoth
Socoh
Roobo
Jedua
Kh. Beit Maqdum
Kh. el-Kum
Beth-shemesh
Bethsames
Hormah ?
T. Masos
Sorech
Shaaraim ?
Libnah ?
Capharabis
Magbish ?
Elam ?
Anab
Ceper(Zach)aria
Harim ?
Azekah
Anab
Madmannah
Bera ?
Ir Nahash
Eglon ?
T. Eton
Moladah ?
Moresheth-gat(h) ?
Mareshah
Marisa
Timnah
Morasthi
Migdal-gad ?
T. Beit Mirsim
Beth-pelet ?
Sansannah
Betogabris, Eleutheropolis
Belzedek ?
Ether
Goshen ?
Thala
T. Halif
En-rimmon
Gallaa
Kefar Dikhriya
Ekron
Accaron
Gath
Saphitha
Lachish
Beer-sheba
Bersabe
Kana ?
Ramoth of the Negeb ?
H. Uza
30
120
110
100
090
080
070
70
150
140
1-16

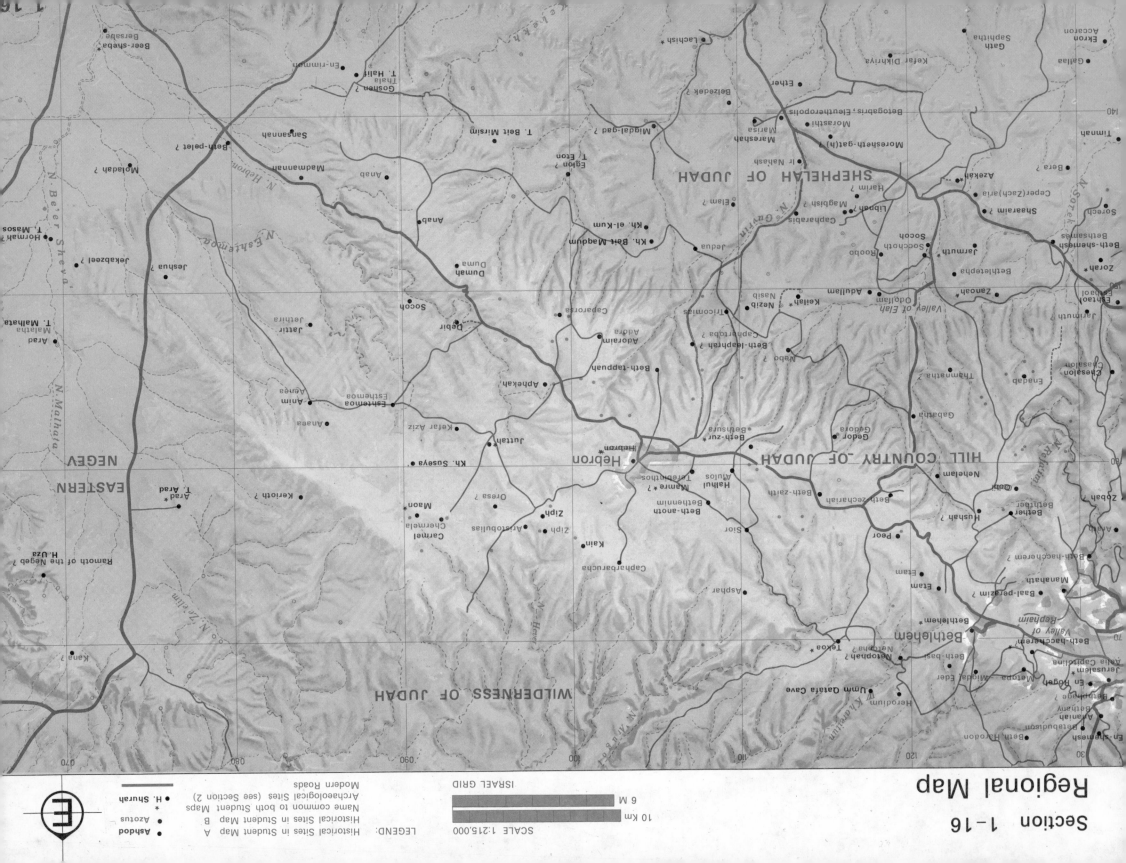

Archaeology

Map No.	Archaeological Period	Date			
2-1	Chalcolithic	4000	-	3150	B.C./B.C.E.
2-2	Early Bronze	3150	-	2200	"
2-3	Middle Bronze	2200	-	1550	"
2-4	Late Bronze	1550	-	1200	"
2-5	Iron Age I	1200	-	1000	"
2-6	Iron Age II	1000	-	586	"
2-7	Persian	586	-	332	"
2-8	Hellenistic (& Hasmonaean)	332	-	37	"
2-9	Herodian (& Early Roman)	37	-	70	A.D./C.E.
2-10	Late Roman & Byzantine	70	-	640	"

This Section is based upon Pictorial Archive's earlier set 'ARCHAEOLOGY SERIES 1—12' (scale 1:250,00) and follows the same basic chronology. Section 2 comprises 10 maps, each indicating the sites of major archaeological finds for all the individual main periods from Chalcolithic to Late Roman and Byzantine. The list is selective, being based upon those published reports which describe significant remains.

The sites represented in these archaeology maps are repeated as 'BACKGROUND SITES' on the maps in Sections 3—13. In this way the primary historical sources (RED) and the background archaeology (BLACK) are combined ON THE SAME MAP, presenting a comprehensive statement on each subject and one which is directly linked to the archaeological slides in the MINI-ARCHIVE. In the Index of Main Names (Section 15-2) each archaeological period is shown above the Sectional titles of all the historical maps, thus providing a quick and simple guide as to which archaeological slides are relevant.

Both modern names (Arabic or Hebrew) and historical names are used in the archaeological maps. When the historical name for the period is not known or is questioned, the modern name is used, appearing in italics. Names shown in brackets are transitional. In Section 2-2 they indicate the later historical name. In Section 2-8 and 2-9 they indicate the earlier historical name.

For example:

Map. No.	Grid Reference 207-206	Grid Reference 197-212
2-1	Tabaqat Fahl	T. Bet Shean
2-2	Tabaqat Fahl (Pehel)	T. Bet Shean (Beth-shan)
2-3	Pehel	Beth-shan
2-8	Pella (Pehel)	Scythopolis, Nysa (Beth-shan)
2-9	Pella	Scythopolis

The same transitional system has been adopted for most of the HISTORICAL maps in Sections 3—13. Some students may find the use of so many different names for the SAME site more than a little confusing. We have therefore introduced the concept of the 'MAIN NAME', which is given in the Index of Main Names (Section 15-2), to which all the Alternative Names (Section 15-1), Grid References (Section 15-3) and the Mini-Archive are cross-indexed. Students are recommended to concentrate on the Main Names rather than on the Alternative Names, many of which are only relevant to specialists.

Notes

Archaeology

SCALE 1:1,500,000
10 Km
6 M
ISRAEL GRID

LEGEND: NAMES < Archaeological • / Historical •

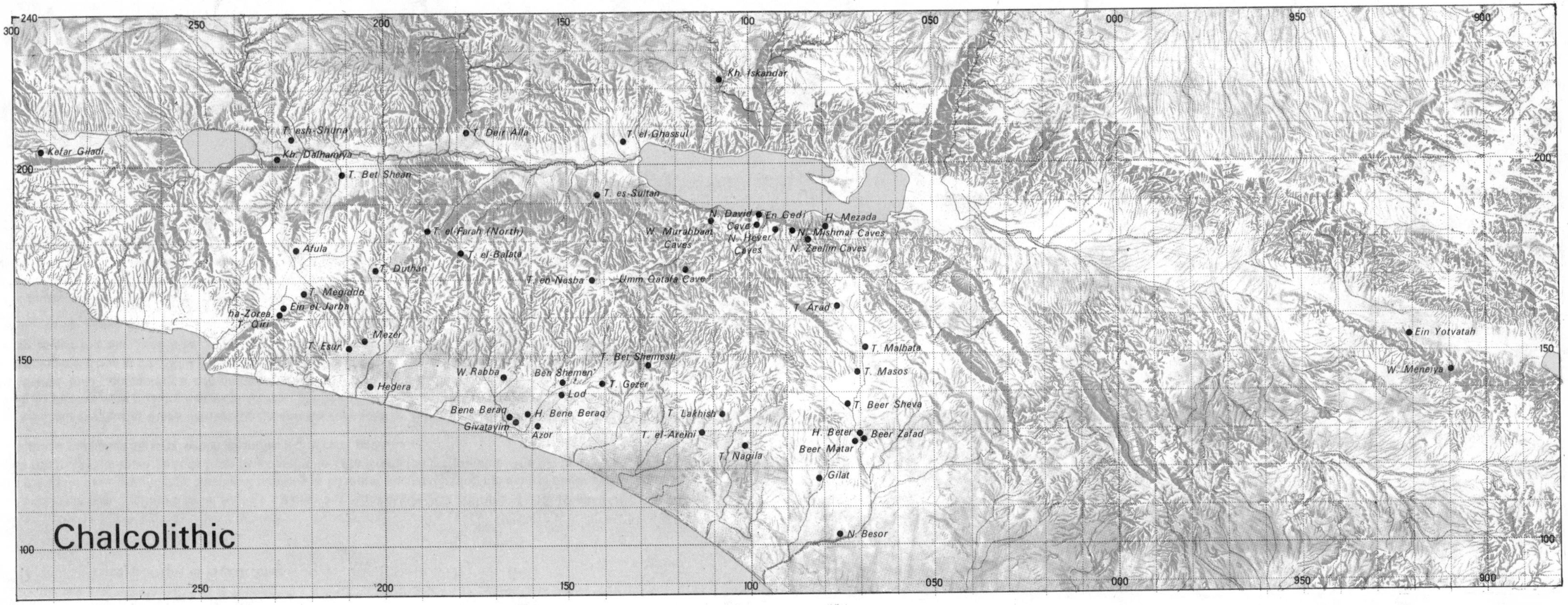
Chalcolithic
Kh. Iskandar
T. esh-Shuna
T. Deir Alla
T. el-Ghassul
Kefar Giladi
Kh. Dalhamiya
T. Bet Shean
T. es-Sultan
N. David
En Gedi
H. Mezada
Cave
T. el-Farah (North)
W. Murabbaat Caves
N. Hever Caves
N. Mishmar Caves
N. Zeelim Caves
Afula
T. el-Balata
T. Duthan
T. en-Nasba
Umm Qatafa Cave
T. Megiddo
Ein el-Jarba
ha-Zorea
T. Qiri
T. Arad
Mezer
T. Esur
T. Malhata
Ein Yotvatah
T. Bet Shemesh
W. Rabba
Ben Shemen
T. Gezer
T. Masos
W. Meneiya
Hedera
Lod
T. Beer Sheva
Bene Beraq
H. Bene Beraq
T. Lakhish
Givatayim
Azor
T. el-Areini
H. Beter
Beer Zafad
Beer Matar
T. Nagila
Gilat
N. Besor

Notes

Section 2 – 2

Archaeology

SCALE 1:1,500.000
10 Km
6 M
ISRAEL GRID

LEGEND: NAMES < *Archaeological* • / Historical •

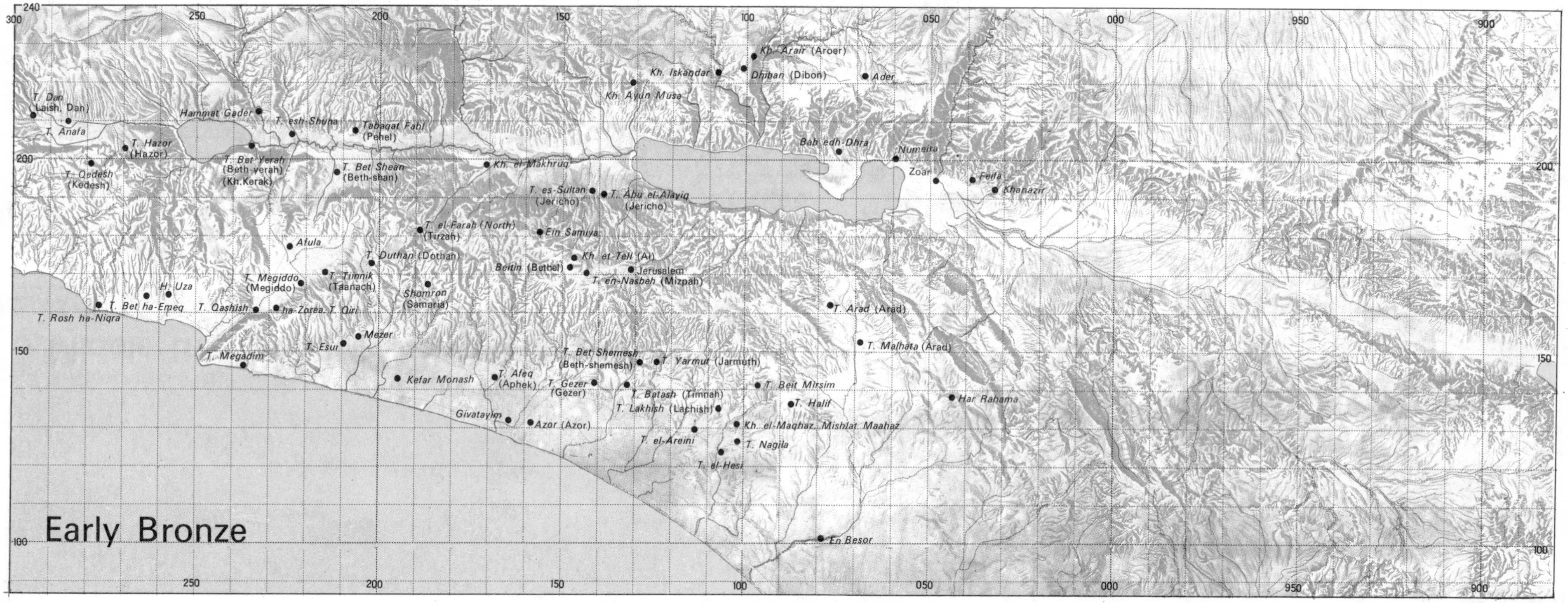
Early Bronze
T. Dan
(Laish, Dan)
T. Anafa
T. Hazor
(Hazor)
T. Qedesh
(Kedesh)
Hammat Gader
T. esh-Shuna
Tabaqat Fahl
(Pehel)
T. Bet Yerah
(Beth-yerah)
(Kh.Kerak)
T. Bet Shean
(Beth-shan)
Kh. el-Makhruq
T. es-Sultan
(Jericho)
T. Abu el-Alayiq
(Jericho)
T. el-Farah (North)
(Tirzah)
Ein Samiya
Afula
T. Duthan (Dothan)
Kh. et-Tell (Ai)
Beitin (Bethel)
Jerusalem
T. en-Nasbeh (Mizpah)
T. Megiddo
(Megiddo)
T. Tinnik
(Taanach)
Shomron
(Samaria)
H. Uza
T. Bet ha-Emeq
T. Qashish
ha-Zorea
T. Qiri
T. Rosh ha-Niqra
Mezer
T. Esur
T. Megadim
Kefar Monash
T. Afeq
(Aphek)
T. Gezer
(Gezer)
T. Bet Shemesh
(Beth-shemesh)
T. Yarmut (Jarmuth)
T. Batash (Timnah)
T. Lakhish (Lachish)
T. Beit Mirsim
T. Halif
Givatayim
Azor (Azor)
Kh. el-Maqhaz
Mishlat Maahaz
T. el-Areini
T. Nagila
T. el-Hesi
En Besor
Kh. Arair (Aroer)
Kh. Iskandar
Dhiban (Dibon)
Ader
Kh. Ayun Musa
Bab edh-Dhra
Numeira
Zoar
Feifa
Khanazir
T. Arad (Arad)
T. Malhata (Arad)
Har Rahama

Notes

Archaeology

SCALE 1:1,500.000
10 Km
6 M
ISRAEL GRID

LEGEND: NAMES < *Archaeological* • / Historical •

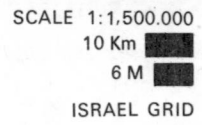

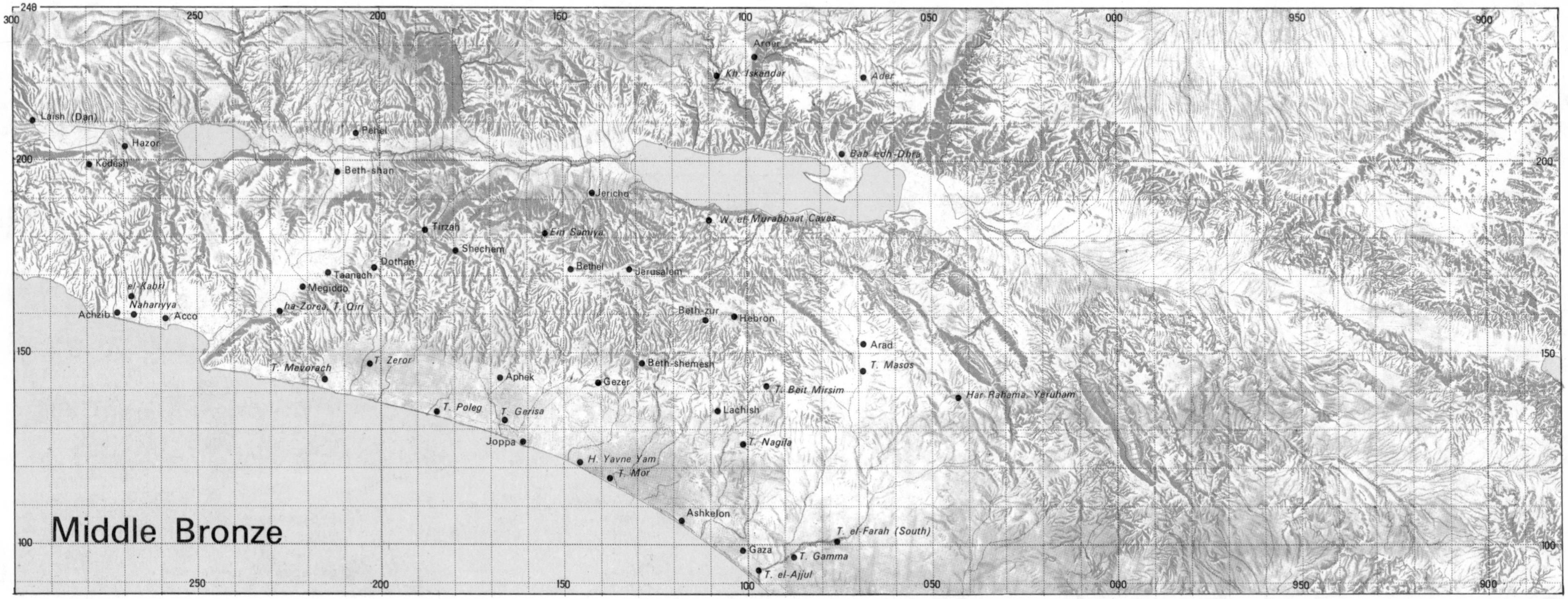
Middle Bronze
Laish (Dan)
Hazor
Kedesh
Pehel
Beth-shan
Jericho
Tirzah
Ein Samiya
Shechem
Dothan
Taanach
Megiddo
el-Kabri
Nahariyya
Achzib
Acco
ha-Zorea, T. Qiri
Bethel
Jerusalem
Beth-zur
Hebron
W. el-Murabbaat Caves
Aroer
Kh. Iskandar
Ader
Bab edh-Dhra
Arad
T. Masos
Har Rahama, Yeruham
T. Mevorach
T. Zeror
Aphek
Gezer
Beth-shemesh
T. Beit Mirsim
Lachish
T. Poleg
T. Gerisa
Joppa
T. Nagila
H. Yavne Yam
T. Mor
Ashkelon
T. el-Farah (South)
Gaza
T. Gamma
T. el-Ajjul

Notes

Section 2 – 4

Archaeology

SCALE 1:1,500.000
10 Km
6 M
ISRAEL GRID

LEGEND: NAMES < *Archaeological* • / Historical •

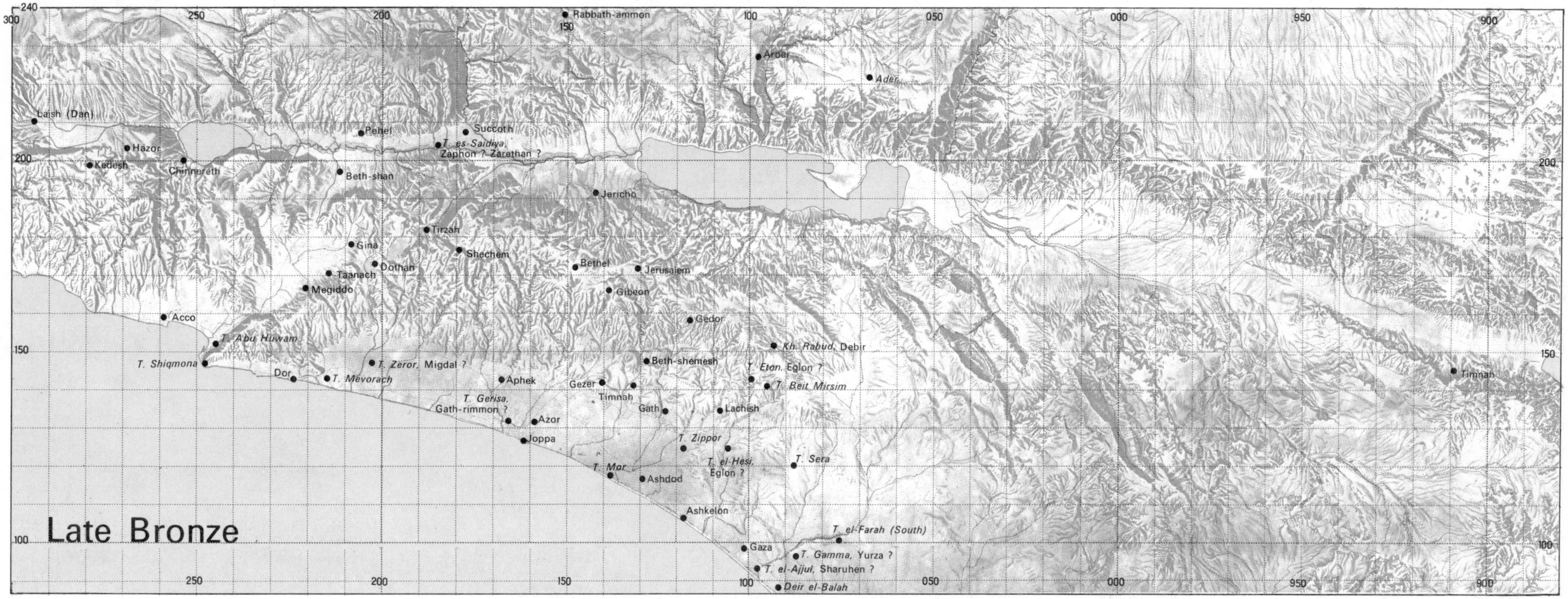

Rabbath-ammon
Aroer
Ader
Laish (Dan)
Pehel
Succoth
T. es-Saidiya, Zaphon ? Zarethan ?
Hazor
Kadesh
Chinnereth
Beth-shan
Jericho
Tirzah
Gina
Shechem
Dothan
Bethel
Jerusalem
Taanach
Megiddo
Gibeon
Acco
Gedor
T. Abu Huwam
Kh. Rabud, Debir
T. Shiqmona
Dor
T. Mevorach
T. Zeror, Migdal ?
Aphek
Beth-shemesh
T. Eton, Eglon ?
T. Beit Mirsim
Gezer
Timnah
Gath
Lachish
T. Gerisa, Gath-rimmon ?
Azor
Joppa
T. Zippor
T. el-Hesi, Eglon ?
T. Sera
T. Mor
Ashdod
Ashkelon
T. el-Farah (South)
Gaza
T. Gamma, Yurza ?
T. el-Ajjul, Sharuhen ?
Deir el-Balah
Timnah
Late Bronze

Notes

Archaeology

SCALE 1:1,500,000
10 Km
6 M
ISRAEL GRID

LEGEND: NAMES < Archaeological • / Historical •

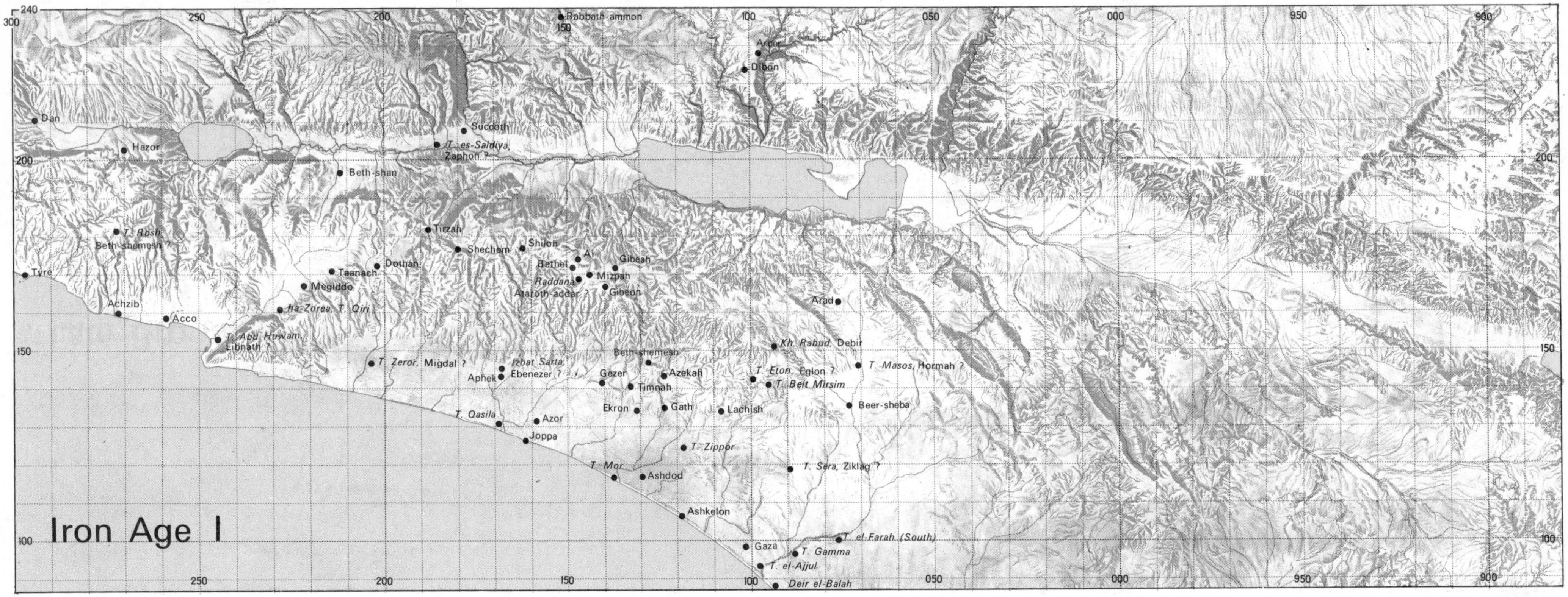
Iron Age I
Dan
Hazor
Succoth
T. es-Saidiya, Zaphon ?
Beth-shan
Rabbath-ammon
Aroer
Dibon
T. Rosh, Beth-shemesh ?
Tyre
Tirzah
Shechem
Shiloh
Ai
Bethel
Gibeah
Dothan
Taanach
Megiddo
Raddana
Mizpah
Ataroth-addar ?
Gibeon
Achzib
Acco
ha-Zorea, T. Qiri
T. Abu Huwam, Libnath ?
Arad
Kh. Rabud, Debir
Beth-shemesh
T. Masos, Hormah ?
T. Zeror, Migdal ?
Izbat Sarta, Ebenezer ?
Aphek
Gezer
Azekah
T. Eton, Eglon ?
T. Beit Mirsim
Timnah
Ekron
Gath
Lachish
Beer-sheba
T. Qasila
Azor
Joppa
T. Zippor
T. Sera, Ziklag ?
T. Mor
Ashdod
Ashkelon
T. el-Farah (South)
Gaza
T. Gamma
T. el-Ajjul
Deir el-Balah
240
300
250
200
150
100
050
000
950
900

Notes

Section 2 – 6
Archaeology

SCALE 1:1,500.000
10 Km
6 M
ISRAEL GRID

LEGEND: NAMES < *Archaeological* • / Historical •

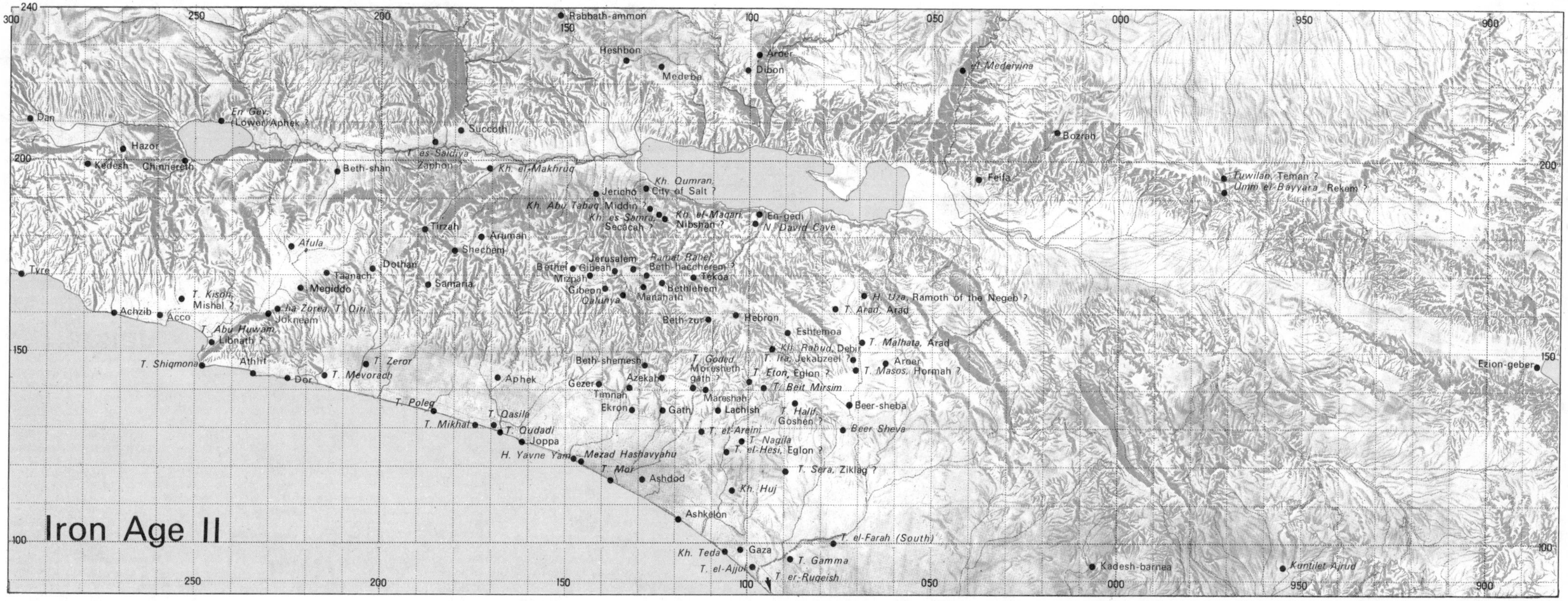

Iron Age II
Rabbath-ammon
Heshbon
Medeba
Aroer
Dibon
el-Medeiyina
Dan
En Gev, (Lower) Aphek ?
Succoth
Hazor
Kedesh
Chinnereth
T. es-Saidiya Zaphon ?
Beth-shan
Kh. el-Makhruq
Bozrah
Feifa
Tuwilan, Teman ?
Umm el-Bayyara, Rekem ?
Jericho
Kh. Qumran, City of Salt ?
Kh. Abu Tabaq, Middin ?
Kh. es-Samra, Secacah ?
Kh. el-Maqari, Nibshan ?
En-gedi
N. David Cave
Tirzah
Aruman
Afula
Shechem
Tyre
Dothan
Taanach
Samaria
Megiddo
Jerusalem
Ramat Rahel, Beth-haccherem ?
Bethel
Gibeah
Mizpah
Gibeon
Qalunya
Manahath
Tekoa
Bethlehem
T. Kison, Mishal ?
Achzib
Acco
Tell Qiri, Jokneam
T. Abu Huwam, Libnath ?
Beth-zur
Hebron
H. Uza, Ramoth of the Negeb ?
T. Arad, Arad
Eshtemoa
Kh. Rabud, Debir
T. Malhata, Arad
T. Ira, Jekabzeel ?
Aroer
T. Masos, Hormah ?
T. Shiqmona
Athlit
Dor
T. Zeror
T. Mevorach
Aphek
Beth-shemesh
T. Goded, Moresheth-gath ?
T. Eton, Eglon ?
T. Beit Mirsim
Gezer
Azekah
Timnah
Mareshah
Ekron
Gath
Lachish
T. Halif, Goshen ?
Beer-sheba
Beer Sheva
T. Poleg
T. Qasile
T. Mikhal
T. Qudadi
Joppa
T. el-Areini
T. Nagila
T. el-Hesi, Eglon ?
H. Yavne Yam
Mezad Hashavyahu
T. Mor
Ashdod
T. Sera, Ziklag ?
Kh. Huj
Ashkelon
T. el-Farah (South)
Kh. Teda
Gaza
T. el-Ajjul
T. Gamma
T. er-Ruqeish
Kadesh-barnea
Kuntilet Ajrud
Ezion-geber

Notes

Section 2 – 7

Archaeology

SCALE 1:1,500.000
10 Km
6 M
ISRAEL GRID

LEGEND: NAMES < *Archaeological* • / Historical •

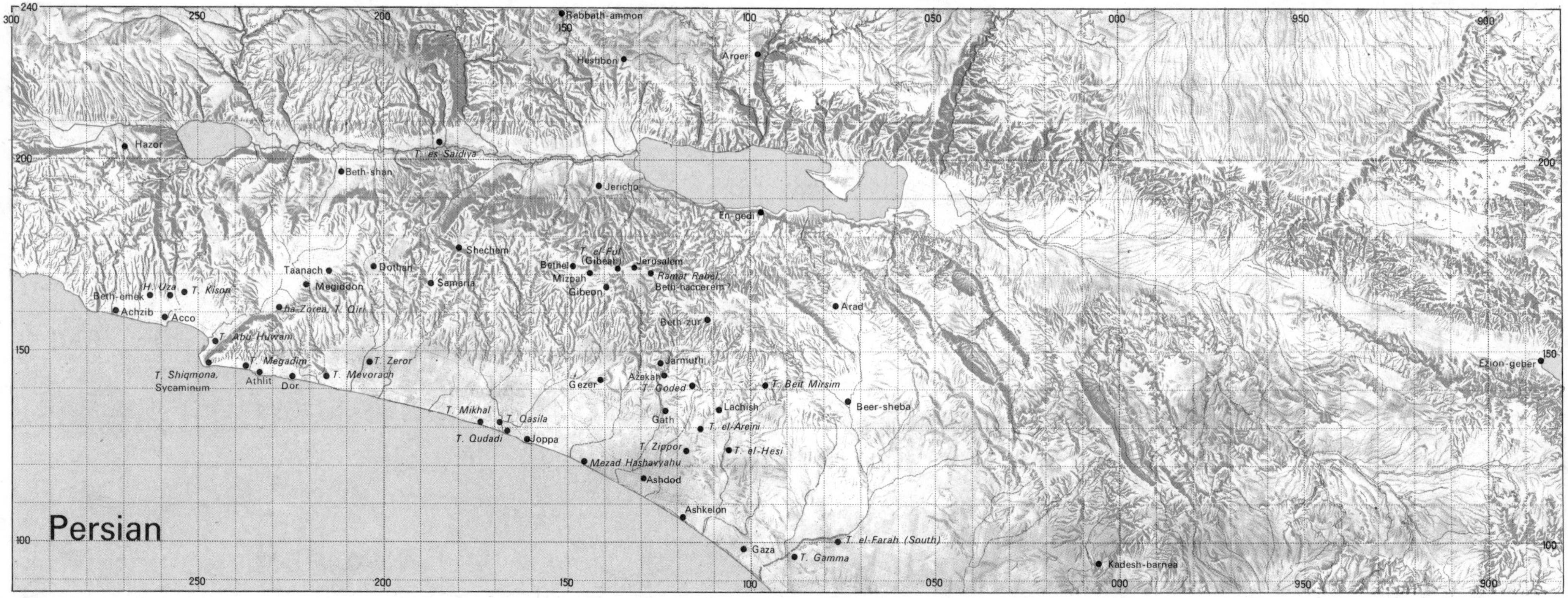

Persian
Hazor
T. es-Saidiya
Beth-shan
Rabbath-ammon
Heshbon
Aroer
Jericho
En-gedi
Shechem
Taanach
Dothan
Megiddon
Samaria
Bethel
T. el-Ful (Gibeah)
Mizpah
Gibeon
Jerusalem
Ramat Rahel, Beth-haccerem?
Beth-emek
H. Uza
T. Kison
Achzib
Acco
ha-Zorea, T. Qiri
T. Abu Huwam
T. Shiqmona, Sycaminum
T. Megadim
Athlit
Dor
T. Mevorach
T. Zeror
Beth-zur
Arad
Jarmuth
Azekah
Gezer
T. Goded
T. Beit Mirsim
Lachish
Beer-sheba
Gath
T. el-Areini
T. Mikhal
T. Qasila
T. Qudadi
Joppa
T. Zippor
T. el-Hesi
Mezad Hashavyahu
Ashdod
Ashkelon
Gaza
T. el-Farah (South)
T. Gamma
Kadesh-barnea
Ezion-geber

Notes

Archaeology

SCALE 1:1,500.000
10 Km
6 M
ISRAEL GRID

LEGEND: NAMES < *Archaeological* • Historical •

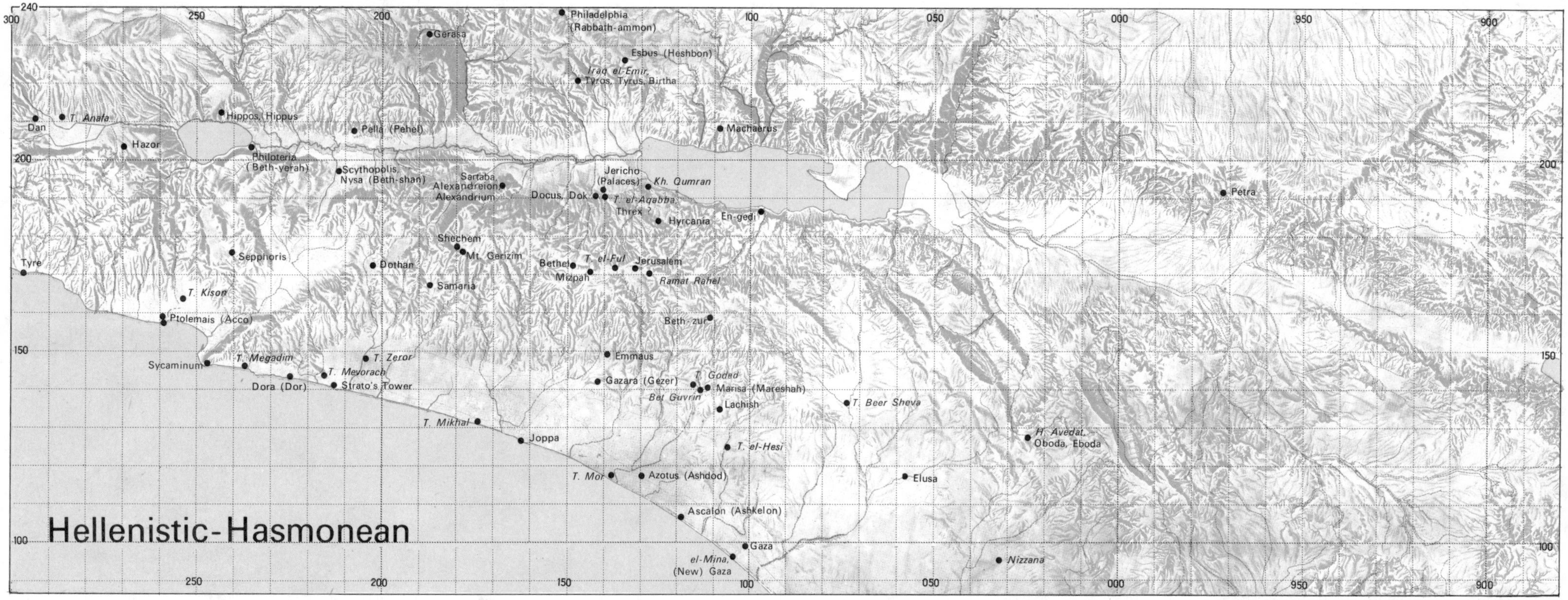

Hellenistic-Hasmonean
Philadelphia (Rabbath-ammon)
Gerasa
Esbus (Heshbon)
Iraq el-Emir, Tyros, Tyrus, Birtha
Dan
T. Anafa
Hippos, Hippus
Pella (Pehel)
Machaerus
Hazor
Philoteria (Beth-yerah)
Scythopolis, Nysa (Beth-shan)
Sartaba, Alexandreion, Alexandrium
Jericho (Palaces)
Kh. Qumran
Docus, Dok
T. el-Aqabba, Threx
Hyrcania
En-gedi
Petra
Shechem
Mt. Gerizim
Sepphoris
Dothan
Tyre
Bethel
T. el-Ful
Jerusalem
Mizpah
Ramat Rahel
Samaria
T. Kison
Ptolemais (Acco)
Beth-zur
Emmaus
Sycaminum
T. Megadim
T. Zeror
T. Mevorach
Dora (Dor)
Strato's Tower
Gazara (Gezer)
T. Goded
Marisa (Mareshah)
Bet Guvrin
Lachish
T. Beer Sheva
T. Mikhal
Joppa
H. Avedat, Oboda, Eboda
T. el-Hesi
T. Mor
Azotus (Ashdod)
Elusa
Ascalon (Ashkelon)
Gaza
el-Mina, (New) Gaza
Nizzana

Notes

Archaeology

SCALE 1:1,500.000
10 Km
6 M
ISRAEL GRID

LEGEND: NAMES < Archaeological • Historical •

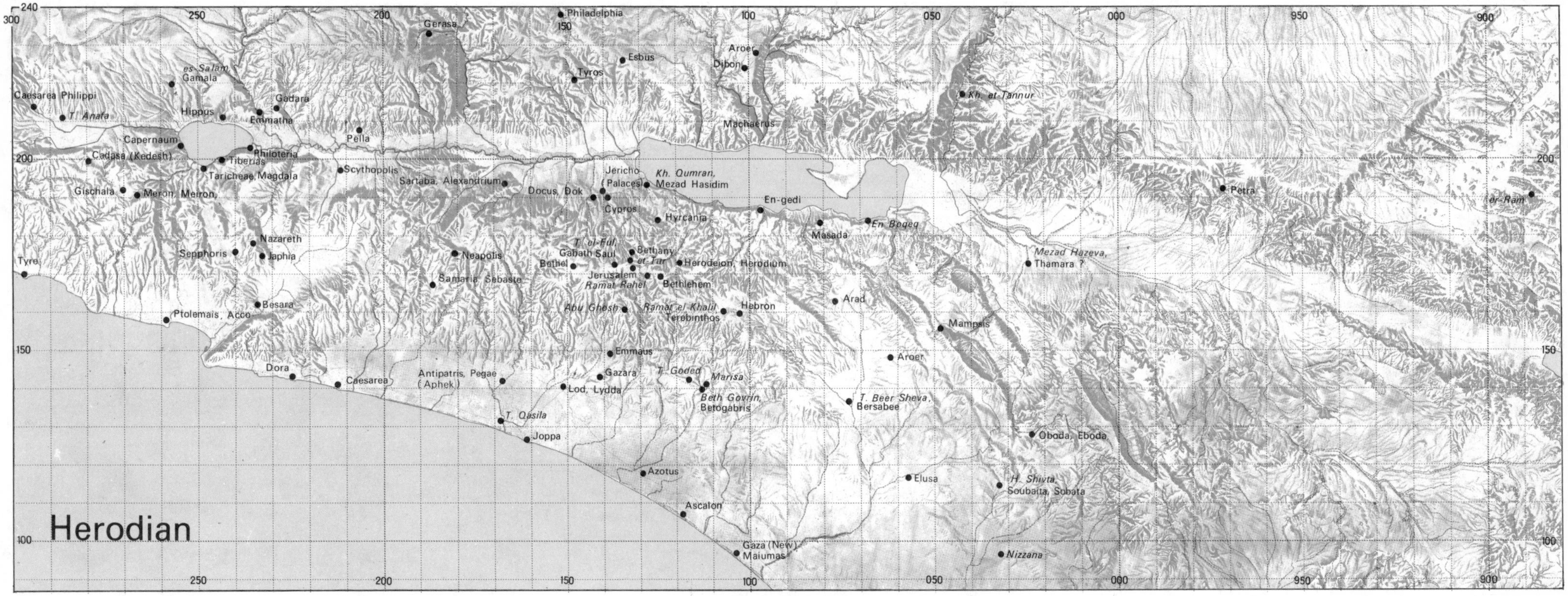
Herodian
Caesarea Philippi
T. Anafa
es-Salam
Gamala
Hippus
Emmatha
Gadara
Pella
Gerasa
Philadelphia
Esbus
Tyros
Aroer
Dibon
Kh. et-Tannur
Machaerus
Capernaum
Cadasa (Kedesh)
Philoteria
Tiberias
Taricheae, Magdala
Gischala
Meron, Meiron,
Scythopolis
Sartaba, Alexandrium
Docus, Dok
Jericho
(Palaces)
Kh. Qumran,
Mezad Hasidim
En-gedi
Cypros
Hyrcania
Masada
En Boqeq
Petra
er-Ram
Nazareth
Sepphoris
Japhia
Tyre
Neapolis
T. el-Ful
Gabath Saul
Bethel
Bethany
et-Tur
Herodeion, Herodium
Jerusalem
Ramat Rahel
Bethlehem
Samaria, Sabaste
Mezad Hazeva,
Thamara ?
Arad
Besara
Ptolemais, Acco
Abu Ghosh
Ramat el-Khalil
Terebinthos
Hebron
Mampsis
Emmaus
Aroer
Dora
Caesarea
Antipatris, Pegae
(Aphek)
Gazara
T. Goded
Marisa
Lod, Lydda
Beth Govrin,
Betogabris
T. Beer Sheva,
Bersabee
T. Qasila
Joppa
Oboda, Eboda
Azotus
Elusa
H. Shivta,
Soubaita, Sobata
Ascalon
Gaza (New),
Maiumas
Nizzana

Notes

Section 2 – 10

Archaeology

SCALE 1:1,500.000
10 Km
6 M
ISRAEL GRID

LEGEND: NAMES < Archaeological • / Historical •

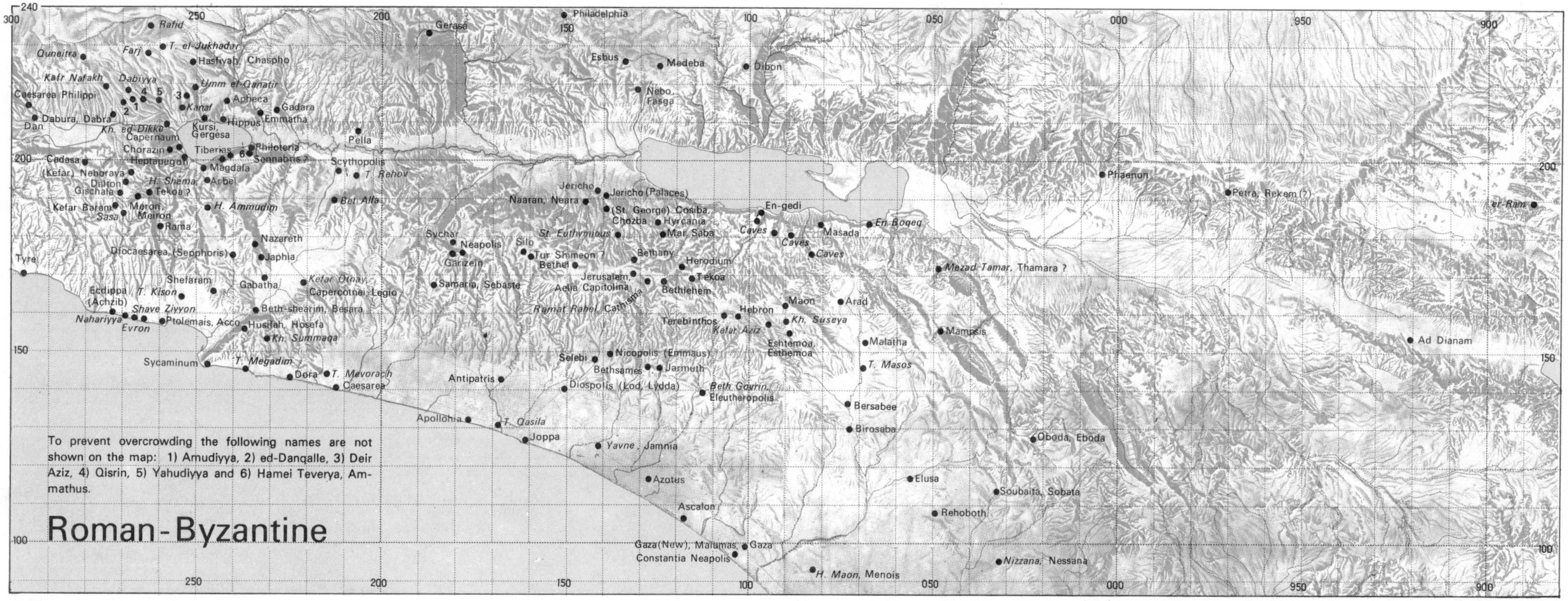

Roman-Byzantine
To prevent overcrowding the following names are not shown on the map: 1) Amudiyya, 2) ed-Danqalle, 3) Deir Aziz, 4) Qisrin, 5) Yahudiyya and 6) Hamei Teverya, Ammathus.
Rafid
T. el Jukhadar
Farj
Quneitra
Hasfiyah, Chaspho
Kafr Nafakh
Dabiyya
Umm el-Qanatir
Caesarea Philippi
Kanaf
Apheca
Gadara
Dan
Dabura, Dabra
Hippus
Emmatha
Kh. ed-Dikke
Kursi, Gergesa
Capernaum
Pella
Chorazin
Tiberias
Philoteria
Sennabris ?
Cadasa
Heptapegon
Scythopolis
(Kefar) Nebboraya
Magdala
T. Rehov
Dalton
H. Shema
Arbel
Gischala
Tekoa ?
Kefar Baram
Meron, Meiron
H. Ammudim
Bet Alfa
Sasa
Rama
Nazareth
Tyre
Diocaesarea (Sepphoris)
Japhia
Shefaram
Gabatha
Kefar Otnay
Ecdippa (Achzib)
T. Kison
Capercotnei, Legio
Shave Ziyyon
Beth-shearim, Besara
Nahariyya
Evron
Ptolemais, Acco
Husifah, Hosefa
Kh. Summaqa
Sycaminum
T. Megadim
Dora
T. Mevorach
Caesarea
Gerasa
Philadelphia
Esbus
Medeba
Dibon
Nebo, Fasga
Sychar
Neapolis
Silo
Garizein
Tur Shimeon ?
Bethel
Samaria, Sebaste
Jericho
Naaran, Neara
Jericho (Palaces)
(St. George) Cosiba, Chozba
Hyrcania
St. Euthymius
Mar Saba
Bethany
Herodium
Jerusalem, Aelia Capitolina
Tekoa
Bethlehem
Ramat Rahel, Cathisma
En-gedi
Caves
Masada
En Boqeq
Hebron
Terebinthos
Kefar Aziz
Maon
Arad
Kh. Suseya
Eshtemoa, Esthemoa
Malatha
T. Masos
Selebi
Nicopolis (Emmaus)
Bethsames
Jarmuth
Antipatris
Diospolis (Lod, Lydda)
Beth Govrin, Eleutheropolis
Bersabee
Apollonia
T. Qasila
Joppa
Birosaba
Yavne, Jamnia
Azotus
Ascalon
Elusa
Gaza(New), Maiumas, Gaza
Constantia Neapolis
H. Maon, Menois
Rehoboth
Soubaita, Sobata
Oboda, Eboda
Nizzana, Nessana
Mezad Tamar, Thamara ?
Mampsis
Phaenon
Petra, Rekem (?)
er-Ram
Ad Dianam

Notes

Section 3 Summary of contents & sources

Early Bronze/Canaanite Period

Map No.	Subject	Primary sources	Regional Map Nos. (Section 1)	Macmillan Bible Atlas Map Nos.	Other references and notes
3-1	**Early Bronze/Canaanite Period**				
	a Important Early Bronze archaeological sites			20,21	
	b Place-names from the Ebla tablets	Ebla tablets (*Tell Mardikh*)			
	c Campaigns of Pepi I in the 'Land of the Sand-dwellers'	Inscription: tomb of Uni, commander, army of Pepi I (*Abydos: Egypt*); ANET 227-8		22	
	This map is an enlargement of map 2-2 (Early Bronze period) in the Archaeology Section. It is repeated here as a useful reference, pending future publication of the tablets recently found at Tell Mardikh in northern Syria. Some of these 'Ebla' sites have been included here, but these are based upon news reports and verbal communication only and are therefore shown in BLACK. Some 'historical' names are used in this map, for simplicity, but without implying that such place-names were necessarily in use during this period.				

Notes

Canaanite (EB) Period

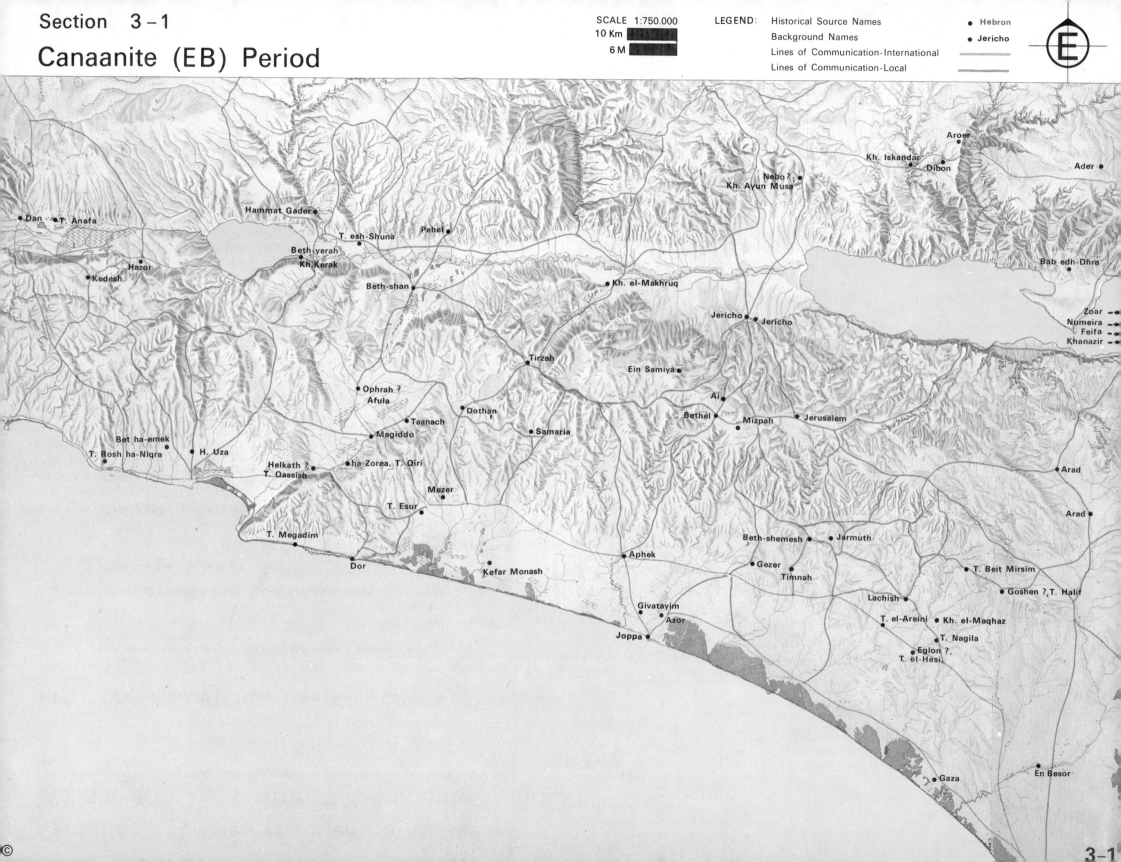

SCALE 1:750.000
10 Km
6 M

LEGEND: Historical Source Names • Hebron
Background Names • Jericho
Lines of Communication-International
Lines of Communication-Local

E

Dan
T. Anafa
Hammat Gader
Kedesh
Hazor
Beth-yerah
Kh.Kerak
T. esh-Shuna
Pehel
Beth-shan
Kh. el-Makhruq
Nebo ?,
Kh. Ayun Musa
Kh. Iskandar
Dibon
Aroer
Ader
Bab edh-Dhra
Zoar
Numeira
Feifa
Khanazir
Jericho
Jericho
Tirzah
Ein Samiya
Ai
Bethel
Mizpah
Jerusalem
Ophrah ?
Afula
Dothan
Taanach
Megiddo
Samaria
Bet ha-emek
T. Rosh ha-Niqra
H. Uza
Helkath ?,
T. Qassish
ha-Zorea, T. Qiri
Mezer
T. Esur
T. Megadim
Dor
Kefar Monash
Aphek
Beth-shemesh
Jarmuth
Gezer
Timnah
Arad
Arad
T. Beit Mirsim
Goshen ?, T. Halif
Lachish
Givatayim
Azor
Joppa
T. el-Areini
Kh. el-Maqhaz
T. Nagila
Eglon ?,
T. el-Hesi,
Gaza
En Besor

Middle and Late Bronze/Canaanite Periods

Map No.	Subject	Primary sources	Regional Map Nos. (Section 1)	Macmillan Bible Atlas Map Nos.	Other references and notes
4-1	**Overview (north) and Egypt's operations in Canaan in the 19th Dynasty**				
	a Overview (north)				
	b Campaign of Seti I (from 4-9 a)				
	c A scribe's satirical description of Canaan in the days of Rameses II (from 4-9 b)				
	d Campaign of Merneptah (from 4-9 c)				
4-2	**Political Centres from the Execration texts**				
	Political Centres from the Execration texts	Execration texts (*Thebes, Sakkara: Egypt*); ANET 328-29; ANEP 593; ANE I: 225-26		23	
4-3	**The Patriarchs: Abraham and Isaac**				
	a Abram's first journey in the Land and his sojourns in Egypt	Genesis 12	13,16	25,26	
	b Abram's return to the Land; Abram and Lot separate	Genesis 13	4	26	
	c Campaign of northern kings; Abram and Melchizedek	Genesis 14	1,8,11,12,15	24	
	d Visit of the three men; Lot's escape from Sodom	Genesis 18, 19	14,15		
	e Abraham in the Negev and at Gerar; birth of Isaac	Genesis 20, 21	3,16	26	
	f Abraham's testing; Sarah's death and burial	Genesis 22, 23	1,16	26	
	g Death and burial of Abraham; Isaac at Gerar	Genesis 25, 26	3,16	26	
4-4	**The Patriarchs: Jacob and Joseph**				
	a Events in Jacob's departure and return to Canaan	Genesis 28, 31-33	1,4,11	27	
	b Jacob's return via Shechem, Bethel and Kiriath-arba	Genesis 34, 35	1,4,11	27	
	c Joseph's trip to Dothan and his sale into Egypt	Genesis 37	1,10	47	
	d The Judah and Tamar affair	Genesis 38	1	cf. 57	
	e Israel goes to Egypt during a severe famine	Genesis 42-46	16		
4-5	**Egypt's expansion into Canaan in the 18th dynasty**				
	a Egypt's expulsion of foreign rulers (Hyksos) and expansion eastward; the battle of Sharuhen	Inscription: tomb of Ahmose, son of Eben, commander, army of Ahmose (*el-Kab: Egypt*); ANET 230-34; 554-55; ANE I: 173-75; ANE II: 89-93	3	28,29	
	b Campaign and city-lists of Thutmose III (for details see 4-6,7)	Inscriptions: Thutmose III (*Karnak, Gebel Barkal, Armant: Egypt*); ANET 22-23; 234-43; ANEP 313; ANE I: 175-82	2,3,5-9	31-34	
	c Campaigns of Amenhotep II	Monuments: Amenhotep II (*Karnak, Memphis, Amada, Elephantine: Egypt*); ANET 245-48	5,6,9	35,36	
4-6	**Detail: campaign of Thutmose III (southern)**				
	Detail: Campaign of Thutmose III (southern)	See 4-5b	3	31	
4-7	**Detail: campaign of Thutmose III (central)**				

Middle and Late Bronze/Canaanite periods

Map No.	Subject	Primary sources	Regional Map Nos. (Section 1)	Macmillan Bible Atlas Map Nos.	Other references and notes
4-8	**The Amarna Age: kings of Canaan and inter-relations**				
	The Amarna Age: kings of Canaan and inter-relations	El-Amarna letters (*Tell el-Amarna: Egypt*); ANET 483-90; ANEP 245; ANE I: 262-77	1,7	37-40	
4-9	**Egypt's operations in Canaan in the 19th Dynasty (northern)**				
	a Campaign of Seti I in the Beth-shan valley and Galilee (see also map 4-1)	Monument: Seti I (*Beth-shan*); reliefs (*Karnak: Egypt*); city-lists (*Egypt*); ANET 253-55; ANEP 320; 322-31; ANE I: 182-83	3,8,9	41,42	
	b A scribe's satirical description of Canaan in the days of Rameses II (see also map 4-1)	Papyrus Anastase I (*Egypt*); ANET 476-78	6-9	45 (cf.43)	
	c Campaign of Merneptah (see also map 4-1)	Victory stele: Merneptah (*Thebes: Egypt*); ANET 376-78; ANEP 342-43; ANE I: 231	2,3,9	46	

Notes

Section 4–1

Canaanite (MB/LB) Period

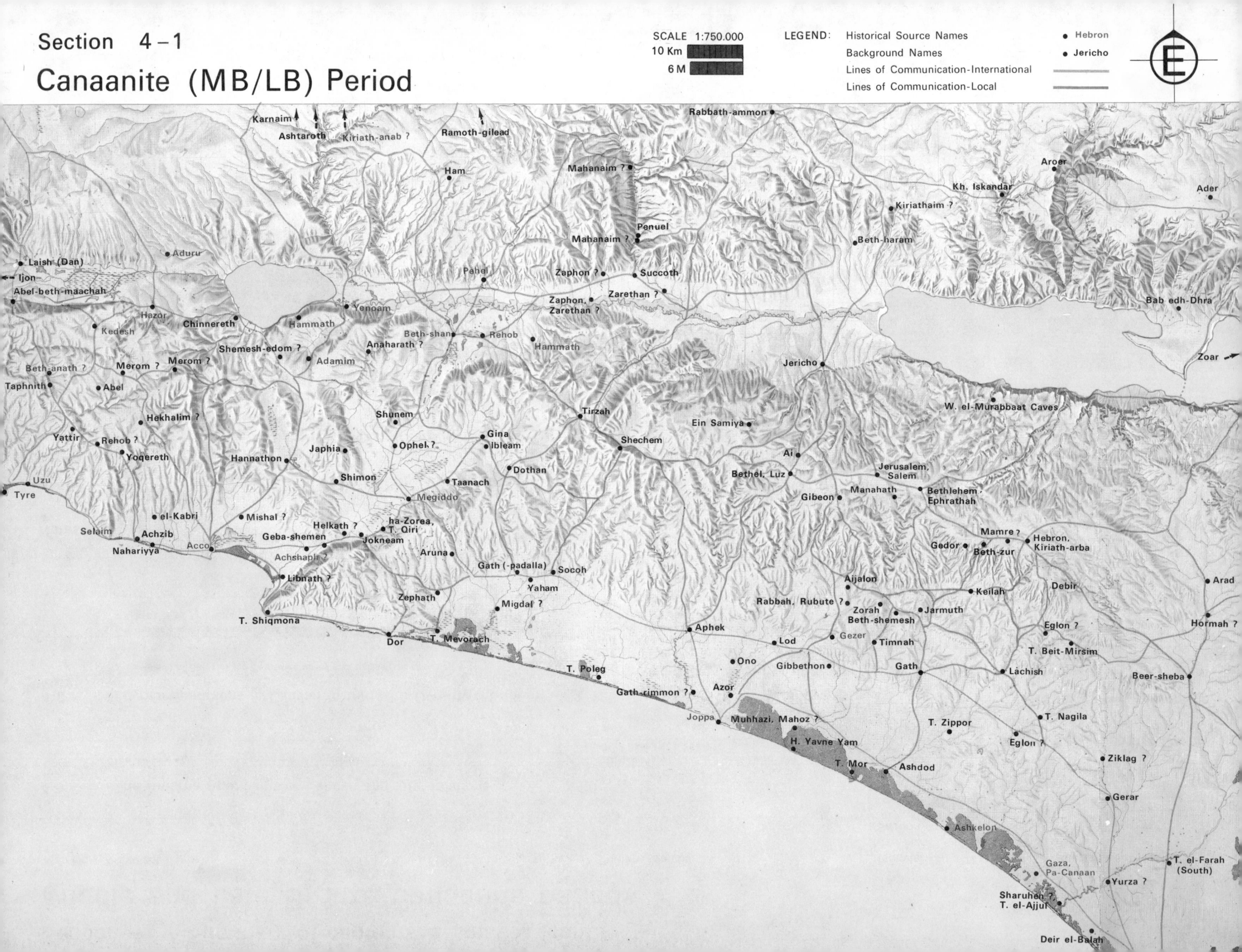

SCALE 1:750.000
10 Km
6 M

LEGEND: Historical Source Names • Hebron
Background Names • Jericho
Lines of Communication-International
Lines of Communication-Local

Karnaim
Ashtaroth
Kiriath-anab ?
Ramoth-gilead
Rabbath-ammon
Ham
Mahanaim ?
Aroer
Kh. Iskandar
Ader
Kiriathaim ?
Penuel
Mahanaim ?
Beth-haram
Aduru
Laish (Dan)
Ijon
Abel-beth-maachah
Pahel
Zaphon ?
Succoth
Zaphon, Zarethan ?
Zarethan ?
Bab edh-Dhra
Yenoam
Hazor
Chinnereth
Hammath
Kedesh
Beth-shan
Rehob
Hammath
Shemesh-edom ?
Anaharath ?
Adamim
Jericho
Zoar
Beth-anath ?
Merom ?
Merom ?
Taphnith
Abel
Hekhalim ?
Shunem
Tirzah
Ein Samiya
W. el-Murabbaat Caves
Yattir
Rehob ?
Yoqereth
Japhia
Ophel ?
Gina
Ibleam
Shechem
Hannathon
Dothan
Ai
Bethel, Luz
Jerusalem, Salem
Uzu
Tyre
Shimon
Taanach
Megiddo
Gibeon
Manahath
Bethlehem, Ephrathah
el-Kabri
Mishal ?
Helkath ?
ha-Zorea, T. Qiri
Selaim
Achzib
Geba-shemen
Jokneam
Mamre ?
Hebron, Kiriath-arba
Nahariyya
Acco
Aruna
Gedor
Beth-zur
Achshaph ?
Gath (-padalla)
Socoh
Libnath ?
Yaham
Aijalon
Debir
Arad
Keilah
Zephath
Rabbah, Rubute ?
Migdal ?
Zorah
Beth-shemesh
Jarmuth
T. Shiqmona
Aphek
Eglon ?
Hormah ?
Dor
T. Mevorach
Lod
Gezer
Timnah
T. Beit-Mirsim
Ono
Gibbethon
Gath
Lachish
Beer-sheba
T. Poleg
Gath-rimmon ?
Azor
Joppa
Muhhazi, Mahoz ?
T. Zippor
T. Nagila
H. Yavne Yam
Eglon ?
Ziklag ?
T. Mor
Ashdod
Gerar
Ashkelon
Gaza, Pa-Canaan
T. el-Farah (South)
Yurza ?
Sharuhen ?, T. el-Ajjul
Deir el-Balah

Section 4 – 2

Canaanite (MB/LB) Period

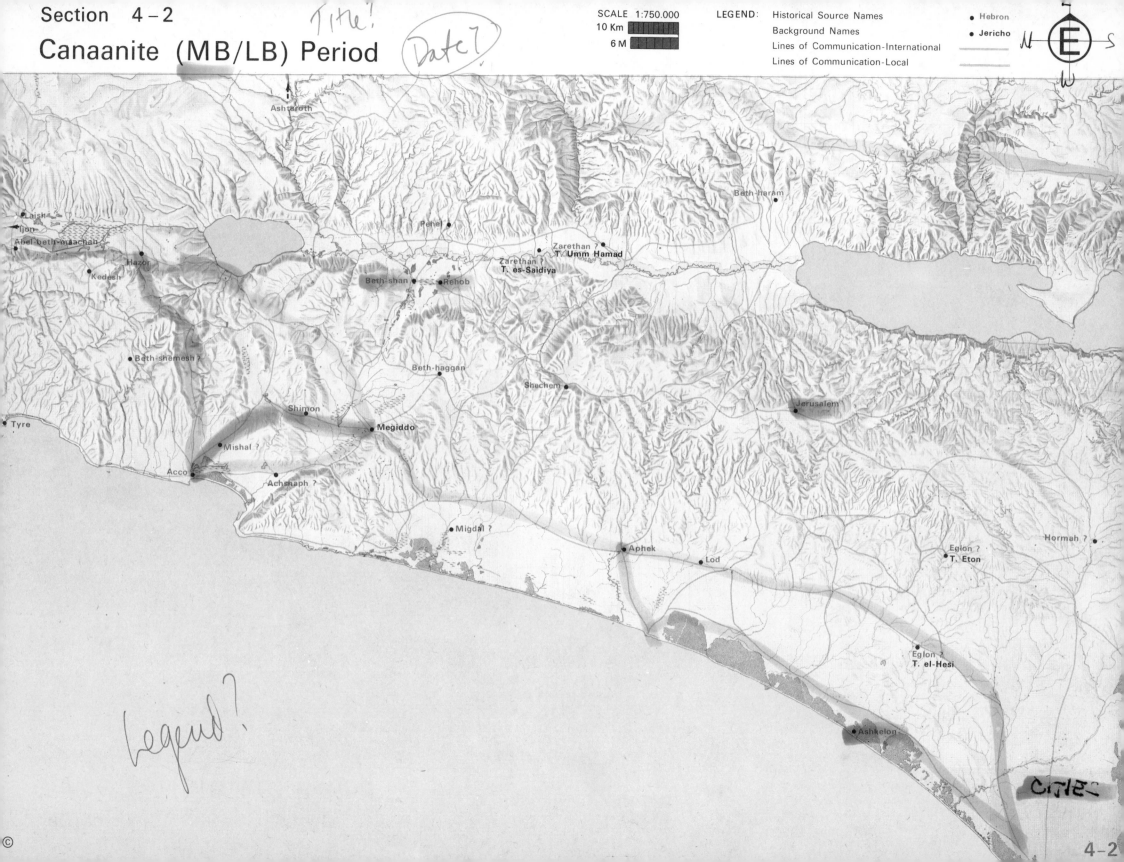

SCALE 1:750.000
10 Km
6 M

LEGEND:
- Historical Source Names — • Hebron
- Background Names — • Jericho
- Lines of Communication-International
- Lines of Communication-Local

Ashtaroth
Laish
Ijon
Abel-beth-maachah
Hazor
Kedesh
Beth-shemesh ?
Tyre
Mishal ?
Acco
Achshaph ?
Shimon
Megiddo
Beth-haggan
Beth-shan
Rehob
Penel
Zarethan ?
T. Umm Hamad
Zarethan ?
T. es-Saidiya
Beth-haram
Shechem
Jerusalem
Migdal ?
Aphek
Lod
Eglon ?
T. Eton
Hormah ?
Eglon ?
T. el-Hesi
Ashkelon

Section 4 – 3

Canaanite (MB/LB) Period

SCALE 1:750.000
10 Km
6 M

LEGEND: Historical Source Names • Hebron
Background Names • Jericho
Lines of Communication-International
Lines of Communication-Local

Ashtaroth
Karnaim
Ramoth-gilead
Beth-arbel
Ham
Mahanaim ?
Penuel
Mahanaim ?
Succoth
Pehel
Zarethan ?
Zarethan ?
Beth-shan
Rehob
Kh. Iskandar
Aroer
Ader
Kiriathaim ?
Beth-haram
Bab edh-Dhra
Zoar
Jericho
W. el-Murabbaat Caves
Tirzah
Ein Samiya
Gina
Shechem
Ai
Dothan
Bethel, Luz
Salem
Jerusalem
Bethlehem
Ephrathah
Taanach
Megiddo
Tamar
Mamre ?
Beth-zur
Hebron,
Kiriath-arba
Arad
Migdal ?
Beth-shemesh
Hormah ?
Aphek
Eglon ?
T. Mevorach
Lod
Gezer
T. Beit Mirsim
T. Poleg
Lachish
Beer-sheba
Gath-rimmon ?
Joppa
T. Nagila
Eglon ?
H. Yavne Yam
T. Mor
Gerar
Ashkelon
T. el-Farah
(South)
Gaza
Yurza ?
Sharuhen ?
T. el-Ajjul
Kadesh-barnea

Canaanite (MB/LB) Period

SCALE 1:750.000
10 Km
6 M

LEGEND:
- Historical Source Names — ● Hebron
- Background Names — ● Jericho
- Lines of Communication-International
- Lines of Communication-Local

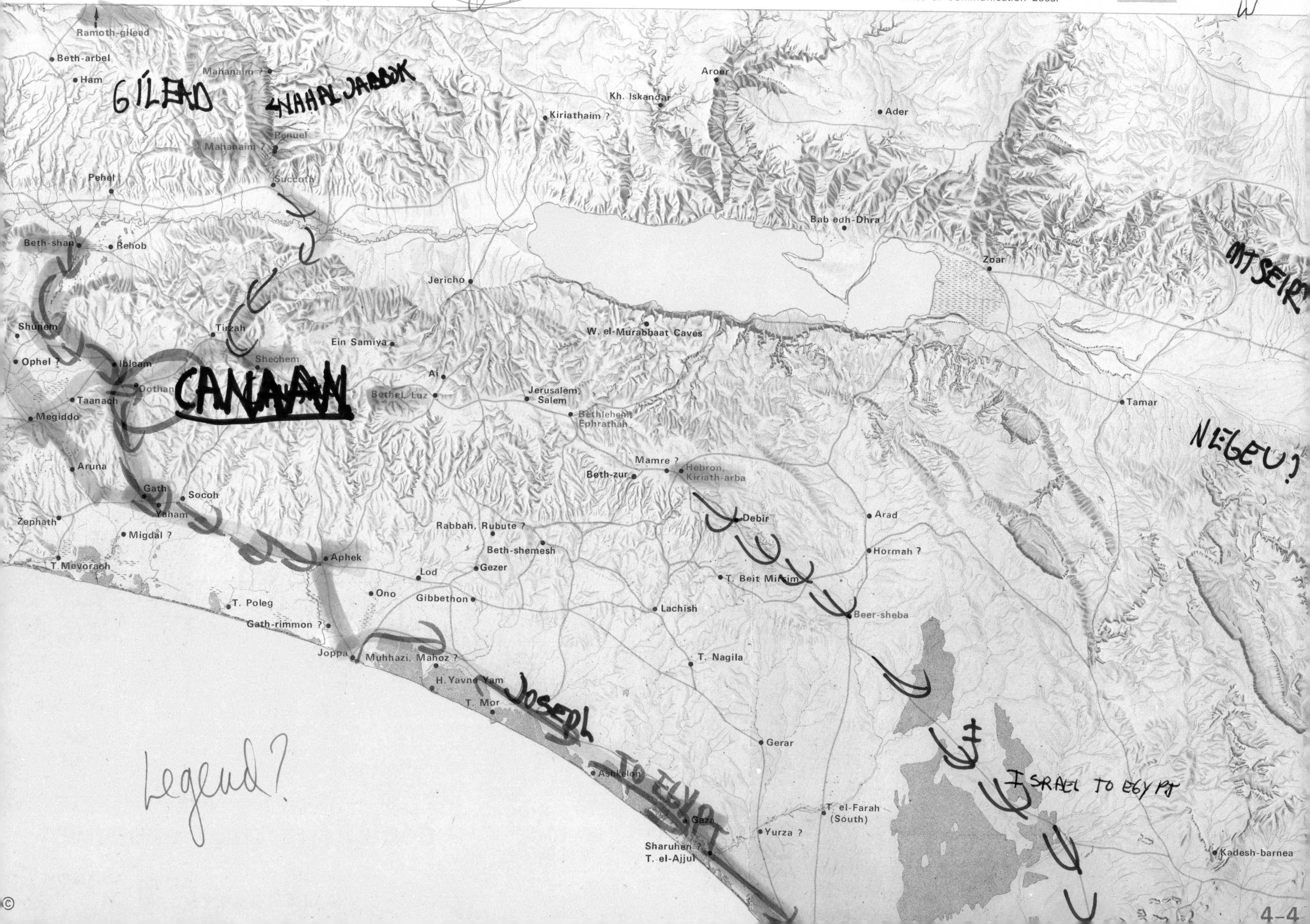
Ramoth-gilead
Beth-arbel
Ham
Mahanaim ?
Penuel
Mahanaim ?
Succoth
Pehel
Beth-shan
Rehob
Shunem
Ophel ?
Ibleam
Tirzah
Shechem
Dothan
Taanach
Megiddo
Aruna
Gath
Socoh
Yaham
Zephath
Migdal ?
T. Mevorach
Aphek
T. Poleg
Gath-rimmon ?
Joppa
Muhhazi, Mahoz ?
H. Yavne Yam
T. Mor
Ono
Lod
Gezer
Gibbethon
Rabbah, Rubute ?
Beth-shemesh
Ein Samiya
Ai
Bethel, Luz
Jericho
Jerusalem, Salem
Bethlehem, Ephrathah
W. el-Murabbaat Caves
Mamre ?
Hebron, Kiriath-arba
Beth-zur
Debir
T. Beit Mirsim
Lachish
Beer-sheba
T. Nagila
Gerar
Ashkelon
Gaza
Sharuhen ? T. el-Ajjul
Yurza ?
T. el-Farah (South)
Arad
Hormah ?
Kadesh-barnea
Tamar
Zoar
Bab edh-Dhra
Aroer
Kh. Iskandar
Kiriathaim ?
Ader
GILEAD
NAHAL JABBOK
CANAAN
MT SEIR
NEGEV?
JOSEPH TO EGYPT
ISRAEL TO EGYPT
Legend?

Section 4 – 5

Canaanite (MB/LB) Period

SCALE 1:750.000
10 Km
6 M

LEGEND:
- • Hebron — Historical Source Names
- • Jericho — Background Names
- Lines of Communication-International
- Lines of Communication-Local

Ashtaroth
Kiriath-enab ?
Rabbath-ammon
Ramoth-gilead
Mahanaim ?
Aroer
Ader
Penuel
Mahanaim ?
Aduru
Laish
Ijon
Abel-beth-maachah
Pehel
Zaphon ?
Succoth
Zarethan ?
Zaphon, Zarethan ?
Hazor
Kedesh
Chinnereth
Hammath
Yenoam
Beth-shan
Rehob
Hammath
Anaharath ?
Shemesh-edom ?
Adamim
Merom ?
Merom ?
Beth-anath ?
Taphnith
Abel
Jericho
Zoar
Shunem
Tirzah
Hekhalim ?
Gina
Ibleam
Shechem
Yattir
Rehob ?
Yodeeth
Ophel ?
Japhia
Hannathon
Dothan
Shimon
Taanach
Bethel, Luz
Jerusalem, Salem
Bethlehem, Ephrathah
Uzu
Tyre
Megiddo
Gibeon
Manahath
Mishal
Helkath ?
Geba-shemen
Jokneam
Achshaph
Aruna
Acco
Hebron, Kiriath-arba
Gedor
Gath
Socoh
Yaham
Libnath ?
Aijalon
Debir
Keilah
Zephath
Rabbah ?
Zorah
Beth-shemesh
Jarmuth
Migdal ?
T. Shiqmona
Aphek
Eglon ?
Dor
T. Mevorach
Lod
Gezer
Timnah
T. Beit Mirsim
Ono
Gibbethon
Gath
Lachish
Gath-rimmon ?
Azor
Joppa
T. Zippor
Mahoz ?
Eglon ?
Ziklag ?
T. Mor
Ashdod
Gerar
Ashkelon
T. el-Farah (South)
Gaza
Yurza ?
Sharuhen ?
T. el-Ajjul
Deir el-Balah

Section 4 – 6

Canaanite (MB/LB) Period

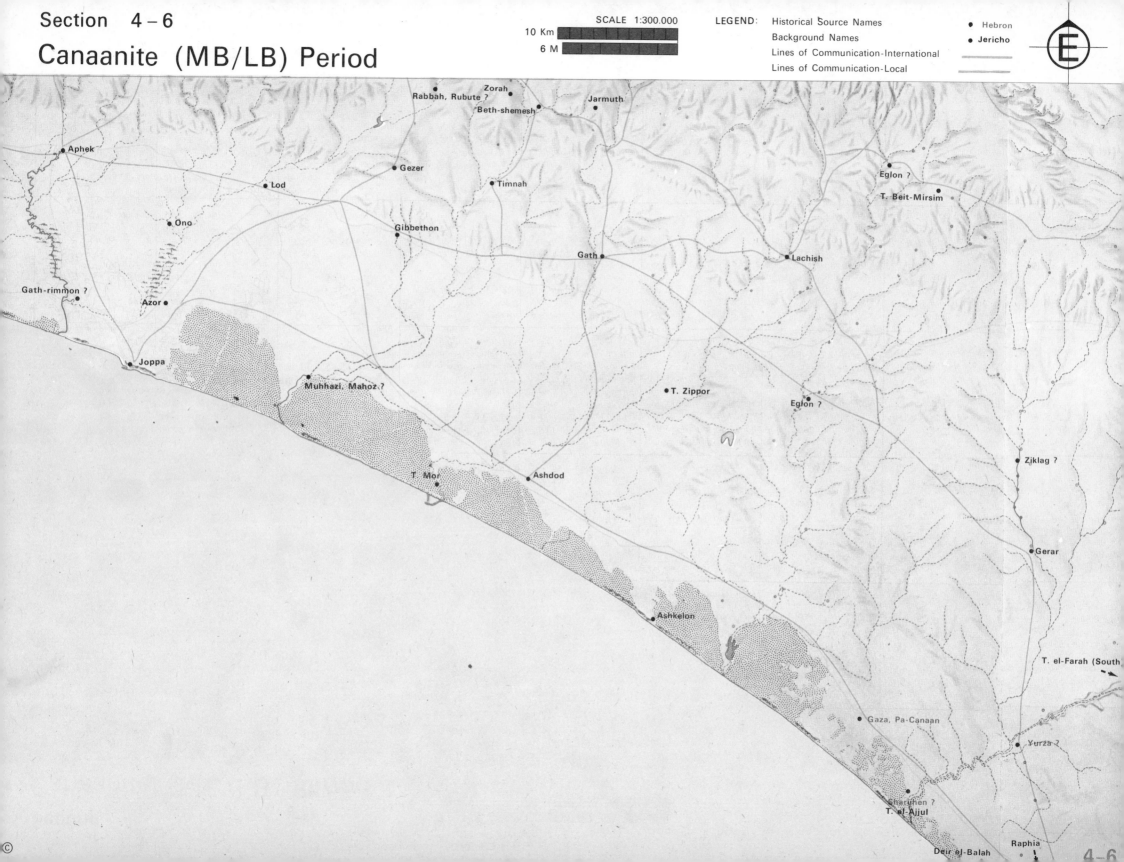

SCALE 1:300.000

10 Km

6 M

LEGEND: Historical Source Names • Hebron
Background Names • Jericho
Lines of Communication-International
Lines of Communication-Local

Zorah
Rabbah, Rubute ?
Beth-shemesh
Jarmuth
Aphek
Gezer
Lod
Timnah
Eglon ?
T. Beit-Mirsim
Ono
Gibbethon
Gath
Lachish
Gath-rimmon ?
Azor
Joppa
Muhhazi, Mahoz ?
T. Zippor
Eglon ?
Ziklag ?
T. Mor
Ashdod
Gerar
Ashkelon
T. el-Farah (South)
Gaza, Pa-Canaan
Yurza ?
Sharuhen ?
T. el-Ajjul
Raphia
Deir el-Balah
©
4–6

Section 4–7

Canaanite (MB/LB) Period

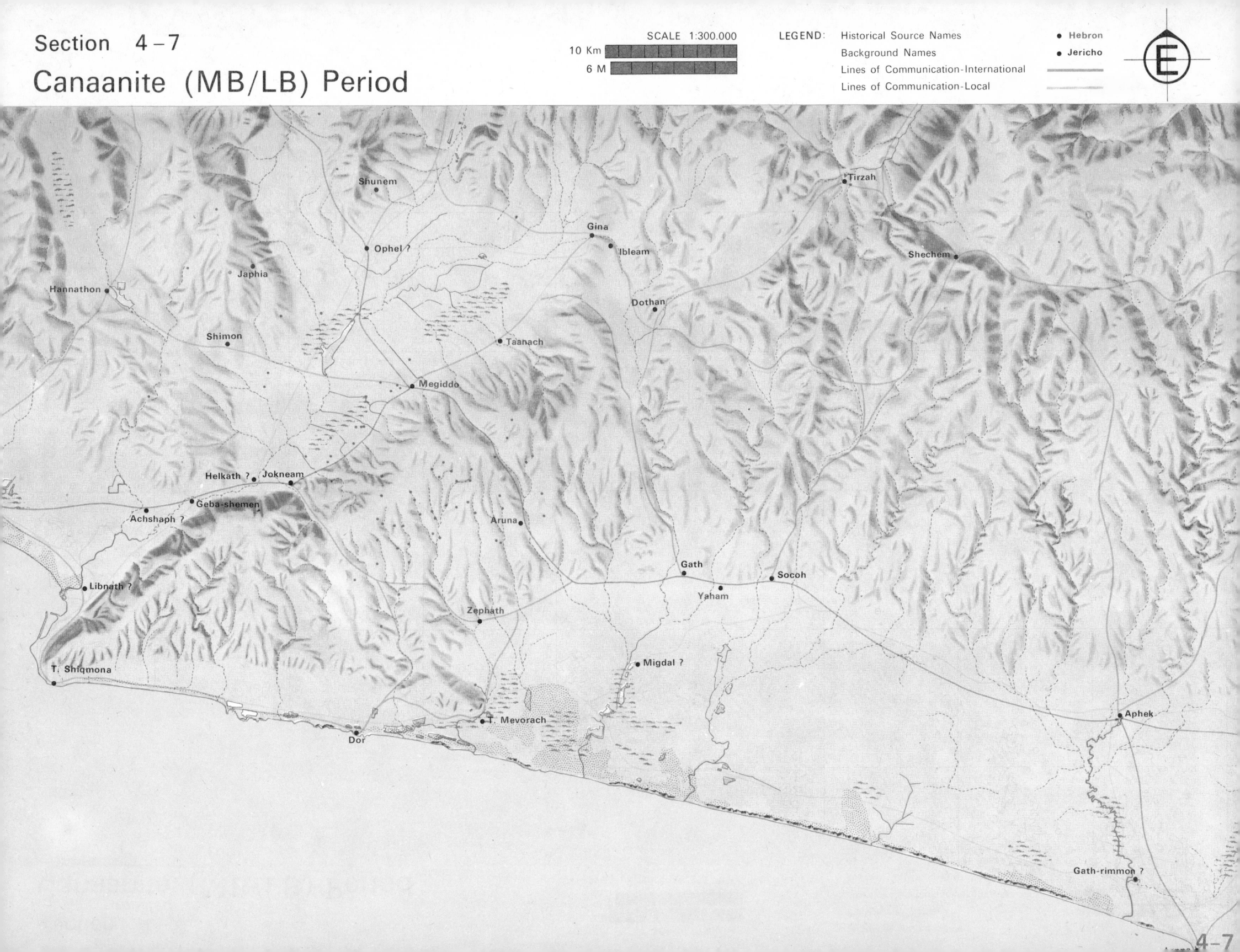

SCALE 1:300.000

10 Km

6 M

LEGEND: Historical Source Names ● Hebron

Background Names ● Jericho

Lines of Communication-International

Lines of Communication-Local

Shunem
Tirzah
Gina
Ophel ?
Ibleam
Shechem
Japhia
Hannathon
Dothan
Shimon
Taanach
Megiddo
Helkath ?
Jokneam
Geba-shemen
Achshaph ?
Aruna
Gath
Socoh
Yaham
Libnath ?
Zephath
Migdal ?
T. Shiqmona
T. Mevorach
Dor
Aphek
Gath-rimmon ?
4–7

Section 4–8

Canaanite (MB/LB) Period

Title? Date?

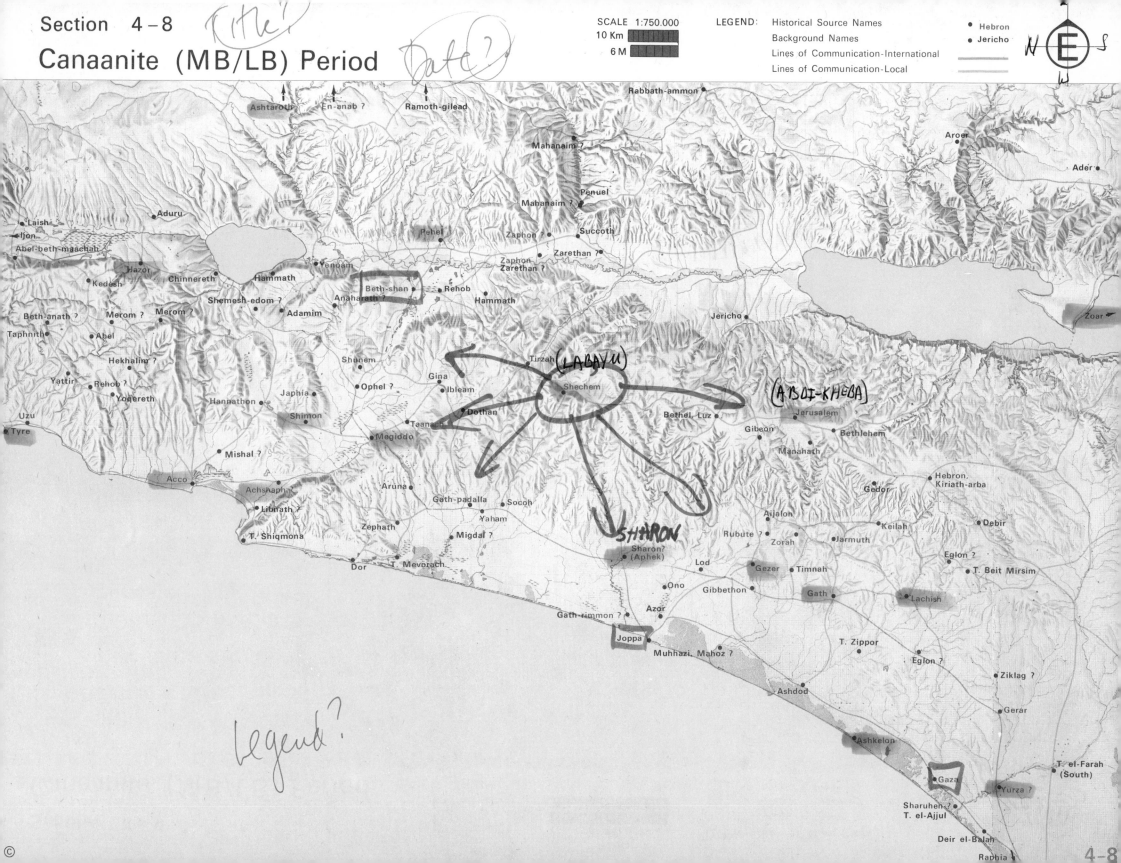

SCALE 1:750.000
10 Km
6 M

LEGEND: Historical Source Names — • Hebron
Background Names — • Jericho
Lines of Communication-International
Lines of Communication-Local

N E S W

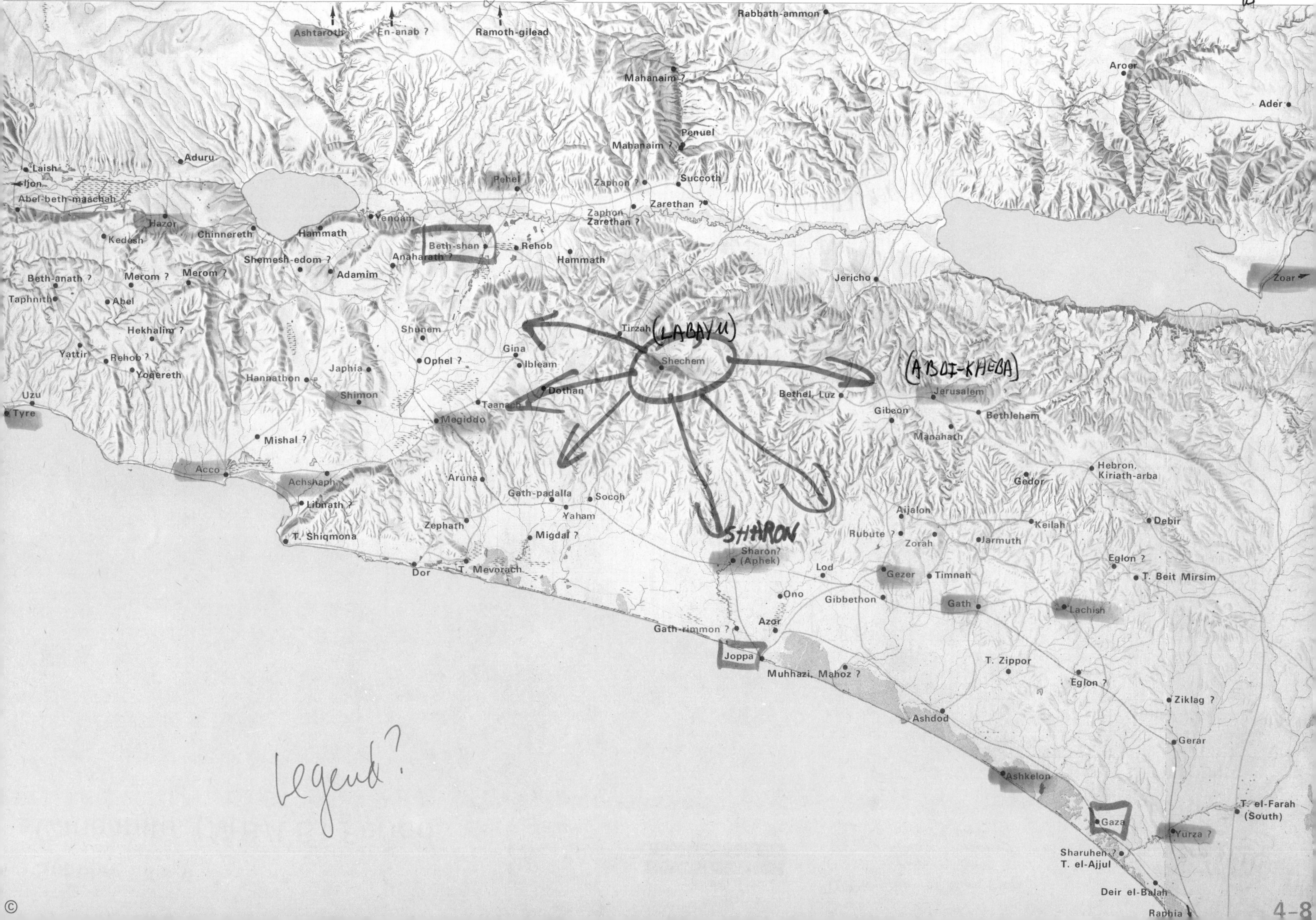

Ashtaroth
En-anab ?
Ramoth-gilead
Rabbath-ammon
Mahanaim ?
Aroer
Ader
Penuel
Mahanaim ?
Succoth
Zaphon ?
Zarethan ?
Zaphon
Zarethan ?
Pehel
Aduru
Laish
Ijon
Abel-beth-maachah
Hazor
Kedesh
Chinnereth
Hammath
Yenoam
Beth-shan
Rehob
Hammath
Anaharath ?
Shemesh-edom ?
Adamim
Beth-anath ?
Merom ?
Merom ?
Taphnith
Abel
Jericho
Zoar
Hekhalim ?
Shunem
Tirzah
(LABAYU)
Shechem
Gina
Ibleam
Ophel ?
Yattir
Rehob ?
Yoqereth
Japhia
Hannathon
Dothan
(ABDI-KHEBA)
Jerusalem
Bethel, Luz
Gibeon
Bethlehem
Uzu
Tyre
Shimon
Taanach
Megiddo
Manahath
Mishal ?
Acco
Achshaph
Aruna
Hebron, Kiriath-arba
Gedor
Gath-padalla
Socoh
Yaham
Libnath ?
Aijalon
Zephath
Keilah
Debir
SHARON
T. Shiqmona
Migdal ?
Rubute ?
Zorah
Jarmuth
Sharon? (Aphek)
Eglon ?
Dor
T. Mevorach
Lod
Gezer
Timnah
T. Beit Mirsim
Ono
Gibbethon
Gath
Lachish
Gath-rimmon ?
Azor
Joppa
T. Zippor
Muhhazi, Mahoz ?
Eglon ?
Ziklag ?
Ashdod
Gerar
Legend?
Ashkelon
T. el-Farah (South)
Gaza
Yurza ?
Sharuhen ?
T. el-Ajjul
Deir el-Balah
Raphia

Section 4 – 9

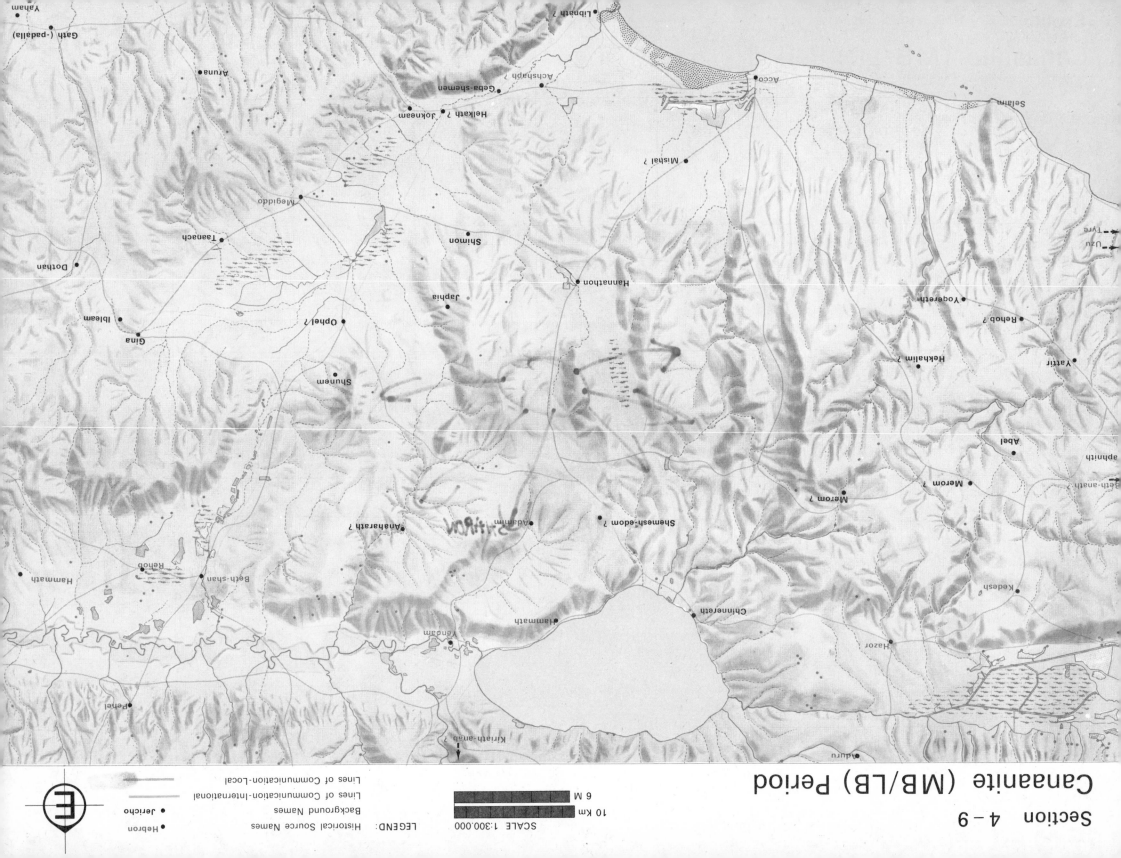

Canaanite (MB/LB) Period

SCALE 1:300.000

10 Km

6 M

LEGEND: Historical Source Names • Hebron
Background Names • Jericho
Lines of Communication-International
Lines of Communication-Local

Aduru
Kiriath-anab ?
Pehel
Hazor
Yenoam
Hammath
Chinnereth
Kedesh
Beth-shan
Rehob
Hammath
Shemesh-edom ?
Adamim
Anaharath ?
Merom ?
Beth-anath ?
Merom ?
aphnith
Abel
Shunem
Yattir
Hekhalim ?
Gina
Ophel ?
Ibleam
Rehob ?
Japhia
Yoqereth
Hannathon
Dothan
Uzu
Tyre
Shimon
Taanach
Megiddo
Mishal ?
Helkath ?
Jokneam
Selaim
Geba-shemen
Acco
Achshaph ?
Aruna
Gath (-padalla)
Libnath ?
Yaham

Section 5 Summary of contents & sources

Israelite Conquest

MAIN BIBLICAL REF.: Numbers 13-14; 20; 21; 32-34
Deuteronomy 1-3; 11; 27
Joshua 1-12

Map No.	Subject	Primary sources	Regional Map Nos. (Section 1)	Macmillan Bible Atlas Map Nos.	Other references and notes
5-1	**Overview (north) and kings of Transjordan and Canaan**				
	a Overview (north)				
	b Western and eastern boundaries of Canaan	Numbers 34.6,10-12 (cf. Ezekiel 47.18,20)		50	
	c Kings and territories in Transjordan (north of the Arnon river)	Joshua 12.1-6			
	d Kings of Canaan	Joshua 12.7-24 (cf. Joshua 10.40; 11.16-20)		63	
5-2	**Overview (south) and Wilderness Wanderings**				
	a Overview (south)				
	b Southern border of Canaan and southern limit of conquest	Numbers 34.1-5; Joshua 11.17; 12.7; 15.1-4 (cf. Ezekiel 47.19; 48.28)		50	
	c Spies in Canaan; proposed entry from the south rejected	Numbers 13; Deuteronomy 1.22-39	16	50	
	d Later attempt to enter Canaan from the south fails	Numbers 14; 21.1-3; 33.40; Deuteronomy 1.41-45 (cf. Joshua 12.14)	16	51	
	e Stations during Wanderings (from Kadesh-barnea to the boundary of Moab)	Numbers 20; 21.4-15; 33.34-44; Deuteronomy 1.6-2.15 (cf. Psalm 90)	15	52	
5-3	**Campaigns in Transjordan and entry into Canaan**				
	a Campaigns in Transjordan: Heshbon, Edrei and Jazer; death of Moses	Numbers 21.13-22.1; 33.45-49; Deuteronomy 2.16-3.11; 3.18-29; 34	11,12	52	
	b Settlement in Transjordan of Reuben, Gad, and half of Manasseh (see also map 6.2)	Numbers 32; Deuteronomy 3.12-17; Joshua 13.7-33	11,12	65,70,71	
	c Entry into Canaan and initial campaigns: Jericho and Ai (for detail see 5-4)	Joshua 1.1-8.29 (cf. Joshua 12.9, 16)	4,12	53,54	
	d Reciting the blessings and curses on Mt. Ebal and Mt. Gerizim	Deuteronomy 11.26-32; 27; Joshua 8.30-35 (cf. Joshua 24.1-28)	4	55	
5-4	**Detail: entry into Canaan and initial campaign: Jericho and Ai**				
	Detail: entry into Canaan and initial campaign: Jericho and Ai	See 5.3 c	4	54	
5-5	**Campaigns in central Canaan: Gibeon and the Shephelah**				
	a Gibeonite strategic positions and deception of Joshua	Joshua 9	13	56	
	b Battle of Gibeon and the valley of Aijalon	Joshua 10.1-15	1	56	
	c Battles in the Shephelah and southern hill-country	Joshua 10.16-39 (cf. Joshua 11.21; 12.10-13, 15-16)	2,16	58	
5-6	**Campaign in northern Canaan: Merom and Hazor**				
	Campaign in northern Canaan: Merom and Hazor	Joshua 11.1-15 (cf. Joshua 12.19-23)	8	62	

Section 5 – 1

Israelite Conquest (LB)

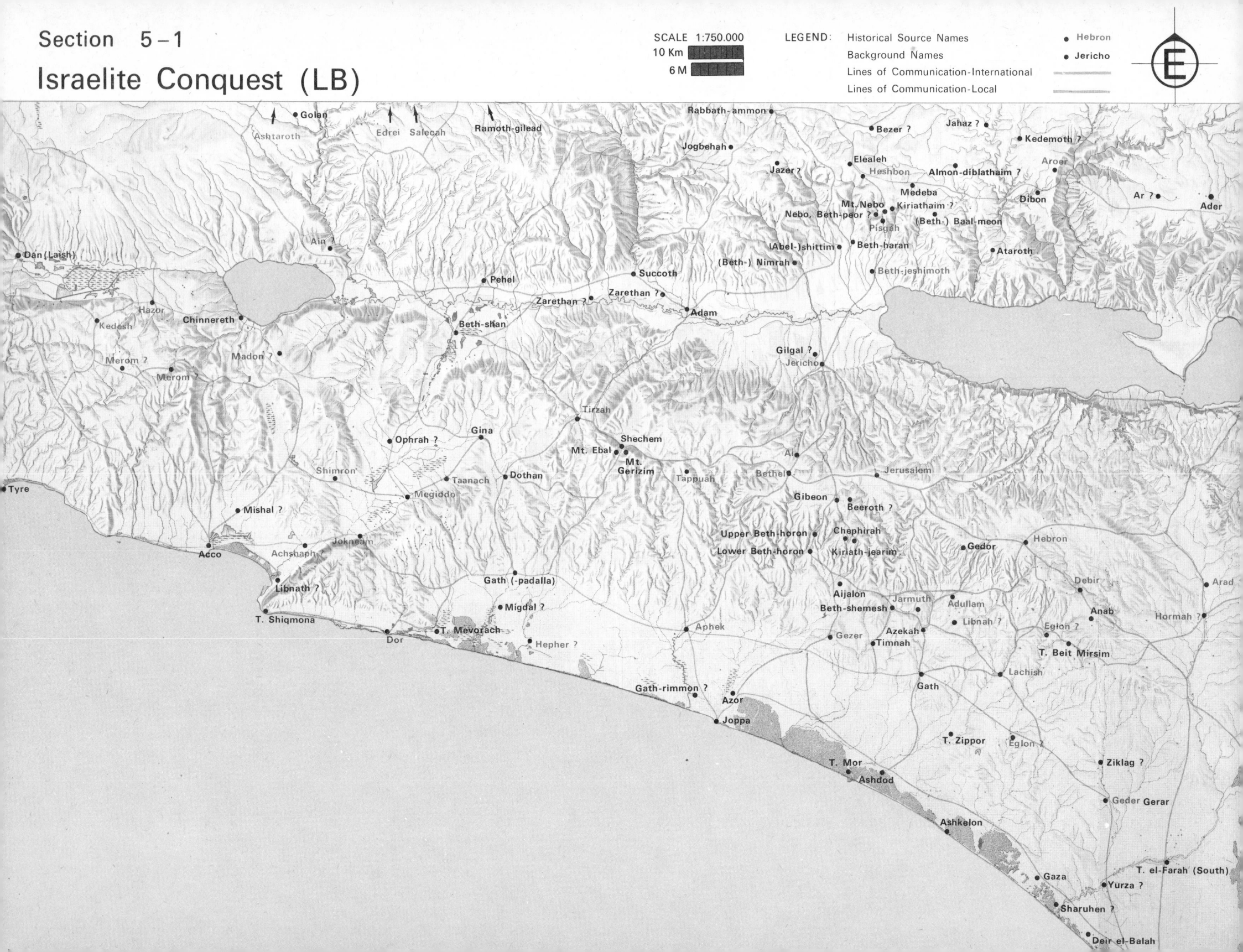

SCALE 1:750.000
10 Km
6 M

LEGEND: Historical Source Names • Hebron
Background Names • Jericho
Lines of Communication-International
Lines of Communication-Local

Golan
Ashtaroth
Edrei
Salecah
Ramoth-gilead
Rabbath-ammon
Bezer ?
Jahaz ?
Kedemoth ?
Jogbehah
Elealeh
Heshbon
Almon-diblathaim ?
Aroer
Jazer ?
Medeba
Dibon
Ar ?
Ader
Mt. Nebo
Nebo, Beth-peor ?
Kiriathaim ?
Pisgah
(Beth-) Baal-meon
(Abel-)shittim
Beth-haran
Ataroth
(Beth-) Nimrah
Beth-jeshimoth
Ain
Dan (Laish)
Pehel
Succoth
Zarethan ?
Zarethan ?
Adam
Hazor
Kedesh
Chinnereth
Beth-shan
Merom ?
Madon ?
Merom ?
Gilgal ?
Jericho
Tirzah
Ophrah ?
Gina
Shechem
Mt. Ebal
Mt. Gerizim
Ai
Shimron
Taanach
Dothan
Tappuah
Bethel
Jerusalem
Tyre
Megiddo
Mishal ?
Gibeon
Beeroth ?
Upper Beth-horon
Chaphirah
Joknéam
Acco
Achshaph ?
Lower Beth-horon
Kiriath-jearim
Gedor
Hebron
Gath (-padalla)
Debir
Arad
Libnath ?
Aijalon
Jarmuth
Adullam
Migdal ?
Beth-shemesh
Anab
T. Shiqmona
Libnah ?
Hormah ?
Aphek
Eglon ?
Dor
T. Mevorach
Azekah
Gezer
Timnah
Hepher ?
T. Beit Mirsim
Lachish
Gath
Gath-rimmon ?
Azor
Joppa
T. Zippor
Eglon ?
Ziklag ?
T. Mor
Ashdod
Geder Gerar
Ashkelon
T. el-Farah (South)
Gaza
Yurza ?
Sharuhen ?
Deir el-Balah

Section 5 – 2

Israelite Conquest (LB)

SCALE 1:750.000
10 Km
6 M

LEGEND: Historical Source Names — Hebron
Background Names — Jericho
Lines of Communication-International
Lines of Communication-Local

Jahaz ?
Kedemoth ?
Almon-diblathaim ?
Aroer
Dibon
Ar ?
Ader
Ije-abarim, Iyim ?
Ataroth
Zoar
Punon
Rekem ?
Zalmonah ?
Tamar
Hebron
Gedor
Keilah
dullam
Debir
Arad
Mt. Halak
Libnah ?
Hormah ?
Eglon ?
T. Beit Mirsim
Lachish
Zippor
Eglon ?
Ziklag ?
Gerar
shkelon
Gaza
T. el-Farah (South)
Yurza ?
Sharuhen ?
Deir el-Balah
Raphia
Mt. Hor?
Hazar-addar, Hezron ?
Kadesh-barnea
Karka ?
Azmon ?
Elath
Ezion-geber
Timnah
Abronah ?
Jotbathah ?

Section 5–3

Israelite Conquest (LB)

SCALE 1:450.000
10 Km
6 M

LEGEND: Historical Source Names • Hebron
Background Names • Jericho
Lines of Communication-International
Lines of Communication-Local

Kenath
Salecah
Edrei
Ramoth-gilead
Rabbah
Rabbath-ammon
Bezer ?
Jahaz ?
Kedemoth ?
Jogbehah
Jazer ?
Elealeh
Heshbon
Almon-diblathaim
Aroer
Medeba
Iyim ?
Dibon (-gad)
Ham
Kamon
Nebo, Beth-peor ?
Mt. Nebo
Kiriathaim ?
Baal-meon, Beon
Pisgah
Jabesh-gilead
Beth-haran
(Abel)shittim
Ataroth
(Beth-) Nimrah
Succoth
Beth-jeshimoth
Pehel
Zarethan ?
T. Umm Hamad
Zarethan ?
T. es-Saidiya
Adam
(Laish)
Zoar
Beth-shan
Rehob
Hammath
Anaharath ?
Gilgal ?
Jericho
Bezek
Shunem
Tirzah
Gina
Ophrah ?
Ibleam
Shechem
Mt. Ebal
Mt. Gerizim
Ai
Dothan
Bethel
Jerusalem
Taanach
Bethlehem
Megiddo
Beeroth ?
Gibeon
Manahath
Chephirah
Kiriath-jearim
Gedor
Hebron
Jokneam
Aruna
Gath(-padalla)
Socoh
Yaham
Aijalon
Debir
Zephath
Migdal-yen ?
Adullam
Keilah
Rabbah, Rubute ?
Zorah
Jarmuth

5-3

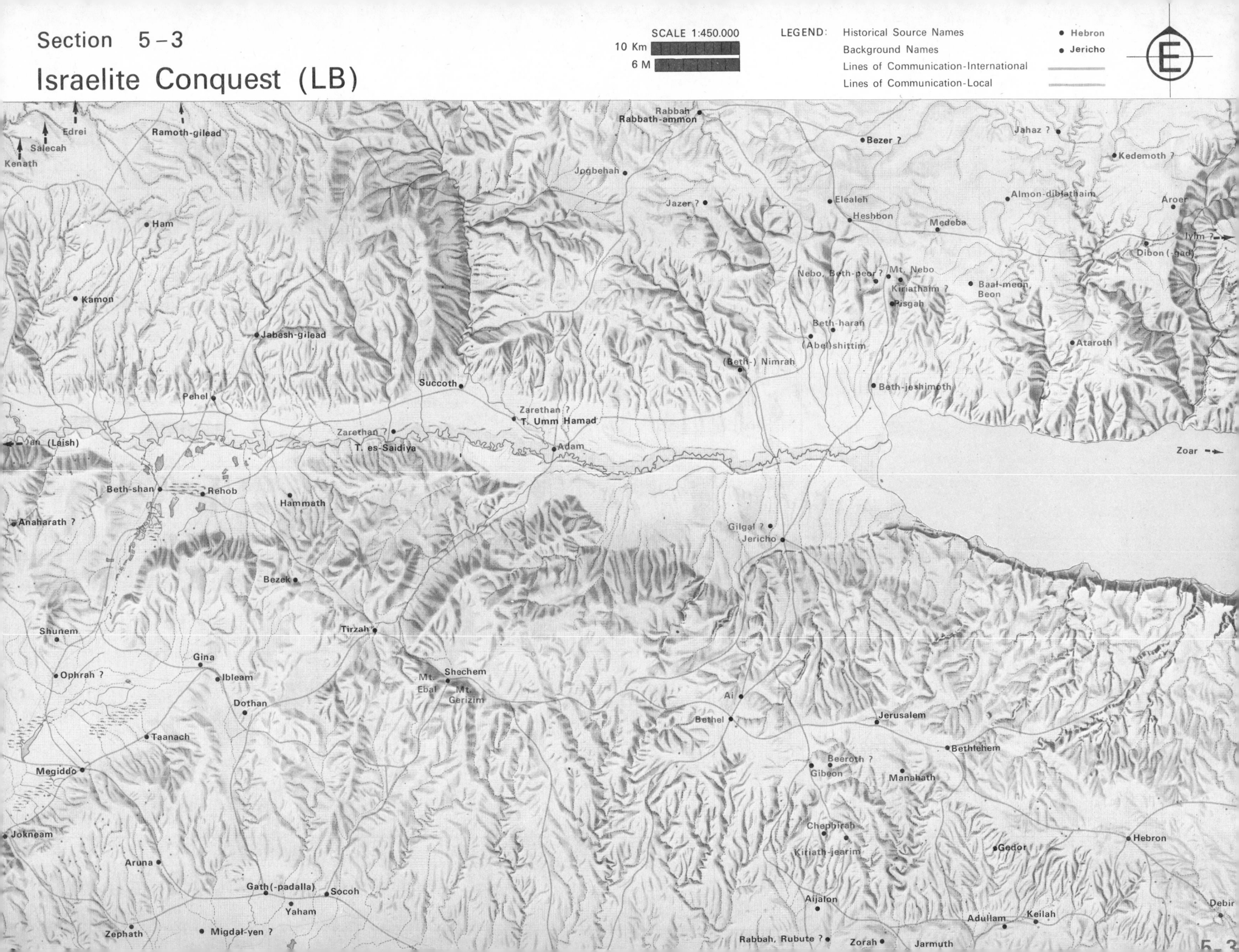

Section 5–4

Israelite Conquest (LB)

SCALE 1:215.000

10 Km

6 M

LEGEND:
- Historical Source Names — Hebron
- Background Names — Jericho
- Lines of Communication-International
- Lines of Communication-Local

(Beth) Nimrah
Beth-jeshimoth
Zarethan ?
Zarethan ?
Adam
W. Nu'eima
Gilgal ?
Jericho
W. 'Auja
W. Samniya
W. Far'a
W. Mukallik (N. Og)
N. Kidron
W. Qilt
W. Suweinit
N. Kidron
Shechem
Mt. Ebal
Mt. Gerizim
Ai
Bethel
Jerusalem
Bethlehem
Gibeon
Beeroth ?
Manahath

Section 5 – 5

Israelite Conquest (LB)

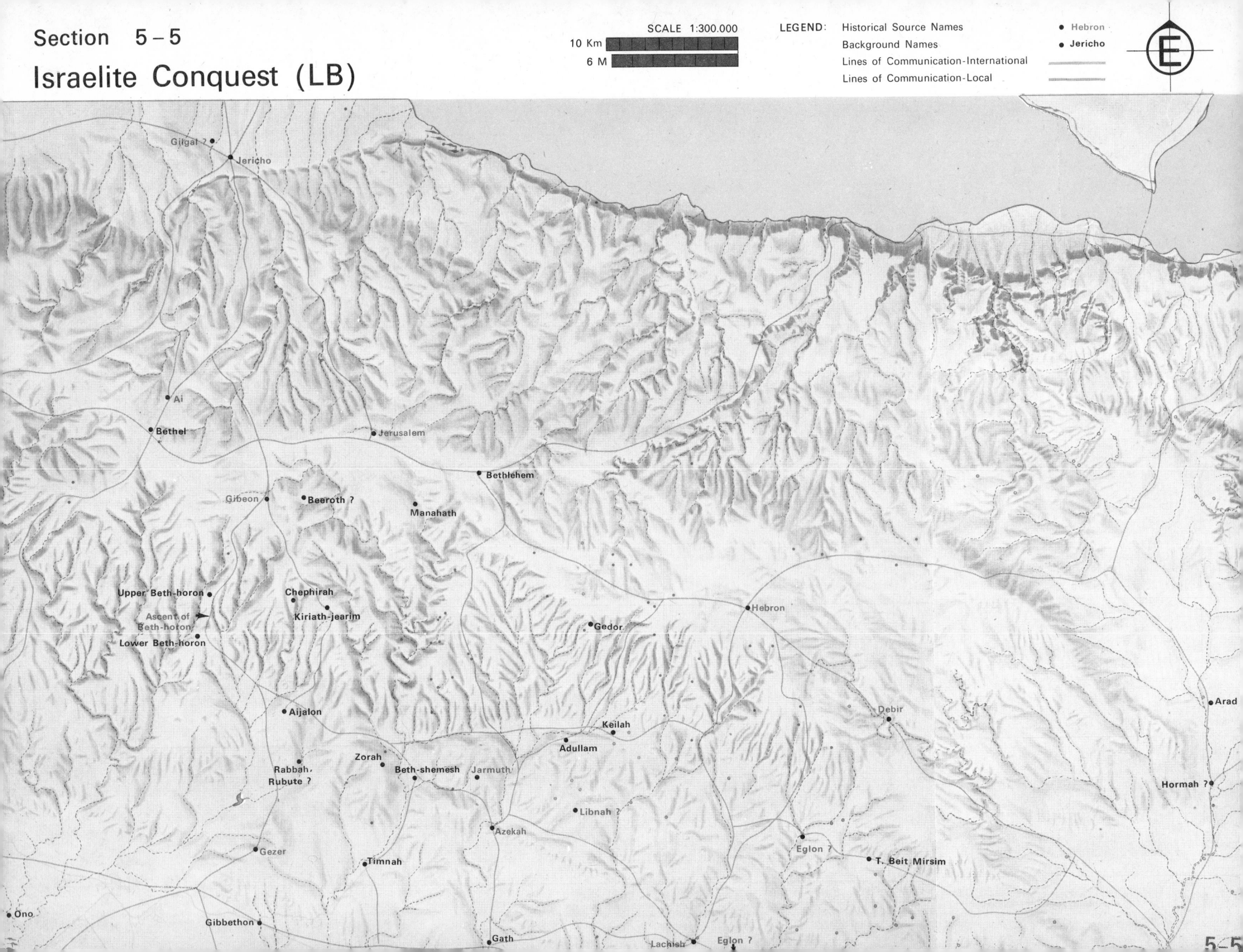

SCALE 1:300.000

10 Km

6 M

LEGEND: Historical Source Names • Hebron

Background Names • Jericho

Lines of Communication-International

Lines of Communication-Local

Gilgal ?
Jericho
Ai
Bethel
Jerusalem
Bethlehem
Gibeon
Beeroth ?
Manahath
Upper Beth-horon
Chephirah
Ascent of Beth-horon
Kiriath-jearim
Lower Beth-horon
Hebron
Gedor
Aijalon
Debir
Arad
Keilah
Adullam
Zorah
Rabbah, Rubute ?
Beth-shemesh
Jarmuth
Hormah ?
Libnah ?
Azekah
Eglon ?
Gezer
Timnah
T. Beit Mirsim
Ono
Gibbethon
Gath
Lachish
Eglon ?
5-5

Israelite Conquest (LB)

SCALE 1:300.000
10 Km
6 M

LEGEND: Historical Source Names • Hebron
Background Names • Jericho
Lines of Communication-International
Lines of Communication-Local

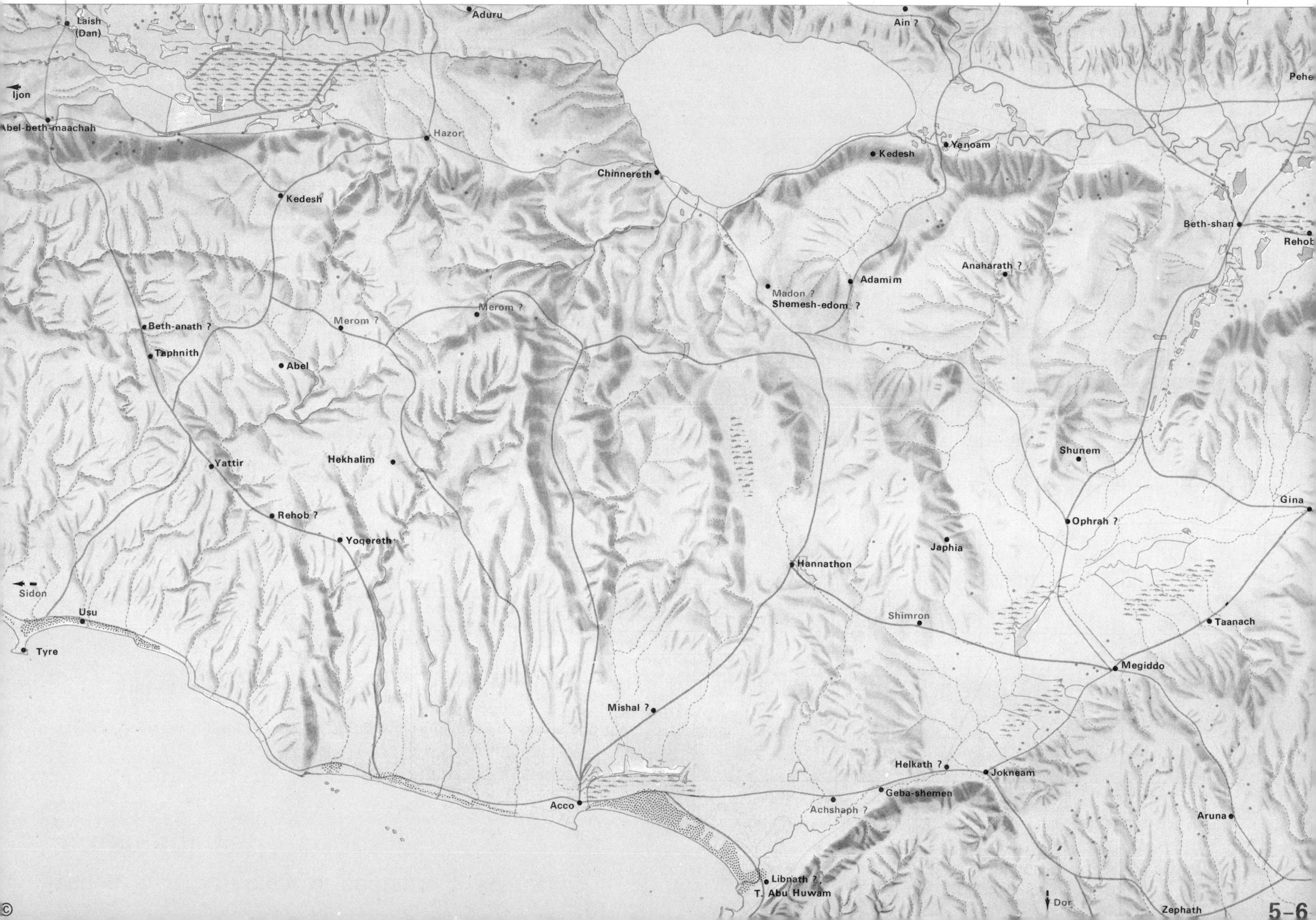

Laish (Dan)
Aduru
Ain ?
Ijon
Pehe
Abel-beth-maachah
Hazor
Yenoam
Kedesh
Chinnereth
Kedesh
Beth-shan
Rehob
Anaharath ?
Adamim
Madon ?
Shemesh-edom ?
Merom ?
Merom ?
Beth-anath ?
Taphnith
Abel
Shunem
Yattir
Hekhalim
Gina
Rehob ?
Ophrah ?
Yoqereth
Japhia
Hannathon
Sidon
Usu
Shimron
Taanach
Tyre
Megiddo
Mishal ?
Helkath ?
Jokneam
Geba-shemen
Acco
Achshaph ?
Aruna
Libnath ?
T. Abu Huwam
Dor
Zephath

Section 6 Summary of contents & sources

Settlement and Judges

MAIN BIBLICAL REF.: Joshua 13 – 21
Judges,
Ruth

Map No.	Subject	Primary sources	Regional Map Nos. (Section 1)	Macmillan Bible Atlas Map Nos.	Other references and notes
6-1	**Overview (north), a preview of regional settlement problems and the book of Ruth**				
	a Overview (north)				
	b Philistine settlement in the coastal plain				
	i) Arrival of the Sea Peoples and cessation of Egyptian rule (journey of Wen Amon)	Reliefs, inscriptions (*Medinet Habu: Egypt*); papyrus Harris I (*Egypt*); journey of Wen-amon, papyrus (*el-Hiba: Egypt*); ANET 25-29, 262-63; ANEP 7, 9, 57, 341, 813; ANE I: 185-86, 16-24	2,3,6	66,67	
	ii) The land that yet remains	Joshua 13.1-6 (cf. Judges 3.1-3)	2,3,6	69	
	c Unconquered Canaanite centres	Judges 1:21, 27-35 (cf. Joshua 15.63; 16.10; 17.11-18)	1,6,9	68	
	d Cities of Refuge	Joshua 20 (cf. Numbers 35.9-34; Deuteronomy 4.41-43)	1,6,9,12,16	108	
	e Levitic cities	Joshua 21 (cf. Numbers 35.1-8; 1 Chronicles 6.54-81)	1,6,9,12,16	108	
	f Story of Ruth, the Moabitess	Ruth	14		
6-2	**Tribal territories and city-lists in Canaan (Tribal territories in Transjordan taken from 5-3 b)**				
	a Initial distributions to the house of Judah and the house of Joseph	Joshua 14.1-5			
	i) **Judah** (for details see maps 6-3, 4, 7)				
	a) Southern border description	See 5-2 b			
	b) Eastern, northern and western border description	Joshua 15.5-12	1,2,4	73,130	
	c) Caleb's inheritance	See 6-3 b			
	d) City-list and districts	Joshua 15.20-63; note LXX Joshua 59a	3,14,16	130	
	ii) Joseph (Ephraim and Manasseh)	Joshua 16.1-4; 17.14-18	1,4,6,9,13	71,73	
	a) **Ephraim**: border description (for details see maps 6-3, 4, 6, 7)	Joshua 16.5-10	1,4,5	71	
	b) **Manasseh**: Machir and the territory of Manasseh (for details see maps 6-5, 6, 7)	Joshua 17.1-13	4,5,6,10,11	65,71	
	b Distribution of other tribal allotments from Shiloh	Joshua 18.1-10 (cf. Joshua 19.51)	4	71	
	i) **Benjamin**				
	a) Border description (between Judah and Joseph)	Joshua 18.11-20	1,4,13	73	
	b) City-list (for details see maps 6-3, 7)	Joshua 18.21-28	1,4,13	73	
	ii) **Simeon**: city-list in Judah (for details see maps 6-3,4; cf. 6-3 d)	Joshua 19.1-9	3,16	130	
	iii) **Zebulun**: border description/city-list (for details see maps 6-5, 6)	Joshua 19.10-16	7	72	
	iv) **Issachar**: city-list/border description (for details see maps 6-5, 6)	Joshua 19.17-23	9	72	
	v) **Asher**: border description/city-list (for detail see map 6-5)	Joshua 19.24-31	6,7	71,72	
	vi) **Naphtali**: border description/city-list (for details see maps 6-5, 6)	Joshua 19.32-39	7,8	71,72	
	vii) **Dan**: city-list and resettlement (for details see maps 6-3, 4, 5, 7)	Joshua 19.40-48	2,8	107	
	viii) Inheritance of Joshua and apostasy after his death (for details see maps 6-4, 7)	Joshua 19.49-50;24.29-33; Judges 2	13		
6-3	**Early developments in and around Judah**				
	a Judah's northern victory at Bezek	Judges 1.1-7	10	57	
	b Caleb's inheritance at Hebron	Judges 1.9-10,20; Joshua 14.6-15; 15.13-14 (cf. Joshua 10.36-37; 11.21)	16	57	
	c Othniel, the judge, and his victory at Debir	Judges 1.11-15; 3.7-11; Joshua 15.15-19 (cf. Joshua 10.38-39; 11.21)	16	57	
	d Kenites and Simeon in the Negev (cf. 6-2 b ii)	Judges 1.16-17	16	57	
	e Developments in the coastal plain	Judges 1.18 (cf. LXX reading 'took not'; Joshua 11.22)	3		
	f Jebus (Jerusalem) is conquered, but inhabitants not driven out	Judges 1.8,21; Joshua 15.63	1	57	
	g Joseph's victory at Bethel	Judges 1.22-26	1	57	

Settlement and Judges

Map No.	Subject	Primary sources	Regional Map Nos. (Section 1)	Macmillan Bible Atlas Map Nos.	Other references and notes
6-4	**Western confrontation: the tribe of Dan and Samson, the judge**				
	a Pressure on Dan and resulting move to the north	Judges 1.34-35; 17-18; Joshua 19.47	2,8	64	
	b Exploits of Samson and the Philistines	Judges 13-16	2,3	79,80	
6-5	**Northern confrontation: Deborah and Barak**				
	a Deborah and Barak against the forces of Sisera	Judges 4,5 (cf. Psalms 83.9-10; Joshua 12.19-23)	7,9	59,60,61	
	b Minor judges: Shamgar and Elon	Judges 3.31; 5.6; 12.11-12		82	
6-6	**Eastern confrontation: Ehud, Gideon and Jephthah**				
	a Ehud and the Moabites	See 6.7 a			
	b Gideon and the Midianites	Judges 6-8 (cf. Psalms 83.9-12)	10,11	75,76	
	c Jephthah and the Ammonites	Judges 10.6-12.7 (cf. 5-3 a)	11,12	78	
	d Minor judge: Jair	Judges 10.3-5		82	
6-7	**Internal confrontation: Abimelech and Benjaminite civil war**				
	a Ehud and the Moabites (from 6-6 a)	Judges 3.12-30	4	74	
	b Rise and fall of Abimelech, son of Gideon	Judges 8.30-9.57	4	77	
	c Atrocity at Gibeah leads to civil war in Benjamin	Judges 19-21	13	81	
	d Minor judges: Tola, Ibzan and Abdon	Judges 10.1-2; 12.8-10,13-15		82	

Notes

Section 6 – 1

Settlement & Judges (Iron I)

SCALE 1:750.000
10 Km
6 M

LEGEND: Historical Source Names • Hebron
Background Names • Jericho
Lines of Communication-International
Lines of Communication-Local

Golan
Ashtaroth, Be-eshterah
Ramoth-gilead
Rabbath-ammon
Mephaath ?
Bezer ?
Jahaz
Kedemoth ?
Jogbehah
Jazer ?
Abel-keramim ?
Heshbon
Aroer
Mahanaim ?
Ramath-mizpeh ?
Dibon
Kamon ?
Penuel
Mahanaim
Jabesh-gilead
Kir-hareseth, Kir of Moab
Dan; Laish
Zaphon ?
Succoth
Zarethan ?
Hazor
Chinnereth
Hammath
Kedesh
Oak in Zaanannim ?
Zaphon ?, Zarethan ?
Adam
Kedesh
Karthan ?
Rakkath
Jarmuth
Remeth
Beth-shan
En-gannim ?
Jokmeam ?
Gilgal ?
Jericho
Beth-anath ?
Adamah ?
Aphekah
Kishion ?
Daberath
En-dor
Bezek
En Harod
Tirzah
Beth-shemesh ?
Arumah
Rimmon
Chesulloth, Chisloth-tabor
Ophrah ?
Ibleam, Bileam
Shechem
Shiloh
Rimmon
Mt. Gerizim
Almon
Alemeth
Anathoth
Ai
Geba
Sidon
Dothan
Lebonah
Bethel
Ramah
Jerusalem, Jebus
Taanach
Shamir
Gibeah
Mizpah
Ataroth-addar ?
Tyre
Rehob ?
Megiddo
Pirathon
Gibeon
Bethlehem, Ephrathah
Abdon
Mishal ?
Achzib
Aphek, Aphik
Helkath ?
ha-Zorea, T. Qiri
Jokneam
Timnath-serah
Upper Beth-horon
Arad
Acco
Lower Beth-horon
Kiriath-jearim
Hebron, Kiriath-arba
Achshaph ?
Juttah
Eshtemoa
Jattir
Libnath ?
Aijalon
Eshtaol
Shaalbim
Debir, Kiriath-sepher
Migdal ?
Har-heres (Beth-shemesh)
Ebenezer ?
Zorah
Hormah, Zephath ?
Libnah ?
Aphek
Azekah
Eglon ?
Dor
Gezer
Timnah
T. Beit Mirsim
Gibbethon
Ekron
Gath
Lachish
Gath-rimmon ?
Azor
Beth-dagon
Beer-she
T. Qasila
Eltekeh ?
Joppa
T. Zippor
Eglon ?
Ziklag ?
T. Mor
Ashdod
Ashkelon
T. el-Farah (South)
Gaza
Yurza ?
Sharuhen ?
Deir el-Balah

Settlement and Judges

LEGEND:
Location certain: Bethel 113 ○
Location probable: Ziklag ? 58 ○
Location undefined: R. Jordan 15 *
Location unknown Eltolad —

Tribes in Canaan

Judah

Southern border: see 5-2 b
Joshua 15.1-5

Eastern, northern and western border
Joshua 15.5-12

29* Salt Sea
15 Mouth of Jordan
30 Beth-hoglah
31 Beth-arabah
— Stone of Bohan
— Valley of Achor
— Debir
— Gilgal (Geliloth)
32* Ascent of Adummim
33 Waters of En-shemesh
34 En-rogel
35 Hinnom valley
36 Jebus(ite), Jerusalem
37 Top of mountain between Hinnom & Rephaim valleys
38 Waters of Nephtoah
39 Mount Ephron
40 Baalah, Kiriath-jearim
41 Mount Seir
42 Mount Jearim, Chesalon
43 Beth-shemesh
44 Timnah
45 Hill north of Ekron
46 Shikkeron
47 Mount Baalah ?
48 Jabneel
49* Great Sea

City list/districts
Joshua 15.20-63

DISTRICT ONE
Joshua 15.21-32

50 Kabzeel ?
51 Eder (Arad)
— Jagur
— Kinah
— Dimonah
52 Adadah (Aroer)
— Kedesh
— Hazor
— Ithnan
— Ziph
— Telem
— Bealoth
— Hazor-hadattah
53 Kerioth ?
— Herzon (Hazor)
— Amam
— Shema
54 Moladah ?
— Hazar-gaddah
— Heshmon
55 Beth-pelet ?
— Hazar-shual
56 Beer-sheba
— Baalah
— Iim, Iyim
— Ezem
— Eltolad
— Chesil (Bethuel)
57 Hormah ?
58 Ziklag ?
59 Madmannah
60 Sansannah
— (Beth-) Lebaoth
— Shilhim
— Ain
— Rimmon

DISTRICT TWO
Joshua 15.33-36

61 Eshtaol
62 Zorah
— Ashnah
63 Zanoah
— En-gannim
— Tappuah
— Enam
64 Jarmuth
65 Adullam
66 Socoh
67 Azekah
68 Shaaraim ?
— Adithaim
— Gederah
— Gederothaim

DISTRICT THREE
Joshua 15.37-41

— Zenan ?
— Hadashah ?
69 Migdal-gad ?
— Dilean
— Mizpeh (Mizpah)
— Joktheel
70 Lachish
— Bozkath
71a Eglon ?
71b Eglon ?
— Cabbon
— Lahmam, Lahmas
— Chitlish
— Gederoth
— Beth-dagon
— Naamah
— Makkedah

DISTRICT FOUR
Joshua 15.42-44

72 Libnah ?
73 Ether
— Ashan
— Iphtah
— Ashnah
74 Nezib
75 Keilah
— Achzib
76 Mareshah

DISTRICT FIVE
Joshua 15.48-51

— Shamir
77 Jattir
78 Socoh
— Dannah
79 Kiriath-sannah, Debir
80 Anab
81 Eshtemoh (Eshtemoa)
82 Anim
83 Goshen ?
— Holon
— Giloh

DISTRICT SIX
Joshua 15.52-54

— Arab
84 Dumah
— Eshan
— Janim, Janum
85 Beth-tappuah
86 Aphekah
— Humtah
87 Kiriath-arba, Hebron
— Zior

DISTRICT SEVEN
Joshua 15.55-57

88 Maon
89 Carmel
90 Ziph
91 Juttah
— Jezreel
— Jokdeam
— Zanoah
92 Kain
— Gibeah
— Timnah

DISTRICT EIGHT
Joshua 15.58-59

793 Halhul
94 Beth-zur
95 Gedor
— Maarath
96 Beth-anoth
— Eltekon

DISTRICT NINE
LXX, Joshua 15.59a

97 Tekoa
98 Ephrathah, Bethlehem
99 Peor
100 Etam
— Kulon, Kulla
— Tatam
101 Sores, Zobah ?
102 Karem (Beth-haccherem ?)
— Gallim
103 Bether
104 Manach (Manahath)

DISTRICT TEN
Joshua 15.60

40 Kiriath-baal, Kiriath-jearim
105 Rabbah ?

DISTRICT ELEVEN
Joshua 15.61-62

31 Beth-arabah
106 Middin ?
107 Secacah ?
108 Nibshan ?
109 City of Salt ?
110 En-gedi

Joseph (Ephraim/Manasseh)

Southern border
Joshua 16.1-4

15* Jordan (river)
111 Jericho (waters, shoulder and city)
112* Wilderness
113 Bethel, Luz
114 Ataroth(-addar) ?
— Territory of Archites
— Territory of Japhletites
115 Lower Beth-horon
116 Gezer
49* Sea

Ephraim

Border description
Joshua 16.5-10

114 Ataroth-addar ?
117 Upper Beth-horon
49* Sea
118 Michmethath
119 Taanath-shiloh
120 Janoah
— Ataroth
121 Naarah (Naaran)
111 Jericho
15* Jordan (river)
122 Tappuah
123* Brook Kanah
49* Sea

Manasseh

General description of territory between tribes of Asher, Ephraim and Issachar
Joshua 17.7-10

118 Michmethath
122 En-tappuah
123* Brook Kanah
49* Sea

Benjamin

Border description
Joshua 18.11-20

15* Jordan (river)
111 Jericho (shoulder)
124 Beth-aven ? (wilderness)
113 Luz, Bethel
114 Ataroth-addar ?
125* Mountain south of Beth-horon
40 Kiariath-baal, Kiriath-jearim
39 Ephron ('westward')
38 Waters of Nephtoah
37 Mountain between Hinnom and Rephaim Valleys
36 Jebus(ite), Jerusalem
34 En-rogel
33 En-shemesh
— Geliloth (Gilgal)
32* Ascent of Adummim
— Stone of Bohan
31 (Beth-)arabah (shoulder)
30 Beth-hoglah (shoulder)
29* Salt Sea
15* Jordan (river)

City list
Joshua 18.21-28

111 Jericho
30 Beth-hoglah
— Emek-keziz ?
31 Beth-arabah
126 Zemaraim ?
113 Bethel
— Avvim
127 Parah
128 Ophrah
— Chephar-ammoni
— Ophni
129 Geba
130 Gibeon
131 Ramah
132 Beeroth ?
133 Mizpeh (Mizpah)
134 Chephirah
135 Mozah
— Rekem
— Irpeel
— Taralah
— Zela
— Haeleph
36 Jebus(ite), Jerusalem
136 Gibeah (Gibeath)
40 Kiriath(-jearim)

Simeon

City list
Joshua 19.1-9

56 Beer-sheba
— Sheba
54 Moladah ?
— Hazar-shual
— Balah
— Ezem
— Eltolad
— Bethul
57 Hormah ?
58 Ziklag ?
— Beth-marcaboth
— Hazar-susah
— Beth-lebaoth
137 Sharuhen ?
— En-rimmon
— Ether
— Ashan
138 Baalath-beer ?
139 Ramah of the Negeb ?

Zebulun

Border description/city list
Joshua 19.10-16

140 Sarid
141 Mareal ? (Maralah)
142 Dabbesheth ?
143* Brook east of Jokneam
144 Chisloth-tabor
145 Daberath
146 Japhia
147 Gath-hepher
— Ethkazin
148 Rimmon
— Neah
149 Hannathon
150* Valley of Iphtahel
— Kattath
— Nahalal
151 Shimron
— Idalah
152 Bethelehem

Issachar

City list/border description
Joshua 19.17-23

153 Jezreel
144 Chesulloth
154 Shunem
155 Hapharaim ?
— Shion
156 Anaharath ?
— Rabbith
157 Kishion ?
— Ebez
158 Remeth ?
159 En-gannim ?
160 En-haddah
— Beth-pazzez
161 Tabor
— Shahazumah
162 Beth-shemesh ?
15* Jordan (river)

Asher

Border description/city list
Joshua 19.24-31

163 Helkath ?
164 Hali
165 Beten ?
166 Achshaph ?
— Allammelech
— Amad
167 Mishal ?
168* Carmel
169* Shihor-libnath ?
170 (Libnath ?)
— Beth-dagon
150* Valley of Iphtahel
171 Beth-emek
172 Neiel
173 Cabul (Kabul)
174 Ebron (Abdon)
— Rehob
175 Hammon
176 Kanah
177 Sidon the Great
— Ramah
178 Tyre
179 Hosah ? (Usu)
180 Mahalab (Mehebel)
181 Achzib
182 Ummah ? (Acco)
183 Aphek
184 Rehob ?

Naphtali

Border description
Joshua 19.32-34

185 Heleph ?
186 Oak in Zaanannim
187 Adami-nekeb
188 Jabneel
189 Lakkum ?
15* Jordan (river)
190 Aznoth-tabor ?
191 Hukkok ?
15* Jordan (river)

City list
Joshua 19.35-39

— Ziddim
— Zer
192 Hammath
193 Rakkath
194 Chinnereth
195 Adamah ?
196 Ramah
197 Hazor
198 Kedesh
— Edrei
— En-hazor
199 Yiron
— Migdal-el
— Horem
200 Beth-anath ?
201 Beth-shemesh ?

Dan

City list
Joshua 19.40-49

62 Zorah
61 Eshtaol
43 Ir-shemesh
202 Shaalabbin
203 Aijalon
— Ithlah
— Elon
44 Timnah
204 Ekron
205 Eltekeh ?
206 Gibbethon
47 Baalath ?
207 Jehud
208 Bene-berak
209 Gath-rimmon ?
210* Me-jarkon
— Rakkon
211 Joppa
212 Leshem, Dan

Settlement & Judges (Iron I)

SCALE 1:750.000
10 Km
6 M

LEGEND: Historical Source Names • Hebron
Background Names • Jericho
Lines of Communication-International
Lines of Communication-Local

Rabbah
Hazor
Beth-shan
Gilgal ?
Ibleam
Shechem
Shiloh
Taanach
Megiddo
Jokneam
Acco
Tyre
Dor
Aphek
Joppa
Ashdod
Gaza

Tribes in Transjordan

General description
Joshua 13.8-13

Reuben

Territory/city list
Joshua 13.15-23

1	Aroer
2•	Valley of Arnon
–	'The city
3	Medeba
4	Heshbon
5	Dibon
–	Bamoth-baal
6	Beth-baal-meon
7	Jahaz ?
8	Kedemoth ?
9	Mephaath ?
10	Kiriathaim ?
–	Sibmah
11	Zereth-shahar ?
12	Beth-peor
13•	Slopes of Pisgah
14	Beth-jeshimoth
15•	Jordan (river)

Gad

Territory
Joshua 13.24-28

16	Jazer ?
–	Aroer
4	Heshbon
17	Ramath-mizpeh ?
18	Betonim
19a	Mahanaim ?
19b	Mahanaim ?
20	Debir (Lo-debar ?)
21	Beth-haram
22	Beth-nimrah
23	Succoth
24a	Zaphon ?
24b	Zaphon ?
15•	Jordan (river)
25•	Sea of Chinnereth

Half-tribe of Manasseh

Territory
Joshua 13.29-31

19a	Mahanaim ?
19b	Mahanaim ?
26•	Towns of Jair (Havvoth-jair)
27	Ashtaroth
28	Edrei

Section 6 – 3

Settlement & Judges (Iron I)

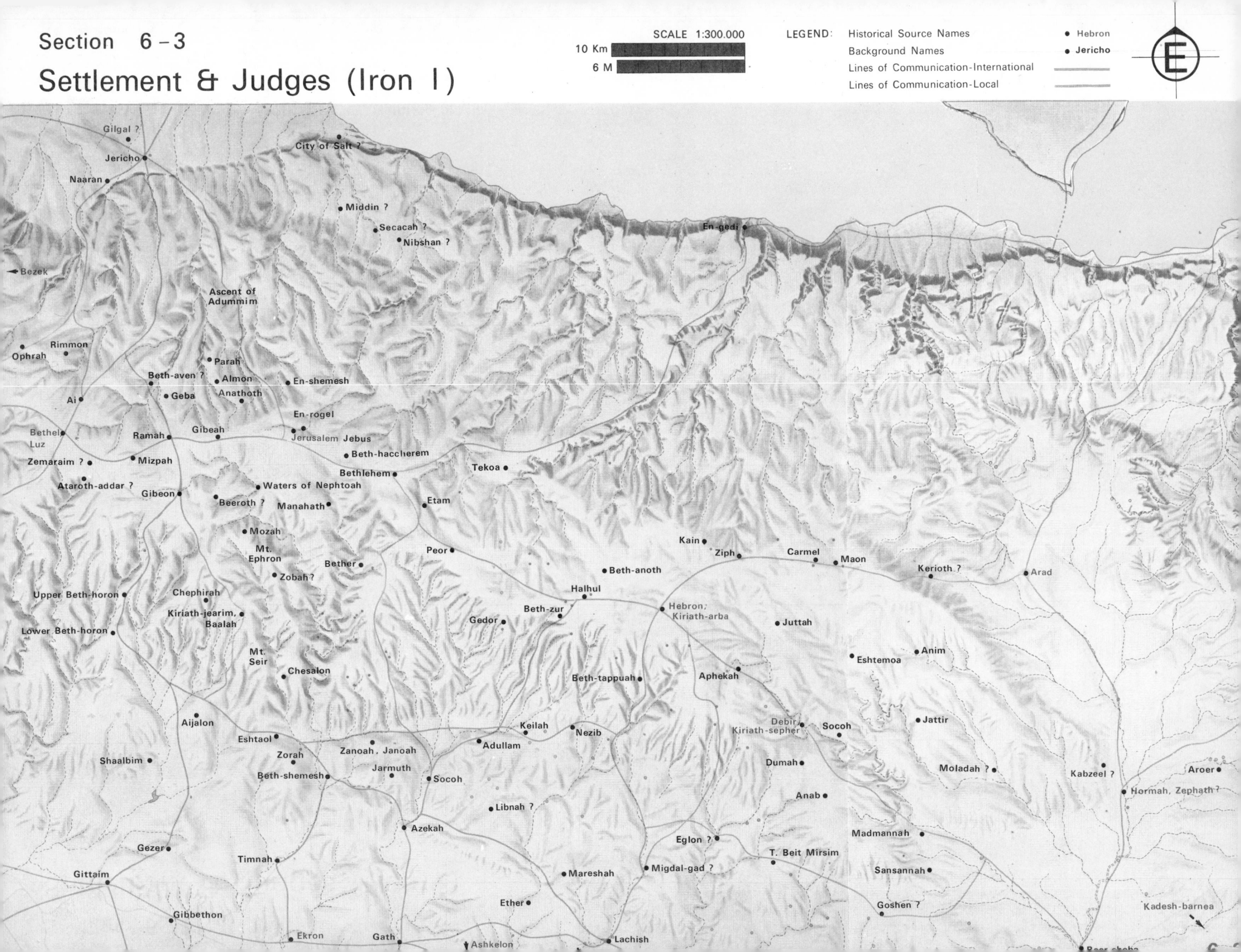

SCALE 1:300.000

10 Km

6 M

LEGEND: Historical Source Names • Hebron

Background Names • Jericho

Lines of Communication-International

Lines of Communication-Local

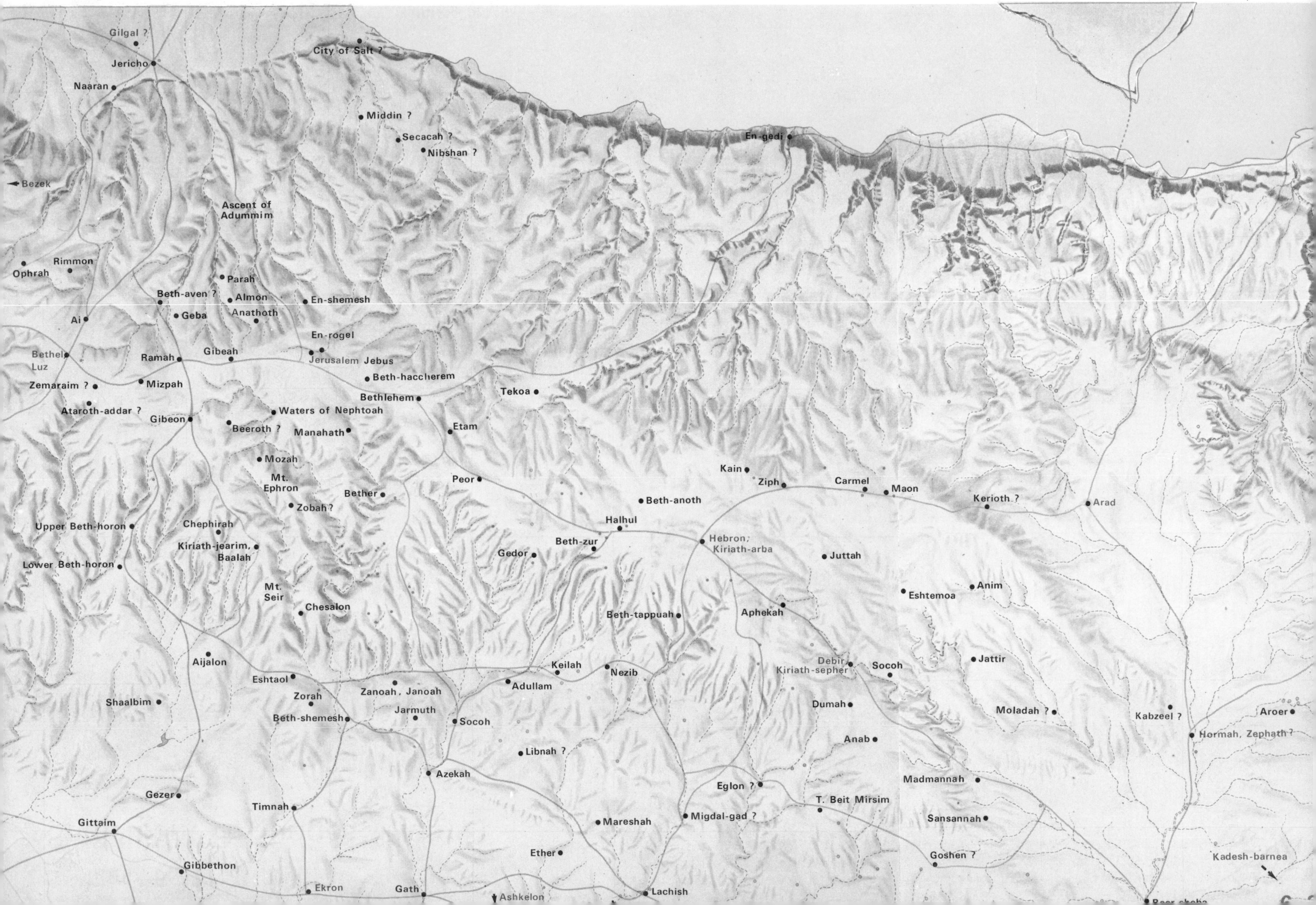

Gilgal ?
Jericho
Naaran
City of Salt ?
Middin ?
Secacah ?
Nibshan ?
En-gedi
Bezek
Ascent of Adummim
Rimmon
Ophrah
Parah
Beth-aven ?
Almon
En-shemesh
Geba
Anathoth
Ai
En-rogel
Bethel
Luz
Ramah
Gibeah
Jerusalem Jebus
Zemaraim ?
Mizpah
Beth-haccherem
Bethlehem
Tekoa
Ataroth-addar ?
Waters of Nephtoah
Gibeon
Beeroth ?
Manahath
Etam
Mozah
Mt. Ephron
Peor
Kain
Ziph
Carmel
Maon
Bether
Beth-anoth
Kerioth ?
Arad
Zobah ?
Halhul
Upper Beth-horon
Chephirah
Kiriath-jearim, Baalah
Beth-zur
Hebron, Kiriath-arba
Juttah
Gedor
Lower Beth-horon
Mt. Seir
Anim
Eshtemoa
Chesalon
Beth-tappuah
Aphekah
Aijalon
Keilah
Nezib
Debir, Kiriath-sepher
Socoh
Jattir
Eshtaol
Adullam
Zorah
Zanoah, Janoah
Shaalbim
Dumah
Jarmuth
Beth-shemesh
Socoh
Moladah ?
Kabzeel ?
Aroer
Hormah, Zephath ?
Anab
Libnah ?
Azekah
Madmannah
Eglon ?
Gezer
T. Beit Mirsim
Timnah
Migdal-gad ?
Mareshah
Sansannah
Gittaim
Ether
Goshen ?
Kadesh-barnea
Gibbethon
Ekron
Gath
Ashkelon
Lachish
Beer-sheba

Section 6 – 4

Settlement & Judges (Iron I)

SCALE 1:300.000

10 Km

6 M

LEGEND: Historical Source Names
Background Names
Lines of Communication-International
Lines of Communication-Local

Hebron

Jericho

E

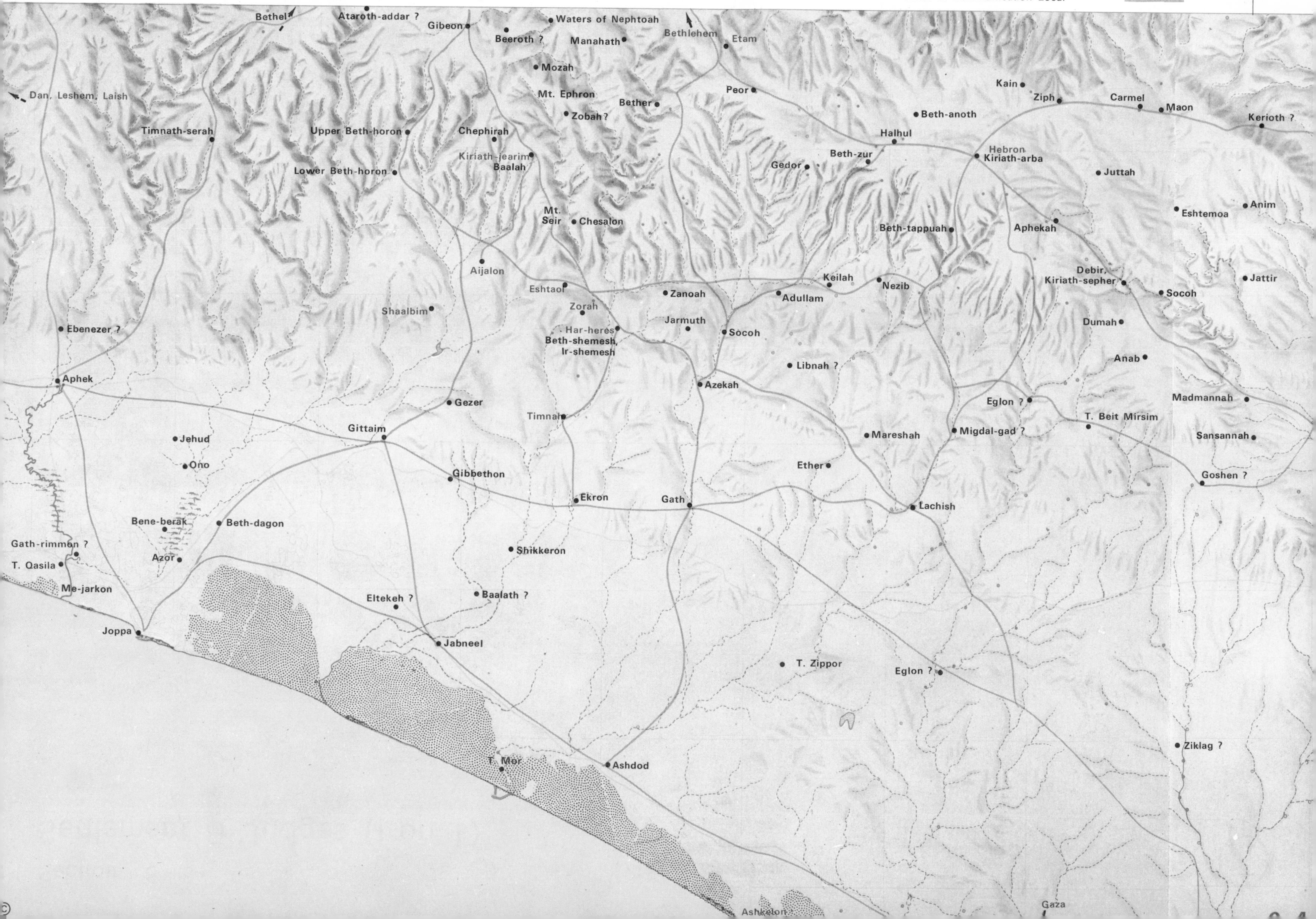

Bethel
Ataroth-addar ?
Gibeon
Beeroth ?
Waters of Nephtoah
Manahath
Bethlehem
Etam
Mozah
Dan, Leshem, Laish
Mt. Ephron
Peor
Bether
Kain
Ziph
Carmel
Maon
Kerioth ?
Zobah ?
Beth-anoth
Timnath-serah
Upper Beth-horon
Chephirah
Halhul
Kiriath-jearim
Baalah
Hebron
Kiriath-arba
Beth-zur
Gedor
Lower Beth-horon
Juttah
Mt. Seir
Chesalon
Eshtemoa
Anim
Beth-tappuah
Aphekah
Aijalon
Keilah
Nezib
Debir,
Kiriath-sepher
Jattir
Eshtaol
Zanoah
Adullam
Socoh
Zorah
Shaalbim
Jarmuth
Dumah
Ebenezer ?
Har-heres
Beth-shemesh,
Ir-shemesh
Socoh
Anab
Libnah ?
Aphek
Azekah
Madmannah
Gezer
Eglon ?
Timnah
T. Beit Mirsim
Gittaim
Jehud
Mareshah
Migdal-gad ?
Sansannah
Ono
Ether
Gibbethon
Goshen ?
Ekron
Gath
Lachish
Bene-berak
Beth-dagon
Gath-rimmon ?
Shikkeron
Azor
T. Qasila
Me-jarkon
Baalath ?
Elteketh ?
Joppa
Jabneel
T. Zippor
Eglon ?
Ziklag ?
T. Mor
Ashdod
Gaza
Ashkelon

Section 6 – 5

Settlement & Judges (Iron I)

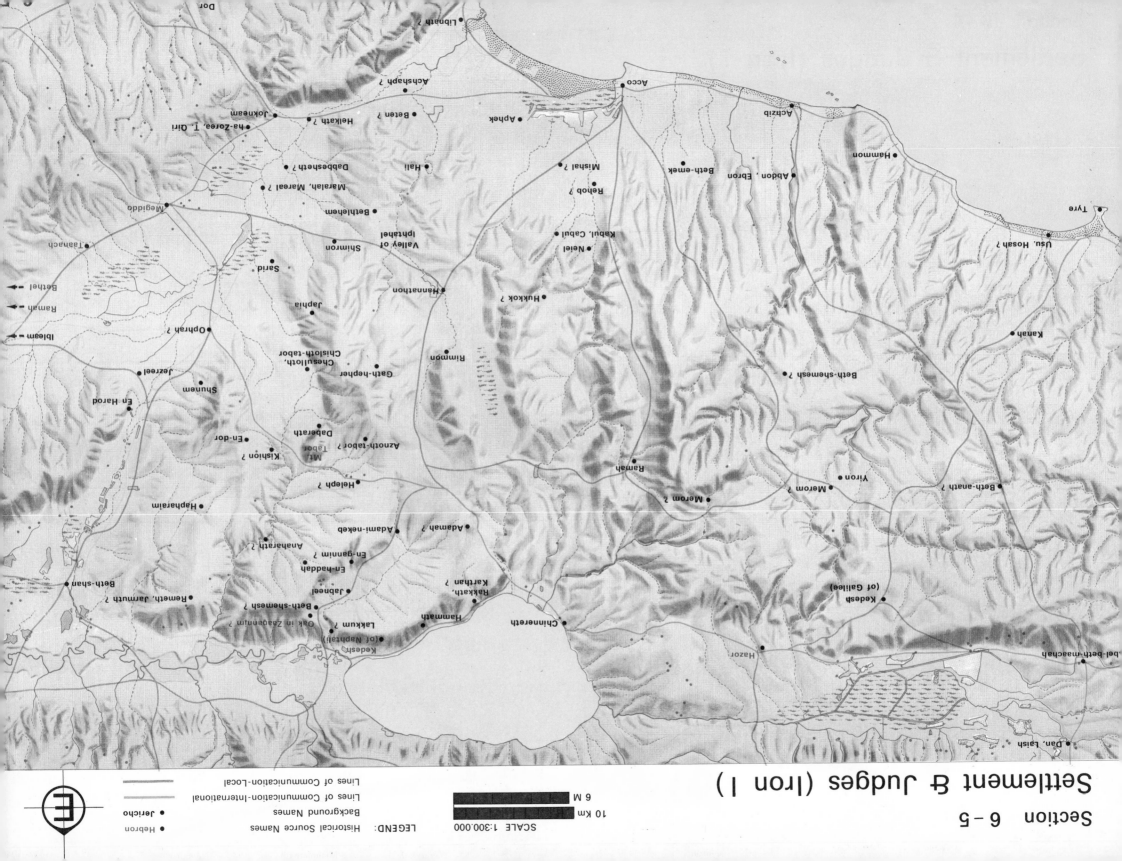

SCALE 1:300.000
10 Km
6 M

LEGEND: Historical Source Names • Hebron
Background Names • Jericho
Lines of Communication-International
Lines of Communication-Local

Dan, Laish
bel-beth-maachah
Hazor
Chinnereth
Kedesh (of Galilee)
Kedesh (of Naphtali)
Lakkum ?
Oak in Zaanannim ?
Hammath
Beth-shemesh ?
Rakkath, Karthan ?
Jabneel
Remeth, Jarmuth ?
Beth-shan
En-haddah
En-gannim ?
Anaharath ?
Adamah ?
Adami-nekeb
Hapharaim
Merom ?
Beth-anath ?
Merom ?
Yiron
Ramah
Heleph ?
Mt. Tabor
Kishion ?
Aznoth-tabor ?
En-dor
Daberath
En Harod
Shunem
Beth-shemesh ?
Gath-hepher
Jezreel
Rimmon
Chesulloth, Chisloth-tabor
Kanah
Ibleam
Ophrah ?
Ramah
Japhia
Hukkok ?
Hannathon
Bethel
Sarid
Neiel
Usu. Hosah ?
Valley of Iphtahel
Shimron
Taanach
Kabul, Cabul
Tyre
Bethlehem
Megiddo
Rehob ?
Maralah, Mareal ?
Abdon, Ebron
Beth-emek
Mishal ?
Hali
Dabbesheth ?
Hammon
ha-Zorea, T. Qiri
Aphek
Helkath ?
Beten ?
Jokneam
Achzib
Acco
Achshaph ?
Libnath ?
Dor

Section 6 – 6

Settlement & Judges (Iron I)

SCALE 1:300.000

10 Km

6 M

LEGEND: Historical Source Names • Hebron

Background Names • Jericho

Lines of Communication-International

Lines of Communication-Local

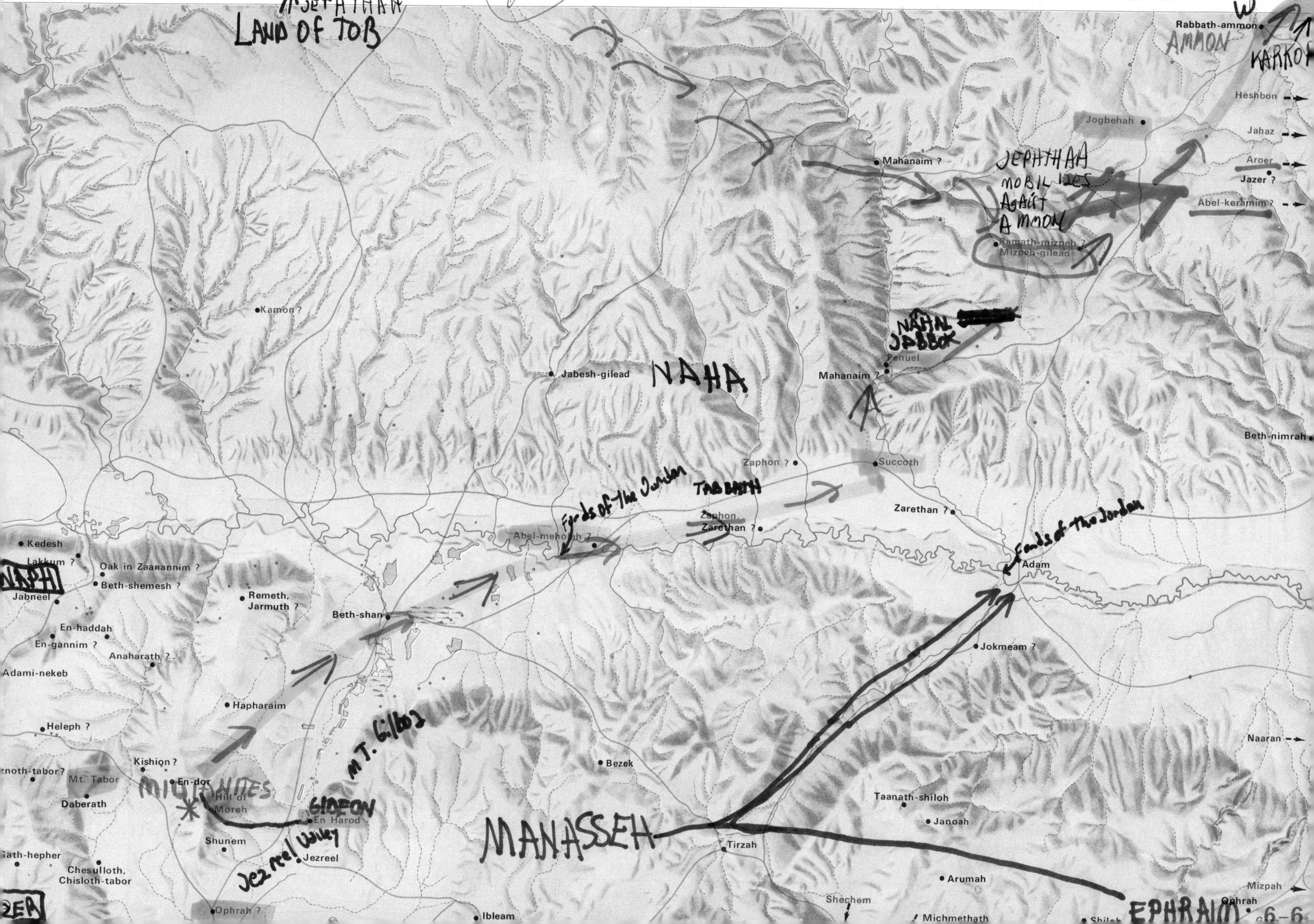

Date?
LAND OF TOB
JEPHTHAH
Rabbath-ammon
AMMON
Heshbon
Jogbehah
Jahaz
Mahanaim ?
Aroer
Jazer ?
Abel-keramim ?
JEPHTHAH MOBILIZES AGAINST AMMON
Ramath-mizpeh ?
Mizpeh-gilead
Kamon ?
NAHAL JABBOK
Penuel
Jabesh-gilead
Mahanaim ?
Beth-nimrah
Zaphon ?
Succoth
Fords of the Jordan
Zaphon, Zarethan ?
Zarethan ?
Abel-meholah ?
Adam
Kedesh
Lakkum ?
Oak in Zaanannim ?
Beth-shemesh ?
Jabneel
Remeth, Jarmuth ?
Beth-shan
En-haddah
En-gannim ?
Anaharath ?
Adami-nekeb
Jokmeam ?
Hapharaim
Heleph ?
Naaran
Kishion ?
Mt. Tabor
En-dor
MIDIANITES
Daberath
Hill of Moreh
GIDEON
En Harod
Bezek
Taanath-shiloh
Janoah
MANASSEH
Shunem
Tirzah
Gath-hepher
Jezreel
Jezreel Valley
Chesulloth, Chisloth-tabor
Arumah
Mizpah
Ophrah ?
Shechem
Ophrah
EPHRAIM
Ibleam
Michmethath
Shiloh

Section 6 – 7

Settlement & Judges (Iron I)

SCALE 1:300.000

10 Km

6 M

LEGEND: Historical Source Names • Hebron

Background Names • Jericho

Lines of Communication-International

Lines of Communication-Local

Jabesh-gilead
Abel-meholah ?
Zaphon, Zarethan ?
Adam
Jokmeam ?
Beth-hoglah ?
Beth-arabah
Gilgal ?
Jericho
City of Salt ?
Naaran
Middin ?
Secacah ?
Nibshan ?
Bezek
Taanath-shiloh
Janoah
Ascent of Adummim
Thebez ? Tirzah
Arumah
Ophrah
Rimmon
Shiloh
Parah
Ibleam
Shechem
Mt. Gerizim
Michmethath
Beth-aven ?
Almon
En-shemesh
Geba
Ai
Anathoth
Dothan
Lebonah
Tappuah
Bethel
Ramah
Gibeah
En-rogel
Jerusalem, Jebus
Beth-haccherem ?
Mizpah
Waters of Nephtoah
Bethlehem
Ephrathah
Ataroth-addar ?
Gibeon
Beeroth ?
Manahath
Etam
Shamir
Pirathon
Mozah ?
Peor
Mt. Ephron
Bether
Zobah ?
Upper Beth-horon
Chephirah
Timnath-serah
Kiriath-jearim, Baalah
Gedor
Lower Beth-horon
Mt. Seir
Chesalon
Aijalon
Eshtaol
Zanoah
Adullam
Shaalbim
Zorah
Jarmuth
Socoh
Migdal ?
Beth-shemesh
Libnah ?
Azekah

Section 7 Summary of contents & sources

Samuel and the United Monarchy

MAIN BIBLICAL REF.: 1 Samuel – 2 Samuel
1 Kings 1.1 – 11.43
1 Chronicles 10 – 2 Chronicles 9

Map No.	Subject	Primary sources	Regional Map Nos. (Section 1)	Macmillan Bible Atlas Map Nos.	Other references and notes
7-1/2	**Overviews, David's census and Solomon's reign**				
	a Overviews (north and south)				
	b The census under David and subsequent developments (from 7-7 f)	2 Samuel 24; 1 Chronicles 21.1-27		106	
	c Solomon's reign, building projects, and districts (from 7-7 g)	1 Kings 2.12-11.43; 2 Chronicles 1-9 (note 1 Kings 4.7-21; 9.15-28; 2 Chronicles 8.1-6, 17-18)	1,6,8	104,105,112,113	
7-3	**Samuel's ministry**				
	a Samuel's birth and childhood at Ramah and Shiloh	1 Samuel 1-3	13		
	b Philistine victory at Ebenezer by Aphek	1 Samuel 4	2,13	83	
	c The Ark in Philistia and its return via Beth-shemesh	1 Samuel 5.1-7.2	2	84	
	d Deliverance from the Philistines at Mizpah	1 Samuel 7.3-14	1	84 (text)	
	e Samuel's circuit	1 Samuel 7.15-17	4	85	
7-4	**Saul's beginning and end**				
	a Call for a king over Israel at Ramah	1 Samuel 8			
	b Samuel anoints Saul of Benjamin as king of Israel	1 Samuel 9-10	4	86	
	c Saul rescues Jabesh-gilead from the Ammonites and is confirmed as king at Gilgal	1 Samuel 11-12	4,10,11	87	
	d Victory over the Philistines at Michmash	1 Samuel 13.1-14.46	13	88,89	
	e Saul's campaign against Amalek, disobedience and rejection	See 7-5 a			
	f David and Saul	See 7-5 b-d			
	g David works for the Philistines at Ziklag	See 7-6			
	h Saul's death and the Philistine victory at Mt. Gilboa	1 Samuel 28-29; 31; 1 Chronicles 10 (cf. 2 Samuel 1.6-10)	2,9	95-97	
7-5	**David and Saul**				
	a Saul's campaign against Amalek; disobedience and rejection (from 7-4 e)	1 Samuel 15	4,16	90	
	b Samuel anoints David as king in Bethlehem	1 Samuel 16	1		
	c David defeats Goliath in the valley of Elah	1 Samuel 17	1	91	
	d David's flight in Judah from Saul	1 Samuel 18-26	1,14,16	92	
	e David's mighty men	1 Samuel 22.1-2; 2 Samuel 23.8-39 (cf. 1 Chronicles 11.10-12.22)	1,16	94	
7-6	**David works for the Philistines at Ziklag (from 7-4 g)**				
	a David's protection of Philistia's southern flank	1 Samuel 27	3,16	93	
	b David's help against Saul rejected by the Philistines at Aphek	1 Samuel 29	2	95	
	c Amalekite raid on Ziklag and the Negev	1 Samuel 30	3,16	93	
	d David's lament for Saul and Jonathan	2 Samuel 1	9		

Samuel and the United Monarchy

Map No.	Subject	Primary sources	Regional Map Nos. (Section 1)	Macmillan Bible Atlas Map Nos.	Other references and notes
7-7	David's reign				
	a David becomes king of Judah and then of 'all Israel' at Hebron	2 Samuel 2.1-5.5a; 1 Chronicles 3.1-4a; 11.1-3; 12.23-40	4,11,14	98,99	
	b A new political capital at Jebus/Jerusalem	2 Samuel 5.5-16; 1 Chronicles 11.4-9; 14.1-7	1	100	
	c Philistine attempt to crush David's united kingdom (via the valley of Rephaim)	2 Samuel 5.17-25; 1 Chronicles 14.8-16	1	100	
	d Jerusalem becomes the religious capital of the united kingdom	2 Samuel 6-7; 1 Chronicles 13; 15-17	1		
	e Administration and expansion of David's kingdom				
	i) Administration	2 Samuel 8.15-18; 20.23-26; 1 Chronicles 18.14-17 (cf. 1 Chronicles 27)		104, 105	
	ii) Western expansion: wars with the Philistines	2 Samuel 8.1; 21.15-22; 1 Chronicles 18.1; 20.4-8	1	102	
	iii) Eastern expansion: Transjordanian wars	2 Samuel 8.2-12; 10-11; 12.26-31; 1 Chronicles 18.2-11; 19.1-20.3	11,12	101,102	
	iv) Southern expansion: wars with Edom	2 Samuel 8.13-14; 1 Chronicles 18.12-13; 1 Kings 11.15-18	15	103	
	f Selected episodes in David's reign				
	i) Dealings with the house of Saul	2 Samuel 2.4b-7; 9; 21.1-14 (cf. 16.1-4; 19.24-30)	1		
	ii) The Bathsheba affair	2 Samuel 11.1-12.25 (cf. Psalm 51)		101	
	iii) The Absalom and Tamar affair	2 Samuel 13-14	4		
	iv) A southern revolt: Absalom's rebellion at Hebron and David's exile in Mahanaim	2 Samuel 15-19	4,11,14	109,110	
	v) A northern revolt: Sheba, son of Bichri, encourages rebellion in the north	2 Samuel 20.1-22	8	111	
	vi) The census and subsequent events	See 7-1 b			
	vii) David prepares for Solomon's building of the Temple	1 Chronicles 21.28-22.19 (cf. 1 Chronicles 23-26)			
	viii) David's last acts: Solomon made king; addresses and prayers	1 Kings 1.1-2.12; 1 Chronicles 28-29; 2 Samuel 23.1-7			
	g Solomon's reign	See 7-1/2 c			

Notes

Section 7 – 1

Samuel & United Monarchy (Iron II)

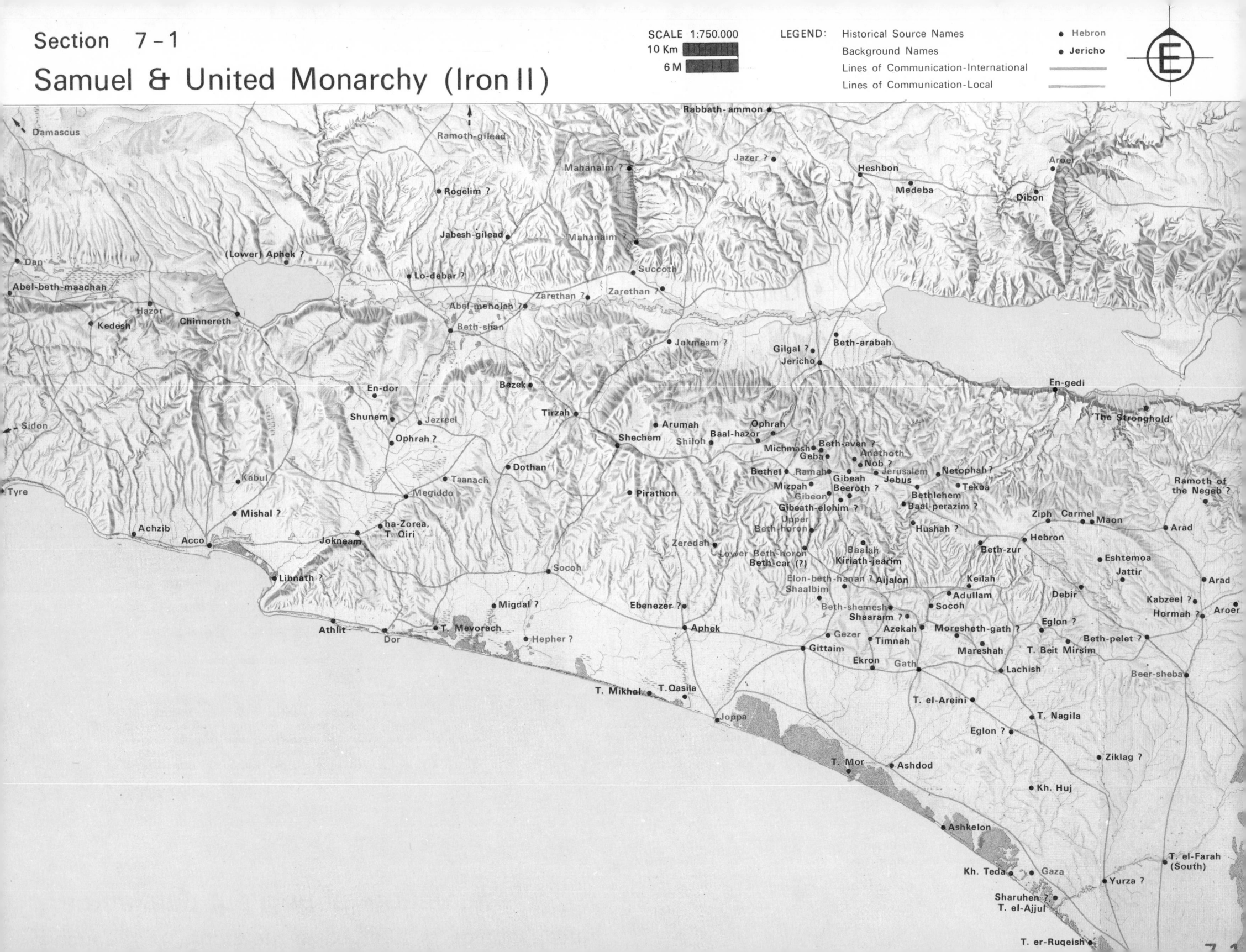

SCALE 1:750.000
10 Km
6 M

LEGEND: Historical Source Names • Hebron
Background Names • Jericho
Lines of Communication-International
Lines of Communication-Local

Damascus
Ramoth-gilead
Rabbath-ammon
Jazer ?
Heshbon
Medeba
Aroer
Dibon
Mahanaim ?
Rogelim ?
Jabesh-gilead
Mahanaim ?
Dan
(Lower) Aphek ?
Succoth
Lo-debar ?
Abel-beth-maachah
Zarethan ?
Zarethan ?
Abel-meholah ?
Hazor
Kedesh
Chinnereth
Beth-shan
Jokmeam ?
Gilgal ?
Beth-arabah
Jericho
En-dor
Bezek
En-gedi
Sidon
Tirzah
Shunem
Jezreel
Arumah
Ophrah
The Stronghold
Shechem
Shiloh
Baal-hazor
Ophrah ?
Michmash
Beth-aven ?
Geba
Anathoth
Nob ?
Dothan
Bethel
Ramah
Jerusalem
Jebus
Netophah ?
Kabul
Taanach
Gibeah
Beeroth ?
Tekoa
Ramoth of the Negeb ?
Tyre
Mizpah
Gibeon
Bethlehem
Megiddo
Pirathon
Gibeath-elohim ?
Baal-perazim ?
Mishal ?
Upper Beth-horon
Ziph
Carmel
Maon
Achzib
ha-Zorea, T. Qiri
Hushah ?
Arad
Acco
Jokneam
Hebron
Zeredah
Baalah
Beth-zur
Lower Beth-horon
Beth-car (?)
Kiriath-jearim
Eshtemoa
Socoh
Jattir
Libnath ?
Elon-beth-hanan ?
Aijalon
Keilah
Arad
Shaalbim
Adullam
Debir
Kabzeel ?
Migdal ?
Ebenezer ?
Beth-shemesh
Socoh
Hormah ?
Aroer
Shaaraim ?
Eglon ?
Athlit
T. Mevorach
Azekah
Moresheth-gath ?
Dor
Aphek
Gezer
Beth-pelet ?
Hepher ?
Timnah
Gittaim
Mareshah
T. Beit Mirsim
Ekron
Gath
Lachish
Beer-sheba
T. Mikhal
T. Qasila
T. el-Areini
Joppa
T. Nagila
Eglon ?
Ziklag ?
T. Mor
Ashdod
Kh. Huj
Ashkelon
T. el-Farah (South)
Kh. Teda
Gaza
Yurza ?
Sharuhen ?
T. el-Ajjul
T. er-Ruqeish

Section 7 – 2

Samuel & United Monarchy (Iron II)

SCALE 1:750.000
10 Km
6 M

LEGEND: Historical Source Names • Hebron
Background Names • Jericho
Lines of Communication-International
Lines of Communication-Local

E

Aroer
Dibon
Bozrah
Teman ?
Feifa
En-gedi
'The Stronghold'
Tamar
Tekoa
Ramoth of the Negeb ?
Ziph
Carmel
Maon
Arad
Hebron
Beth-zur
Eshtemoa
Arad
Debir
Jattir
Keilah
Adullam
Kabzeel ?
Hormah ?
Aroer
Eglon ?
Mareshah
Beth-pelet ?
Baalath-beer ?
Moresheth-gath?
T. Beit Mirsim
Lachish
Beer-sheba
T. el-Areini
T. Nagila
Eglon ?
Ziklag ?
Kh. Huj
T. el-Farah (South)
Yurza ?
Gaza
Kh. Teda
Sharuhen ?
T. el-Ajjul
T. er-Ruqeish
Hazar-addar ?
Elat
Ezion-geber

©

Section 7 – 3

Samuel & United Monarchy (Iron II)

SCALE 1:300.000

10 Km

6 M

LEGEND: Historical Source Names • Hebron

Background Names • Jericho

Lines of Communication-International

Lines of Communication-Local

Gilgal ?
Naaran
Tirzah
Arumah
Ophrah
Shiloh
Baal-hazor
Shechem
Michmash
Beth-aven ?
Geba
Anathoth ?
Jeshanah
Nob ?
Gibeah
Bethel
Ramah
Jerusalem, Jebus
Tappuah
Netophah ?
Tekoa
Mizpah
Bethlehem
Gibeon
Beeroth ?
Manahath
Baal-perazim ?
Gibeath-elohim ?
Pirathon
Hushah ?
Timnath-serah
Upper Beth-horon
Zeredah
Kiriath-jearim
Baalah
Beth-zur
Hebron
Beth-car ?
Lower Beth-horon
Aijalon
Keilah
Adullam
Shaalbim
Beth-shemesh
Socoh
Ebenezer ?
Shaaraim ?
Aphek
Azekah
Eglon ?
Gezer
Timnah
Moresheth-gath ?
Mareshah
Gittaim
Ekron
Gath
Lachish
Ashkelon
Gaza

Section 7 – 4

Samuel & United Monarchy (Iron II)

SCALE 1:450.000
10 Km
6 M

LEGEND: Historical Source Names • Hebron
Background Names • Jericho
Lines of Communication-International
Lines of Communication-Local

Mahanaim ?
Rabbath-ammon
Jabesh-gilead
Mahanaim ?
Succoth
Lo-debar ?
Zarethan ?
Zarethan ?
Adam
Abel-meholah ?
Hazor
Beth-shan
Jokmeam ?
Beth-arabah
Gilgal ?
Naaran
Bezek
En-dor
Shunem
Jezreel
Tirzah
Arumah
Ophrah ?
Ibleam
Shechem
Shiloh
Ophrah
Baal-hazor
Michmash
Beth-aven ?
Geba
Anathoth
Dothan
Bethel
Ramah
Nob ?
Jerusalem, Jebus
Gibeah
Taanach
Mizpah
Netophah ?
Bethlehem
Tekoa
Megiddo
Gibeon
Beeroth ?
Manahath
Gibeath-elohim ?
Baal-perazim ?
Pirathon
Hushah ?
Jokneam
ha-Zorea, T. Qiri
Upper Beth-horon
Timnath-serah
Zeredah
Kiriath-jearim, Baalath
Lower Beth-horon
Hebron
Beth-zur
Socoh
Aijalon
Keilah
Shaalbim
Adullam
Migdal ?
Ebenezer ?
Beth-shemesh
Socoh
Shaaraim ?
Athlit
Azekah
Dor
T. Mevorach
Aphek
Gezer
Hepher ?
Timnah
Moresheth-gath ?
Mareshah
Gittaim
Ekron
Gath
Lachish
T. Mikhal
T. Qasila

©

Section 7 – 5

Samuel & United Monarchy (Iron II)

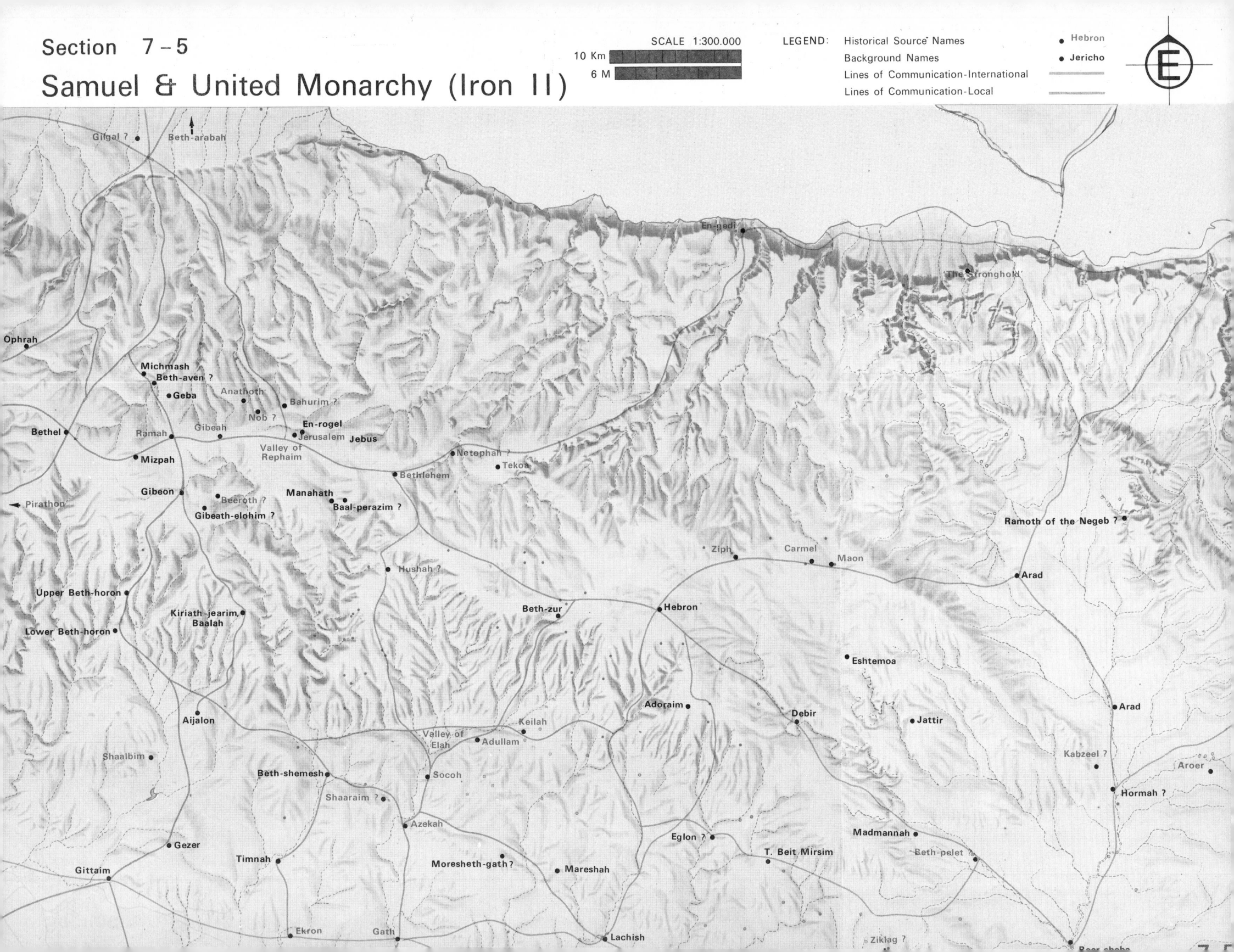

SCALE 1:300.000
10 Km
6 M

LEGEND: Historical Source Names • Hebron
Background Names • Jericho
Lines of Communication-International
Lines of Communication-Local

Gilgal ?
Beth-arabah
Ophrah
Michmash
Beth-aven ?
Geba
Anathoth
Nob ?
Bahurim ?
En-rogel
Jerusalem
Jebus
Bethel
Ramah
Gibeah
Mizpah
Valley of Rephaim
Netophah ?
Tekoa
Bethlehem
Gibeon
Beeroth ?
Gibeath-elohim ?
Manahath
Baal-perazim ?
Pirathon
Ramoth of the Negeb ?
Ziph
Carmel
Maon
Arad
Hushah ?
Upper Beth-horon
Kiriath-jearim, Baalah
Lower Beth-horon
Beth-zur
Hebron
Eshtemoa
Adoraim
Debir
Arad
Jattir
Aijalon
Keilah
Valley of Elah
Adullam
Shaalbim
Kabzeel ?
Aroer
Beth-shemesh
Socoh
Hormah ?
Shaaraim ?
Azekah
Madmannah
Eglon ?
Gezer
T. Beit Mirsim
Beth-pelet
Timnah
Moresheth-gath ?
Mareshah
Gittaim
Ekron
Gath
Lachish
Ziklag ?
En-gedi
'The Stronghold'

Section 7 – 6

Samuel & United Monarchy (Iron II)

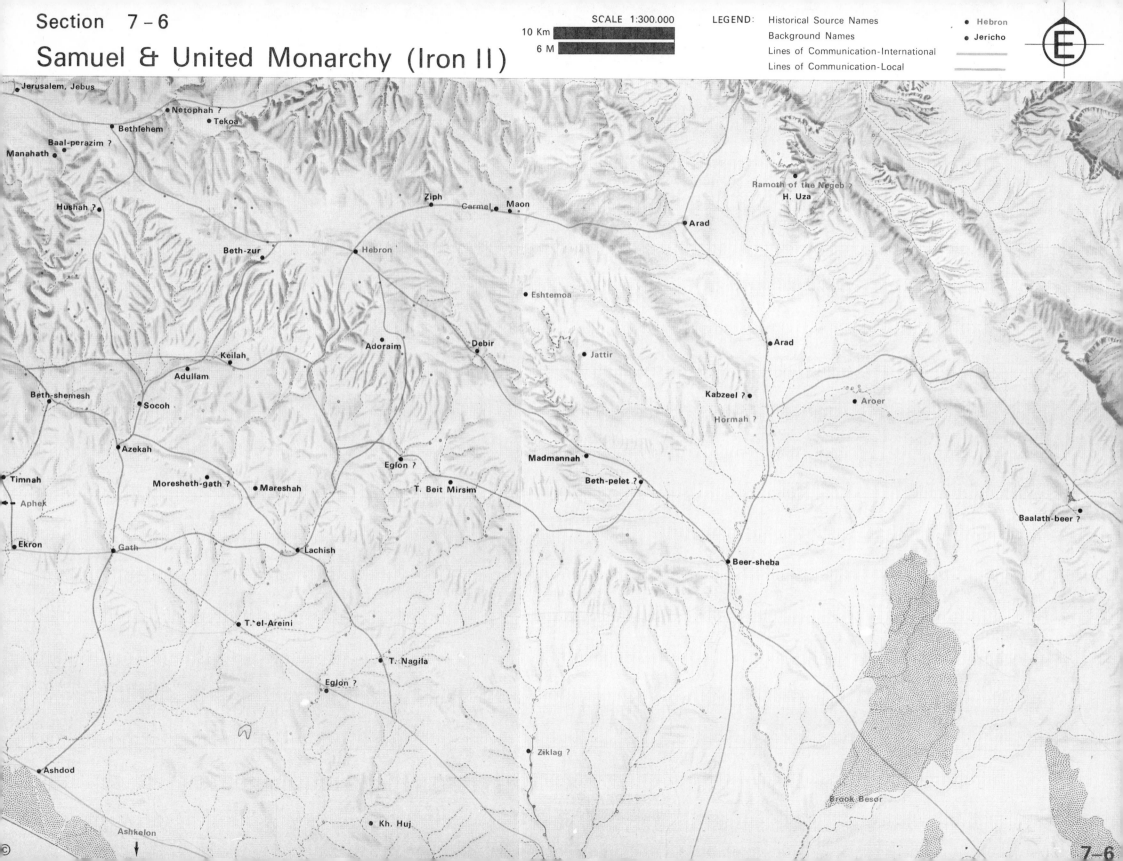

SCALE 1:300.000

10 Km

6 M

LEGEND: Historical Source Names • Hebron

Background Names • Jericho

Lines of Communication-International

Lines of Communication-Local

E

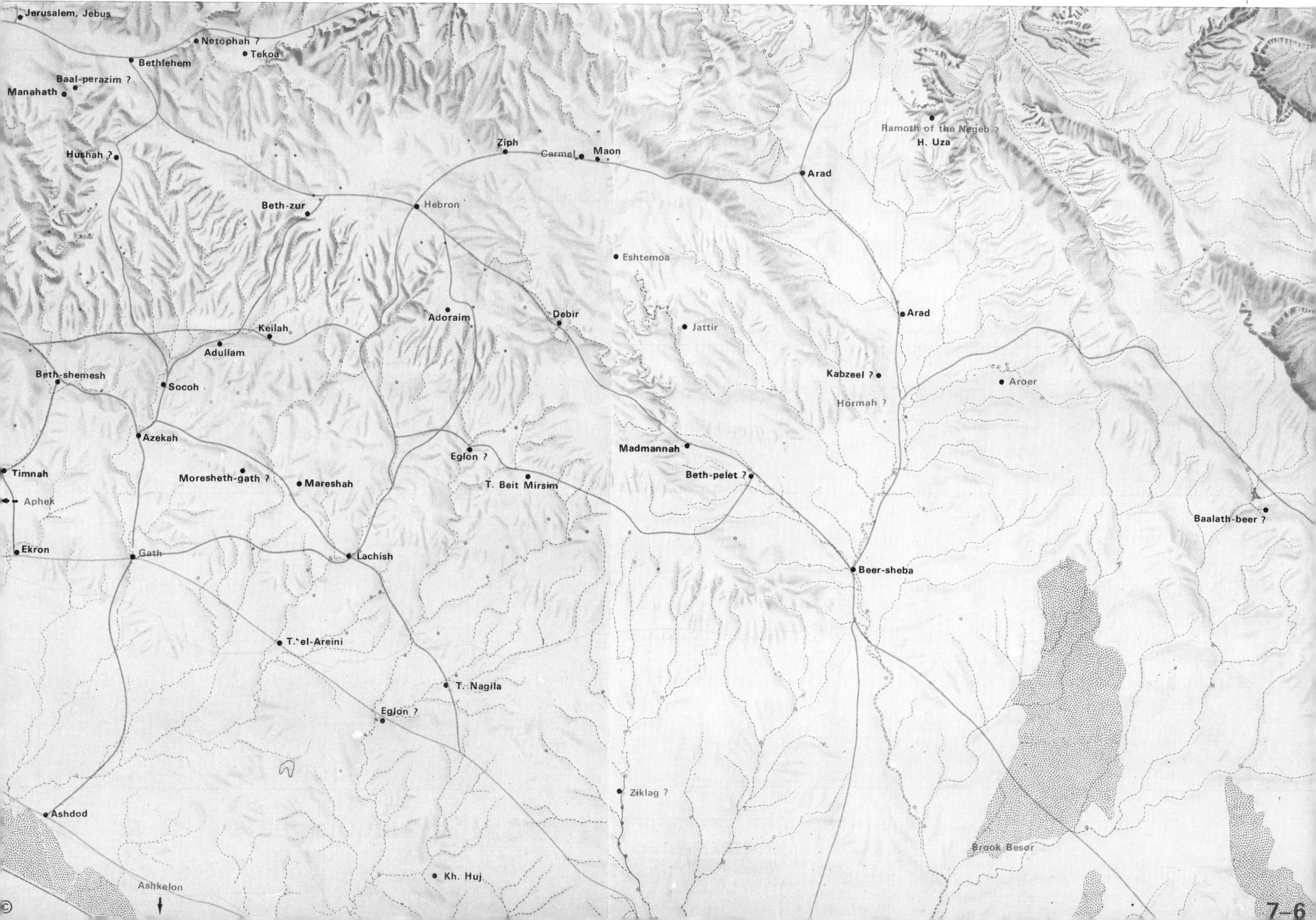

Jerusalem, Jebus
Netophah ?
Tekoa
Bethlehem
Baal-perazim ?
Manahath
Hushah ?
Beth-zur
Ziph
Carmel
Maon
Arad
Ramoth of the Negeb ?
H. Uza
Hebron
Eshtemoa
Adoraim
Debir
Jattir
Arad
Keilah
Adullam
Beth-shemesh
Socoh
Kabzeel ?
Hormah ?
Aroer
Azekah
Madmannah
Eglon ?
Timnah
Moresheth-gath ?
Mareshah
T. Beit Mirsim
Beth-pelet ?
Aphek
Baalath-beer ?
Ekron
Gath
Lachish
Beer-sheba
T. el-Areini
T. Nagila
Eglon ?
Ziklag ?
Ashdod
Brook Besor
Kh. Huj
Ashkelon

©

Section 7 – 7

Samuel & United Monarchy (Iron II)

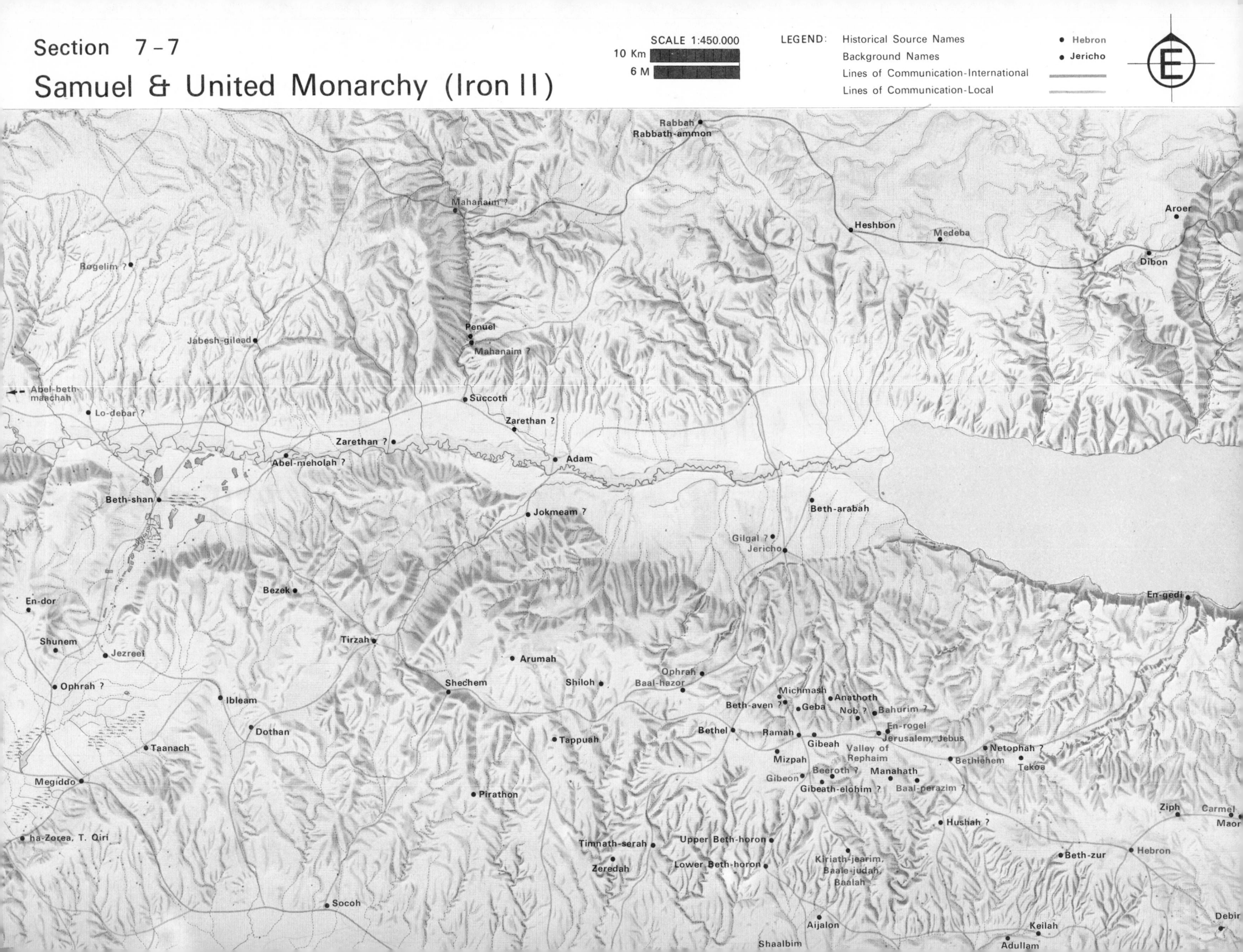

SCALE 1:450.000

10 Km

6 M

LEGEND: Historical Source Names • Hebron

Background Names • Jericho

Lines of Communication-International

Lines of Communication-Local

Rabbah
Rabbath-ammon
Mahanaim ?
Heshbon
Medeba
Aroer
Dibon
Rogelim ?
Penuel
Mahanaim ?
Jabesh-gilead
Abel-beth-maachah
Succoth
Lo-debar ?
Zarethan ?
Zarethan ?
Abel-meholah ?
Adam
Beth-shan
Jokmeam ?
Beth-arabah
Gilgal ?
Jericho
Bezek
En-dor
En-gedi
Tirzah
Shunem
Jezreel
Arumah
Ophrah
Baal-hazor
Shiloh
Shechem
Ophrah ?
Michmash
Anathoth
Ibleam
Beth-aven ?
Geba
Nob ?
Bahurim ?
Dothan
Bethel
Ramah
En-rogel
Jerusalem, Jebus
Tappuah
Gibeah
Valley of Rephaim
Netophah ?
Taanach
Mizpah
Bethlehem
Tekoa
Gibeon
Beeroth ?
Manahath
Megiddo
Gibeath-elohim ?
Baal-perazim ?
Pirathon
Ziph
Carmel
Maor
Hushah ?
ha-Zorea, T. Qiri
Timnath-serah
Upper Beth-horon
Kiriath-jearim, Baale-judah, Baalah
Beth-zur
Hebron
Zeredah
Lower Beth-horon
Socoh
Aijalon
Keilah
Debir
Shaalbim
Adullam

Section 8 Summary of contents & sources

Divided Kingdom 'A'

MAIN BIBLICAL REF.: 1 Kings 11.26-2 Kings 10.31
2 Chronicles 10.1-22.9

ABBREVIATIONS: *(Jud.)* King of Judah (southern Kingdom)
(Isr.) King of Israel (northern Kingdom)

Map No.	Subject	Primary sources	Regional Map Nos. (Section 1)	Macmillan Bible Atlas Map Nos.	Other references and notes
8-1	**Overview (north) and Elijah's ministry**				
	a Overview (north)				
	b Elijah's ministry under Ahab (from 8-5 d; cf. 8-5 e-h and 8-6 a)	1 Kings 17-19, 21	6,10	128	
	c Elijah's ministry under Ahaziah and his translation (from 8-5 i)	1 Kings 22.51-53; 2 Kings 1.2-2.18	4	128	
8-2	**Division of the Kingdom and Shishak's campaign in Israel (northern Kingdom)**				
	a **Jeroboam** *(Isr.)*: northern tribes declare independence at Shechem	1 Kings 11.26-12.24; 2 Chronicles 10.1-11.4	13	118	
	b **Jeroboam** *(Isr.)*: capitals in Shechem and Penuel (central Israel and Transjordan); religious shrines at Bethel and Dan (frontiers)	1 Kings 12.25-14.20 (note 'Tirzah' in 14.17)	8,11,13	118	
	c **Jeroboam** *(Isr.)*: continual war between Israel and Judah; pharaoh Shishak subdues capitals of Judah and Israel and controls northern international trade routes (see also 8-3 b)	1 Kings 14.25-28,30; 2 Chronicles 12.2-12, city-lists, Shishak *(Karnak: Egypt)*; ANET 263-64; ANEP 349; ANE I: 187; Kitchen 1973: Pars. 252-60; 398-415	1,4,5,10,11	120	
8-3	**Judah under Rehoboam and Shishak's campaign in Judah (southern Kingdom)**				
	a **Rehoboam** *(Jud.)*: rule from Jerusalem and defence strategy of the southern tribes (see 8-4 a for detail)	1 Kings 14.21-24, 29-31; 2 Chronicles 11.5-23; 12.1, 13-16	1	118,119	
	b **Rehoboam** *(Jud.)*: continual war between Israel and Judah; pharaoh Shishak subdues Jerusalem and controls international trade routes in the Negev (see also 8-2 c)	1 Kings 14.25-28,30; 2 Chronicles 12.2-12; city-lists, Shishak *(Karnak: Egypt)*; ANET 263-64; ANEP 349; ANE I: 187; Kitchen 1973: Pars. 252-60, 398-415	1,16	120	
8-4	**Judah-Israel border disputes, Ethiopian threat to Judah and internal political strife in Israel**				
	a **Rehoboam** *(Jud.)*: defence strategy in Judah (detail of 8-3 a)	2 Chronicles 11.5-23	1	119	
	b **Abijah** *(Jud.)*: rule; Judah's military thrust into southern Israel via Bethel	1 Kings 15.1-8; 2 Chronicles 13	13	121	
	c **Asa** *(Jud.)*: rule; Judah meets the threat of Zerah the Ethiopian near Mareshah	1 Kings 15.9-15; 2 Chronicles 14-15 (cf. 2 Chronicles 16.7-10)	2, 3	122	
	d **Baasha** *(Isr.)*: new ruling house in Tirzah with the murder of **Nadab** (Jeroboam's son) at Gib-bethon	1 Kings 15.25-34	2, 4		
	e **Asa** *(Jud.)* and **Baasha** *(Isr.)*: Israel controls northern approach to Jerusalem (see also 8-5 a); Israel-Judah border established north of Mizpah and Geba	1 Kings 15.16-24; 2 Chronicles 16.1-14	13	123	
	f **Elah, Zimri; Tibni** and **Omri** *(Isr.)*: Zimri destroys the house of Baasha, but dies in siege of Tirzah; Omri overcomes Tibni and establishes a new ruling house at Tirzah	1 Kings 16.1-23	4		
8-5	**Israel's relations with Syria (Aram-Damascus) and Sidon, internal apostasy under Ahab and Jezebel, Elijah's ministry**				
	a **Baasha** *(Isr.)*: king of Damascus conquers the northern approaches to Israel in response to Judah's request (see also 8-4 e)	1 Kings 15.16-21; 2 Chronicles 16.1-5	8,13	124	
	b **Omri** *(Isr.)*: Samaria becomes Israel's third and final capital	1 Kings 16.24-28	13	125	
	c **Ahab** *(Isr.)*: summary of Ahab's rule with Jezebel of Sidon (see also 8-6 a)	1 Kings 16.29-34			
	d **Ahab** *(Isr.)*: Elijah's ministry under Ahab	See 8-1 b			
	e **Ahab** *(Isr.)*: siege of Samaria by Damascus-led league of kings fails	1 Kings 20.1-21	10	126	
	f **Ahab** *(Isr.)*: battle of Aphek ends in concessions by a united Syria under Damascus	1 Kings 20.22-43	8	126	
	g **Ahab** *(Isr.)*: three-year truce between Syria and Israel to meet the common threat of Assyria in northern Syria (twelve kings against Shalmaneser III of Assyria at Qarqar)	1 Kings 22.1; monument of Shalmaneser III *(Calah: Assyria)* and other inscriptions; ANET 276-81; ANEP 351-65, 443; ANE I: 188-92		127	
	h **Ahab** *(Isr.)* and **Jehoshaphat** *(Jud.)*: war again with Syria at the battle of Ramoth-gilead (cf. 8-5 f); death of Ahab	1 Kings 22.2-40; 2 Chronicles 18	11	126	
	i **Ahaziah** and **J(eh)oram** *(Isr.)*: Elijah's closing ministry	See 8-1 c			

Divided Kingdom 'A'

Map No.	Subject	Primary sources	Regional Map Nos. (Section 1)	Macmillan Bible Atlas Map Nos.	Other references and notes
8-6	Israel and Judah's relations with Moab and Edom				
	a **Ahab** *(Isr.)*: Jericho rebuilt by Hiel of Bethel	1 Kings 16.34	4		
	b **Jehoshaphat** *(Jud.)*: rule and expansion (see also 8-6 e and 8-5 h)	1 Kings 22.41-50; 2 Chronicles 17,19,20.31-21.1		(cf. 130)	
	c **Ahab/Ahaziah/J(eh)oram** *(Isr.)*: Mesha, king of Moab, revolts against Israel and conquers the Medeba plateau/mishor (cf. 5-3 b; 6-1 e; 6-6 a; 9-1 k)	2 Kings 1.1; 3.1-5; Moabite stone *(Dibon: Transjordan)*; ANET 320-21; ANEP 274; ANE 1:209-10	12,15	131	
	d **J(eh)oram** *(Isr.)* and **Jehoshaphat** *(Jud.)*: Israel and Judah join in a campaign against Moab	2 Kings 3.6-27	15,16	132	
	e **Jehoshaphat** *(Jud.)*: Moab's campaign to Judah via En-gedi fails	2 Chronicles 20.1-30	14,15	133	
	f **J(eh)oram** *(Jud.)*: rule; Edomite revolt succeeds; attacks from Arabs (Edom) and Philistia (Libnah)	2 Kings 8.16-27; 2 Chronicles 21	1		
8-7	Elisha, J(eh)oram, Jehu and Israel's relations with Syria and Assyria				
	a Elisha's call and ministry (see also 8-6 d and 8-7 c); Jehu, son of Nimshi, anointed king of Israel	1 Kings 19.15-21; 2 Kings 2.1-9.10; 13.14-21; 2 Chronicles 21.11-15	10	129	
	b **J(eh)oram** *(Isr.)*: Syria's incursion and siege of Samaria	2 Kings 6-7	10		
	c Elisha predicts victories and cruelty of Hazael of Syria	2 Kings 8.7-15 (cf. 1 Kings 19.15-17; 9.1 d)			
	d **J(eh)oram, Jehu** *(Isr.)* and **Ahaziah** *(Jud.)*: war with Syria at Ramoth-gilead; house of Jehu established with murder of J(eh)oram (Ahab's son), Jezebel, Ahaziah and prophets of Baal	2 Kings 8.28-10.31; 2 Chronicles 22.1-9 (cf. 1 Kings 21)	10,11	134	
	e **Jehu** *(Isr.)*: Shalmaneser III of Assyria attacks Damascus and regions of Hauran and Galilee, receiving tribute from Israel, Tyre and Sidon	Inscriptions: Shalmaneser III *(Calah: Assyria)*; ANET 280-81; ANEP 361-65; ANE I: 191-92; other Assyrian sources	6,8	135	
8-8	Approaches to Samaria and regional settlement reflected in Samaria ostraca				
	a Samaria: strategic regions and communication routes	For use with 8-2,4,5,7 and 9-1,4, 5	4,5,10,13		
	b Settlements in the Samaria ostraca (from 9-1 f)	Samaria ostraca; ANET 321; ANE I: 211	4,13	137	
	Kitchen, K. A. 1973 *The Third Intermediate Period in Egypt (1100-650 B.C.).* Warminster, England: Aris & Phillips.				

Notes

Section 8–1

Divided Kingdom A (Iron II)

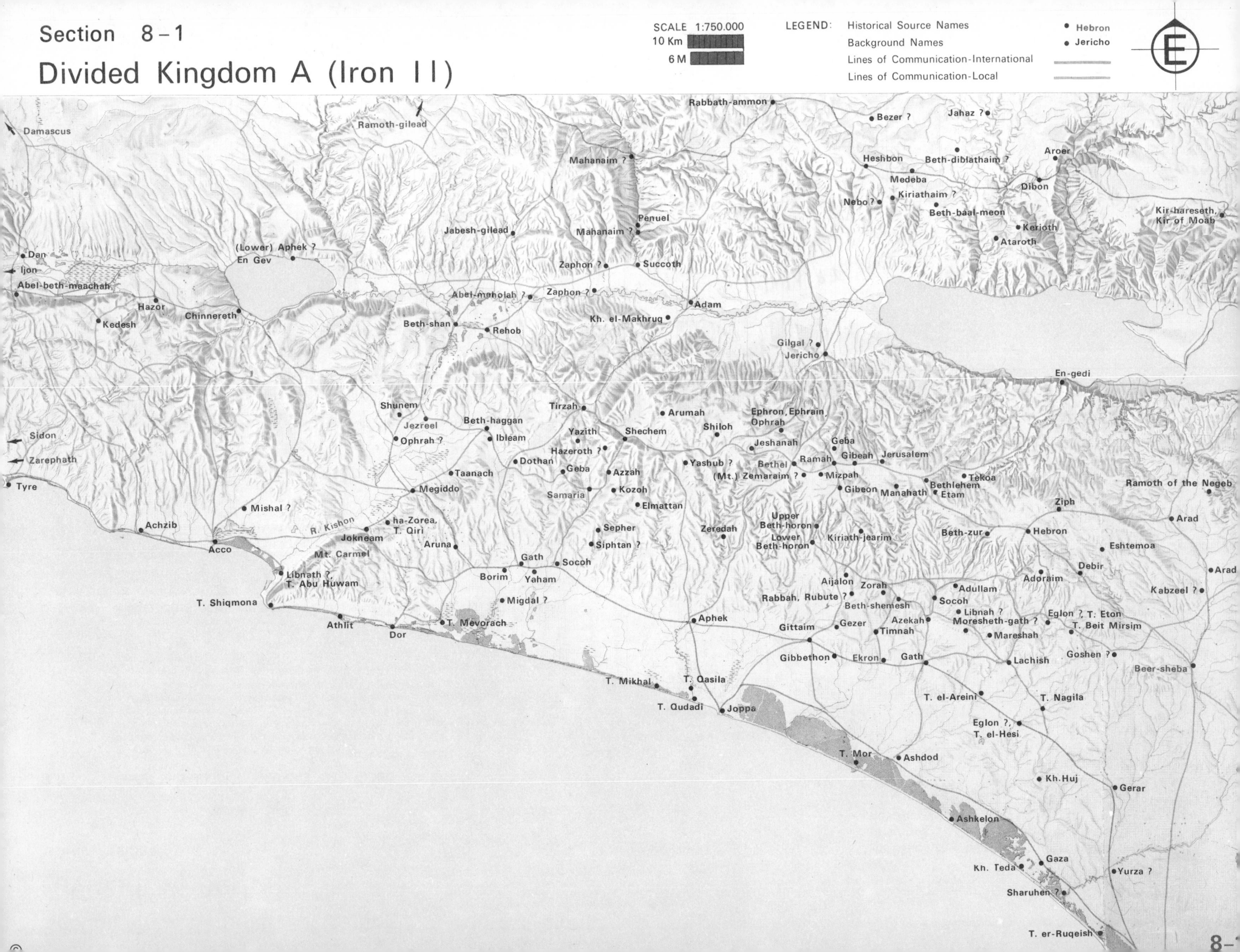

SCALE 1:750.000
10 Km
6 M

LEGEND: Historical Source Names — ● Hebron
Background Names — ● Jericho
Lines of Communication-International
Lines of Communication-Local

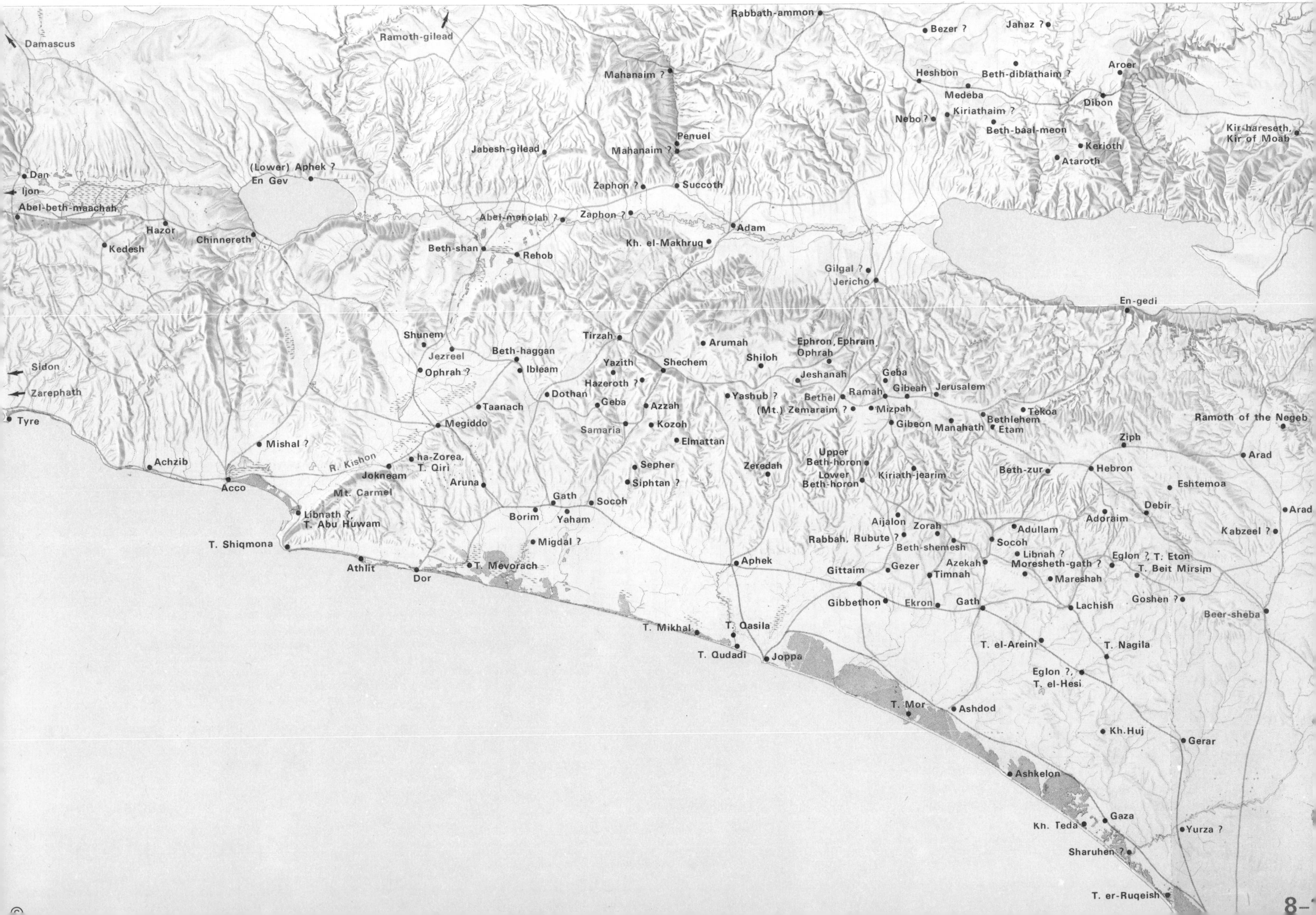

Damascus
Ramoth-gilead
Rabbath-ammon
Bezer ?
Jahaz ?
Heshbon
Beth-diblathaim ?
Aroer
Medeba
Dibon
Nebo ?
Kiriathaim ?
Beth-baal-meon
Kir-hareseth,
Kir of Moab
Kerioth
Ataroth
Mahanaim ?
Penuel
Mahanaim ?
Jabesh-gilead
(Lower) Aphek ?
En Gev
Dan
Ijon
Abel-beth-maachah
Hazor
Kedesh
Chinnereth
Zaphon ?
Succoth
Abel-meholah ?
Zaphon ?
Adam
Kh. el-Makhruq
Beth-shan
Rehob
Gilgal ?
Jericho
En-gedi
Shunem
Jezreel
Beth-haggan
Ibleam
Ophrah ?
Tirzah
Yazith
Shechem
Arumah
Shiloh
Ephron, Ephrain,
Ophrah
Jeshanah
Geba
Gibeah
Jerusalem
Sidon
Zarephath
Tyre
Hazeroth ?
Dothan
Geba
Azzah
Yashub ?
Bethel
Ramah
(Mt.) Zemaraim ?
Mizpah
Taanach
Megiddo
Samaria
Kozoh
Elmattan
Gibeon
Manahath
Bethlehem
Etam
Tekoa
Ramoth of the Negeb
Mishal ?
Achzib
R. Kishon
ha-Zorea,
T. Qiri
Jokneam
Aruna
Acco
Mt. Carmel
Sepher
Siphtan ?
Zeredah
Upper
Beth-horon
Lower
Beth-horon
Kiriath-jearim
Beth-zur
Hebron
Ziph
Arad
Eshtemoa
Gath
Socoh
Borim
Yaham
Libnath ?,
T. Abu Huwam
Debir
Arad
Adoraim
Aijalon
Zorah
Adullam
Kabzeel ?
Rabbah, Rubute ?
Beth-shemesh
Socoh
T. Shiqmona
Migdal ?
Libnah ?
Moresheth-gath ?
Eglon ?, T. Eton
T. Beit Mirsim
Azekah
Athlit
Dor
T. Mevorach
Aphek
Gittaim
Gezer
Timnah
Mareshah
Gibbethon
Ekron
Gath
Lachish
Goshen ?
Beer-sheba
T. Mikhal
T. Qasila
T. Qudadi
Joppa
T. el-Areini
T. Nagila
Eglon ?,
T. el-Hesi
T. Mor
Ashdod
Kh. Huj
Gerar
Ashkelon
Kh. Teda
Gaza
Yurza ?
Sharuhen ?
T. er-Ruqeish

Section 8-2

Divided Kingdom A (Iron II)

SCALE 1:600.000
10 Km
6 M

LEGEND:
Historical Source Names
Background Names
Lines of Communication-International
Lines of Communication-Local

• Hebron
• Jericho

E

Rabbath-ammon
Bezer ?
Beth-diblathaim ?
Heshbon
Medeba
Mahanaim ?
Kiriathaim ?
Nebo ?
Beth-baal-meon
Penuel
Mahanaim ?
Dan
(Lower) Aphek ?,
En-Gev
Zaphon ?
Succoth
Abel-beth-maachah
Hazor
Zaphon ?
Adam
Kedesh
Chinnereth
Abel-meholah ?
Kh. el-Makhruq
Beth-shan
Rehob
Gilgal ?
Jericho
Shunem
Jezreel
Tirzah
Arumah
Ephron, Ephrain,
Ophrah
Sidon
Ophrah ?
Beth-haggan
Ibleam
Yazith
Shechem
Shiloh
Jeshanah
Geba
Hazeroth ?
Dothan
Geba
Yashub ?
Bethel
Ramah
Gibeah
Jerusalem
Tyre
Taanach
Azzah
Shamir
(Mt.) Zemaraim ?
Mizpah
Bethlehem
Tekoa
Megiddo
Kozoh
Gibeon
Manahath
Mishal ?
Elmattan
Achzib
Jokneam
ha-Zorea, T. Qiri
Upper Beth-horon
Sepher
Kiriath-jearim
Acco
Aruna
Zeredah
Siphtan ?
Lower Beth-horon
Libnath ?,
T. Abu Huwam
Gath
Socoh
Borim
Yaham
Aijalon
Adullam
Rabbah, Rubute ?
Zorah
Socoh
Migdal ?
Beth-shemesh
T. Shiqmona
Azekah
Athlit
Dor
T. Mevorach
Aphek
Gezer
Gittaim
Timnah
Moresheth-gath ?
Gibbethon
Ekron
Gath
T. Qasila
T. Mikhal
T. Qudadi
Joppa
8-2
T. Mor
Gaza
Sharuhen

Section 8 – 3

Divided Kingdom A (Iron II)

SCALE 1:600.000
10 Km
6 M

LEGEND: Historical Source Names • Hebron
Background Names • Jericho
Lines of Communication-International
Lines of Communication-Local

Penuel
Mahanaim ?
Succoth
Kerioth
Ataroth
Kir-hareseth, Kir of Moab
Horonaim ?
Bozrah
Kh. el-Makhruq
Gilgal ?
Jericho
Zoar
Feifa
En-gedi
Arumah
Shiloh
Ophrah
Jeshanah
Geba
Yashub ?
Bethel
Gibeah
Jerusalem
(Mt.) Zemaraim ?
Mizpah
Bethlehem
Tekoa
Gibeon
Manahath
Etam
Tamar
Elmattan
Ziph
Ramoth of the Negeb ?
Upper Beth-horon
Arad (Rabba/Great)
Kiriath-jearim
Hebron
Zeredah
Lower Beth-horon
Beth-zur
Eshtemoa
Aijalon
Adullam
Adoraim
Debir
Arad (of Jerahmeel)
Rabbah, Rubute ?
Kabzeel ?
Zorah
Socoh
Aroer
Beth-shemesh
Aphek
Azekah
Eglon ?, T. Eton
Gezer
Moresheth-gath ?
Mareshah
T. Beit Mirsim
Baalath-beer ?
Gittaim
Timnah
Gibbethon
Ekron
Gath
Lachish
Goshen ?
Beer-sheba
T. Mikhal
T. Qasila
T. el-Areini
T. Qudadi
Joppa
T. Nagila
Eglon ?,
T. el-Hesi
Ziklag ?
T. Mor
Ashdod
Kh. Huj
Gerar
Ashkelon
Hazar-addar ?
Sharuhen ?
Kadesh-barnea
Gaza
Kh. Teda
8-3

©

Section 8 – 4

Divided Kingdom A (Iron II)

SCALE 1:300.000

10 Km

6 M

LEGEND: Historical Source Names • Hebron
Background Names • Jericho
Lines of Communication-International
Lines of Communication-Local

E
Gilgal ?
Jericho
Naaran
En-gedi
Tirzah
Ephron, Ephrain
Ophrah ?
Michmash
Jeshanah
Geba
Anathoth
En-shemesh
Ananiah
Bethel
Ramah
Gibeah
Jerusalem
(Mt.) Zemaraim ?
Mizpah
Ataroth-addar ?
Birzaith
Gibeon
Waters of Nephtoah
Beeroth ?
Manahath
Bethlehem
Tekoa
Etam
Mozah
Bether
Peor
Zobah ?
Kain
Ziph
Carmel
Maon
Kerioth ?
Arad
Ramoth of the Negeb ?
Beth-anoth
Halhul
Hebron
Beth-zur
Gedor
Juttah
Upper Beth-horon
Chephirah
Timnath-serah
Kiriath-jearim
Lower Beth-horon
Eshtemoa
Anim
Chesalon
Beth-tappuah
Aphekah
Adoraim
Aijalon
Debir
Socoh
Jattir
Arad
Eshtaol
Keilah
Nezib
Zanoah
Adullam
Shaalbim
Rabbah ?
Zorah
Beth-shemesh
Jarmuth
Socoh
Dumah
Kabzeel ?
Shaaraim ?
Libnah ?
Anab
Azekah
Madmannah
Eglon ?
Gezer
Timnah
T. Beit Mirsim
Moladah ?
Gittaim
Moresheth-gath ?
Mareshah
Migdal-gad ?
Beth-pelet ?
Sansannah
Ether
Goshen ?
Gibbethon
Ekron
Gath
Lachish
Gerar
Beer-sheba

Section 8 – 5

Divided Kingdom A (Iron II)

SCALE 1:450.000
10 Km
6 M

LEGEND: Historical Source Names • Hebron
Background Names • Jericho
Lines of Communication-International
Lines of Communication-Local

Ramoth-gilead
amascus
Mahanaim ?
(Upper) Aphek
Jabesh-gilead
Penuel
Mahanaim ?
(Lower) Aphek ?
En Gev
Dan
Zaphon ?
Succoth
Lo-debar ?
Ijon
Abel-beth-maachah,
Abel-maim
Hazor
Zaphon ?
Adam
Abel-meholah ?
Chinnereth
Kedesh
Kh. el-Makhruq
Beth-shan
Rehob
Tirzah
Arumah
Shunem
Jezreel
Beth-haggan
Shechem
Shiloh
Ophrah ?
Ibleam
Yazith
Hazeroth ?
Sidon
Dothan
Yashub ?
Geba
Azzah
Taanach
Samaria
Tyre
Megiddo
Kozoh
Elmattan
Mishal ?
Jokneam
ha-Zorea, T. Qiri
Sepher
Achzib
Siphtan ?
Acco
Aruna
Gath
Socoh
Borim
Yaham
Libnath ?,
T. Abu Huwam

Section 8 – 6

Divided Kingdom A (Iron II)

SCALE 1:450.000
10 Km
6 M

LEGEND: Historical Source Names • Hebron
Background Names • Jericho
Lines of Communication-International
Lines of Communication-Local

Rabbath-ammon
Bezer ?
Jahaz ?
City of Moab ?
Jazer ?
Elealah
Heshbon
Medeba
Beth-diblathaim ?
Almon-diblathaim ?
Aroer
Dibon
Ar ?
Ije-abarim ?
Nebo ?
Kiriathaim ?
Beth-baal-meon
Madmen ?
Kir-hareseth
Kir of Moab
Kerioth
Ataroth
Hauronen
Horonaim ?
Bozrah
Sela
Gilgal ?
Jericho
Zoar
Feifa
En-gedi
Ezion-geber
Ophrah
Geba
Bethel
Ramah
Gibeah
Jerusalem
(Mt.)
Zemaraim ?
Mizpah
Bethlehem
Tekoa
Tamar
Gibeon
Samaria
Manahath
Etam
Ramoth of the Negeb ?
Ziph
Arad
Upper
Beth-horon
Lower
Beth-horon
Kiriath-jearim
Hebron
Beth-zur
Eshtemoa
Aijalon
Adoraim
Debir
Arad
Rabbah ?
Zorah
Adullam
Libnah ?
Beer-sheba
Beth-shemesh
Socoh
Kabzeel ?
Aroer

Section 8 – 7

Divided Kingdom A (Iron II)

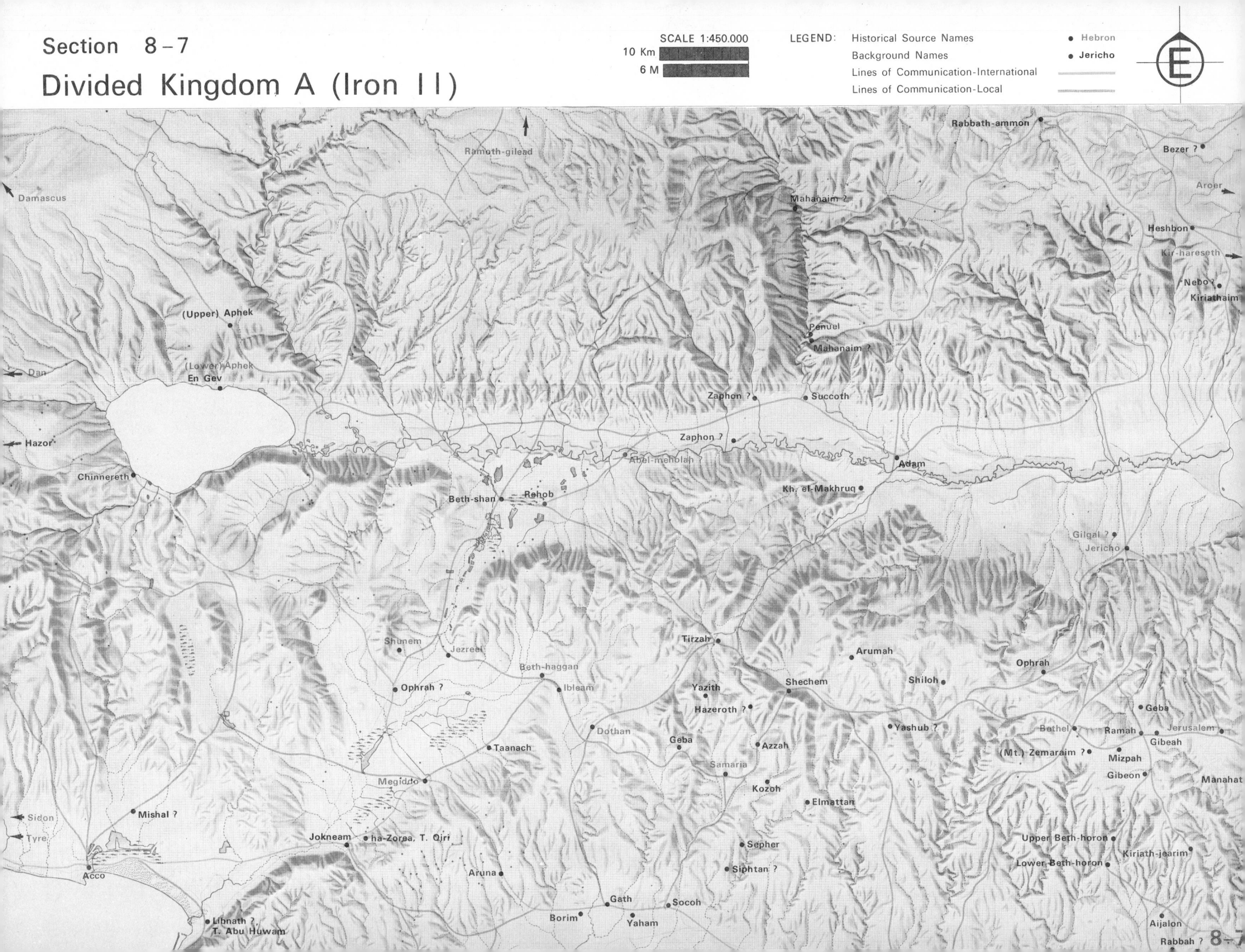

SCALE 1:450.000
10 Km
6 M

LEGEND: Historical Source Names • Hebron
Background Names • Jericho
Lines of Communication-International
Lines of Communication-Local

Rabbath-ammon
Bezer ?
Aroer
Damascus
Ramoth-gilead
Mahanaim ?
Heshbon
Kir-hareseth
Nebo ?
Kiriathaim
(Upper) Aphek
Penuel
Mahanaim ?
(Lower) Aphek
En Gev
Dan
Zaphon ?
Succoth
Zaphon ?
Hazor
Abel-meholah
Adam
Chinnereth
Beth-shan
Rehob
Kh. el-Makhruq
Gilgal ?
Jericho
Shunem
Jezreel
Tirzah
Arumah
Ophrah
Beth-haggan
Shiloh
Ophrah ?
Ibleam
Yazith
Shechem
Hazeroth ?
Geba
Yashub ?
Bethel
Ramah
Jerusalem
Dothan
Geba
Gibeah
Taanach
Azzah
(Mt.) Zemaraim ?
Mizpah
Samaria
Gibeon
Megiddo
Kozoh
Manahat
Elmattan
Mishal ?
Sidon
Tyre
Jokneam
ha-Zorea, T. Qiri
Upper Beth-horon
Sepher
Kiriath-jearim
Acco
Aruna
Siphtan ?
Lower Beth-horon
Gath
Socoh
Borim
Yaham
Libnath ?
T. Abu Huwam
Aijalon
Rabbah ?

Divided Kingdom A (Iron II)

Title & date?

SCALE 1:300.000
10 Km
6 M

LEGEND:
- Historical Source Names • Hebron
- Background Names • Jericho
- Lines of Communication-International
- Lines of Communication-Local

N E S W

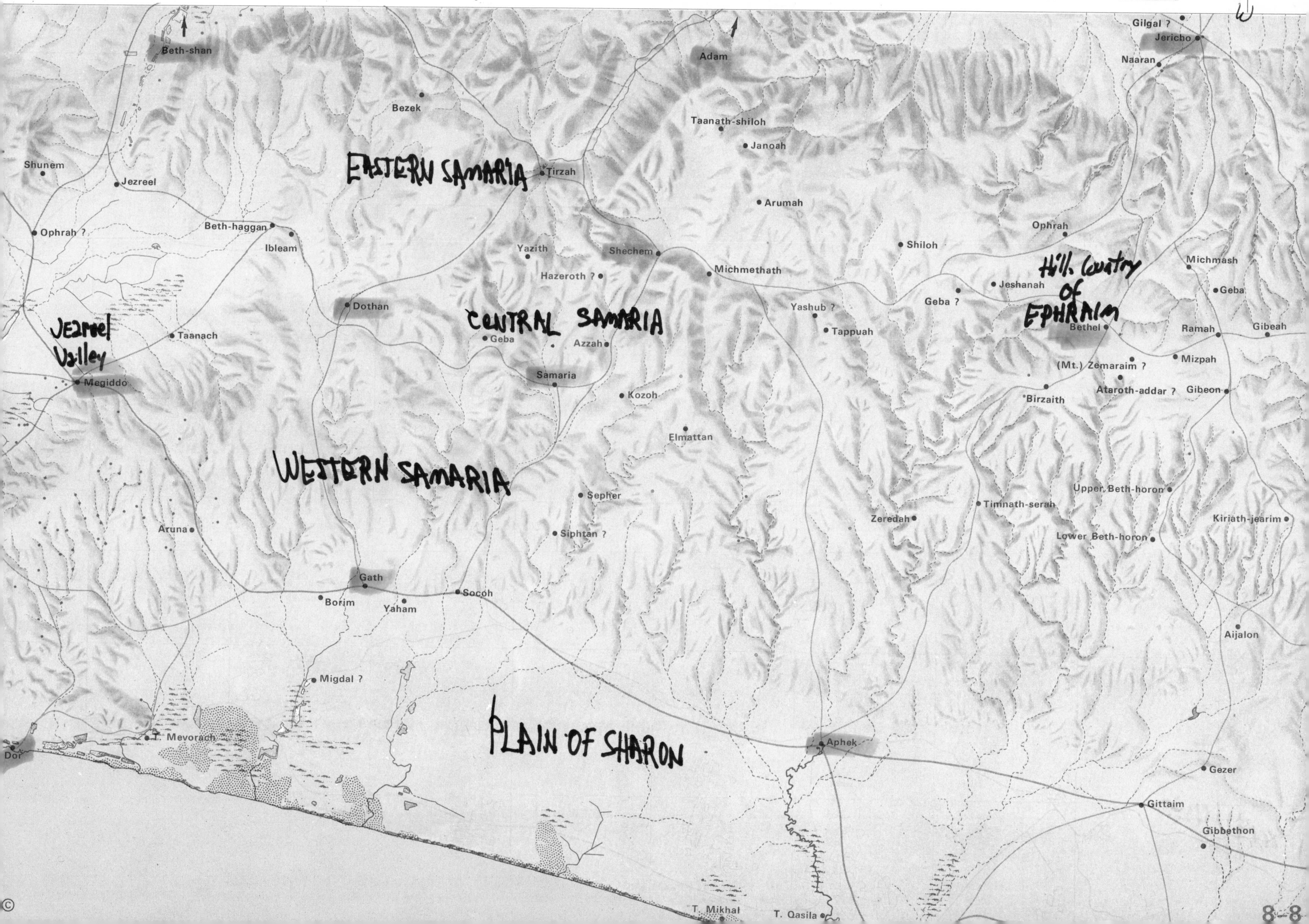

Beth-shan
Adam
Gilgal ?
Jericho
Naaran
Bezek
Taanath-shiloh
Janoah
Shunem
Jezreel
EASTERN SAMARIA
Tirzah
Arumah
Ophrah ?
Beth-haggan
Ibleam
Yazith
Shechem
Michmethath
Shiloh
Ophrah
Hazeroth ?
Hill Country of EPHRAIM
Jeshanah
Michmash
Geba ?
Geba
Dothan
Yashub ?
Tappuah
Jezreel Valley
Taanach
CENTRAL SAMARIA
Geba
Azzah
Bethel
Ramah
Gibeah
Mizpah
Megiddo
Samaria
(Mt.) Zemaraim ?
Kozoh
Birzaith
Ataroth-addar ?
Gibeon
Elmattan
WESTERN SAMARIA
Sepher
Upper Beth-horon
Timnath-serah
Zeredah
Kiriath-jearim
Aruna
Siphtan ?
Lower Beth-horon
Gath
Borim
Yaham
Socoh
Aijalon
Migdal ?
PLAIN OF SHARON
T. Mevorach
Dor
Aphek
Gezer
Gittaim
Gibbethon
T. Mikhal
T. Qasila

Section 9 Summary of contents & sources

Divided Kingdom 'B'

MAIN BIBILCAL REF.: 2 Kings 10.32 – 25.26
2 Chronicles 22.10 – 36.21
Prophets of the period

Map No.	Subject	Primary sources	Regional Map Nos. (Section 1)	Macmillan Bible Atlas Map Nos.	Other references and notes
9-1/2	**Overviews, internal politics and wars prior to major Assyrian invasions (Israel, Syria/Aram, Judah, Edom and Philistia)**				
	a Overview (north = 9-1)				
	b Overview (south = 9-2)				
	c **Athaliah** and **J(eh)oash** (*Jud.*): civil strife, reform and apostasy; Hazael of Damascus takes Gath and threatens Jerusalem	2 Kings 11-12; 2 Chronicles 22.10-24.27	1		
	d **Jehu** and **Jehoahaz** (*Isr.*): Syrian oppression and the loss of major routes in Galilee, Transjordan and coastal plain weakens Israel and threatens Judah; a 'saviour' to bring relief from Syria	2Kings 10.32-36; 12.17-18; 13.1-9, 20-23; 2 Chronicles 24.23-25 (cf. 8-7 c and Amos 1.3-5; 6.1-3)	8,9,11,12	136	
	e **J(eh)oash, Jeroboam II** and **Zachariah** (*Isr.*): Aphek victory predicted; Assyrian pressure on Syria brings relief to Israel; Israelite victories at Lo-debar and Karnaim and her control extended over Transjordan and Syria; Shallum kills Zachariah, ending the rule of the house of Jehu	2 Kings 13.10-25; 14.23-29; 15.8-12; Amos; Hosea; monuments: Adadnirari III (*Calah, Sabaa: Assyria*); ANET 281-282; ANEP 444; ANE I: 192-193 (cf. Jonah)	8,9,11	138,140,142	
	f Settlements in the Samaria ostraca	See 8-8 b			
	g **Amaziah** (*Jud.*): victory in Edom campaign; defeat at Beth-shemesh by **J(eh)oash** (*Isr.*) and his sacking of Jerusalem	2 Kings 14.1-22; 2 Chronicles 25	1,15	139	
	h **Shallum, Menahem, Pekahiah** and **Pekah** (*Isr.*): civil strife in Israel	2 Kings 15.13-28	4		
	i **Uzziah/Azariah** and **Jotham** (*Jud.*): western and southern expansion of Judah and building projects; Judah's control extended to Transjordan (victory over Ammonites and tribute from them)	2 Kings 15.1-7, 32-38; 2 Chronicles 26, 27 (cf. Isaiah 1-6)	2	141,142	
	j **Ahaz** (*Jud.*) and **Pekah** (*Isr.*): Israel's league with Rezin of Syria against Judah; Judah's apostasy and threat from Syria; revolt in Edom (see 9-3 for Philistine incursions and settlement)	2 Kings 15.37; 16.1-6; 2 Chronicles 28.1-19 (see 9-3 a for 2 Chronicles 28.18); Isaiah 7-12; 17 (see 9-6 c for Isaiah 10.28-32)	1,2	144	
	k Moabite settlement in Transjordan as reflected in Isaiah and Jeremiah (place-names in black: cf. 8-6 c)	Isaiah 15-16; Jeremiah 48.1-49.6		155	
9-3	**Warnings in the Shephelah: Philistine conquests and Micah, the prophet**				
	a **Ahaz** (*Jud.*): Philistine incursions and settlement	2 Chronicles 28.18 (from 9-1 j)	2	145	
	b Setting of the prophecy of Micah	Micah (NB chapter 1)	2,16	143	
9-4	**The campaigns and provincial organization of Tiglath-pileser III of Assyria**				
	The campaigns: 1) Philistia, 2) Galilee and Gilead, and 3) Damascus; partial deportation of populations in Galilee, Gilead and Damascus; murder of **Pekah** (*Isr.*); submission of **Hoshea** (*Isr.*) and **Ahaz** (*Jud.*) to Assyria; Assyrian provincial organization (including Damascus, Karnaim, Gilead, Megiddo and Dor) and tributaries	2 Kings 15.29-31; 16.7-20; 2 Chronicles 28.20-27 (cf. 1 Chronicles 5.6, 25-26; Isaiah 9.1-7; Ezekiel 47.17-18); annals, reliefs: Tiglath-pileser III (*Calah: Assyria*); ANET 282-84; ANEP 445; ANE I: 193-94; lists and administrative documents (*Assyria*)	2,3,6,8	146,147,148,150	
9-5	**Fall of Samaria, Assyrian expansion under Shalmaneser V and Sargon II**				
	a **Hoshea** (*Isr.*): collaboration with Egypt, rebellion and capture; Assyrian invasion and the fall of Samaria (Shalmaneser V and Sargon II); Assyrian resettlement programme and provincial organization	2 Kings 17; 18.9-12; annals, lists, reliefs: Sargon II (*Khorsabad, Asshur: Assyria*); ANET 284-85; ANEP 446; ANE I: 195-96	10	149 ,150,151	
	b Sargon II's coastal campaigns in response to Egyptian-inspired revolts at: 1) Gaza and Raphia, and 2) Ashdod, Gibbethon, Ekron and Gath (not Azekah); provinces of Samaria and Ashdod	Isaiah 20 (cf. Isaiah 18 and 19); ANET 284-87; ANEP 446; ANE I: 195-98	2,3	149	

Divided Kingdom 'B'

Map No.	Subject	Primary sources	Regional Map Nos. (Section 1)	Macmillan Bible Atlas Map Nos.	Other references and notes
9-6	**Resistance of Hezekiah of Judah against Sennacherib of Assyria**				
	a **Hezekiah** (*Jud.*): rule; expansionist policy toward Gaza and Edom; religious revival in Judah and Jerusalem; revolt from Assyrian rule and preparation for Assyrian invasion (including the building of the Siloam tunnel, known as 'Hezekiah's tunnel')	2 Kings 18.1-8; 20; 1 Chronicles 4.38-43; 2 Chronicles 29.1-32.8, 23-33; Isaiah 38-39 (cf. Isaiah 22.8-11); Siloam inscription (*Jerusalem*); ANET 321; ANEP 275; ANE I:212	1,3	152	
	b Sennacherib's campaign along the coast (cf. map 9-1) and in the Shephelah of Judah; a written threat to Hezekiah, 'a prisoner in Jerusalem . . . like a bird in a cage' (cf. 9-6 c); Judah delivered from Sennacherib	2 Kings 18.13-19.37; 2 Chronicles 32.1, 9-22; Isaiah 30, 36-37 (cf. Isaiah 31-35); Micah 1.10-16 (cf. 9-3 b); annals: Sennacherib (*Nineveh: Assyria*); ANET 287-8; ANEP 371-4; ANE I: 199-201; Kitchen 1973: Pars. 126-37; 345-54; Naaman 1974	2	153,154	
	c A possible Assyrian threat to Jerusalem from the north	Isaiah 10.28-32	1	154	
	d **Manasseh** (*Jud.*): rule; religious apostasy in the wake of Sennacherib's campaign	2 Kings 21.1-18; 2 Chronicles 33.1-20		155	
	e Assyria's expansion into Lower Egypt via Philistia and the western Negev under Esarhaddon; rebellions in Tyre and Sidon suppressed (covered on map 9-1, but not necessarily in red)	Annals: Esarhaddon; Assyrian documents; Babylonian Chronicle on the days of Esarhaddon; ANET 289-94, 533-34; ANEP 447-9; ANE I: 201-2; ANE II 52-53		146,156	
	f Ashurbanipal's campaigns against Egypt, Arabia (via Transjordan) and Tyre, prior to the rapid decline and fall of Assyria (cf. map 9-1/2)	Annals: Ashurbanipal; ANET 294-301; ANEP 10, 63, 167,170			
	g Egypt's confrontation with the Scythians who retreat via Ashkelon; invasion of Psammtik I of Egypt: the siege and fall of Ashdod (according to Herodotus)	Herodotus, *The Histories*: I.105; II.157 (cf. Jeremiah 47.1)	3		
	h **Amon** (*Jud.*): rule; religious apostasy increases	2 Kings 21.19-26; 2 Chronicles 33.21-25 (cf. Jeremiah 23)			
	i **Josiah** (*Jud.*): rule; religious reform and Judah's last period of expansion with the decline of Assyria; the fall of Nineveh; pharoah Neco's northern march to help Assyria results in Josiah's death at Megiddo (cf. map 9-1); the message of the prophet Zephaniah; Jeremiah's ministry begins; beginning of a four-year Egyptian control of Palestine prior to Babylonian invasions	2 Kings 22.1-23.30 (cf. 1 Kings 13:1-3); 2 Chronicles 34-35; Zephaniah: note 2.1-7 (cf. Nahum, Jeremiah 1-20; 47); Letter from Mezad Hashavyahu; Babylonian Chronicle; ANET 303-5, 568; ANEP 808; ANE I: 202-3; ANE II: 121	2,3,6,13	158,159	
9-7	**The rise of Babylon, Judah's closing years and the fall of Jerusalem**				
	a Shallum/**Jehoahaz** and Eliakim/**Jehoiakim** (*Jud.*): pharaoh Neco deports Jehoahaz to Egypt making Jehoiakim king; heavy tribute to Egypt and wasteful domestic policies; Jeremiah's warnings and imprisonment	2 Kings 23.31-37; 2 Chronicles 36.1-4; Jeremiah 22.1-23; 26; 35; 45	1,2,3,12,15		
	b **Jehoiakim** (*Jud.*): fall of Assyria (battle of Carchemish) and Babylonian expansion to Philistia; confrontation with Egypt; Judah submits to Babylon for three years, but then rebels; raids on Judah; Egypt's influence in the region is limited; the ministry of Jeremiah and message of Habbakuk	2 Kings 24.1-7; 2 Chronicles 36.5-8; Jeremiah 25 (cf. Jeremiah 48.1-51.58); 36; 46 (cf. Jeremiah 47); Habbakuk 1-3; Babylonian Chronicle; ANET 308; ANE I:205	3	160,161	
	c (Je)Coniah/**Jehoiakin** (*Jud.*): Nebuchadnezzar besieges Jerusalem; Jehoiakin's surrender and deportation with nobles and skilled labour class; Mattaniah/**Zedekiah** appointed king of Judah	2 Kings 24.8-17; 2 Chronicles 36.9-10 (cf. 2 Kings 25.27-30); Jeremiah 22.24-30 (cf. Jeremiah 24; 52.31-34); Babylonian Chronicle: siege of Jerusalem; ANET 568-9; ANEP 807; ANE I: 203; ANE II: 122		161	
	d Mattaniah/**Zedekiah** (*Jud.*): lack of decisive action, unrest and rebellion in Judah; the conquest of Judah; the fall of Jerusalem and additional deportations to Babylon	2 Kings 24.18-25.21; 2 Chronicles 36.11-21; Jeremiah 21, 24, 27-34, 37.1-39.10; 51.59-52.30 (cf. Ezekiel 1-24); Lachish ostraca; ANET 321-2; ANEP 279; ANE I: 212-4	1,2	162,163	
	e Edomite invasion of the Negev	Obadiah; Psalm 137.7; Lamentations 4.21-22; Arad ostraca; ANET 568-9; ANEP 807; ANE II: 122;	15,16	162	
	f Administration in Judah after the fall of Jerusalem; the remnant left in the Land; flight to Egypt	2 Kings 25.22-26; Jeremiah 39.11-44.30; Nehemiah 11.20, 25-36 (cf. Lamentations)	1,2,3,16	164,165	

Kitchen, K. A.
1973 *The Third Intermediate Period in Egypt (1100-650 B.C.)* Warminster, England: Aris & Phillips.

Naaman, N.
1974 Sennacherib's *Letter to God* on His Campaign to Judah. *Bulletin of the American Schools of Oriental Research* 214: 26-28.

Divided Kingdom B (Iron II)

SCALE 1:750.000
10 Km
6 M

LEGEND: Historical Source Names • Hebron
Background Names • Jericho
Lines of Communication-International
Lines of Communication-Local

E

Rabbath-ammon
Mephaath ?
Bezer ?
Jahaz ?
Beth-gamul
Kedemoth ?
Karnaim
Damascus
Beth-arbel
Mahanaim ?
Jazer ?
Elealeh
Heshbon
Beth-diblathaim ?
Aroer
Medeba
Dibon
Nebo ?
Kiriathaim ?
Beth-baal-meon
Madmen ?
Kerioth
Kir-hareseth
Kir of Moab
Dan
(Lower) Aphek ?
En Gev
Ijon
Lo-debar ?
Succoth
Abel-beth-maachah
Abel-meholah ?
Zaphon ?
Hazor
Chinnereth
Adam
Kedesh
Beth-shan
Gilgal ?
Jericho
City of Salt ?
Merom ?
Merom ?
Yiron
En-gedi
N. David Cave
Tirzah
Gath-hepher
Jezreel
Arumah
Kanah
Shechem
Hazor
(A)Rumah
Ophrah ?
Ibleam
Michmash
Anathoth
Sidon
Aiath,
Ayyah ?
Ananiah
Jotbah
Hannathon
Geba
Jerusalem
Uzu
Janoah
Dothan
Geba
Ramah
Nob ?
Tappuah
Bethel
Gibeah
Beth-haccherem ?
Tyre
Taanach
Tekoa
Mizpah
Megiddo
Samaria
Bethlehem
Gibeon
Mishal ?
Qalunya
Manahath
Ziph
Ramoth of the Negeb ?
Achzib
ha-Zorea,
T. Qiri
Upper
Beth-horon
Jokneam
Arad
Acco
Lower
Beth-horon
Beth-zur
Hebron
Libnath ?
Beth-leaphrah ?
Adoraim
Debir
Arad
Zanoah
Aijalon
Zorah
Jarmuth
Jeshua ?
Migdal ?
Adullam
Neballat
Beth-shemesh
Socoh
(Je)Kabzeel ?
T. Shiqmona
Hormah ?
Aroer
Gimzo
Libnah ?
Athlit
T. Mevorach
Aphek
Hadid
Azekah
Eglon ?, T. Eton
Moladah ?
Dor
Gezer
Moresheth-gath ?
Lod
Timnah
T. Beit Mirsim
Gittaim
Mareshah
Ono
Beth-pelet ?
Gibbethon
Ekron
Gath
T. Poleg
Goshen ?
Lachish
Bene-berak
Beer-sheba
Beth-dagon
T. Mikhal
T. Qasila
Azor
T. el-Areini
T. Qudadi
Eltekeh ?
Joppa
Jabneh
Jabneel
T. Nagila
Eglon ?,
T. el-Hesi
Mezad Hashavyahu
H. Yavne Yam
T. Mor
Ashdod
Ziklag ?
Ashdod-yam
Kh. Huj
Gerar
Ashkelon
Gaza
Kh. Teda
Arzani,
Yurza ?
Sharuhen ?
T. el-Ajjul
T. er-Ruqeish
9-1

Section 9-2

Divided Kingdom B (Iron II)

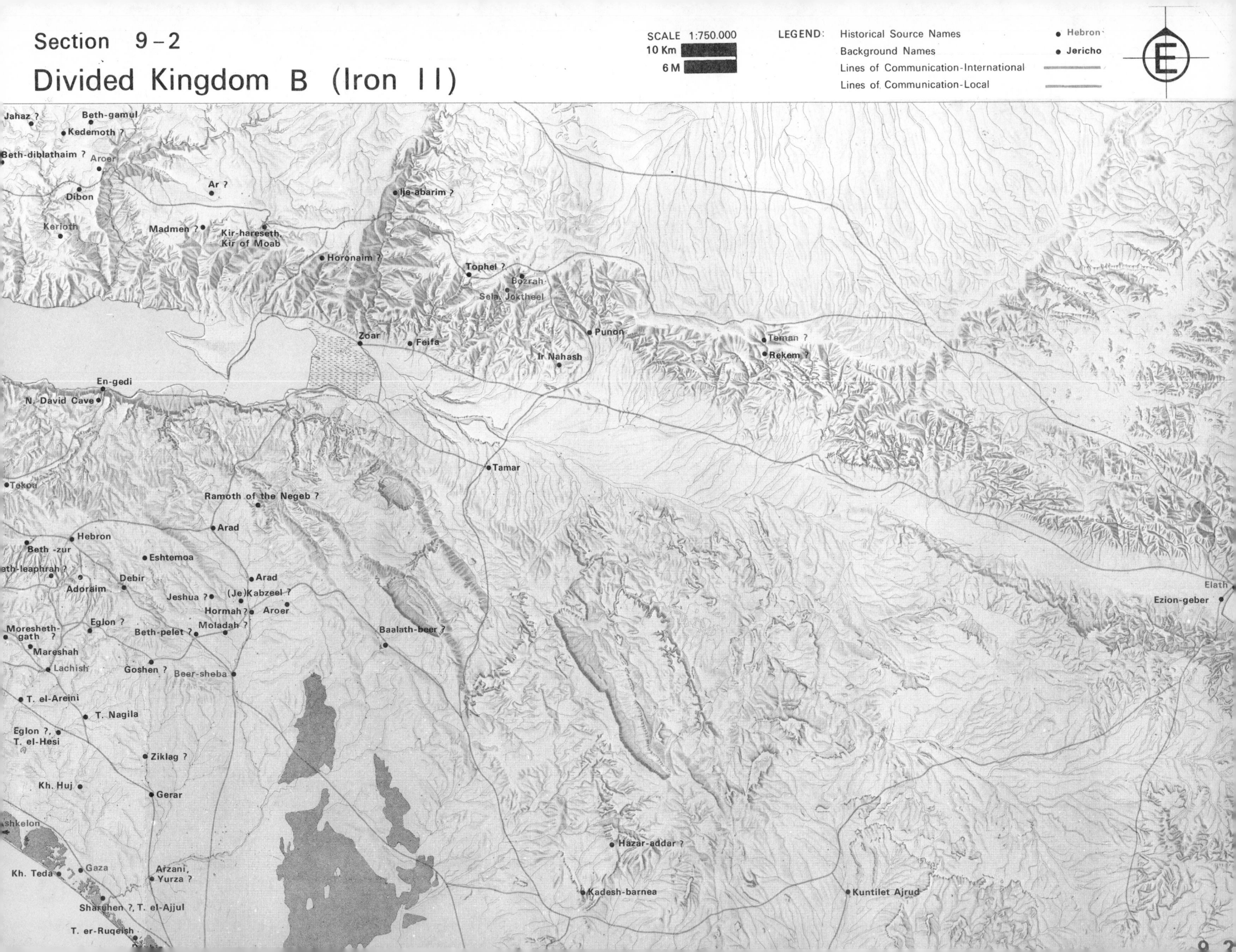

SCALE 1:750.000
10 Km
6 M

LEGEND: Historical Source Names • Hebron
Background Names • Jericho
Lines of Communication-International
Lines of Communication-Local

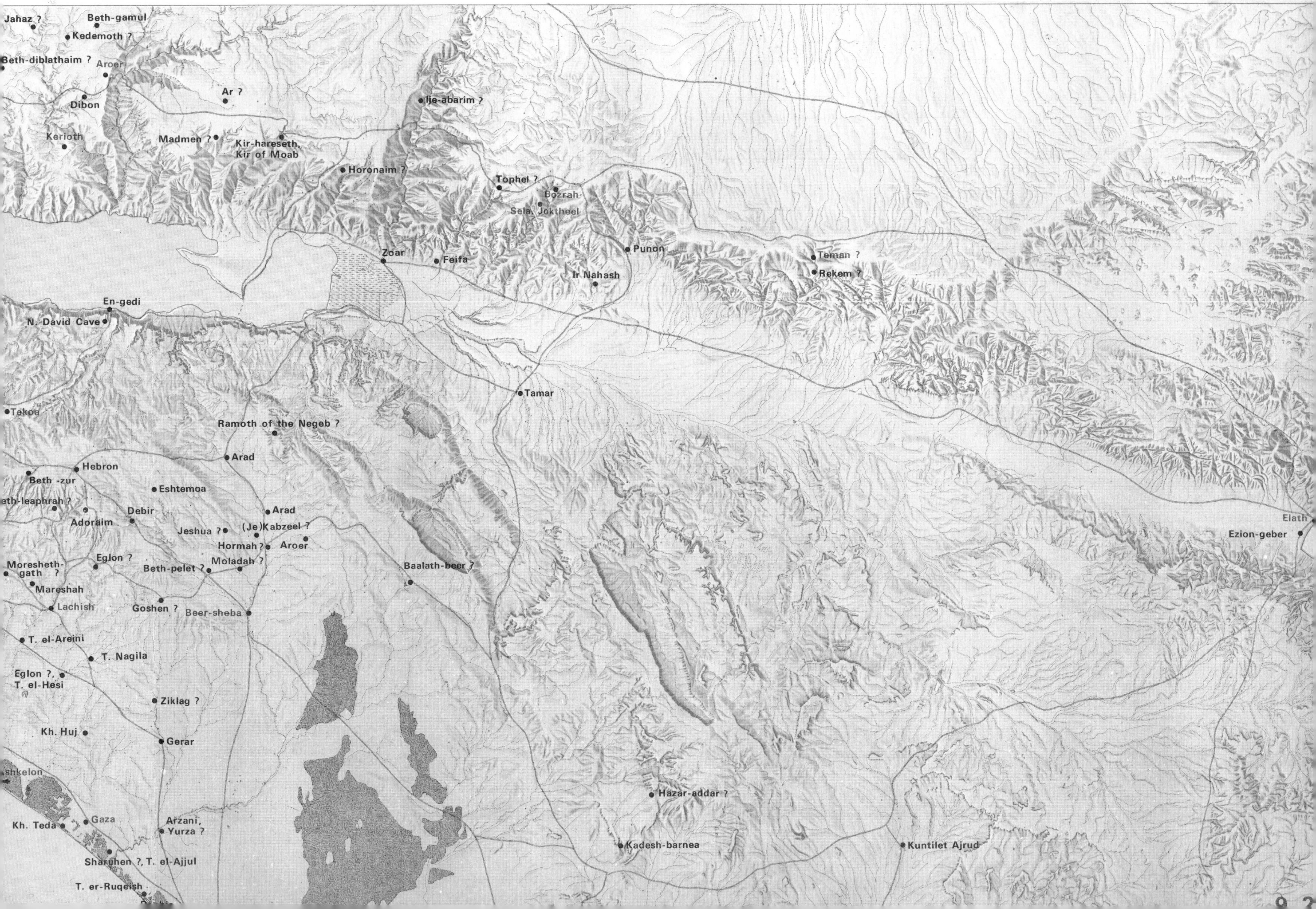

Jahaz ?
Beth-gamul
Kedemoth ?
Beth-diblathaim ?
Aroer
Ar ?
Dibon
Ije-abarim ?
Kerioth
Madmen ?
Kir-hareseth,
Kir of Moab
Horonaim ?
Tophel ?
Bozrah
Sela, Joktheel
Zoar
Feifa
Punon
Teman ?
Rekem ?
Ir Nahash
En-gedi
N. David Cave
Tamar
Tekoa
Ramoth of the Negeb ?
Arad
Hebron
Beth -zur
eth-leaphrah ?
Eshtemoa
Debir
Adoraim
Arad
Jeshua ?
(Je)Kabzeel ?
Hormah ?
Aroer
Eglon ?
Moladah ?
Beth-pelet ?
Baalath-beer ?
Moresheth-
gath ?
Mareshah
Lachish
Goshen ?
Beer-sheba
T. el-Areini
T. Nagila
Eglon ?,
T. el-Hesi
Ziklag ?
Kh. Huj
Gerar
shkelon
Kh. Teda
Gaza
Arzani,
Yurza ?
Sharuhen ?, T. el-Ajjul
T. er-Ruqeish
Hazar-addar ?
Kadesh-barnea
Kuntilet Ajrud
Elath
Ezion-geber

Section 9 – 3

Divided Kingdom B (Iron II)

SCALE 1:300.000

10 Km

6 M

LEGEND: Historical Source Names • Hebron
Background Names • Jericho
Lines of Communication-International
Lines of Communication-Local

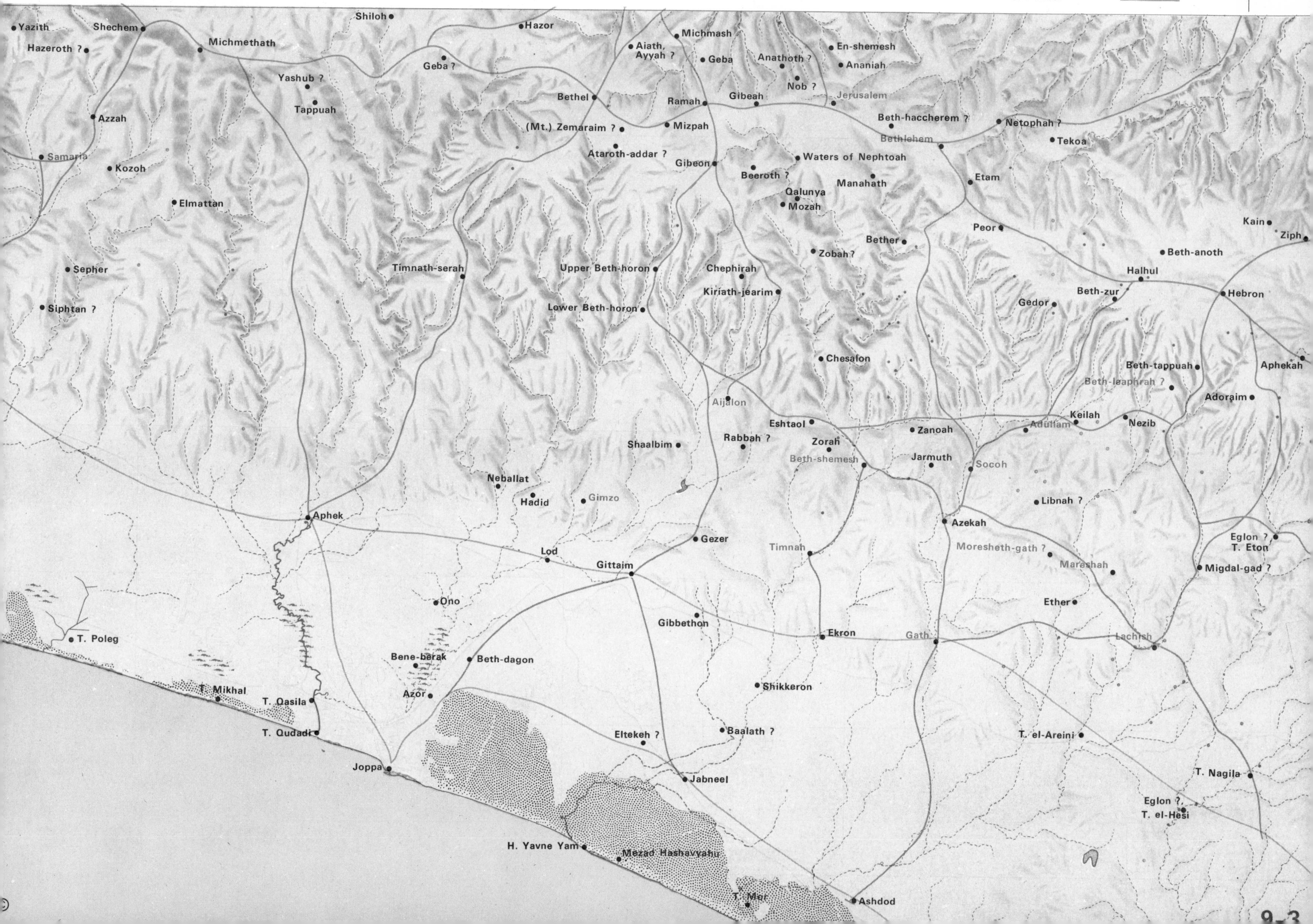

Yazith
Shechem
Hazeroth ?
Michmethath
Shiloh
Hazor
Geba ?
Yashub ?
Tappuah
Bethel
Aiath, Ayyah ?
Michmash
Geba
Anathoth ?
Nob ?
En-shemesh
Ananiah
Gibeah
Jerusalem
Ramah
(Mt.) Zemaraim ?
Mizpah
Ataroth-addar ?
Gibeon
Beeroth ?
Waters of Nephtoah
Manahath
Qalunya
Mozah
Beth-haccherem ?
Netophah ?
Bethlehem
Tekoa
Etam
Azzah
Samaria
Kozoh
Elmattan
Kain
Ziph
Peor
Bether
Zobah ?
Beth-anoth
Halhul
Hebron
Beth-zur
Gedor
Sepher
Siphtan ?
Timnath-serah
Upper Beth-horon
Lower Beth-horon
Chephirah
Kiriath-jearim
Chesalon
Beth-tappuah
Beth-leaphrah ?
Aphekah
Adoraim
Aijalon
Eshtaol
Rabbah ?
Zorah
Beth-shemesh
Zanoah
Jarmuth
Socoh
Adullam
Keilah
Nezib
Shaalbim
Neballat
Hadid
Gimzo
Libnah ?
Azekah
Aphek
Gezer
Lod
Gittaim
Timnah
Moresheth-gath ?
Mareshah
Eglon ?
T. Eton
Migdal-gad ?
Ono
Ether
Gibbethon
Ekron
Gath
Lachish
T. Poleg
Bene-berak
Beth-dagon
T. Mikhal
T. Qasila
Azor
Shikkeron
T. Qudadi
Eltekeh ?
Baalath ?
T. el-Areini
Joppa
Jabneel
T. Nagila
Eglon ?
T. el-Hesi
H. Yavne Yam
Mezad Hashavyahu
T. Mor
Ashdod

Section 9–4
Divided Kingdom B (Iron II)

SCALE 1:750.000
10 Km
6 M

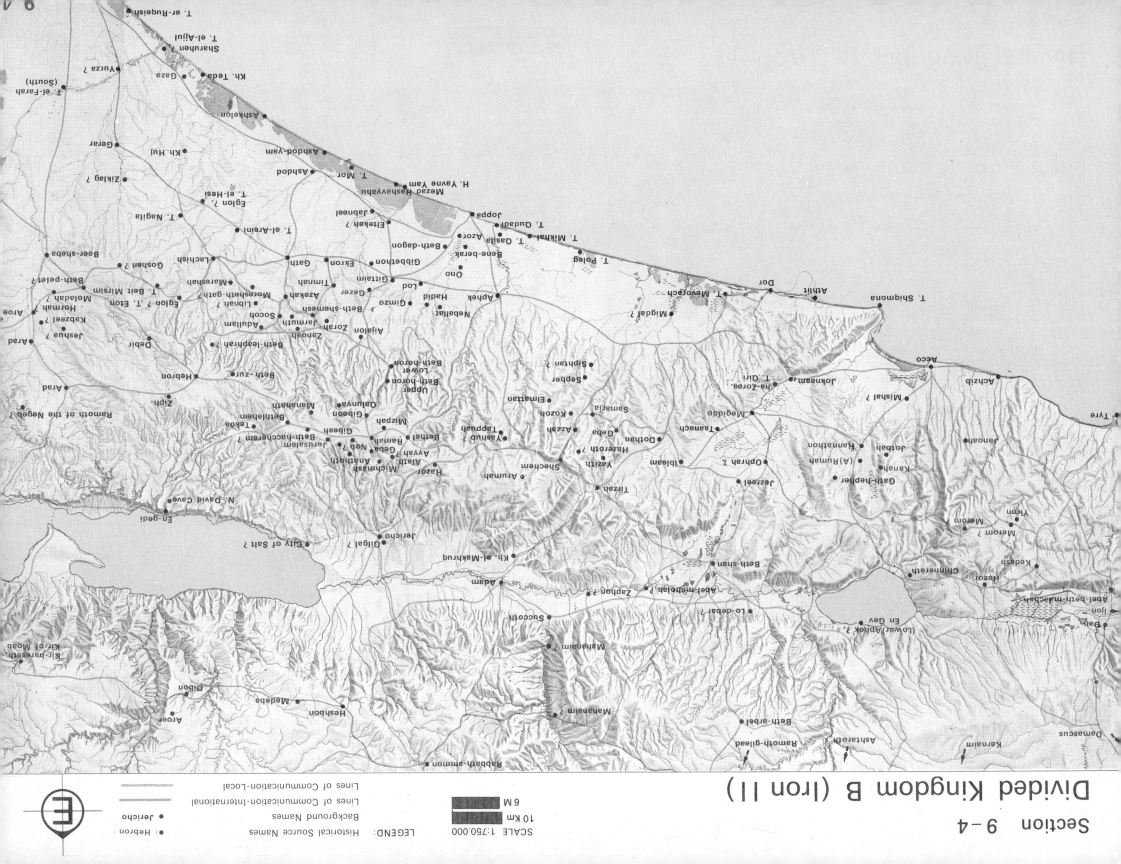

LEGEND: Historical Source Names — Hebron
Background Names — Jericho
Lines of Communication-International
Lines of Communication-Local

Rabbath-ammon
Damascus
Karnaim
Ashtaroth
Ramoth-gilead
Beth-arbel
Mahanaim ?
Heshbon
Medeba
Aroer
Dibon
Kir-hareseth, Kir of Moab
Mahanaim ?
(Lower) Aphek ?, En Gev
Dan
Ijon
Abel-beth-maachah
Lo-debar ?
Succoth
Abel-meholah ?
Zaphon ?
Adam
Hazor
Chinnereth
Kedesh
Beth-shan
Kh. el-Makhruq
Gilgal ?
City of Salt ?
Jericho
Merom ?
Merom ?
Yiron
En-gedi
N. David Cave
Tirzah
Gath-hepher
Jezreel
Arumah
Kanah
(A)Rumah
Ophrah ?
Ibleam
Yazith
Shechem
Hazor
Aiath, Ayyah ?
Michmash
Anathoth
Jotbah
Hannathon
Hazeroth ?
Geba
Nob ?
Jerusalem
Janoah
Dothan
Yashub ?
Tappuah
Bethel
Ramah
Beth-haccherem ?
Geba
Azzah
Gibeah
Tekoa
Taanach
Mizpah
Bethlehem
Tyre
Megiddo
Samaria
Kozoh
Gibeon
Qalunya
Manahath
Ramoth of the Negeb ?
Elmattan
Ziph
Mishal ?
Upper Beth-horon
Arad
Achzib
ha-Zorea, T. Qiri
Jokneam
Sepher
Beth-zur
Hebron
Acco
Siphtan ?
Lower Beth-horon
Beth-leaphrah ?
Debir
Aijalon
Zanoah
Jeshua ?
Arad
Zorah
Jarmuth
Adullam
Kabzeel ?
Migdal ?
Neballat
Beth-shemesh
Socoh
Hormah ?
Aroer
T. Shiqmona
Gimzo
Libnah ?
Eglon ? ,T. Eton
Moladah ?
Athlit
Aphek
Hadid
Gezer
Azekah
Moresheth-gath ?
T. Beit Mirsim
T. Mevorach
Dor
Lod
Timnah
Mareshah
Beth-pelet ?
Gittaim
Ono
Gibbethon
Ekron
Gath
Goshen ?
T. Poleg
Lachish
Beer-sheba
Bene-berak
Beth-dagon
T. Mikhal
T. Qasila
Azor
T. el-Areini
T. Qudadi
Elteke ?
Joppa
Jabneel
T. Nagila
Eglon ?, T. el-Hesi
Mezad Hashavyahu
H. Yavne Yam
T. Mor
Ashdod
Ziklag ?
Ashdod-yam
Kh. Huj
Gerar
Ashkelon
T. el-Farah (South)
Kh. Teda
Gaza
Yurza ?
Sharuhen ?, T. el-Ajjul
T. er-Ruqeish

Section 9 – 5

Divided Kingdom B (Iron II)

SCALE 1:450.000

10 Km

6 M

LEGEND: Historical Source Names • Hebron

Background Names • Jericho

Lines of Communication-International

Lines of Communication-Local

E

(Lower)Aphek ?,
En Gev
Lo-debar ?
Succoth
Zaphon ?
Adam
Abel-meholah ?
Chinnereth
Kh. el-Makhruq
Beth-shan
City of Salt ?
Gilgal ?
Jericho
Taanath-shiloh
Janoah
Tirzah
Jezreel
Gath-hepher
Kanah
Arumah
Ophrah
(A)Rumah
Ophrah ?
Ibleam
Yazith
Shechem
Hazor
Aiath, Ayyah ?
Michmash
Jotbah
Hazeroth ?
Michmethath
Anathoth
Hannathon
Geba
Geba ?
Ananiah
Yashub ?
Lebonah
Nob ?
Jerusalem
Dothan
Bethel
Ramah
Geba
Tappuah
Azzah
Gibeah
Beth-haccherem ?
Taanach
Mizpah
Bethlehem
Samaria
Megiddo
Gibeon
Kozoh
Pirathon
Manahath
Elmattan
Qalunya
Mishal ?
ha-Zorea, T. Qiri
Timnath-serah
Upper Beth-horon
Jokneam
Sepher
Zeredah
Lower Beth-horon
Siphtan ?
Aijalon
Zanoah
Adulla
Jarmuth
Zorah
Socoh
Migdal ?
Neballat
Beth-shemesh
Hadid
Gimzo
T. Shiqmona
Athlit
T. Mevorach
Aphek
Azekah
Dor
Gezer
Timnah
Lod
Gittaim
Ono
Gibbethon
Ekron
Gath
T. Poleg
Bene-berak
Beth-dagon
Azor
T. Qasila
T. Qudadi
Eltekeh ?
Jabneel
Joppa
Mezad Hashavyahu
H. Yavne Yam
Ashdod-yam
Asdudimmu
Gaza
Raphi
Lab
9–5

Section 9 – 6

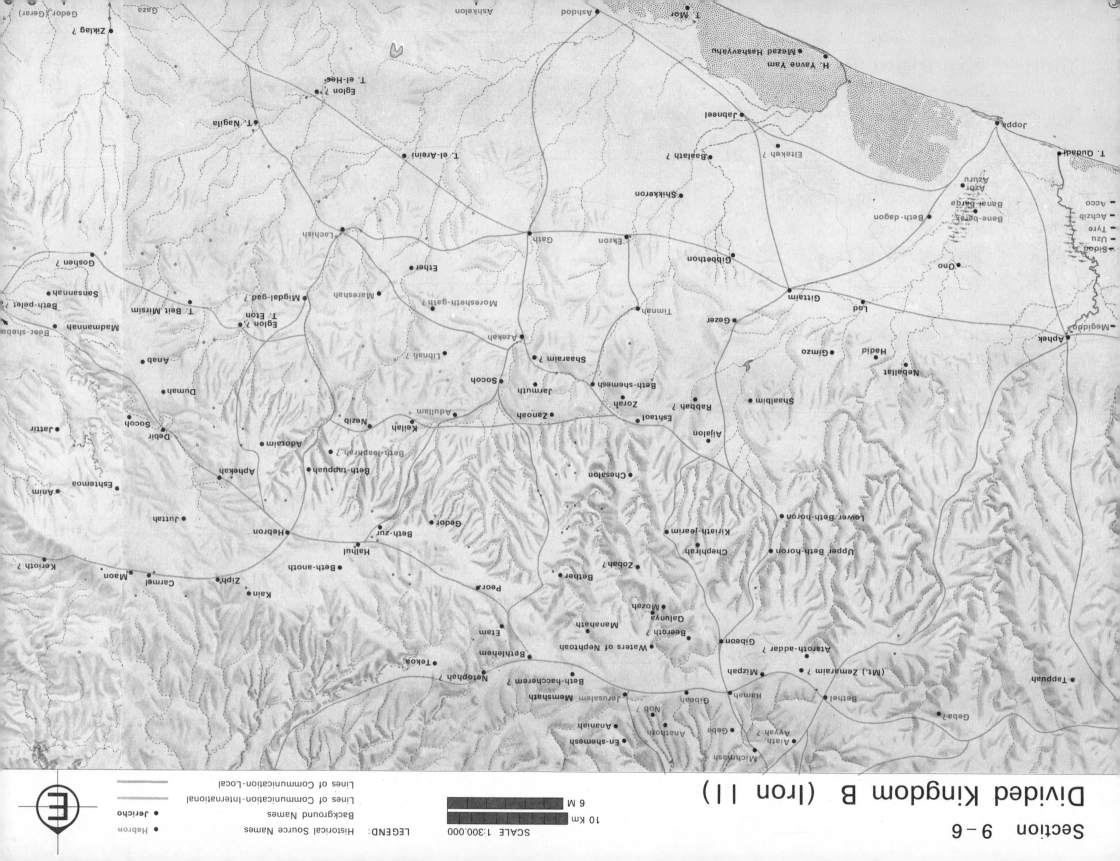

Divided Kingdom B (Iron II)

SCALE 1:300.000

10 Km

6 M

LEGEND: Historical Source Names • Hebron

Background Names • Jericho

Lines of Communication-International

Lines of Communication-Local

Michmash
Aiath, Ayyah ?
Geba
Anathoth
En-shemesh
Ananiah
Nob ?
Geba ?
Bethel
Ramah
Gibeah
Jerusalem
Memshath
Tappuah
(Mt.) Zemaraim ?
Mizpah
Beth-haccherem ?
Netophah ?
Tekoa
Ataroth-addar ?
Waters of Nephtoah
Bethlehem
Gibeon
Beeroth ?
Etam
Manahath
Qalunya
Mozah
Kain
Peor
Ziph
Carmel
Maon
Bether
Zobah ?
Beth-anoth
Kerioth ?
Upper Beth-horon
Chephirah
Halhul
Kiriath-jearim
Beth-zur
Hebron
Gedor
Lower Beth-horon
Juttah
Eshtemoa
Anim
Chesalon
Beth-tappuah
Aphekah
Beth-leaphrah ?
Adoraim
Aijalon
Debir
Keilah
Socoh
Jattir
Nezib
Eshtaol
Zanoah
Adullam
Rabbah ?
Zorah
Shaalbim
Dumah
Jarmuth
Beth-shemesh
Socoh
Neballat
Shaaraim ?
Anab
Hadid
Gimzo
Libnah ?
Azekah
Aphek
Beer-sheba
Megiddo
Madmannah
Eglon ?
T. Eton
Gezer
Lod
Timnah
T. Beit Mirsim
Beth-pelet ?
Moresheth-gath ?
Gittaim
Mareshah
Migdal-gad ?
Sansannah
Ono
Ether
Goshen ?
Gibbethon
Sidon
Uzu
Ekron
Gath
Tyre
Lachish
Achzib
Bene-berak
Beth-dagon
Banai-barqa
Acco
Shikkeron
Azor
Azuru
Eltekeh ?
Baalath ?
T. Qudadi
T. el-Areini
Joppa
Jabneel
T. Nagila
Eglon ?
T. el-Hesi
H. Yavne Yam
Mezad Hashavyahu
Ziklag ?
T. Mor
Ashdod
Ashkelon
Gaza
Gedor (Gerar)

Section 9–7

Divided Kingdom B (Iron II)

SCALE 1:300.000

10 Km

6 M

LEGEND: Historical Source Names • Hebron
Background Names • Jericho
Lines of Communication-International
Lines of Communication-Local

E

Gilgal ?
City of Salt ?
Jericho
Middin ?
Secacah ?
Nibshan ?
En-gedi
N. David Cave
Ophrah
Shiloh
Hazor
Michmash
Aija, Ayyah ?
Geba
Anathoth
En-shemesh
Ananiah
Shechem
Nob ?
Rumah
Bethel
Ramah
Gibeah
Jerusalem
Beth-haccherem ?, Ramat Rahel
Netophah ?
(Mt.) Zemaraim ?
Mizpah
Tekoa
Bethlehem
Ataroth-addar ?
Waters of Nephtoah
Samaria
Gibeon
Beeroth ?
Manahath
Etam
Qalunya
Mozah
Ramoth of the Negeb
Kain
Peor
Ziph
Carmel
Maon
Bether
Beth-anoth
Kerioth ?
Arad
Zobah ?
Halhul
Upper Beth-horon
Chephirah
Beth-zur
Kiriath-arba
Hebron
Kiriath-jearim
Gedor
Lower Beth-horon
Anim
Eshtemoa
Chesalon
Beth-tappuah
Aphekah
Arad
Debir
Aijalon
Keilah
Nezib
Socoh
Jattir
Eshtaol
Zanoah
Adullam
Rabbah ?
Zorah
Jeshua ?
Shaalbim
Dumah
(Je)Kabzeel ?
Jarmuth
Socoh
Beth-shemesh
Neballat
Anab
Shaaraim ?
Libnah ?
Hadid
Gimzo
Azekah
Eglon ?
Madmannah
Moladah ?
Gezer
T. Beit Mirsim
Timnah
Lod
Moresheth-gath ?
Beth-pelet ?
Gittaim
Mareshah
Migdal-gad ?
Sansannah
Ether
Ono
Goshen ?
Gibbethon
Ekron
Gath
Lachish
Beer-sheba
Ashdod
Ashkelon
Gaza
Ziklag ?
Shikkeron
©
9-7

Section 10 Summary of contents & sources

Persian Period

MAIN BIBLICAL REF.: Ezra; Nehemiah
Prophets of the period

Map No.	Subject	Primary sources	Regional Map Nos. (Section 1)	Macmillan Bible Atlas Map Nos.	Other references and notes
10-1	**Overview, the 'Return' and Persian administration**				
	a Overview (north)				
	b Selected historical background (place-names in black)				
	i) The remnant in Judah from the Babylonian and Persian periods	Nehemiah 11.20, 25-36 (cf. Jeremiah 40; Daniel; Esther)	1,16	165	
	ii) Persian policy reference Tyre, Sidon and other cities of the coast	*Periplus* (Pseudo-Scyláx): see Avi-Yonah 1977:28-31; Eshumun'azar of Sidon; ANET 662			
	iii) Return to the land of Judah and the rebuilding of the Temple and Jerusalem under Jeshua, Zerubbabel, Ezra and Nehemiah (see map 10-2)	2 Chronicles 36.22-23; Ezra; Nehemiah (cf. Haggai; Malachi; Zechariah)	13	168,169,170	
	c Persian rule ends with the conquests of Alexander the Great; sieges of Tyre and Gaza; legendary visit to Jerusalem; revolt of Samaria and resettlement by Macedonians; penetration to Jericho	Arrian, *Anabasis* II; Diodorus XVII; Plutarch, *Life of Alexander* 25; Pliny, *Natural History* XII 117; Curtius Rufus IV; GLAJJ 447-9 Ant. **XI** 313-47/**XI** viii.3-7	3	172,173,174	
10-2	**Land of Judah and administrative districts during the 'Return' (from 10.1 b iii)**				
		Ezra 2.1-35; 3.1-7; Nehemiah 2.9-4.23; 7.6-38	1	171	

Avi-Yonah, M.
1977 *The Holy Land from the Persian to the Arab Conquest (536 B.C.-A.D. 640): A Historical Geography*. Grand Rapids, Michigan: Baker Book House

Notes

Section 10–1

Persian Period

SCALE 1:750.000
10 Km
6 M

LEGEND: Historical Source Names • Hebron
Background Names • Jericho
Lines of Communication-International
Lines of Communication-Local

E

Dium
Gerasa
Rabbath-bene-ammon
Aroer
Heshbon
Birtha, Tyros
Gedor
T. es-Saidiya
Hazor
Beth-shan
Senaah ?
Jericho
En-gedi
Aqraba
Apherema, Ephraim
Hazor
Michmash
Azmaveth
Ayyah ?
Geba
Ananiah
Shechem, Sichem
Mt. Gerizim, Garizeim
Bethel
Ramah
Nob ?
Beth-haccherem ?
Beeroth ?
Jerusalem
Netopha ?
Tekoa
Mizpah
Gibeon
Beeroth ?
Bethlehem
Samaria
Dothan
Taanach
Megiddon
Tyre
H. Uza
T. Kison
Beth-emek
Achzib, Ecdippa
Acco, Ake
ha-Zorea
T. Qiri
Beth-haccherem ?
Upper Beth Horon
Timnah, Thamna
Chephirah
Lower Beth Horon
Kiriath-jearim
Beth-zur
Kiriath-arba, Hebron
Arad
Nebo ?
T. Abu Huwam
Arbatta, Narbata
Haramatha, Ramathaim, Aramathea
Zanoah
Adullam
Jeshua ?
T. Megadim
T. Shiqmona
H. Migdal Malha
T. Zeror
Zorah
Keilah
Jekabzeel ?
Adaroth
Neballat
Hadid
Jarmuth
Magbish ?
Moladah ?
T. Mevorach
Aphek
Elam ?
Dor, Doros, Dora
Gezer
Azekah
Harim ?
Crocodilon Polis
Strato's Tower
Lod
T. Goded
Beth-pelet ?
Ono
Gittaim
T. Beit Mirsim
Mareshah, Marisa
Lachish
En-rimmon ?
Beer-sheb
T. Qasila
Accaron, Ekron
Gath
T. Mikhal
T. el-Areini
T. Qudadi
Joppa
Jabneh, Jamnia
T. Zippor
T. el-Hesi
Port of Jamnia
Mezad Hashavyahu
Ziklag ?
Ashdod, Azotus
Ashdod-yam, Azotus Paralius
Ashkelon, Ascalon
Gaza
T. Gamma
T. el-Farah (South)

Section 10–2

Persian Period

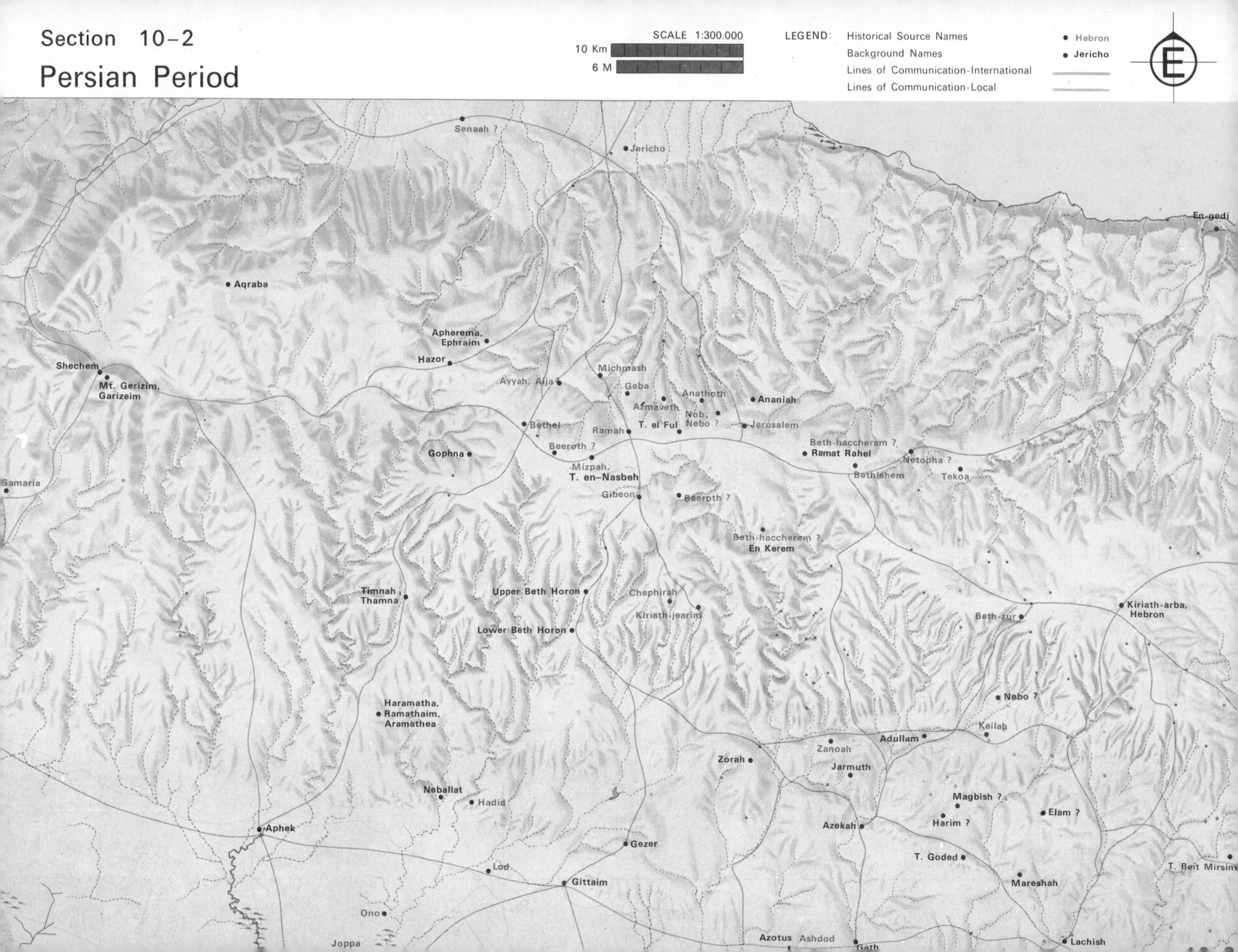

SCALE 1:300.000

10 Km

6 M

LEGEND: Historical Source Names • Hebron

Background Names • Jericho

Lines of Communication-International

Lines of Communication-Local

Senaah ?
Jericho
En-gedi
Aqraba
Apherema,
Ephraim
Hazor
Shechem
Mt. Gerizim,
Garizeim
Michmash
Geba
Ayyah, Aija
Anathoth
Azmaveth
Ananiah
Nob,
Nebo ?
Bethel
Ramah
T. el Ful
Jerusalem
Beeroth ?
Gophna
-Mizpah,
T. en-Nasbeh
Beth-haccherem ?
Ramat Rahel
Netopha ?
Bethlehem
Tekoa
Samaria
Gibeon
Beeroth ?
Beth-haccherem ?
En Kerem
Timnah,
Thamna
Upper Beth Horon
Chephirah
Kiriath-jearim
Lower Beth Horon
Kiriath-arba,
Hebron
Beth-zur
Nebo ?
Haramatha,
Ramathaim,
Aramathea
Keilah
Adullam
Zanoah
Zorah
Jarmuth
Neballat
Hadid
Magbish ?
Elam ?
Harim ?
Azekah
Aphek
Gezer
T. Goded
Lod
Gittaim
T. Beit Mirsim
Mareshah
Ono
Joppa
Azotus
Ashdod
Gath
Lachish

Section 11 Summary of contents & sources
Hellenistic and Hasmonaean Periods

MAIN HISTORICAL REF.: 1 and 2 Maccabees, Judith
Ant. **XII** 1-**XIV** 491 / **XII** i.1-**XIV** xvi.4
Wars **I** 54-357 / **I** ii.3-xviii.3
Selected writings of Greek historians

Map No.	Subject	Primary sources	Regional Map Nos. (Section 1)	Macmillan Bible Atlas Map Nos.	Other references and notes
11-1	**Overview and the Hellenistic cities**				
	a Overview (north)			181	
	b Development of Hellenistic Greek cities				
11-2	**Hellenistic rule in Palestine I**				
	a Struggle of Alexander's successors	Diodorus, *Bibliotheca Historica* XVIII 43; IXX 58-59, 79-86; 90-100; XX 73-76, 113; Appianus Syriaca LII; GLAJJ 174-181; (cf. 1 Maccabees 1.1-9) *Ant.* **XII** 1-9 / **XII** i.1		175,176	
	b Zenon's circuit in Ptolemaic Palestine	Archive of Zenon		177	
11-3	**Hellenistic rule in Palestine II**				
	a Antiochus III: Seleucid campaign in Palestine (Fourth Syrian War)	Polybius, *Histories* V 68-71, 80-86; GLAJJ 112-113		179	
	b Antiochus III: Seleucid conquest of Palestine (Fifth Syrian War)	Polybius, *Histories* XV 13, 25; XVI 18-19, 22, 39; GLAJJ 113-115; *Ant* **XII** 133-146 / **XII** iii.3-4	10	180	
11-4	**Hasmonaean Revolt I: Mattathias and Judas Maccabaeus**				
	a Antiochus IV: enforced Hellenization, despoiling the Temple, and persecution of faithful Jews kindles the Maccabaean revolt	1 Maccabees 1-2; Diodorus, *Bibliotheca Historica* XXXIV - XXXV; Polybius quoted in *Ant.* (below); GLAJJ 115-116; 181-185 (cf. 2 Maccabees 4-7) *Ant.* **XII** 234-85 / **XII** iv.2-vi.4	1	184,185	
	b Maccabaean defence of the approaches to Jerusalem against the Seleucid forces: battles of Beth-horon, Emmaus and Beth-zur	1 Maccabees 3.1-4.35 (cf. 2 Maccabees 8.1-29, 34-36 and 11.1-21, 34-38, 27-33) *Ant.* **XII** 286-315 / **XII** vii.1-5	1	186,187,188	
	c Purification and rededication of the Temple	1 Maccabes 4.36-61 (cf. 2 Maccabees 10.1-8) *Ant.* **XII** 316-326 / **XII** vii.6-7		188	
11-5	**Hasmonaean Revolt II: Judas Maccabaeus**				
	Rescue operations: Idumaea, Gilead and Galilee	1 Maccabees 5.1-54; 2 Maccabees 12.10-31 (cf. 2 Maccabees 10.15-23) *Ant* **XII** 327-49 / **XII** viii.1-5	9,11	189,190	
11-6	**Hasmonaean Revolt III: Judas Maccabaeus**				
	a Campaigns in the coastal plain and Idumaea	1 Maccabees 5.55-68; 2 Maccabees 12.3-9, 32-45 *Ant* **XII** 350-53 / **XII** viii.6	2	191	
	b News of the Seleucid defeat in Judaea reaches Antiochus V; Judas besieges the citadel (Acra) in Jerusalem	1 Maccabees 6.1-27 (cf. 2 Maccabees 1.11-17; 9) *Ant.* **XII** 354-66 / **XII** ix.1-3		192	
	c Seleucid victory at Beth-zacharia, Beth-zur and Jerusalem	1 Maccabees 6.28-54; 2 Maccabees 13.1-17 *Ant.* **XII** 367-78 / **XII** ix.4-5	1	192	
	d Religious freedom granted by Antiochus V	1 Maccabees 6.55-63 (cf. 2 Maccabees 11.13-33;13.18-23 *Ant.* **XII** 379-88 / **XII** ix.6-7			
	e Demetris I; Bacchides, Alcimus' actions and Nicanor's defeat at Capharsalama	1 Maccabees 7.1-32 (cf. 2 Maccabees 14.1-22) *Ant.* **XII** 389-405 / **XII** x.1-4	1	193	

Section 11 Summary of contents & sources (cont.)
Hellenistic and Hasmonaean Periods

Map No.	Subject	Primary sources	Regional Map Nos. (Section 1)	Macmillan Bible Atlas Map Nos.	Other references and notes
11-7	**Hasmonaean Revolt IV: Judas Maccabaeus and Jonathan**				
	a Nicanor's final defeat at Adasa	1 Maccabees 7.33-50; 2 Maccabees 15.25-36; *Ant* **XII** 406-12 / **XII** x.5	1	194	
	b Alliance between Judas and Rome	1 Maccabees 8; *Ant.* **XII** 414-19 / **XII** x.6	1		
	c Bacchides victory, Judas' death at Elasa	1 Maccabees 9.1-22; *Ant.* **XII** 420-34 / **XII** xi.1-2	13	195,196	
	d Retreat to the wilderness under Jonathan	1 Maccabees 9.23-33; *Ant.* **XIII** 1-8 / **XIII** i.1-2		197	
	e Skirmishes with Nabataeans and with Bacchides	See 11-8 a below			
	f Fortresses built or strengthened by Bacchides	1 Maccabees 9.50-53; *Ant.* **XIII** 14-17 / **XIII** i.3	1,4	197	
	g Jonathan's victory at Beth-basi; return to Michmash	1 Maccabees 9.54-73; *Ant.* **XIII** 22-34 / **XIII** i.5-6	1	198	
11-8	**Hasmonaean Revolt V: Jonathan**				
	a Skirmishes with Nabataeans and with Bacchides (from 11-7 e)	1 Maccabees 9.33-49; *Ant.* **XIII** 8-14, 18-21 / **XIII** i.2-4	12		
	b Concessions by competing Seleucid rulers (Alexander Balas and Demetrius I); Jonathan made High Priest	1 Maccabees 10.1-66; *Ant.* **XIII** 35-61, 80-5 / **XIII** ii.1-4; iv.1-2	1,6	199	
	c Jonathan's coastal campaign and international politics (Alexander Balas, Demetrius II and Ptolemy VI)	1 Maccabees 10.67-11.19; *Ant* **XIII** 86-119 / **XIII** iv.3-8	2	200	
	d Religious and territorial concessions by Demetrius II to Jonathan	Maccabees 11.20-37; *Ant* **XIII** 120-30 / **XIII** iv.9		199	
	e Jonathan's relations with competing Seleucid rulers (Demetrius II, Antiochus VI), Rome and Sparta	1 Maccabees 11.28-12.38; *Ant* **XIII** 131-70, 174-86 / **XIII** v.1-9, 11	8	201-204	
	f Trypho's campaign in Judaea and Jonathan's capture and death	1 Maccabees 12.39-13.30; *Ant* **XIII** 187-212 / **XIII** vi.1-6	6,2,	205	
11-9	**Hasmonaean Independence I: Simon, John Hyrcanus and Aristobulus I**				
	a Simon: Hasmonaean independence: new political, territorial and religious realities	1 Maccabees 13.31-16.24; *Ant.* **XIII** 213-29 / **XIII** vi.7-vii.4	1,2	206,207	
	b John Hyrcanus: expansion into Transjordan, Idumaea, Samaria and coastal plain	*Ant.* **XIII** 230-300 / **XIII** viii.1-x.7; *War* **I** 54-69 / **I** ii.3-8	10,12,16	208,209,210	
	c Aristobulus I: war on the Ituraeans and expansion into Galilee	*Ant.* **XIII** 301-19 / **XIII** xi.1-3; *War* **I** 70-84 / **I** iii.1-6		212	
	d Book of Judith (place-names in black)	Judith	10	211	
11-10 (north) and 11-11 (south)	**Hasmonaean Independence II: Alexander Jannaeus, Alexandra, Hyrcanus II and Aristobulus II**				
	a Alexander Jannaeus: unsuccessful campaign against Ptolemais; battles of Asochis and Asophon	*Ant.* **XIII** 320-55 / **XIII** xii.1-xiii.2; *War* **I** 85-6 / **I** iv.1-2	4,6		
	b Alexander Jannaeus: campaigns in Transjordan and the coastlands; the extent of his kingdom	*Ant.* **XIII** 356-64, 374, 387-97 / **XIII** xiii.3, 5; xv.1-4; *War* **I** 87, 99-106 / **I** iv.2, 7-8	3,5,8	213	
	c Alexander Jannaeus: the struggle against foreign and internal enemies; his death	*Ant* **XIII** 372-83, 398-404 / **XIII** xiii.5-xiv.2; *War* **I** 88-98, 105, 106 / **I** iv.3-6, 8	4,8		
	d Alexandra Salome: increasing internal strife and external threats	*Ant.* **XIII** 405-32 / **XIII** xvi.1-6; *War* **I** 107-19 / **I** v.1-4			
	e Hyrcanus II and Aristobulus II: the fraternal war; Antipater (the Idumaean), the Nabataeans and Rome	*Ant* **XIV** 1-33 / **XIV** i.1-ii.3; *War* **I** 120-30 / **I** vi.1-3	4		

Hellenistic and Hasmonaean Periods

Map No.	Subject	Primary sources	Regional Map Nos. (Section 1)	Macmillan Bible Atlas Map Nos.	Other references and notes
11-12	**Hasmonaean internal strife and Decline I**				
	a Pompey's campaign against Aristobulus II and the fall of Jerusalem	*Ant.* **XIV** 34-73 / **XIV** iii.1-iv.4		214,215	
		War **I** 131-154 / **I** vi.4-viii.6			
	b Territorial reorganization by Pompey; Antipater's arrangement between Rome and the Nabataeans	*Ant.* **XIV** 74-81 / **XIV** iv.4-v.1	2,5,9	216	
		War **I** 155-159 / **I** vii.7-viii.1			
	c Gabinius, governor of Syria: further attempts at reorganization and unsuccessful revolts	*Ant.* **XIV** 82-104 / **XIV** v.2-vi.4	4,12	216	
		War **I** 160-78 / **I** viii.2-7			
11-13	**Hasmonaean internal strife and Decline II**				
	a Crassus, Cassius, the Parthian threat and Antipater of Idumaea	*Ant.* **XIV** 105-122 / **XIV** vii.1-3			
		War **I** 179-82 / **I** viii.8-9			
	b Julius Caesar in the east; the Jews and the rise of Antipater and his family	*Ant.* **XIV** 123-270 / **XIV** vii.4-xi.1	1,5	217	
		War **I** 183-217 / **I** ix.1-x.10			
	c Cassius' oppression, Antipater's assasination, Mark Antony, Parthian invasion, Herod's flight to Rome	*Ant.* **XIV** 271-380 / **XIV** xi.2-xiv.3	4,14	218	
		War **I** 218-81 / **I** xi.1-xiv.3			
	d Herod, the king, returns to conquer Galilee and Judaea and to frustrate Hasmonaean power	*Ant.* **XIV** 381-491 / **XIV** xiv.4-xvi.4	1,4,5,6,9,14	219	
		War **I** 282-357 / **I** xi.4-xviii.3			

Notes

Section 11–1

Hellenistic-Hasmonean Period

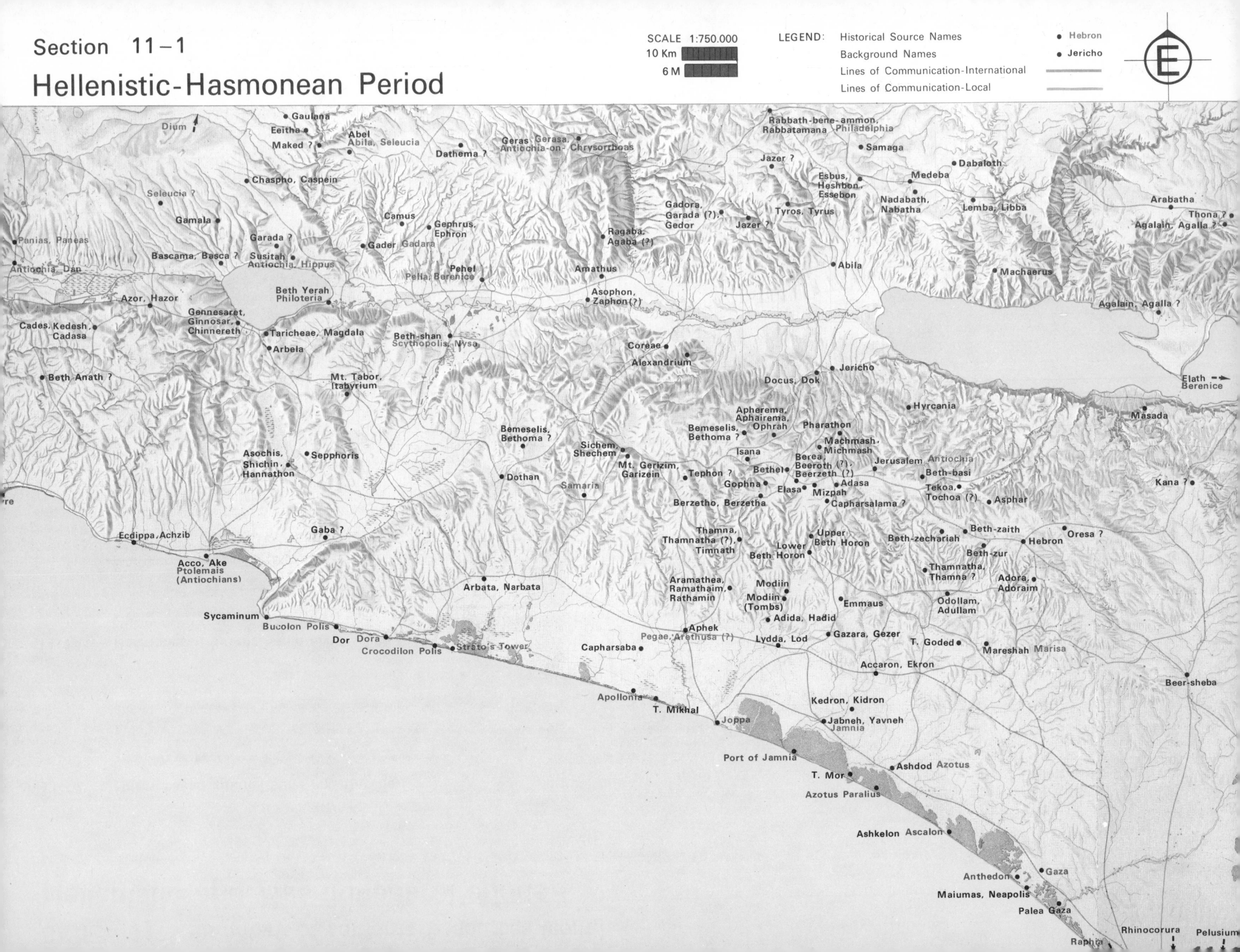

SCALE 1:750.000
10 Km
6 M

LEGEND: Historical Source Names • Hebron
Background Names • Jericho
Lines of Communication-International
Lines of Communication-Local

Gaulana
Dium
Eeitha
Maked ?
Abel
Abila, Seleucia
Dathema ?
Geras Gerasa, Antiochia-on- Chrysorrhoas
Rabbath-bene-ammon, Rabbatamana Philadelphia
Samaga
Jazer ?
Dabaloth
Esbus, Heshbon, Essebon
Medeba
Chaspho, Caspein
Seleucia ?
Gamala
Camus
Gephrus, Ephron
Gadora, Garada (?), Gedor
Tyros, Tyrus
Jazer ?
Nadabath, Nabatha
Lemba, Libba
Arabatha
Thona ?
Agalain, Agalla ?
Panias, Paneas
Garada ?
Gader Gadara
Ragaba, Agaba (?)
Bascama, Basca ?
Susitah, Antiochia, Hippus
Antiochia, Dan
Pehel
Pella, Berenice
Amathus
Abila
Machaerus
Azor, Hazor
Beth Yerah Philoteria
Asophon, Zaphon (?)
Agalain, Agalla ?
Cades, Kedesh, Cadasa
Gennesaret, Ginnosar, Chinnereth
Taricheae, Magdala
Arbela
Beth-shan Scythopolis, Nysa
Coreae
Alexandrium
Jericho
Docus, Dok
Elath Berenice
Beth Anath ?
Mt. Tabor, Itabyrium
Hyrcania
Masada
Apherema, Aphairema, Ophrah
Pharathon
Bemeselis, Bethoma ?
Bemeselis, Bethoma ?
Machmash, Michmash
Sichem, Shechem
Isana
Berea, Beeroth (?), Beerzeth (?)
Jerusalem Antiochia
Asochis, Shichin, Hannathon
Sepphoris
Mt. Gerizim, Garizein
Tephon ?
Bethel
Beth-basi
Dothan
Samaria
Gophna
Elasa
Adasa
Mizpah
Tekoa, Tochoa (?)
Asphar
Kana ?
Berzetho, Berzetha
Capharsalama ?
Ecdippa, Achzib
Gaba ?
Thamna, Thamnatha (?), Timnath
Upper Beth Horon
Lower Beth Horon
Beth-zechariah
Beth-zaith
Hebron
Oresa ?
Beth-zur
Acco, Ake Ptolemais (Antiochians)
Thamnatha, Thamna ?
Arbata, Narbata
Aramathea, Ramathaim, Rathamin
Modiin
Modiin (Tombs)
Adora, Adoraim
Emmaus
Odollam, Adullam
Sycaminum
Bucolon Polis
Adida, Hadid
Dor Dora
Crocodilon Polis
Strato's Tower
Aphek
Pegae, Arethusa (?)
Capharsaba
Lydda, Lod
Gazara, Gezer
T. Goded
Mareshah Marisa
Accaron, Ekron
Beer-sheba
Apollonia
T. Mikhal
Kedron, Kidron
Joppa
Jabneh, Yavneh
Jamnia
Port of Jamnia
Ashdod Azotus
T. Mor
Azotus Paralius
Ashkelon Ascalon
Gaza
Anthedon
Maiumas, Neapolis
Palea Gaza
Rhinocorura
Pelusium
Raphia

Section 11–2

Hellenistic-Hasmonean Period

SCALE 1:750.000
10 Km
6 M

LEGEND:
Historical Source Names • Hebron
Background Names • Jericho
Lines of Communication-International
Lines of Communication-Local

Lacasa
Naveh
Eeitha
Abila
Gerasa
Rabbath-bene-ammon, Philadelphia
Tyros
Camus
Gephrus
Panias
Dan
Hippus
Gadara
Abila
Pella
Petra
Philoteria
Cadasa
Cades
Nysa, Scythopolis, Beth-shan
Beth Anath ?
Jericho
Berenice, Elath
En-gedi
Mt. Tabor
Acrabeta
Apherema
Shechem
Mt. Gerizim, Garizein
Samaria
Bethel
Jerusalem
Tyre
T. Kison
Arad
Thamna, Timnah
Lower Beth Horon
Beth-zur
Hebron
Ecdippa, Achzib
Acco, Ptolemais
Narbata, Arbatta
Aramathea
Adora
Keilah
T. Zeror
Sycaminum
Pegae
Gazara
Lod, Lydda
Bucolon Polis
Dora
Crocodilon Polis
Strato's Tower
T. Goded
Mareshah Marisa
Beer-sheba
Apollonia
T. Mikhal
Joppa
Jamnia, Jabneh
Port of Jamnia
Ashdod Azotus
T. Mor
Azotus Paralius
Ashkelon Ascalon
Anthedon
Gaza
T. Gamma
Palea Gaza
Raphia
Pelusium

Section 11–3

Hellenistic-Hasmonean Period

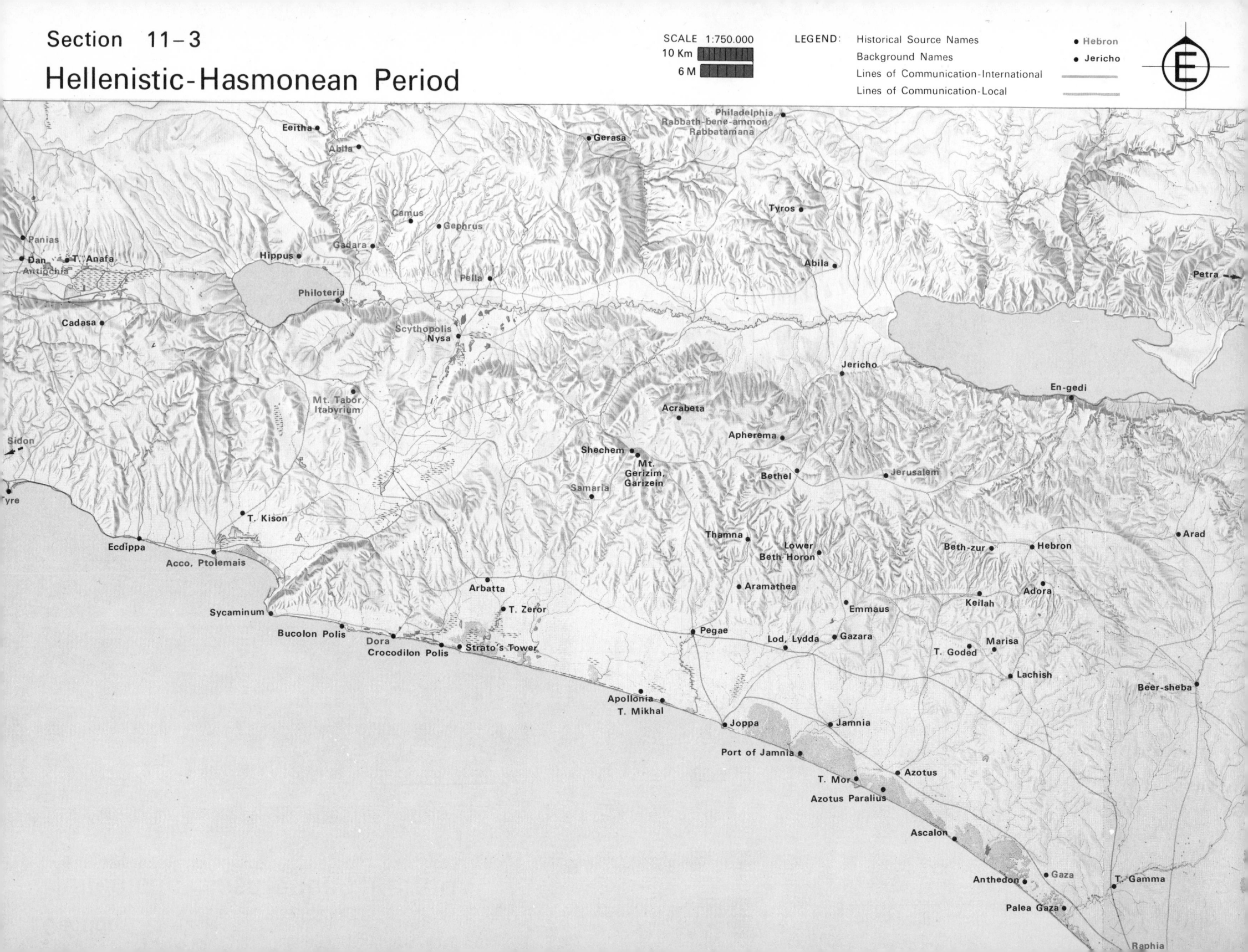

SCALE 1:750.000
10 Km
6 M

LEGEND: Historical Source Names • Hebron
Background Names • Jericho
Lines of Communication-International
Lines of Communication-Local

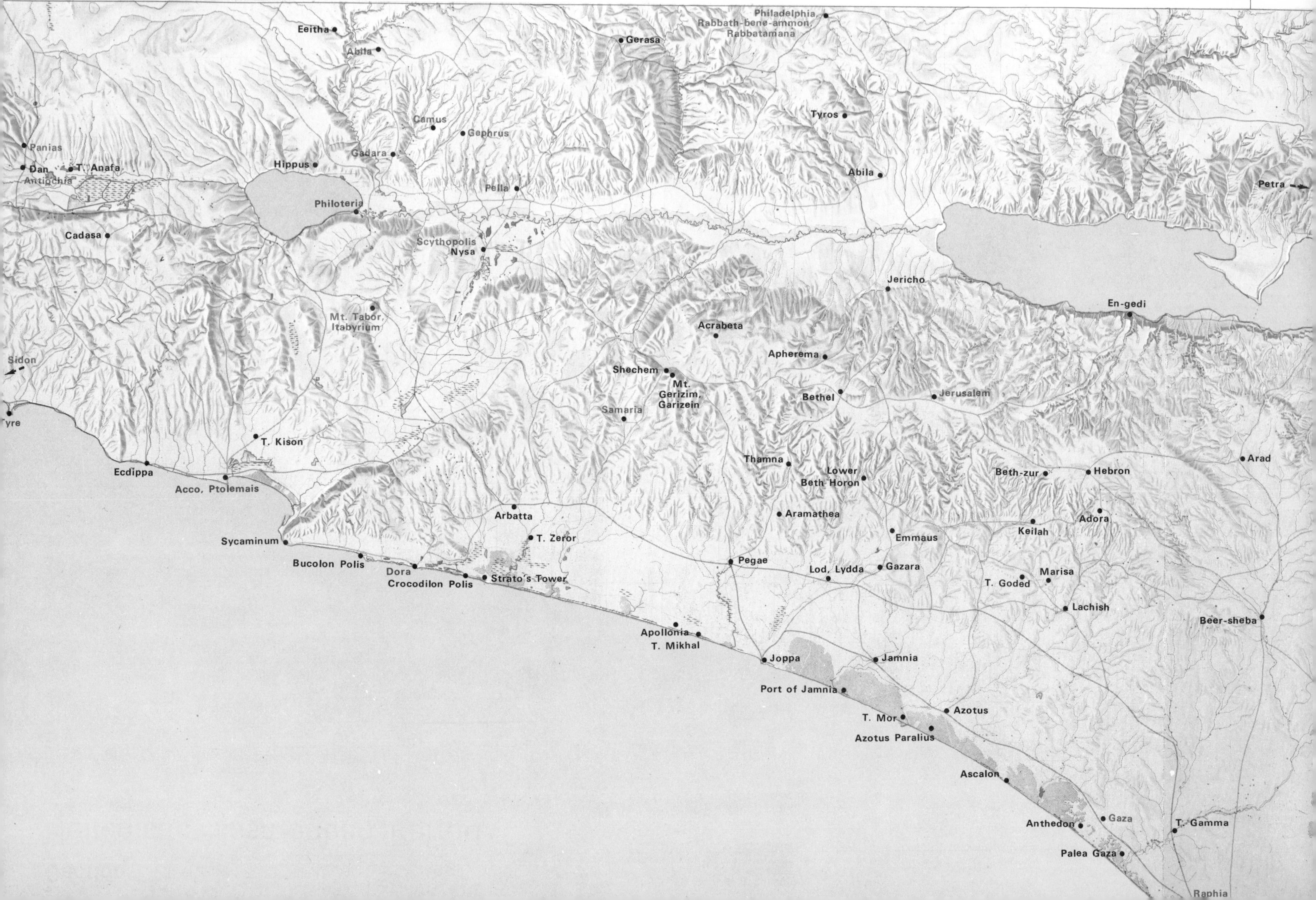

Eeitha
Gerasa
Philadelphia, Rabbath-bene-ammon, Rabbatamana
Abila
Camus
Gephrus
Tyros
Panias
Gadara
Hippus
Dan
T. Anafa
Antiochia
Pella
Abila
Petra
Philoteria
Cadasa
Scythopolis
Nysa
Jericho
Mt. Tabor, Itabyrium
En-gedi
Acrabeta
Apherema
Sidon
Shechem
Mt. Gerizim, Garizein
Bethel
Jerusalem
Samaria
Tyre
T. Kison
Thamna
Arad
Ecdippa
Lower Beth Horon
Beth-zur
Hebron
Acco, Ptolemais
Arbatta
Aramathea
Adora
Keilah
Emmaus
Sycaminum
T. Zeror
Bucolon Polis
Pegae
Lod, Lydda
Gazara
Dora
Crocodilon Polis
Strato's Tower
Marisa
T. Goded
Lachish
Beer-sheba
Apollonia
T. Mikhal
Joppa
Jamnia
Port of Jamnia
Azotus
T. Mor
Azotus Paralius
Ascalon
Gaza
Anthedon
T. Gamma
Palea Gaza
Raphia

Section 11–4

Hellenistic-Hasmonean Period

SCALE 1:300.000
10 Km
6 M

LEGEND:
Historical Source Names — Hebron
Background Names — Jericho
Lines of Communication-International
Lines of Communication-Local

Coreae
Jericho
Acrabeta
Pharathon
Apherema
Shechem
Mt. Gerizim, Garizein
Machmas
Lebonah
Bethel
Antiochia Jerusalem
T. el-Ful
Beth-basi
Berea
Gophna
Mizpah
Adasa
Ramat Rahel
Elasa
Samaria
Berzetho
Tekoa
Capharsalama ?
Upper Beth Horon
Beth-zechariah
Thamna
Kiriath-jearim
Bethsura Beth-zur
Hebron
Lower Beth Horon
Aramathea, Ramathaim
Adora
Odollam
Keilah
Modiin
Modiin (Tombs)
Emmaus
Adida
Pegae
Gazara, Gezer
T. Goded
Lod, Lydda
Marisa
Yehud
Apollonia
Joppa
Jamnia
Accaron
Azotus
Lachish

Section 11–5

Hellenistic-Hasmonean Period

SCALE 1:600.000
10 Km
6 M

LEGEND: Historical Source Names • Hebron
Background Names • Jericho
Lines of Communication-International
Lines of Communication-Local

Philadelphia
Raphon
Carnaim
Bosor
Dathema ?
Alema
Charax
Bozrah, Bostra
Dathema ?
Gerasa
Maked
Maker ?
Abila
Chaspho, Caspein
Jazer ?
Medeba
Tyros
Jazer ?
Baal-meon
Ephron
Panias
Gadara
Dan, Antiochia
T. Anafa
Hippus
Pella
Philoteria
Cadasa
Gennesaret
Scythopolis, Beth-shan
Caves
Arbela
Jericho
Mt. Tabor, Itabyrium
Acrabeta
Apherema
Machmas
Shechem
Mt. Gerizim, Garizein
Antiochia
Jerusalem
Beth-basi
Bethel
Gophna
Adasa
Tekoa
Samaria
Berea
Berzetho
Capharsalama ?
T. Kison
Thamna
Beth-zechariah
Lower Beth Horon
Kiriath-jearim
Ecdippa
Ptolemais
Arbatta
Aramathea, Ramathaim
Modiin
Odollam
Emmaus
Sycaminum
Adida
Bucolon Polis
Pegae
Gazara
Dora
Lydda, Lod
T. Goded
Strato's Tower
Accaron
Apollonia
T. Mikhal
Joppa
Jamnia
Port of Jamnia

Section 11–6

Hellenistic-Hasmonean Period

SCALE 1:300.000

10 Km

6 M

LEGEND: Historical Source Names • Hebron

Background Names • Jericho

Lines of Communication-International

Lines of Communication-Local

E
Apherema
Shechem
Mt. Gerizim, Garizein
Machmas
Bethel
Berea
T. el-Ful
Antiochia, Jerusalem
Beth-basi
Gophna
Adasa
Ramat Rahel
Elasa
Tekoa
Samaria
Berzetho, Berzetha
Capharsalama ?
Upper Beth Horon
Thamna
Kiriath-jearim
Beth-zechariah
Beth-zaith
Hebron
Beth-zur, Bethsura
Lower Beth Horon
Aramathea, Ramathaim
Adora
Adullam, Odollam
Keilah
Modiin
Modiin (Tombs)
Emmaus
Adida
Pegae
Gazara
Lydda, Lod
T. Goded
Marisa
Accaron
Lachish
Apollonia
T. Mikhal
Joppa
Jamnia
Port of Jamnia

©

Section 11–7

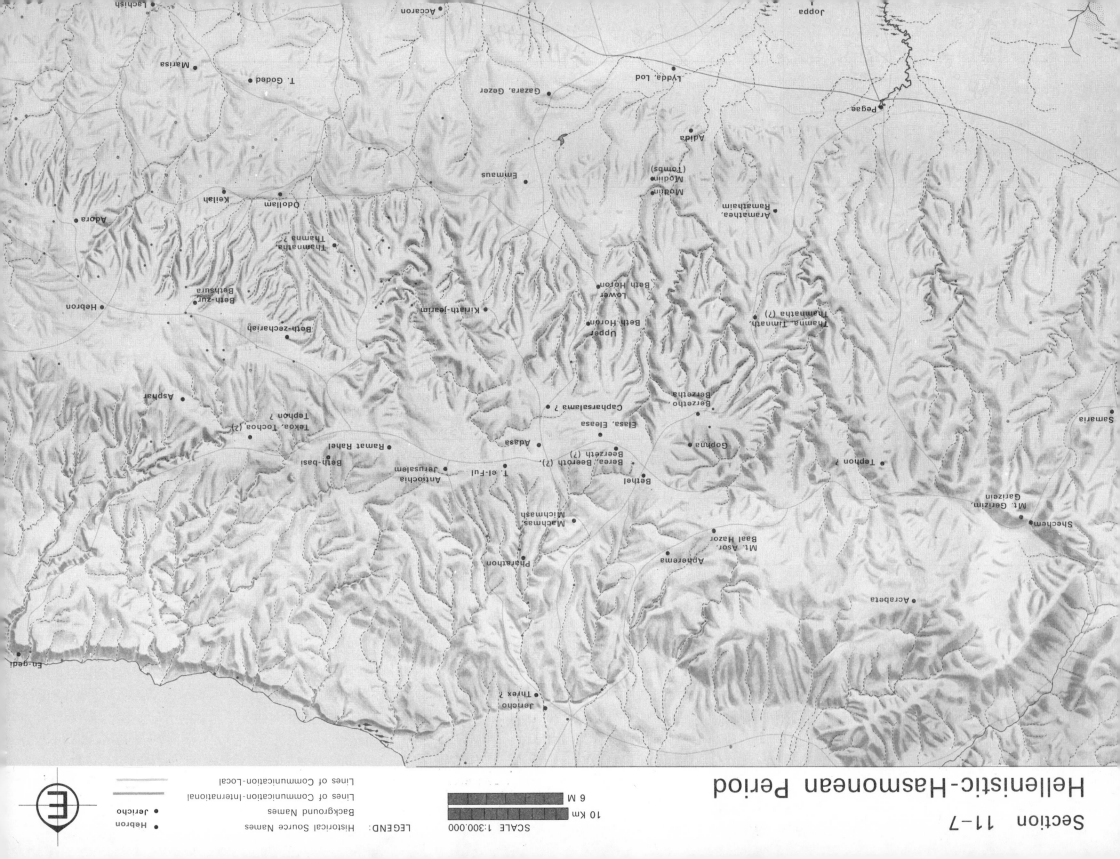

Hellenistic-Hasmonean Period

SCALE 1:300.000
10 Km
6 M

LEGEND: Historical Source Names — • Hebron
Background Names — • Jericho
Lines of Communication-International
Lines of Communication-Local

Jericho
Threx ?
En-gedi
Acrabeta
Apherema
Mt. Asor, Baal Hazor
Pharathon
Shechem
Mt. Gerizim, Garizein
Machmas, Michmash
Bethel
Tephon ?
Berea, Beeroth (?), Beerzeth (?)
T. el-Ful
Antiochia
Jerusalem
Beth-basi
Gophna
Adasa
Ramat Rahel
Samaria
Elasa, Eleasa
Tekoa, Tochoa (?)
Tephon ?
Berzetho, Berzetha
Capharsalama ?
Asphar
Upper Beth Horon
Thamna, Timnath, Thamnatha (?)
Beth-zechariah
Kiriath-jearim
Hebron
Lower Beth Horon
Beth-zur, Bethsura
Thamnatha, Thamna ?
Aramathea, Ramathaim
Adora
Odollam
Keilah
Modiin
Modiin (Tombs)
Emmaus
Adida
Pegae
Gazara, Gezer
T. Goded
Lydda, Lod
Marisa
Joppa
Accaron
Lachish

Section 11–8

Hellenistic-Hasmonean Period

SCALE 1:600.000
10 Km
6 M

LEGEND: Historical Source Names — • Hebron
Background Names — • Jericho
Lines of Communication-International
Lines of Communication-Local

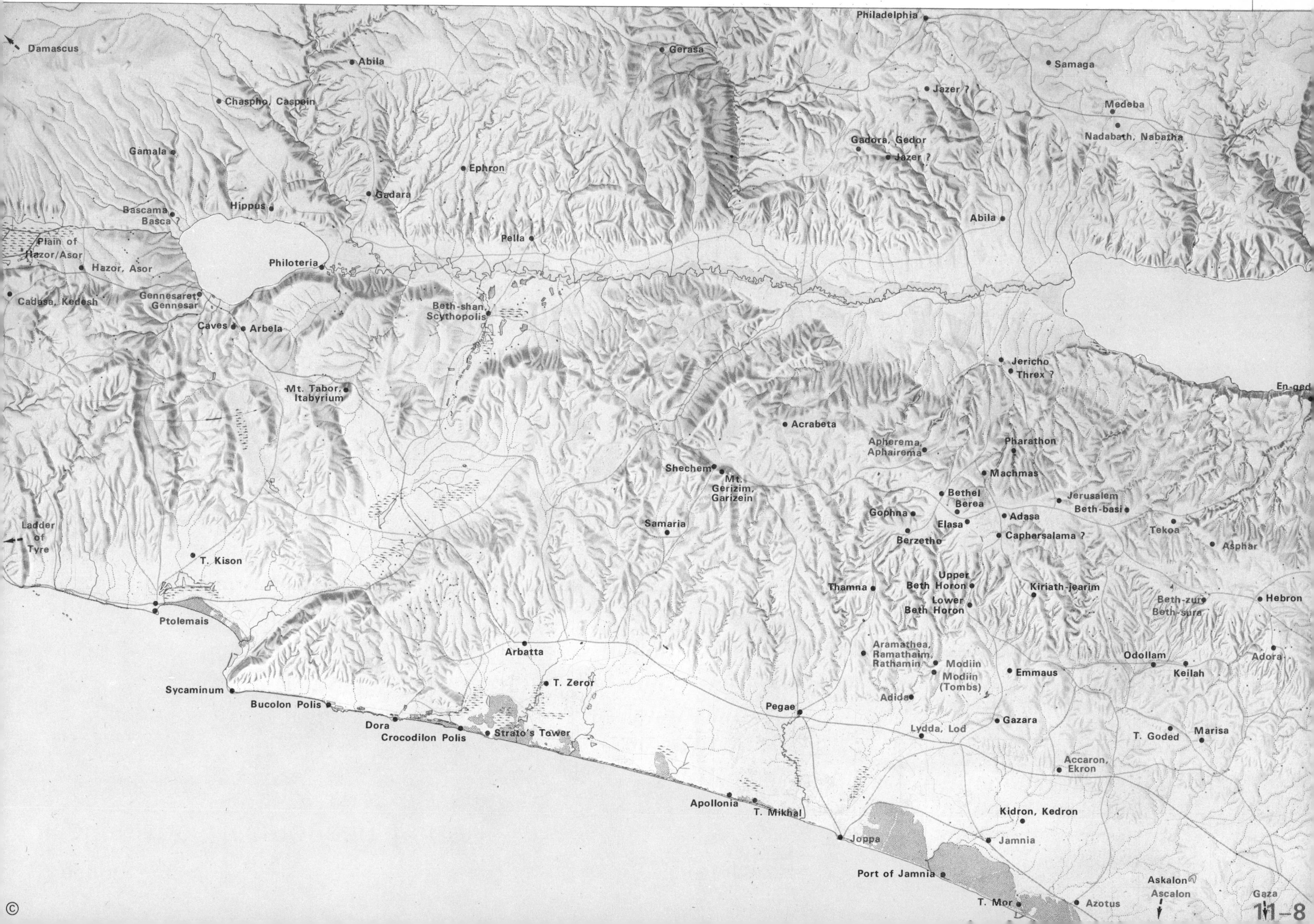

Damascus
Abila
Chaspho, Caspein
Gamala
Ephron
Gadara
Hippus
Bascama
Basca ?
Plain of
Hazor/Asor
Hazor, Asor
Cadasa, Kedesh
Gennesaret,
Gennesar
Caves
Arbela
Philoteria
Pella
Beth-shan,
Scythopolis
Mt. Tabor,
Itabyrium
Gerasa
Philadelphia
Samaga
Jazer ?
Medeba
Nadabath, Nabatha
Gadora, Gedor
Jazer ?
Abila
Jericho
Threx ?
En-ged
Acrabeta
Apherema,
Aphairema
Pharathon
Machmas
Shechem
Mt.
Gerizim,
Garizein
Bethel
Berea
Jerusalem
Beth-basi
Gophna
Elasa
Adasa
Samaria
Berzetho
Capharsalama ?
Tekoa
Asphar
Ladder
of
Tyre
T. Kison
Upper
Beth Horon
Thamna
Lower
Beth Horon
Kiriath-jearim
Beth-zur
Beth-sura
Hebron
Ptolemais
Arbatta
Aramathea,
Ramathaim,
Rathamin
Modiin
Modiin
(Tombs)
Emmaus
Odollam
Keilah
Adora
T. Zeror
Sycaminum
Bucolon Polis
Adida
Pegae
Dora
Crocodilon Polis
Strato's Tower
Gazara
Lydda, Lod
T. Goded
Marisa
Accaron,
Ekron
Apollonia
T. Mikhal
Kidron, Kedron
Joppa
Jamnia
Port of Jamnia
Askalon
Ascalon
T. Mor
Azotus
Gaza

Section 11–9

Hellenistic-Hasmonean Period

SCALE 1:750.000
10 Km
6 M
LEGEND: Historical Source Names
Background Names
Lines of Communication-International
Lines of Communication-Local
Hebron
Jericho
E
Gaulan
Philadelphia
Gerasa
Samaga
Abila
Aesora ?
Dabaloth
Medeba
Esbus
Seleucia ?
Gamala
Gadora
Rabbath Moab
Lemba
Thona
Agalain ?
Ragaba
Panias
Gadara
Hippus
Abila
Beth-ramatha
Dan,
T. Anafa
Antiochia
Amathus
Pella
Philoteria
Agalain ?
Salem ?
Cadasa
Gennesaret
Taricheae
Beth-shan
Scythopolis
Choba ?
Arbela
Belmain,
Belman
Cola,
Conas, Kona
Mezad Hasidim,
Kh. Qumran
Jericho
Gischala
Threx ?
Mt. Tabor,
Itabyrium
Docus Dok
En-gedi
(G)Araba
Dabaritta
Salem
Acrabeta,
Aqraba, Ekrebel
Esdraelon
Gerasa
Apherema
Balamo
Sichem
Shechem
Machmas
Asochis
Sepphoris
Mt.
Gerizim,
Garizein
Chusi ?
Bethel
Jerusalem
Mahalol
Geba
Dothan
Gophna
Samaria
Tekoa
Capercotnei
Sur
Aristobulias
T. Kison
Upper
Beth Horon
Kiriath-jearim
Arad
Geba ?
Thamna
Cyamon
Lower
Beth Horon
Beth-zur
Hebron
Ecdippa
Ptolemais
Acco, Ocina
Aramathea
Malatha
Adora
Arbatta
Modiin
Emmaus
T. Zeror
Adida
Sycaminum
Pegae
Gazara
Marisa
Bucolon Polis
Lydda, Lod
Dora
T. Goded
Strato's Tower
Crocodilon Polis
Capharsaba
Accaron
Beer-sheba
Apollonia
T. Mikhal
Kidron, Kedron
Joppa
Jamnia Jemnaan
Port of Jamnia
Azotus
T. Mor
Azotus Paralius
Orda
Ascalon
Gaza
Anthedon
Raphia

Section 11–10
Hellenistic-Hasmonean Period

SCALE 1:750.000
10 Km
6 M

LEGEND: Historical Source Names • Hebron
Background Names • Jericho
Lines of Communication-International
Lines of Communication-Local

Damascus
Gaulana
Dium
Abila
Philadelphia
Gerasa
Samaga
Dabaloth
Esbus
Medeba
Tyros
Nadabath
Lemba, Libba
Arabatha
Gadora
Garada
Thona, Athone ?
Agalain, Agalla
Seleucia ?
Gamala
Ragaba, Agaba (?)
Panias
Garada ?
Hippus
Gadara
Beth-ramatha
Machaerus
Dan
T. Anafa
Antiochia
Amathus
Pella
Philoteria
Asophon
Agalain, Agalla ?
Cadasa
Gennesaret
Taricheae
Scythopolis
Coreae
Arbela
Alexandrium
Mezad Hasidim, Kh. Qumran
Gischala
Jericho
Threx ?
Mt. Tabor, Itabyrium
Docus, Dok
En-gedi
Acrabeta
Hyrcania
(G)Araba
Salem
Masada
Esdraelon
Bemeselis, Bethoma ?
Bemeselis, Bethoma ?
Apherema
Sichem, Shechem
Mt. Gerizim, Garizein
Machmas
Sepphoris
Asochis
Bethel
T. el-Ful
Jerusalem
Dothan
Ramat Rahel
Gophna
Kana ?
Samaria
Tekoa
Tyre
Aristobulias
Gaba ?
Kiriath-jearim
Thamna
Lower Beth Horon
Beth-zur
Hebron
Ecdippa
Ptolemais
Arbata
Aramathea
Zanoah
Malatha
Adora
Modiin
Keilah
Emmaus
T. Zeror
Sycaminum
Adida
Pegae
Arethusa ?
Dora
Lydda, Lod
T. Goded
Strato's Tower
Marisa
Chab(ph)arsaba
Accaron
Bersabee, Beer-sheba
Apollonia
T. Mikhal
Joppa
Jamnia
Port of Jamnia
Azotus
T. Mor
Azotus Paralius
Orda
Ascalon
Gaza
Anthedon
Raphia
Rhinocorur

Section 11–11

Hellenistic-Hasmonean Period

SCALE 1:750.000
10 Km
6 M

LEGEND: Historical Source Names
Background Names
Lines of Communication-International
Lines of Communication-Local

• Hebron
• Jericho

E
Philadelphia
Gerasa
Samaga
Dabaloth
Essebon, Esbus
Medeba
Tyros
Nadabath
Lemba, Libba
Gadora
Garada ?
Ragaba, Agaba (?)
Beth-ramatha
Amathus
Machaerus
Asophon
Arabatha
Thona, Athone ?
Agalain , Agalla ?
Kh. et-Tannur
Oronaim
Gobolis
Agalain, Agalla ?
Coreae
Alexandrium
Mezad Hasidim, Kh. Qumran
Jericho
Docus
Threx ?
Zoara
Petra
En-gedi
Salem
Acrabeta
Hyrcania
Masada
Apherema
Sichem, Shechem
Mt. Gerizim, Garizein
Machmas
Bethel
T. el-Ful
Jerusalem
Ramat Rahel
Gophna
Samaria
Tekoa
Kana ?
Aristobulias
Thamna
Kiriath-jearim
Lower Beth Horon
Beth-zur
Hebron
Aramathea
Modiin
Zanoah
Adora
Malatha
Emmaus
Keilah
Adida
Pegae
Arethusa ?
Lydda, Lod
T. Goded
Marisa
Chab(ph)arsaba
Accaron
Bersabee, Beer-sheba
Apollonia
T. Mikhal
Joppa
Jamnia
Oboda
Orybda ?
Arydda ?
Port of Jamnia
T. Mor
Azotus
Elusa
Alousa, Alusa ?
Azotus Paralius
Orda
Ascalon
Gaza
Anthedon
Nessana
Raphia
Rhinocorura

Section 11–12

Hellenistic-Hasmonean Period

SCALE 1:750.000
10 Km
6 M

LEGEND: Historical Source Names • Hebron
Background Names • Jericho
Lines of Communication-International
Lines of Communication-Local

Damascus
Dium
Abila
Gerasa
Philadelphia
Samaga
Dabaloth
Esbus
Medeba
Nadabath
Lemba, Libba
Arabatha
Thona ?
Agalain ?
Gamala
Panias
Gadora
Tyros
Ragaba
Gadara
Hippus
Beth-ramatha
Antiochia, Dan
Amathus
Pella
Machaerus
Petra
Philoteria
Cadasa
Gennesaret
Taricheae
Arbela
Scythopolis
Coreae
Alexandrium
Mezad Hasidim,
Kh. Qumran
Gischala
Mt. Tabor,
Itabyrium
Jericho
Threx ?
En-gedi
(G)Araba
Esdraelon
Salem
Acrabeta
Hyrcania
Masada
Apherema
Sepphoris
Sichem,
Shechem
Isana
Machmas
Asochis
Mt. Gerizim,
Garizein
Dothan
Bethel
T. el-Ful
Jerusalem
Ramat Rahel
Samaria
Gophna
Tekoa
yre
Gaba ?
Ecdippa
Thamna
Lower
Beth Horon
Kiriath-jearim
Hebron
Ptolemais
Arbatta
Aramathea
Zanoah
Adora
Modiin
Emmaus
Keilah
Sycaminum
T. Zeror
Adida
Arethusa ?
Dora
Strato's Tower
Capharsaba
Lydda, Lod
T. Goded
Marisa
Accaron
Bersabee,
Beer-sheba
Apollonia
T. Mikhal
Joppa
Jamnia
Port of Jamnia
Azotus
T. Mor
Azotus Paralius
Ascalon
Orda
Anthedon
Gaza
Raphia
Pelusium

Section 11–13

Hellenistic-Hasmonean Period

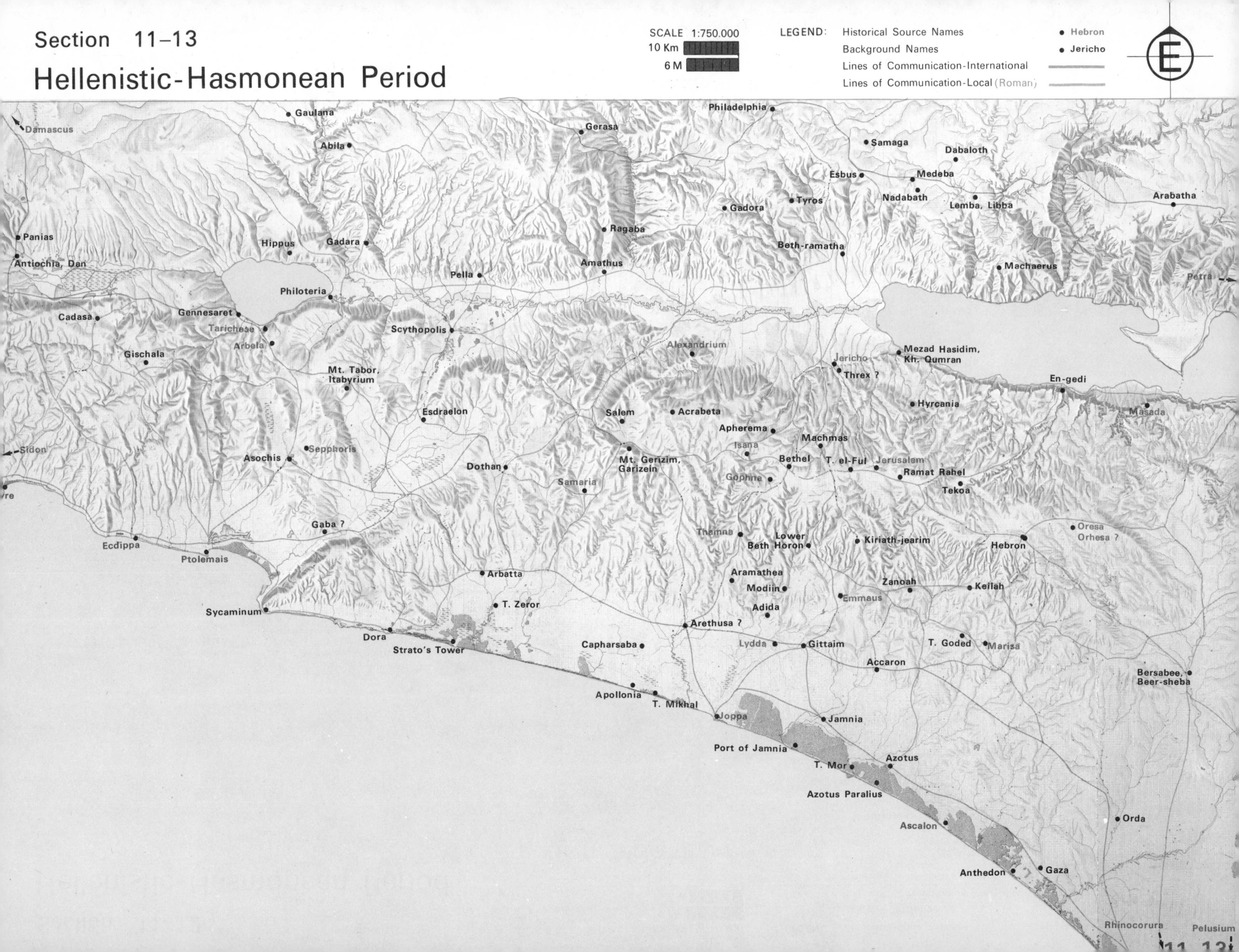

SCALE 1:750.000
10 Km
6 M

LEGEND: Historical Source Names • Hebron
Background Names • Jericho
Lines of Communication-International
Lines of Communication-Local (Roman)

Damascus
Gaulana
Abila
Gerasa
Philadelphia
Samaga
Dabaloth
Esbus
Medeba
Nadabath
Lemba, Libba
Arabatha
Tyros
Gadora
Ragaba
Panias
Hippus
Gadara
Beth-ramatha
Antiochia, Dan
Amathus
Pella
Machaerus
Petra
Philoteria
Gennesaret
Cadasa
Tarichеae
Scythopolis
Arbela
Alexandrium
Gischala
Mezad Hasidim,
Kh. Qumran
Jericho
Threx ?
Mt. Tabor,
Itabyrium
En-gedi
Hyrcania
Masada
Esdraelon
Salem
Acrabeta
Apherema
Machmas
Isana
Sidon
Sepphoris
Asochis
Bethel
T. el-Ful
Jerusalem
Ramat Rahel
Dothan
Mt. Gerizim,
Garizein
Gophna
Samaria
Tekoa
Gaba ?
Thamna
Lower
Beth Horon
Kiriath-jearim
Hebron
Oresa
Orhesa ?
Ecdippa
Ptolemais
Arbatta
Aramathea
Modiin
Zanoah
Keilah
Emmaus
Adida
T. Zeror
Sycaminum
Arethusa ?
Dora
Strato's Tower
Capharsaba
Lydda
Gittaim
T. Goded
Marisa
Accaron
Bersabee,
Beer-sheba
Apollonia
T. Mikhal
Joppa
Jamnia
Port of Jamnia
Azotus
T. Mor
Azotus Paralius
Ascalon
Orda
Anthedon
Gaza
Rhinocorura
Pelusium

Section 12 Summary of contents & sources
Herodian Period

MAIN BIBLICAL REF.: The Four Gospels and the Acts of the Apostles
MAIN HISTORICAL REF.: *Ant.* **XV** 1 – **XX** 258/**XV** i.1 – **XX** xi.1
War **I** 358 – **VII** 455/**I** xviii.4 – **VII** xi.5

Map No.	Subject	Primary sources		Regional Map Nos. (Section 1)	Macmillan Bible Atlas Map Nos.	Other references and notes
12-1	**Overview and administration in Jewish territory**					
	a Overview (north)					
	b Jewish administrative organization in Judaea, Across-the-Jordan (Peraea) and Galilee during the Herodian period	*War* **III** 54-56	**III** iii.5			
		Pliny, *Natural History* V.70 (GLAJJ, 1974, 468-481)				
		War **II** 252, 566-568, 629	**II** xiii.2, xx.4, xxi.7			
		War **IV** 413	**IV** vii.3			
		Note Avi-Yonah 1977: 94-101				
12-2	**Reign of king Herod: selected passages**					
	a Mark Antony grants Cleopatra territory at Herod's expense	*Ant.* **XV** 88-107	**XV** iv.1-4	4		
		War **I** 359-363	**I** xviii.4-5			
	b Earthquake of 31 B.C./B.C.E and Herod's war with the Arabs (Nabataeans)	*Ant.* **XV** 108-160	**XV** v.1-5	12		
		War **I** 364-385	**I** xix.1-6			
	c Herod's rule confirmed and his territory enlarged by Octavian	*Ant.* **XV** 183-217	**XV** vi.5-vii.3		220	
		War **I** 386-397	**I** xx.1-3			
	d Additional territorial grants to Herod by Augustus (Octavian); Herod's war with the Arabs (Nabataeans)	*Ant.* **XV** 342-364	**XV** x.1-3	8,13	220	
		War **I** 398-406	**I** xx.4-xxi.3			
	e Herod erects temples and palaces, builds cities, and fortifies strategic positions	*Ant.* **XV** 267-341, 363-364, 380-425	**XV** viii.1-ix.6, x.3, xi 1-7	5,8,13,14	220,221	
		Ant. **XVI** 12-15, 136-159	**XVI** ii.1, v.1-4			
		War **I** 401-428	**I** xxi.1-12			
		Appian, *Civil Wars*				
	f Conflict and settlement programme in Trachonitis and Batanaea (These regions not covered in Student Maps or Manual)	*Ant.* **XVI** 271-99, 335-55	**XVI** ix, x.8-9		220	
		Ant. **XVII** 23-28	**XVII** ii.1-2			
	g Herod's last days, his last will, death and burial	*Ant.* **XVII** 146-199	**XVII** vi.1-viii.3			
		War **I** 647-673	**I** xxxiii.1-9	14		
	h Birth of John the Baptist and Jesus in Judaea; the flight to Egypt	**Luke 1.5-2.40; Matthew 1.18-2.20**		6,13	225	
12-3	**Sons of Herod and direct rule by Rome in Judaea**					
	a Events following Herod's death: rebellions in Judaea; actions of Archelaus, Sabinius and Varus; Herod's last will debated before Augustus	*Ant.* **XVII** 200-316	**XVII** viii.4-xi.3	1,4,7		
		War **II** 1-92	**II** i.1-vi.2			
	b Augustus divides Herod's kingdom between Archelaus (ethnarch), Herod Antipas and Philip (tetrarchs)	*Ant.* **XVII** 317-320	**XVII** xi.4	5,13	222	
		War **II** 93-100	**II** vi.3			
	c Joseph, Mary and Jesus return from Egypt to Nazareth in Galilee	**Matthew 2.19-23**		6	226	
	d Archelaus' rule and exile; direct Roman rule in Judaea; Salome's territories	*Ant.* **XVII** 321-323, 339-344, 354-355	**XVII** xi.5, xiii.1-2, 5	4,8,9		
		Ant. **XVIII** 1-10, 26-38	**XVIII** i.1, ii.1-3			
		War **II** 111,117-119, 167-168	**II** vii.1, viii.1, ix.1			
	e Pilate's ten-year term as procurator of Judaea under Tiberius	*Ant.* **XVIII** 54-64, 85-95	**XVIII** iii.1-3, iv.1-3	1		
		War **II** 169-177	**II** ix.2-4			
	f Administrative organization during Jesus' ministry (cf. maps 12-4 to 10)	**Luke 3.1-3**			229	
	g Philip's death; Herod (Antipas), Herodias, John the Baptist and Roman-Arab relations; Agrippa I's travels under Tiberius; his rise under emperor Gaius Caligula and the exile of Herod (Antipas) and Herodias	*Ant.* **XVIII** 106-129, 143-204, 224-256	**XVIII** iv.6-v.3, vi.1-7, vi.10-vii.2	12	227	
		War **II** 178-183	**II** ix.5-6			
		Matthew 14.3-12; Mark 6.17-29; Luke 3.19-20				

Herodian Period

Map No.	Subject	Primary sources	Regional Map Nos. (Section 1)	Macmillan Bible Atlas Map Nos.	Other references and notes
12-4	The four Gospels	**Matthew, Mark, Luke, John** *Ant.* **XVIII** 119 **XVIII** v.2		225-237	
12-5	Detail: central Judaea, southern Peraea				
12-6	Detail: Samaria, northern Peraea, Beth-shan/Scythopolis valley				
12-7	Detail: Upper and Lower Galilee				
12-8	Detail: Sea of Galilee and environs				
12-9	Detail: central and western Judaea (Shephelah)				
	These detail regional maps (12-5 to 9) contain place-names of the four Gospels in red and a wide variety of important background names in black. These background names come mainly from section 12-11 to 13 and 13-5. Because of varying views on the chronology of the Gospels, no one system is presented here. The maps are designed for use in a variety of teaching contexts.				
12-10	Agrippa I and II, later procurators, the Acts of the Apostles				
	a Early ministry of Jesus' disciples in Judaea, Samaria and Syria; Saul's (Paul) conversion	**Acts 1-11; Luke 24.50-52; 2 Corinthians 11.30-33; Galatians 1.11-20**	1,5	238,242	
	b Reign of (Herod) Agrippa I				
	i) Gaius Caligula's attempt to erect his statue in Jerusalem and Agrippa I's mediation	*Ant.* **XVIII** 257-309 **XVIII** viii.1-9 *War* **II** 184-203 **II** x.1-5	8		
	ii) On Gaius Caligula's assassination Agrippa I mediates between Claudius and the Senate; Agrippa I's kingdom confirmed and enlarged; Claudius' decree regarding Jews	*Ant.* **XIX** 236-291 **XIX** iv.1-v.3 *War* **II** 204-217 **II** xi.1-5 **Acts 11.28**	8	249	
	iii) Agrippa I's return to Jerusalem and events during his four-year reign	*Ant.* **XIX** 292-342 **XIX** vi.1-viii.1 *War* **II** 218 **II** xi.6	13		
	iv) Agrippa I's treatment of Christians and events surrounding his death at Caesarea	*Ant.* **XIX** 343-359 **XIX** viii.2-ix.1 *War* **II** 219 **II** xi.6; **Acts 12.1-25**	5		
	c Later procurators; the kingdom of (Herod) Agrippa II				
	i) Events during the terms of Fadus, Alexander and Cumanus during the reign of Claudius	*Ant.* **XIX** 360-366 **XIX** ix.2 *Ant.* **XX** 1-16, 97-136 **XX** i.1-3, v.1-vi.3 *War* **II** 220-246 **II** xi.6-xii.7	1,2,6,13	250	
	ii) Paul's first missionary journey; the Council of Jerusalem; Paul's second missionary journey	**Acts 13.1-18.21; Galatians 1.21-2.10**	13	245,246	
	iii) Felix' term under Claudius and Nero; Agrippa II's territory enlarged	*Ant.* **XX** 137-181 **XX** vii.1-viii.8 *War* **II** 247-270 **II** xii.8-xiii.7	8,13	250	
	iv) Paul's third missionary journey, his arrest in Jerusalem and defence at Caesarea	**Acts** 27–28 –26.32	1,5	247,248	
	v) Festus' term under Nero; Paul's defence before Festus and Agrippa II; his appeal to 'Caesar' (Nero) and his voyage to Rome	*Ant.* **XX** 182-196 **XX** viii.9-11 *War* **II** 271 **II** xiv.1	6,13	248	

Herodian Period

Map No.	Subject	Primary sources			Regional Map Nos. (Section 1)	Macmillan Bible Atlas Map Nos.	Other references and notes
12-11	**First Revolt against Rome (complete)**						
	a Abuses of the procurators Albinus and Florus; outbreak of the revolt in Caesarea and Jerusalem	*Ant.*	**XX** 197-223, 252-258	**XX** ix.1-7; xi.1	6,8,13	251	
		War	**II** 272-332	**II** xiv.1-xv.6			
	b Agrippa II's appeal; rebels capture Masada and Jerusalem; massacre of Jews in Caesarea leads to violence throughout Judaea and Syria	*War*	**II** 333-498	**II** xvi.1-xviii.8	5,7-9,12,14	251	
		Life	17-27	4-6			
	c Cestius Gallus' campaign to suppress the revolt ends in his disastrous defeat at Beth Horon	*War*	**II** 499-565	**II** xviii.9-xx.4	1,5,6	251	
		Life	24	6			
	d Josephus' defence of Galilee; his problems, etc.	See	12-12 a				
	e Rebels prepare for war in Judaea; their attacks on Ascalon repulsed	*War*	**II** 566-567, 647-654	**II** xx.4, xxii.1-2	3,14	251	
		War	**III** 1-28	**III** i.1-ii.3			
	f Vespasian's western Lower Galilee campaign, etc.	See	12-12 b				
	g Massacre of Samaritans at Mt. Gerizim	*War*	**III** 307-315	**III** vii.32	4	253	
	h Joppa again destroyed by the Romans	*War*	**III** 414-427	**III** ix.2-3	5	253	
	i Vespasian's eastern Lower Galilee campaign, etc.	See	12-12 c				
	j Final Roman campaigns in the north, etc.	See	12-12 d				
	k Internal strife in Jerusalem and Judaea	*War*	**IV** 121-409	**IV** iii.1-vii.2	2,5,14	253	
	Note Vespasian's coastal campaign: Jamnia and Azotus	*War*	**IV** 130	**IV** iii.2			
	l Initial stages of Roman campaign in Peraea and Judaea	See	12-13 b-f				
	m Vespasian becomes emperor; Titus' return to Caesarea	*War*	**IV** 585-663	**IV** x.1-xi.5	5,13	255	
	n Events during the siege of Jerusalem by Titus	See	12-13 g-k				
	o Titus' departure after Jerusalem is razed	*War*	**VII** 1-25	**VII** i.1-ii.1		256	
	p Later events and campaigns; Machaerus and Masada	See	12-13 l-n				
12-12	**Detail of Galilee: Josephus' defence and Vespasian's campaigns (from 12-11 d, f, i, j)**						
	a Josephus' defence of Galilee; his problems with local leaders and the general population	*War*	**II** 569-646	**II** xx.5-xxi.10	6-10,13	252	
		Life	28-406	7-73			
	Note towns fortified by Josephus	*War*	**II** 572-576	**II** xx.6	6-10	252	
		Life	187-188	37			
	b Vespasian's western Lower Galilee campaign: submission of Sepphoris. siege of Jotapata and surrender of Josephus	*War*	**III** 29-69, 110-413	**III** ii.4-iv.2, vi.1-ix.1, 5-6	6	252	
		Life	407-413	74			
	Note descriptions of Galilee, Peraea, Samaria, Judaea and the territory of Agrippa II	*War*	**III** 35-58	**III** iii.1-5		252	
			Pliny, *Natural History* V.66-73 in GLAJJ 468-81				
	c Vespasian's eastern Lower Galilee campaign: Tiberias and Taricheae	*War*	**III** 443-542	**III** ix.7-x.10	8,9	252	
	Note descriptions of Jordan valley and lake and plain of Gennesar	*War*	**III** 506-521	**III** x.7-8			
			Pliny, *Natural History* V.66-73 in GLAJJ 468-81				
	d Final Roman campaigns in the north: Gamala, Mt. Tabor, Gischala	*War*	**IV** 1-120	**IV** i.1-ii.5	8	252	
12-13	**Detail of Judaea: defence and defeat of Judaea and Jerusalem**						
	a Preparatory measures	See	12-11 g, h, k				
	b Roman campaign in Peraea	*War*	**IV** 410-439	**IV** vii.2-6	4,6,8	254	
	c Romans secure all approaches to Jerusalem; Nero's death delays Vespasian's campaign	*War*	**IV** 440-502	**IV** viii.1-ix.2	1,4		
	Note descriptions of Jordan valley, Jericho, Dead Sea	*War*	**IV** 451-485	**IV** viii.2-4			
			Pliny, *Natural History* V.66-73 in GLAJJ 468-81				
	d Internal strife in Judaea and in Rome	*War*	**IV** 503-549	**IV** ix.3-9	14	254	
	e Roman campaigns north and south of Jerusalem	*War*	**IV** 550-555	**IV** ix.9	13,14	255	
	f Internal strife in Jerusalem increases	*War*	**IV** 556-584	**IV** ix.10-12	6,13,14		
		War	**V** 1-38	**V** i.1-5			
	g Titus prepares for siege of Jerusalem; early skirmishes	*War*	**V** 39-135	**V** 1.6-iii.5	1,13	255	
	h Description of Jerusalem and the Temple	*War*	**V** 136-247	**V** iv.1-v.8		256	
	i First and second walls of the city breached	*War*	**V** 248-361	**V** vi.1-ix.2		256	
	j Last days of Jerusalem and the 2nd Temple	*War*	**V** 420-**VI**.442	**V** x.1-**VI** x.1	1,13	256	
		Life	417-421	75			

Herodian Period

Map No.	Subject	Primary sources		Regional Map Nos. (Section 1)	Macmillan Bible Atlas Map Nos.	Other references and notes
12-13	Detail of Judaea: defence and defeat of Judaea and Jerusalem (Cont.)					
	k Siege and fall of Machaerus in Peraea	*War* **VII** 163-209	**VII** vi.1-4	15	255	
	l Land sold, taxes levied and Roman army veterans placed at Emmaus	*War* **VII** 216-218	**VII** v.6			
	m Siege and fall of Masada	*War* **VII** 252-408	**VII** viii.1-x.1	14	255,257	
	Note description of Masada	*War* **VII** 280-303	**VII** viii.3-4			
	n Repercussions of the revolt on other Jewish communities in the eastern Mediterranean	*War* **VII** 407-455	**VII** x.1-xi.5			
	Avi-Yonah, M. 1977 *The Holy land From the Persian to the Arab Conquest (536 B.C.-A.D. 640): A Historical Geography*. Grand Rapids, Michigan: Baker Book House.					

Notes

Herodian Period

SCALE 1:750.000
10 Km
6 M

LEGEND: Historical Source Names • Hebron
Background Names • Jericho
Lines of Communication-International
Lines of Communication-Local (Roman)

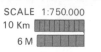

Damascus
Bathyra ?
Canatha
Dium, Diospolis
Abila
Abila
Philadelphia
Gerasa
Lake Phiale
Seleucia ?
Gamala
Sogane
Esbus
Medeba
Dibon
Gadora, Gadara, Gedor
Tyros
Agrippina ?
Ragaba
Zia
Panias, Caesarea Philippi, Neronias
Dan
Daphne
Chalcis
Thella
Julias, Bethsaida (?)
Bethsaida ?
Hippus
Emmatha
Gadara
Gergesa (Kursi)
Pella
Amathus
Abila, Abel
Livias, Julias, Beth-ramatha
Bethennabris
Besimoth
Baaras
Machaerus
Gabalis
Petra
Callirrhoe
Capernaum, Capharnaum, Cepharnocus
Chorazin
Kh. Harrawi
Philoteria
Tiberias
Sennabris ?
Agrippina ?
Salim ?
Aenon ?
Aenon, Bethany ?
Cadasa, Cydasa
Jamnith
Gennesaret
Ammathus, Hammath
Acchabare
Taricheae, Migdal
Gebul ?
Scythopolis, Beth-shan
Coreae
Archelais
Gischala, Gush Halab
Sepph
Caves
Arbela
Adamah
Hapharaim ?
Alexandrium
Meroth ?
Tekoa ?, H. Shema
Meron, Meroth ?
Mt. Tabor, Itabyrium
Phasaelis
Neara
Jericho
Cypros
Zoara
Bersabe
Selame
Beth Netofa
Dabaritta
En-gedi
(G) Araba, Gabara
Acrabeta, Aqraba
Hyrcania
Masada
En Boqeq
Baca ?
Exaloth
Nain
Aenon ?
Salim ?
Gerasa
Apherema, Ephraim
(N) Ain, Pheretae
Berytus
Platana
Sidon
Cana
Ruma
Nazareth
Ginae
Baddan
Sychar
Shechem
Tirathana ?
Anuathu Borcaeus
Michmash
Sogane
Jotapata
Japhia
Beth-haccherem
Sepphoris, Zippori
Mabartha, Neapolis
Mt. Gerizim
Bethela
Bethphage ?
Bethany
Rama
Jerusalem
Herodium
Gelil
Saab, Saba
Mt. Asamon
Asochis
Geba
Samaria, Sebaste
Gophna
Gabath Saul, T. el-Ful
Ramat Rahel
Bethlehem
Tyre
Chabulon, Kabul
Simonias
Capercotnei, Kefar Otnay
Thekoue, Tekoa
Apharatha ?
Gabaon
Besara, Beth-shearim
Arus ?
Emmaus
Thamna, Timnath
Upper Beth Horon
Emmaus ?
Alulos
Arad
Gaba ?
Anabtah
Beth Rimah
Lower Beth Horon
Kiriath-jearim
Terebinthos
Hebron
Ecdippa
Kefar Aziz
Ptolemais, Acco
Sappho
Narbata
Arbatta
Birat Soreqah
Beth Laban
Caphartoba ?
Arimathea, Aramathea
Tibetah
Zanoah
Keilah
Adora
Caphethra, Caparorsa
Malatha
Kefar Qesem
Emmaus
Bethletepha
Adida
Tower of Aphek
Capharabis
Burgatah
Antipatris
Gamzo
Dora
Strato's Tower, Caesarea
Capharsaba
Lydda, Lod
Betogabris
Belzedek ?
Ono
Accaron, Ekron
Bene-berak
Saalis, Chaalis
Beer-sheba
Apollonia
Joppa
Jamnia, Jabneh
Azotus, Ashdod
Beror Hayil
Azotus Paralius
Iarda ?
Ascalon
Gaza
Anthedon, Agrippias
Rhinocorura
Pelusium
Raphia

©

Section 12-2

Herodian Period

SCALE 1:750.000
10 Km
6 M

LEGEND:
- Historical Source Names
- Background Names
- Lines of Communication-International
- Lines of Communication-Local (Roman)

Hebron
Jericho
Damascus
Bathyra ?
Canatha
Dium, Diospolis
Abila
Philadelphia
Gerasa
Esbus, Essebonitis
Medeba
Tyros
Gadora, Gadara
Arabatha
Gamala
Sogane
Panias
Dan
Hippus
Emmatha
Gadara
Ragaba
Beth-ramatha
Abila
Thella
Bethsaida ?
Bethsaida ?
Pella
Amathus
Machaerus
Petra
Capernaum
Chorazin
Philoteria
Callirrhoe
Cadasa
Gennesaret
Ammathus
Sepph
Taricheae
Agrippina, Cochaba ?
Gebul ?
Scythopolis
Arbela
Gischala
Meroth ?
Bersabe
Meron, Meroth (?)
Beth Netofa
Mt. Tabor, Itabyrium
Coreae
Alexandrium
Phasaelis
Jericho
Cypros
Mezad Hasidim, Kh. Qumran
En-gedi
(G)Araba, Gabara
Baca ?
Exaloth
Nain
Esdraelon
Acrabeta
Hyrcania
Masada
En Boqeq
Barytus
Platana
Sidon
Sogane
Cana
Nazareth
Japhia
Ginae
Sychar
Anuathu Borcaeus
Apherema
Michmash
Bethany
Beth-haccherem
Asochis
Sepphoris
Mt. Gerizim
Bethela
Bethphage ?
Herodium
Jerusalem
Bethlehem
Chabulon
Simonias
Samaria, Sebaste
Gophna
Tekoa
Tyre
Kefar Otnay, Capercotnei
Besara
Beth-haccherem ?, En Kerem
Gaba ?
Ecdippa
Anabtah
Thamna
Lower Beth Horon
Beth Rimah
Kiriath-jearim
Terebinthos
Hebron
Ptolemais
Narbata
Birat Soreqah
Beth Laban
Aramathea
Zanoah
Keilah
Adora
Malatha
Kefar Qesem
Emmaus
Bethletepha
Sycaminum
Adida
Antipatris
Dora
Strato's Tower, Caesarea
Capharsaba
Lydda
Betogabris
Accaron
Beer-sheba
Apollonia
Joppa
Jamnia
Port of Jamnia
Azotus
Azotus Paralius
Iarda ?
Ascalon
Anthedon, Agrippias
Gaza
Pelusium

Section 12–3

Herodian Period

SCALE 1:600.000
10 Km
6 M

LEGEND: Historical Source Names — Hebron
Background Names — Jericho
Lines of Communication-International
Lines of Communication-Local (Roman)

E
Damascus
Abila
Gerasa
Philadelphia
Gabalis
Petra
Esbus
Medeba
Dibon
Tyros
Gadora
Baal-meon
Agrippina ?
Zia
Ragaba
Gamala
Sogane
Panias, Caesarea
Caesarea Philippi
Hippus
Gadara
Emmatha, Hammat Gader
Julias
Bethsaida (?)
Bethsaida ?
Thella
Abila, Abel
Beth-ramatha, Julias
Livias
Amathus
Bethennabris, Beth Nimrin
Machaerus
Baaras, Baaru
Callirrhoe
Pella
Chorazin
Capernaum, Kefar Nahum
Philoteria
Kh. Harrawi
Heptapegon
Gennesaret, Ginnosar
Ammathus
Tiberias
Cadasa
Jamnith
Acchabare
Taricheae, Magdala, Migdal Nunnayah
Agrippina, Cochaba ?
Gebul ?
Scythopolis
Arbela
Gischala, Gush Halab
Sepph
Meron, Meroth ?
Meroth ?
H. Shema, Tekoa ?
Kefar Hananiya
Bersabe
Hapharaim ?
Coreae
Alexandrium, Sartaba
Archelais
Zoar
Mezad Hasidim, Kh. Qumran
Jericho
Cypros
Phasaelis
Neara
Mt. Tabor, Itabyrium
Beth Netofa
Beth Dagon
Selame
Tubani
En-gedi
Baca ?
(G)A raba, Gabara
Nain
Exaloth
Esdraelon
Acrabeta, Aqraba
Hyrcania
Sogane, Kefar Signa(?)
Nazareth
Sepphoris
Japhia
Ginae, Ginnay
Baddan
Gerasa
Apherema
Sychar, En Soker ?
Tirathana ?
Shechem
Mt. Gerizim
Anuathu Borcaeus
Michmash
Jotapata
Beth-haccherem
Asochis
Tarbenet
Geba
Bethel
To Tetarton
Bethany
Bethphage ?
Jerusalem
Herodium
Chabulon
Berytus
Sidon
Tyre
Simonias
Capercotnei, Kefar Otnay
Samaria, Sebaste
Gophna
Beth-haccherem ?, Ramat Rahel
Bethlehem
Tekoa
Gabaon
Malatha
Betoaenea, Beth Yannai (?)
Beth-haccherem ?, En Kerem
Besara
Arus ?
Ecdippa, Achzib
Gaba ?
Anabtah
Thamna
Beth Rimah
Upper Beth Horon
Lower Beth Horon
Terebinthos
Hebron
Ptolemais
Seredah
Kiriath-jearim
Sappho
Narbata
Birat Soreqah
Beth Laban
Aramathea
Zanoah
Keilah
Adora
Emmaus
Bethletepha
Kefar Qesem
Sycaminum
Geba
Tower of Aphek
Adida
Burgatah
Antipatris
Dora
Caesarea, Strato's Tower
Lydda, Lod
Betogabris, Eleutheropolis
Belzedek ?
Onus
Accaron
Serifin
Apollonia
Saalis
Joppa
Jamnia
Ascalon
Port of Jamnia
Gaza
Anthedon
Azotus
Beror Hayil

Section 12–4

Herodian Period

SCALE 1:600.000
10 Km
6 M

LEGEND: Historical Source Names ● Hebron
Background Names ● Jericho
Lines of Communication-International
Lines of Communication-Local (Roman)

Philadelphia
Gerasa
Abila
Damascus
Esbus
Medeba
Dibon
Tyros
Gadora
Agrippina ?
Zia
Baal-meon
Gamala
Sogane
Caesarea Philippi
Hippus
Gadara
Ragaba
Emmatha,
Hammat Gader
Gergesa
Abila, Abel
Beth-ramatha,
Livias, Julias
Amathus
Bethennabris,
Beth Nimrin
Machaerus
Baaras, Baaru
Bethsaida ?
Thella
Pella
Capernaum,
Kefar Nahum
Chorazin
Philoteria
Kh. Harrawi
Callirrhoe
Heptapegon
Gennesaret
Ammathus
Cadasa
Jamnith
Tiberias
Agrippina,
Cochaba ?
Gebul ?
Salim ?
Aenon ?
Acchabare
Taricheae,
Magdala,
Magadan, Dalmanutha
Sepph
Scythopolis,
Beth-shan
Coreae
Alexandrium,
Sartaba
Archelais
Gischala,
Gush Halab
Arbela
Meron,
Meroth ?
Hapharaim ?
Mezad Hasidim,
Kh. Qumran
Meroth ?
Kefar
Hananiya
H. Shema,
Tekoa (?)
Bersabe
Mt. Tabor,
Itabyrium
Jericho
Cypros
Neara
Phasaelis
Beth Netofa
Beth Dagon
Selame
Tubani
En-gedi
Hyrcania
(G)Araba,
Gabara
Nain
Aenon ?
Salim ?
Acrabeta
Baca ?
Exaloth
Esdraelon
Baddan
Gerasa
Ephraim
Cana
Nazareth
Ginae,
Ginnay
Sychar
Jacob's Well
Anuathu
Borcaeus
Machmas
Sogane
Sepphoris
Japhia
Shechem
Mt.
Gerizim,
Garizein
Bethany
Jotapata
Bethel
Gabath
Saul
Bethphage ?
Herodium
Beth-haccherem
Asochis,
Shichin
Tarbenet
Geba
Rama
Jerusalem
Geba
Bethlehem
Chabulon
Gophna
Simonias
Samaria, Sebaste
Beth-haccherem ?,
Ramat Rahel
Tekoa
Berytus
Capercotnei,
Kefar Otnay
Gabaon
Sidon
Betoaenea,
Beth Yannai(?)
Emmaus
Beth-haccherem ?,
En Kerem
Tyre
Arus ?
Emmaus ?
Besara
Thamna
Upper
Beth Horon
Terebinthos
Hebron
Ecdippa
Gaba ?
Anabtah
Beth Rimah
Lower
Beth Horon
Kiriath-jearim
Seredah
Sappho
Ptolemais, Acco
Narbata
Beth Laban
Birat Soreqah
Aramathea
Arimathea
Zanoah
Keilah
Adora
Kefar Qesem
Emmaus
Bethletepha
Sycaminum
Geba
Tower of Aphek
Adida, Hadid
Burgatah
Antipatris
Dora
Lydda, Lod
Betogabris
Caesarea,
Strato's Tower
Accaron
Belzedek ?
Onus
Serifin
Apollonia
Saalis
Joppa
Jamnia
Ascalon
Port of Jamnia
Gaza
Anthedo
Azotus

Section 12–5
Herodian Period

SCALE 1:215.000

10 Km

6 M

LEGEND:
- Historical Source Names • Hebron
- Background Names • Jericho
- Lines of Communication-International
- Lines of Communication-Local (Roman)

Livias, Julias, Beth-ramatha
Abila
Bethennabris, Beth Nimrin
Machaerus
Baaras
W. Zarqa
Besimoth
Aenon Bethany (?)
Callirrhoe
Bethabara
Choba ?
Coreae
Archelais
Alexandrium, Sartaba
W. Nu'eima
Beth-hakkoz
Jericho (Ericha)
Mezad Hasidim, Kh. Qumran
Phasaelis
W. 'Auja
Jericho (Tulul Abu el-Alayiq)
W. Mukallik (Og)
Neara
Docus
Cypros
N. Kidron
Chozba
W. Qilt
Kh. Karm Atrad
W. Samniya
W. Murabba'at
Hyrcania
Acrabeta, Aqraba
Gerasa
Apherema Ephraim
(N)Ain Pheretae, Pharathon
N. Kidron
W. Suweinit
Shiloh
Tur Shimeon
Kefar Yatma
Michmash
Ailamon
Beth Harodon
Anuathu Borcaeus
Geba
Anathoth
Isana
Bethany
Azmaveth
Bethphage ?
Herodium
W. Khareitun
Jeshub
Bethel
Gabath Saul, T. el-Ful
Jerusalem
Rama
Migdal Eder
Berea
Beth-haccherem ?, (Ramat Rahel)
Gophna
Mizpah
Tekoa

Section 12–6

Herodian Period

SCALE 1:215.000
10 Km
6 M
LEGEND: Historical Source Names
Background Names
Lines of Communication-International
Lines of Communication-Local (Roman)
Hebron
Jericho
E
Hammat Pella
Pella
Amathus
Taralah
Gesher
R. JORDAN
N. Tavor
Agrippina, Cochaba ?
Gebul ?
Scythopolis, Beth-shan
Rehob
Aenon ?
Salim ?
Bethmaela
Choba ?
Coreae
Cola
Abelmea
Alexandrium, Sartaba
N. Harod
Hapharaim ?
Gelbus
Bezek
W. Far'a
Neoran
Thena
Beth Dagon
Salaba
Thebez
Tubani
Araba
Jano
Bethacath
Nain
Acrabeta, Aqraba
Aenon ?
Salim ?
Esdraelon
Gerasa
Baddan
Ginae, Ginnay
Tur Lozah
Sychar En Soker
Jacob's Well
Belemoth
Shechem
Tirathana ?
Awartha
Shiloh
Mt. Gerizim
Mabartha
Kefar Yatma
Macher
Anuathu Borcaeus
Hivria
Merrus
Sanur
Dothaim
Jeshub
Geba
Sebaste, Samaria
Capercotnei, Kefar Otnay
Kefar Silah
Fahma
Betoaenea, Beth Yannai(?)

Herodian Period

SCALE 1:215.000

10 Km

6 M

LEGEND: Historical Source Names • Hebron
Background Names • Jericho
Lines of Communication-International
Lines of Communication-Local (Roman)

E

H. Shurah
Capernaum, Kefar Nahum
Chorazin
N. Korazim
N. Dishon
Heptapegon
Gennesaret, Ginnosar
Philoteria
Kefar Agon
Gesher
Sennabris ?
Ammathus, Hammath
Tiberias
Kefar Menori
Cadasa
Qisyon
Rosh Pinna
Jamnith
Kefar Neboraya
Sayydatah
Bethmaus
Sergunin
Kefar Yamma
Ullama
N. Tavor
Agrippina, Cochaba ?
Gebul ?
Scythopolis, Beth-shan
Alma
Dalton
Biri
Sepph
Acchabare
N. Ammud
N. Zalmon
Migdal Nunnayah, Taricheae Magdala, Magadan, Dalmanutha
Huqoq
Arbela
H. Sarona
Adamah
N. Harod
Kefar Hittaya
Qarne Hittim
Meroth ?
Safsofah
Gischala, Gush Halab
Meron, Meroth ?
H. Shema, Tekoa (?)
Parod
Mamliah
Kefar Shabtay
Hapharaim ?
Bet Alfa
Kefar Nimrah
Lubiya
Bersabe
Kefar Hananiya
Kefar Baram
Mashkanah
H. Ammudim, Kefar Uziel (?)
Mearaia
Ailabo
Mt. Tabor, Itabyrium
Neoran
Sasa
Beth Netofa
Aendor, En Dor
Beth Dagon
Selame
Turan ?
Dabaritta
Tubani
Rama
Kefar Yohannah
En Teena
En Tab ?
Nain
N. Keziv
Shezor
Baca ?
(G)Araba, Gabara
Garis ?
Exaloth
Esdraelon
Gath Hepher
Abel ?
Rimmon
Rani ?
Mafshetah
Caparasima
Cana
Nazareth
Ginae
Sogane
Ruma
N. Iphtahel
Jotapata
Sepphoris
Japhia
Jokereth
Mt. Asamon
Kefar Mandi
Aitalo
Ginneigar
Beth-haccherem
Asochis, Shichin
Janoah
Cochaba ?
Tarbenet
Mahalol
Gelil
Saab
Zenitah
Simonias
Gabatha
Chabulon
Kefar Tamartah
Sidon
Beth Hobaya
Apharatha ?
Tyre
Gaaton
Abelim
Bethlehem
Hivria
Capercotnei, Kefar Otnay
Hanotah
Shefaram
Kefar Amiqo
Kefar Yasif
Pi Masoba
Bezet
Kabrita
Ushah
Ardasqus
N. Kishon
N. Iron
Tibon
Kefar Sasay
Besara
N. Keziv
Ecdippa
Ptolemais, Acco
Gaba ?
Caesarea
12-7

Section 12–8

Herodian Period

SCALE 1:215.000

10 Km

6 M

LEGEND: Historical Source Names • Hebron
Background Names • Jericho
Lines of Communication-International
Lines of Communication-Local (Roman)

Kafr Nafakh
Gamala
El Al
Yaarut
Camus
Ephron
Dabiyya
Amudiyya
Qisrin
Sogane
Apheca
Ram Baraq
ed-Danqalle, Ghadriyya
Kanaf
Gadara
Emmatha, Hammat Gader
Iyyon
Dabra, Dabura
Hippus
Kefar Harub
Gergesa
Kursi
R. JORDAN
Julias
Bethsaida ?
Thella
Kh. er-Rafid
Kh. ed-Dikke
N. Hazor
Kefar Semah ?
Philoteria
Kefar Agon
Sennabris ?
Gesher
H. Shurah
Capernaum, Kefar Nahum
Chorazin
N. Korazim
Kh. Harrawi
N. Dishon
Heptapegon
Gennesaret, Ginnosar
Ammathus, Hammath
Tiberias
Kefar Menori
N. Tavor
Cadasa
Qisyon
Rosh Pinna
Sayydatah
Agrippina, Cochaba ?
Gebul ?
Jamnith
Kefar Neboraya
Migdal Nunnayah, Taricheae
Magdala, Magadan, Dalmanutha
Bethmaus
Sergunin
Kefar Yamma
Ullama
Alma
Dalton
Biri
Sepph
Acchabare
N. Ammud
N. Zalmon
Arbela
Scythopolis, Beth-shan
Huqoq
H. Sarona
Adamah
Kefar Hittaya
Qarne Hittim
Meroth ?
Safsofah
Gischala, Gush Halab
Meron, Meroth ?
H. Shema, Tekoa (?)
Mamliah
Kefar Shabtay
Hapharaim ?
Parod
Kefar Nimrah
Lubiya
Bersabe
Kefar Hananiya
Kefar Baram
Mearaia
Mashkanah
H. Ammudim, Kefar Uziel (?)
Ailabo
Mt. Tabor, Itabyrium
Neoran
Sasa
Beth Netofa
Aendor, En Dor
Beth Dagon
Selame
Dabaritta
Tubani
Rama
Kefar Yohannah
Turan ?
En Teena
En Tab ?
Nain
Shezor
Garis ?, Kafr Kanna
Baca ?
(G)Araba, Gabara
N. Kezív
Gath Hepher
Exaloth
Esdraelon
Abel ?
Rimmon
Rani ?
Mafshetah
(Ca)parasima
Cana
Nazareth
Sogane
Ruma
N. Iphtah

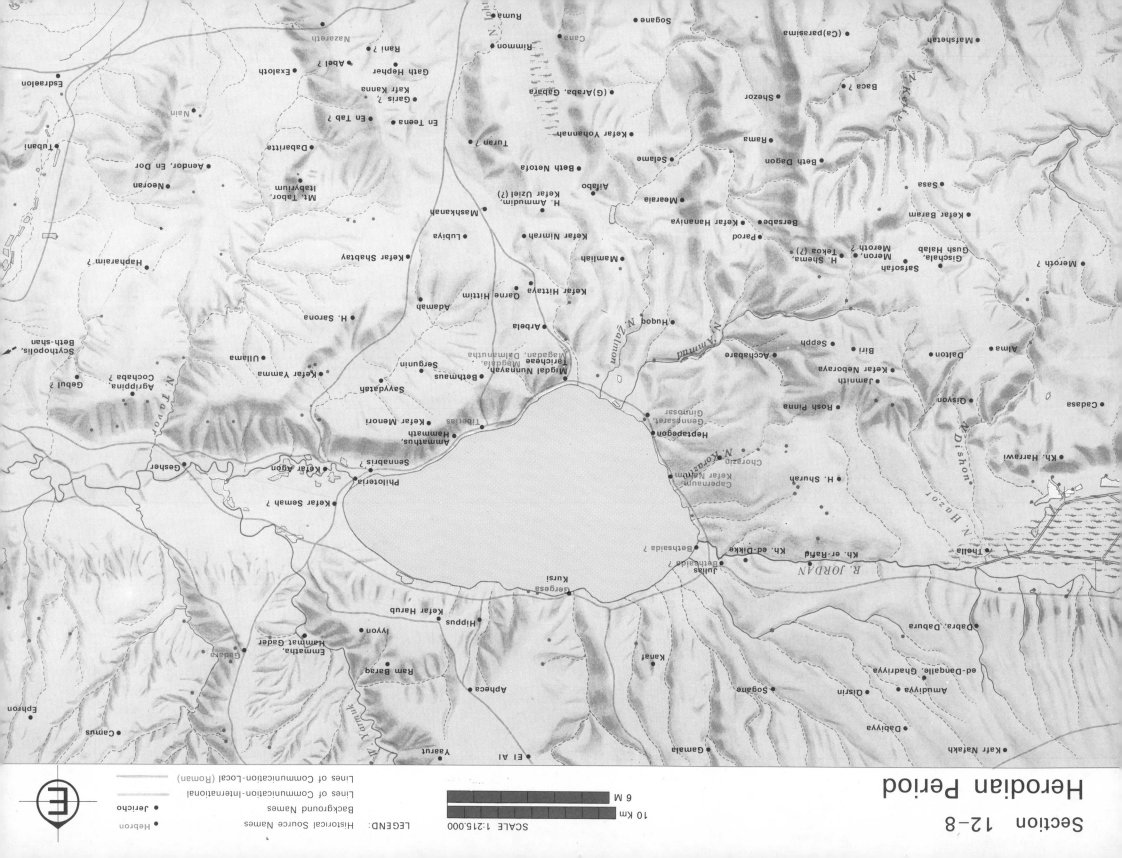

Herodian Period

SCALE 1:215.000
10 Km
6 M

LEGEND:
- Historical Source Names • Hebron
- Background Names • Jericho
- Lines of Communication-International
- Lines of Communication-Local (Roman)

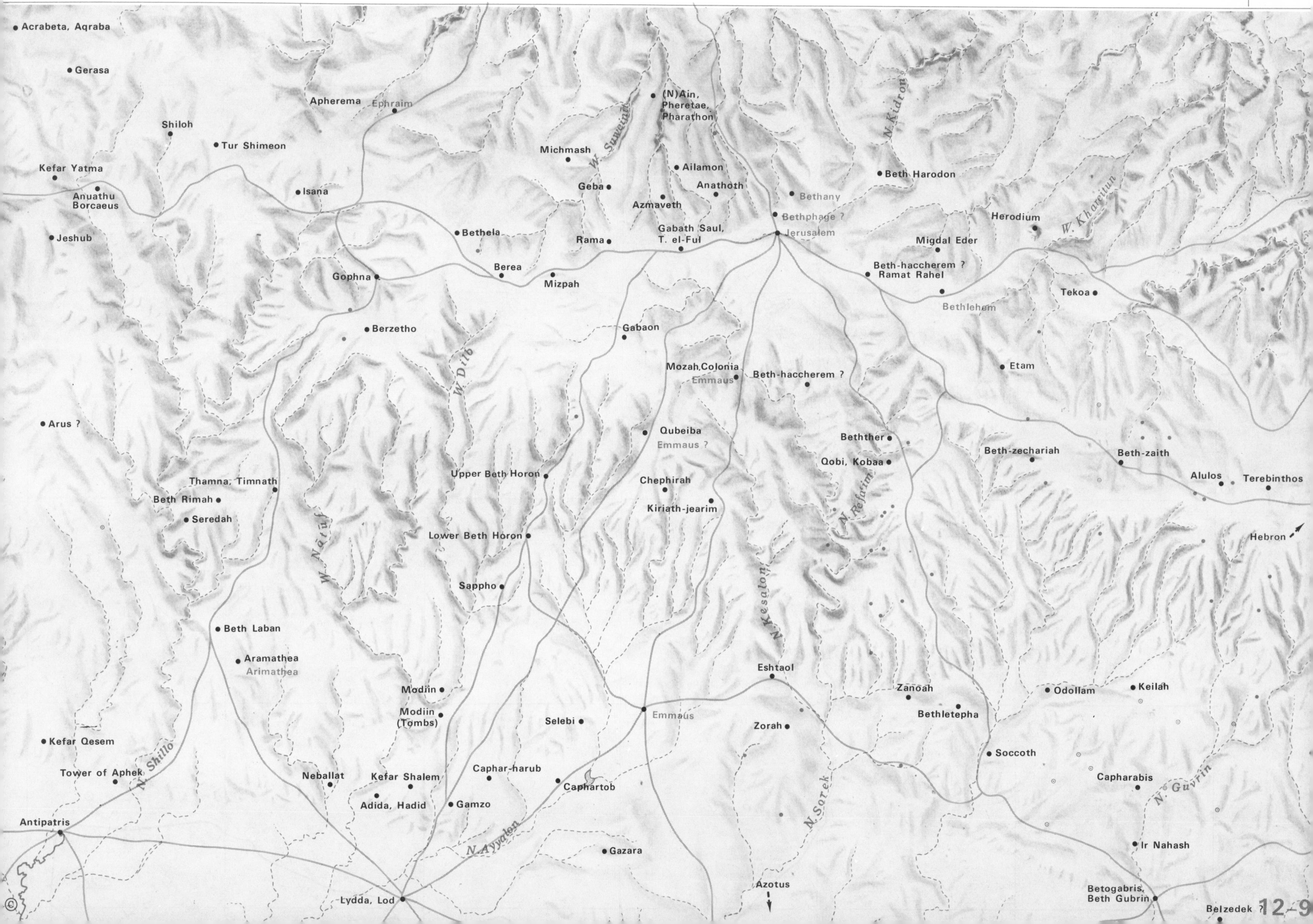

Acrabeta, Aqraba
Gerasa
Apherema
Ephraim
Shiloh
Tur Shimeon
Kefar Yatma
Anuathu Borcaeus
Isana
Jeshub
Bethela
Gophna
Berea
Mizpah
Berzetho
Michmash
W. Suweinit
(N)Ain, Pheretae, Pharathon
Ailamon
Geba
Anathoth
Azmaveth
Rama
Gabath Saul, T. el-Ful
Bethany
Bethphage ?
Jerusalem
N. Kidron
Beth Harodon
Herodium
W. Khareitun
Migdal Eder
Beth-haccherem ? Ramat Rahel
Bethlehem
Tekoa
Gabaon
W. Dilb
Mozah, Colonia
Emmaus
Beth-haccherem ?
Etam
Arus ?
Qubeiba
Emmaus ?
Bethther
Qobi, Kobaa
Beth-zechariah
Beth-zaith
Alulos
Terebinthos
Upper Beth Horon
Thamna, Timnath
Beth Rimah
Seredah
Chephirah
Kiriath-jearim
N. Refaim
Hebron
Lower Beth Horon
W. Natuf
N. Kesalon
Sappho
Beth Laban
Aramathea
Arimathea
Eshtaol
Modiin
Modiin (Tombs)
Selebi
Emmaus
Zanoah
Bethletepha
Odollam
Keilah
Zorah
Soccoth
Kefar Qesem
N. Shillo
Tower of Aphek
Neballat
Kefar Shalem
Adida, Hadid
Caphar-harub
Gamzo
Caphartob
N. Sorek
Capharabis
N. Guvrin
Antipatris
N. Ayyalon
Gazara
Ir Nahash
Azotus
Lydda, Lod
Betogabris, Beth Gubrin
Belzedek ?

Section 12–10

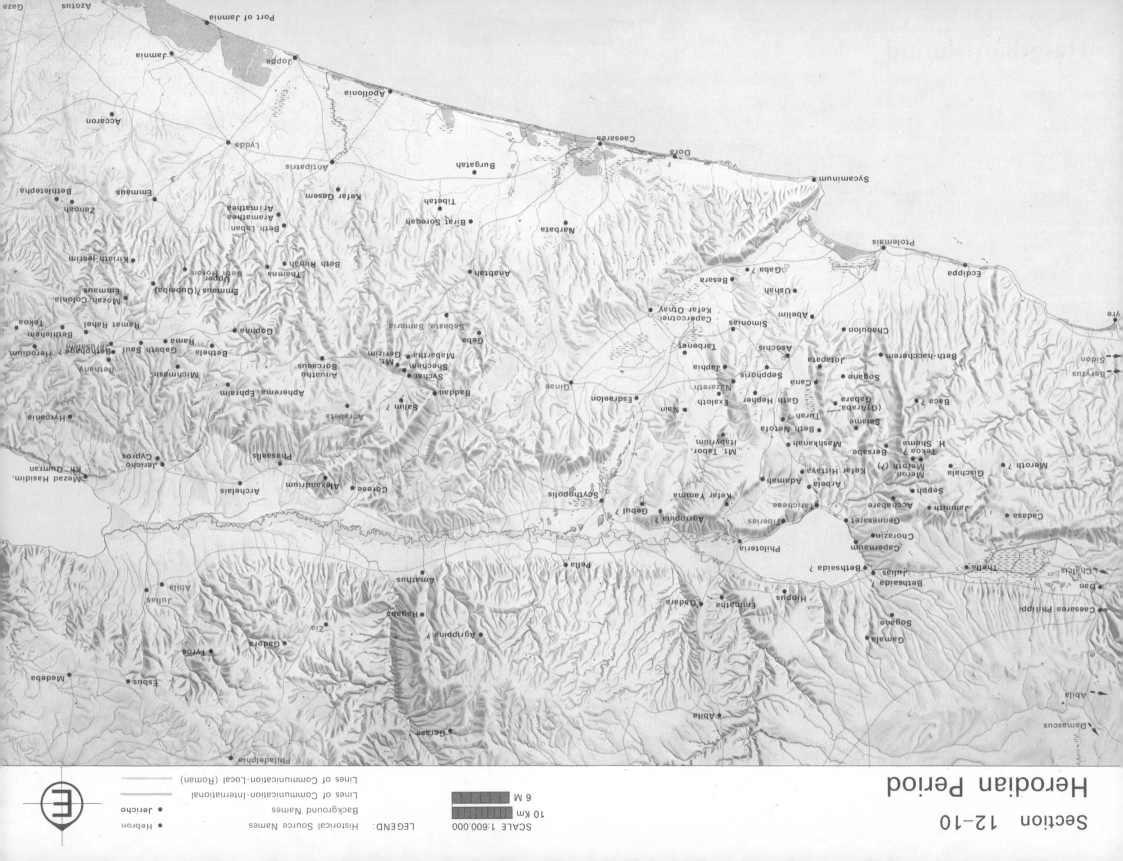

Herodian Period

SCALE 1:600.000
10 Km
6 M

LEGEND: Historical Source Names • Hebron
Background Names • Jericho
Lines of Communication-International
Lines of Communication-Local (Roman)

Damascus
Abila
Abila
Philadelphia
Gerasa
Esbus
Medeba
Tyros
Gadora
Gamala
Sogane
Agrippina ?
Zia
Ragaba
Caesarea Philippi
Hippus
Emmatha
Gadara
Julias
Abila
Dan
Bethsaida ?
Julias
Bethsaida ?
Amathus
Chalcis
Thella
Pella
Capernaum
Philoteria
Chorazin
Gennesaret
Tiberias
Cadasa
Jamnith
Acchabare
Taricheae
Agrippina ?
Gebul ?
Sepph
Kefar Yamma
Scythopolis
Arbela
Adamah
Coreae
Alexandrium
Archelais
Gischala
Meron, Meroth (?)
Kefar Hittaya
Mezad Hasidim, Kh. Qumran
Meroth ?
Jericho
Cypros
Tekoa ?, H. Shema
Bersabe
Mashkanah
Mt. Tabor, Itabyrium
Phasaelis
Beth Netofa
Selame
Turan ?
Hyrcania
(G)Araba, Gabara
Nain
Acrabeta
Baca ?
Gath Hepher
Exaloth
Salim ?
Esdraelon
Baddan
Apherema, Ephraim
Nazareth
Ginae
Cana
Berytus
Sogane
Sepphoris
Sychar
Anuathu Borcaeus
Michmash
Japhia
Shechem
Mt. Gerizim
Bethany
Sidon
Jotapata
Mabartha
Bethela
Gabath Saul
Bethphage ?
Herodium
Beth-haccherem
Asochis
Tarbenet
Jerusalem
Rama
Geba
Bethlehem
Chabulon
Gophna
Sebaste, Samaria
Ramat Rahel
Tekoa
Simonias
yre
Abelim
Capercotnei, Kefar Otnay
Mozah, Colonia, Emmaus
Emmaus ?(Qubeiba)
Ushah
Upper Beth Horon
Thamna
Besara
Kiriath-jearim
Anabtah
Beth Rimah
Ecdippa
Gaba ?
Ptolemais
Beth Laban
Aramathea, Arimathea
Narbata
Birat Soreqah
Zanoah
Tibetah
Kefar Qesem
Emmaus
Bethletepha
Sycaminum
Burgatah
Antipatris
Dora
Lydda
Caesarea
Accaron
Apollonia
Joppa
Jamnia
Port of Jamnia
Azotus
Gaza

Section 12-11

Herodian Period

SCALE 1:750.000
10 Km
6 M

LEGEND: Historical Source Names • Hebron
Background Names • Jericho
Lines of Communication-International
Lines of Communication-Local (Roman)

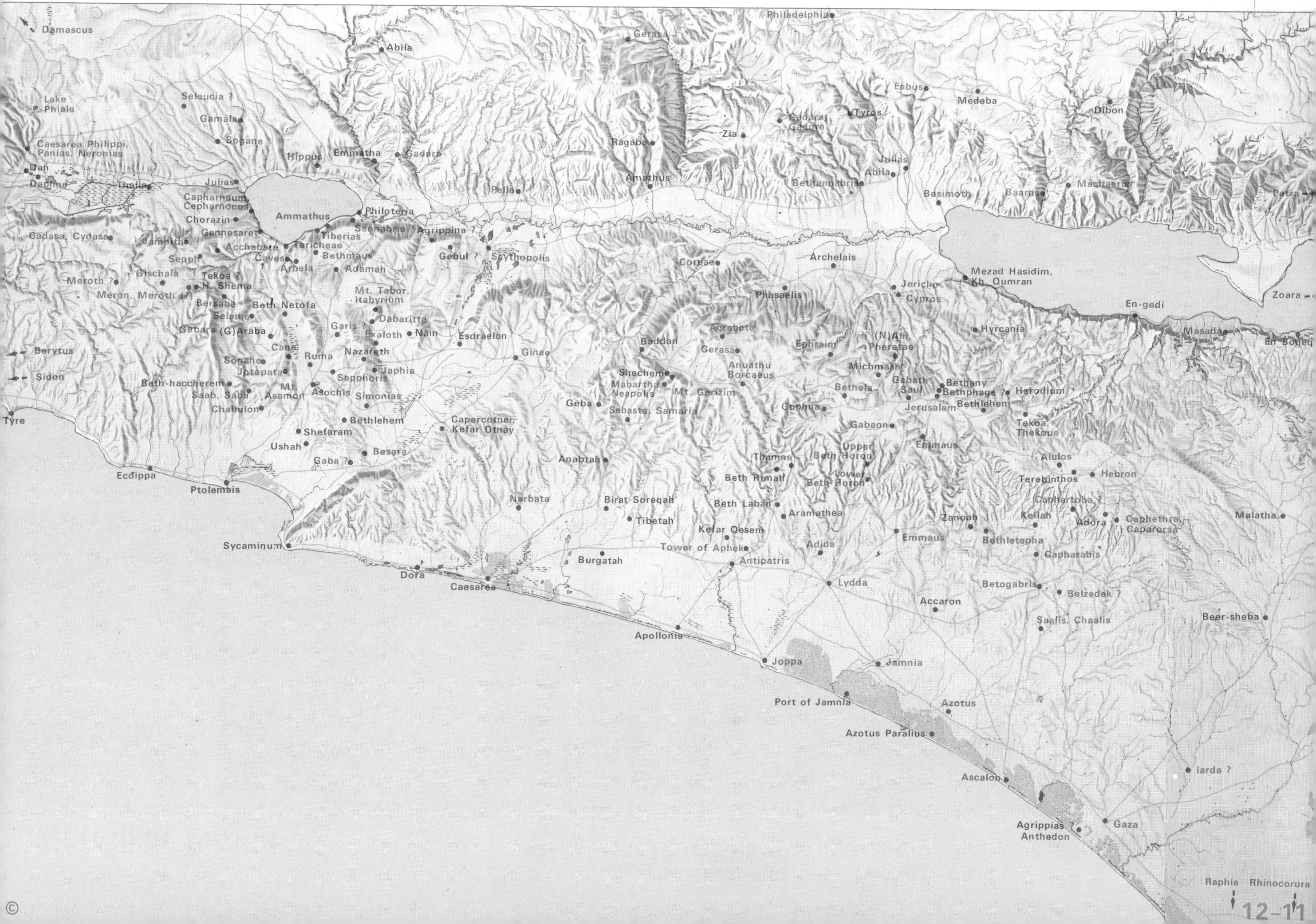

Damascus
Philadelphia
Abila
Gerasa
Lake Phiale
Seleucia ?
Gamala
Sogane
Caesarea Philippi, Panias, Neronias
Dan
Daphne
Thella
Julias
Hippus
Emmatha
Gadara
Capharnaum, Cephamocus
Chorazin
Gennesaret
Ammathus
Philoteria
Pella
Ragaba
Amathus
Esbus
Medeba
Dibon
Gadara, Gadore
Tyros
Zia
Julias
Abila
Bethennabris
Besimoth
Baaras
Machaerus
Petra
Cadasa, Cydasa
Jamnith
Acchabare
Taricheae
Tiberias
Sennabris ?
Agrippina ?
Gebul ?
Scythopolis
Bethmaus
Caves
Arbela
Adamah
Sepph
Gischala
Tekoa ?
H. Shema
Meroth ?
Meron, Meroth (?)
Bersabe
Beth Netofa
Selame
Mt. Tabor, Itabyrium
Dabaritta
Garis ?
Exaloth
Nain
Gabara (G)Araba
Cana
Esdraelon
Ginae
Berytus
Sidon
Sogane
Ruma
Nazareth
Jotapata
Japhia
Sepphoris
Beth-haccherem
Saab, Saba
Mt. Asamon
Asochis
Simonias
Chabulon
Tyre
Bethlehem
Capercotnei, Kefar Otnay
Shefaram
Ushah
Besara
Gaba ?
Ecdippa
Ptolemais
Sycaminum
Dora
Caesarea
Narbata
Burgatah
Corea
Archelais
Mezad Hasidim, Kh. Qumran
Jericho
Cypros
Phasaelis
Zoara
En-gedi
Acrabeta
Hyrcania
Masada
En Boqeq
Baddan
Gerasa
Ephraim
(N)Ain, Pheretae
Michmash
Shechem
Mabartha, Neapolis
Mt. Gerizim
Anuathu Borcaeus
Gabath Saul
Bethany
Bethphage ?
Herodium
Bethela
Jerusalem
Bethlehem
Geba
Sebaste, Samaria
Gophna
Gabaon
Tekoa, Thekoue
Emmaus
Anabtah
Thamna
Upper Beth Horon
Lower Beth Horon
Beth Rimah
Alulos
Hebron
Terebinthos
Birat Soreqah
Tibetah
Beth Laban
Aramathea
Capharitoba ?
Kellah
Zanoah
Adora
Caphethra, Caparorsa
Malatha
Kefar Qesem
Emmaus
Bethletepha
Adida
Tower of Aphek
Antipatris
Capharabis
Lydda
Betogabris
Belzedek ?
Accaron
Saafis, Chaalis
Beer-sheba
Apollonia
Joppa
Jamnia
Port of Jamnia
Azotus
Azotus Paralius
Ascalon
Iarda ?
Agrippias Anthedon
Gaza
Raphia
Rhinocorura
12-11

Section 12-12
Herodian Period

SCALE 1:300.000
10 Km
6 M

LEGEND:
- • Hebron — Historical Source Names
- • Jericho — Background Names
- Lines of Communication-International
- Lines of Communication-Local (Roman)

Kafr Nafakh
Dabiyya
Gamala
Umm el-Qanatir
Camus
Ephron
Deir Aziz
Amudiyya
Qisrin
Sogane
Apheca
Ram Baraq
Caesarea Philippi,
Panias, Neronias
ed-Danqalle, Ghadriyya
Kanaf
Hammat Gader,
Emmatha
Gadara
Shuqayyif,
Masharfawi
Ayyanosh
Kh. el-Asaliya
Hippus
Iyyon
Dabra, Dabura
Kefar Harub
Dan
Daphne
Gergesa
(Kursi)
Kh. er-Rafid
Bethsaida ?
Julias
Thella
Kh. ed-Dikke
Pella
Kefar Semah ?
Capharnaum,
Cepharnocus
Philoteria
Kefar Agon
H. Shurah
Gesher
Kh. Harrawi
Chorazin
Sennabris ?
Heptapegon
Ammathus
Kefar Menori
Rosh Pinna
Gennesaret
Tiberias
Agrippina,
Cochaba ?
Cadasa, Cydasa
Qisyon
Jamnith
Bethmaus
Sayydatah
Kefar Yamma
Gebul ?
Kefar Neboraya
Magdala,
Tarichaeae
Sergunin
Ullama
Scythopolis
Alma
Dalton
Biri
Acchabare
Sepph
Caves
Arbela
Huqoq
H. Sarona
Adamah
Kefar Hittaya
Gischala
Safsofah
Meroth ?
Tekoa ?
H. Shema
Mamliah
Kefar Shabtay
Hapharaim ?
Meron,
Meroth ?
Kefar Nimrah
Lubiya
Parod
Bersabe
H. Ammudim
Kefar Baram
Mearaia
Ailabo
Mashkanah
Mt. Tabor,
Itabyrium
Sasa
Neoran
Beth Dagon
Selame
Beth Netofa
Dabaritta
Turan ?
Rama
En Teena
Tubani
Araba
Kefar Yohannah
En Tab ?
Nain
Shezor
Baca ?
(G)Araba, Gabara
Garis ?
Esdraelon
Gath Hepher
Exaloth
Rimmon
Rani ?
Ginae
Mafshetah
Cana
Nazareth
(Ca)parasima
Sogane
Ruma
Jotapata
Sepphoris
Japhia
Jokereth
Mt. Asamon
Aitalo
Ginneigar
Janoah
Beth-haccherem
Asochis
Mahalol
Tarbenet
Gelil
Saab, Saba
Cochaba ?
Simonias
Zenitah
Chabulon
Gabatha
Apharatha ?
Beth Hobaya
Kefar Tamartah
Tyre
Gaaton
Abelim
Bethlehem
Hivria
Hanotah
Capercotnei,
Kefar Otnay
Kefar Amiqo
Shefaram
Pi Masoba
Bezet
Kabrita
Ardasqus
Ushah
Kefar Sasay
Tibon
Besara
Ecdippa
Gaba ?
Caesarea

Section 12-13
Herodian Period

SCALE 1:450.000
10 Km
6 M

LEGEND: Historical Source Names • Hebron
Background Names • Jericho
Lines of Communication-International
Lines of Communication-Local (Roman)

Gerasa
Philadelphia
Esbus
Medeba
Dibon
Petra
Tyros
Gadora, Gadara
Zia
Ragaba
Julias
Abila
Bethennabris
Amathus
Taralah
Besimoth
Machaerus
Baaras
Scythopolis
Coreae
Archelais
Alexandrium
Mezad Hasidim,
Kh. Qumran
Phasaelis
Neara
Jericho
Cypros
Zoara
En-gedi
Hyrcania
Masada
En Boqeq
Acrabeta
Baddan
Gerasa
Apherema
Ephraim
(N)Ain, Pheretae
Michmash
Shechem
Mt.
Gerizim
Mabartha,
Neapolis
Anuathu
Borcaeus
Bethany
Bethphage ?
Bethela
Gabath Saul
Jerusalem
Herodium
Dothaim
Geba
Sebaste, Samaria
Gophna
Bethlehem
Tekoa
Gabaon
Emmaus
Ziph
Chermela, Carmel
Arad
Anabtah
Thamna
Upper
Beth Horon
Beth Rimah
Lower
Beth Horon
Alulos
Terebinthos
Hebron
Jettan
Kefar Aziz
Esthemoa
Anaea
Birat Soreqah
Tibetah
Beth Laban
Aramathea
Caphartoba ?
Adora
Caphethra,
Caparorsa
Malatha
Zanoah
Keilah
Bethletepha
Kefar Qesem
Emmaus
Tower of Aphek
Adida
Burgatah
Capharabis
Antipatris
Anab
Caesarea
Lydda
Betogabris
Belzedek ?
Thala
En-rimmon ?
Joppa
Jamnia
Accaron
Azotus
Ascalon
Beer-sheba
©
12-13

Section 13 Summary of contents & sources
Late Roman and Byzantine Periods

Map No.	Subject	Primary sources	Regional Map Nos. (Section 1)	Macmillan Bible Atlas Map Nos.	Other references and notes
13-1	**Overview and urbanization under Roman rule**				
	a Overview (north)				
	b Development of the municipal system in the Late Roman period	Avi-Yonah 1977: 108-17			
	c City territories and the development of the Roman road system	Avi-Yonah 1977:118-87			
13-2	**Annexation of the Nabataean kingdom and establishment of the Roman province of Arabia**				
	Annexation of the Nabataean Kingdom and establishment of the Roman province of Arabia	Writings of Dio Cassius			
13-3	**Bar Kokhba Revolt I**				
	Early developments and the establishment of Jewish independence	Documents and archaeological finds from the Judaean Wilderness; writings of Dio Cassius and Eusebius; Talmudic sources	1,13,14	259	
13-4	**Bar Kokhba Revolt II**				
	Roman campaigns in the third and fourth years of the revolt; the fall of Jerusalem and Bethther; the last stand in caves in the Judaean Wilderness	Documents and archaeological finds from the Judaean Wilderness; writings of Dio Cassius and Eusebius; Talmudic sources	1,13,14	260	
13-5	**Centre of Jewish life moves to Galilee and the Golan**				
	a Jewish settlement in the north after the Bar Kokhba Revolt (place-names in black)	Talmudic and Rabbinic sources	6,7,8,9,		
	b The movement of the Sanhedrin in Galilee	Babylonian Talmud, Rosh ha-Shanah, 31 b	7,8		
	c List of Priestly courses and their seats in Galilee (place-names in black)	Avi-Yonah 1962: 137-139; Klein 1901; SHY 1977: 162-63	7		

NB

Due to overcrowding or the lack of historical relevance, only selected archaeological sites from the Late Roman/Byzantine period (Section 2-10) appear on the maps of this section.

Avi-Yonah, M

1962 A List of Priestly Courses from Caesarea. *Israel Exploration Journal* 12: 137-39.

1977 *The Holy Land from the Persian to the Arab Conquest (536 B.C.-A.D. 640): A Historical Geography*. Grand Rapids, Michigan: Baker Book House.

Klein, S.

1901 Die Barajta der 24 Priesterabteilungen. *Beiträge zur Geographie und Geschichte Galiläas.* Leipzig.

SHY

1977 *Sefer ha-Yishuv* ed. S. Klein. (Hebrew) Jerusalem.

Section 13–1

Roman-Byzantine Period

SCALE 1:750.000
10 Km
6 M

LEGEND: Historical Source Names • Hebron
Background Names • Jericho
Lines of Communication-International
Lines of Communication-Local (Roman)

E

Rafid
Gaulan
Zeizin
Dium
Bostra
Philadelphia
Ziza (Fort)
Maschana ?
Yaduda
Cochaba
Abila
Gerasa
Maanith
T. el-Jukhadar
Farj
Arbela
Jazer ?
Elealeh
Chedaron
Quneitra
Caspein, Hasfiyah
Capitolias
Esbus
Medeba
Nob
Ramoth ?
Lake Phiale
Seleucia ?
Enganna
Gadora
Dibon
Rabbath Moab, Areopolis
Kafr Nafakh
Dabiyya
Gamala
Umm el-Qanatir
Yaarut
Erga
Baun
Jazer ?
Beelmaus
Amudiyya
Qisrin
Ephron
Zia
Nebo, Fasga
Agaltain ?
Charachmoba
Caesarea Philippi, Panias
ed-Danqalle, Ghadriyya
Sogane
Kanaf
Apheca
Ram Baraq
Iyyon
Gadara
Ragaba
Beth Peor, Phogor
Cariatha
Dan
Dabra, Dabura
Ayyanosh
Hippus
Emmatha, Hammat Gader
Jabesh-gilead
Livias, Julias
Abila
Tholla
Julias
Gergesa, Chorsia
Kefar Harub
Amathus
Machaerus
Pella
Capernaum
Philoteria, Beth-yerah
Kefar Semah ?
Kh. Harrawi
Chorazin
Kefar Agon
Gesher
Mazraa, Agaltain (?)
Cadasa
Qisyon
Tiberias
Gebul ?
Salumias
Aenon ?
Bethagla
Alma
Taricheae
Agrippina ?
Kefar Neboraya
Scythopolis, Beth-shan
Bethmaela
Magdalsenna
Archelais
Mezad, Kh. Qumran
Gischala
Conas
Abelmea
Coreae
Jericho, Hiericho
Meroth ?
H. Shema
Bet Alfa
Noarath
Kefar Hananiya
Phasaelis
Kefar Baram
Meron
Mashkanah
Bersabe
Mt. Tabor
Bezek
Aser
Chozba
En-gedi
Sasa
H. Ammudim
Aendor
Araba
Saleba
Eduma
Hyrcania
Beth Netofa
Dabira, Helenopolis (?)
Naim, Nain
Maledomnei
Masada
En Boqeq
Baca ?
Esdraelon, Jezreel
Bethacath
Thebez
Salem, Sanim
Acrabeta, Aqaba
St. Euthymious
(G)Araba
Gabara
Exaloth
Sulem
Mar Saba
Mafshetah
Suhmata
(Ca)parisima
Nazareth
Ginae
Apherema
Remmon
Arbela ?
Japhia
Silo
Machmas
Mt. Ebal
Tur Shimeon
Isana
Bethany, Lazarium
Miiliya
Saab
Sepphoris, Diocaesarea
Mahalol
Tarbenet
Neapolis
Mt. Gerizim
Bethel
Jerusalem, Aelia Capitolina
Beth-haccherem
Janua ?
Anuathu Borcaeus
Geba
Herodium
Simonias
Sarid
Cathisma
Tyre
Dothaim
Thaanach
En Naqura
Chabulon
Bethlehem, Soraia
Gabatha
Fahma
Sebaste
Gophna
Bethlehem
Tekoa
Legio
Kefar Othnay
Aruir
Capharbarucha
Shefaram
Betoanaea, Beth-anath
Sior
Ziph
Chermela
Ardasqus
Addara ?
Ushah
Capercotnei, Maximianopolis
Ataroth
Bethther
Bethennim
Maon
Arad
Ecdippa
Kefar Sasay
Tibon
Besara, Beth-shearim
Aenam
Thamna
Alulos
Terebinthos
Kh. Susya
Gantah
Apheraea
Anabtah
Gaba ?
Cimona
Beth Horon
Gidora
Seredah
Beth-zur
Hebron
Jettan
Gedru
Caphargamala
Chasalon
Anaea
Ptolemais
Gabatha
Esthemoa
Anaea
Narbata
Birat Soreqah
Betoannaba
Apedno
Enadab
Kh. Summaqa
Jethira
Aramathea
Bethsarisa
Alus
Adollam
Tricomias ?
Malatha
Castra Samaritanorum
Tibetah
Jarimuth ?
Haifa
Modiin
Selebi
Cela
Nasib
Kefar Qesem
Geba
Mearath Telimon
Capparetaea
Tower of Aphek
Caphar-harub
Emmaus, Nicopolis
Saraa
Bethletepha
Jedna
Certha
Calecaelea
Galgulis
Betoannaba
T. Masos
Magdiel
Soran
Bethariph
Adida
Sorech
Ir Nahash
Antipatris
Gazara
Bera ?
Dora
Rantia
Caesarea
Capharsaba
Lydda, Diospolis
Gittham
Betogabris, Eleutheropolis
Thala, Thella
Onus
Accaron
Gallaa
En-rimmon, Eremmon ?
Bersabee
Beth Dagon
Geth
Saalis
Apollonia, Sozusa
Kedron, Gedrus
Birosaba
Joppa
Jamnia
Bareca
Agla
Port of Jamnia
Sapheir
Azotus
Cariathmaus
Azotus Paralius
Gerara
Ascalon
Orda
Sarafia, Diocletianupolis
Birsama
Asalea
Gaza
Anthedon
Maiumas, Constantia, Neapolis
Menois, Maon
(Migdal) Thanatha
Sycomazon
Raphia

Section 13–2

Roman-Byzantine Period

SCALE 1:750.000
10 Km
6 M

LEGEND: Historical Source Names • Hebron
Background Names • Jericho
Lines of Communication-International
Lines of Communication-Local (Roman)

Esbus
Medeba
Beth Horon
Muhai
Qalat el-Hasa
Jurf ed-Darawish
Kh. el-Aqraba
Valtha
Dibon
Rabbath Moab
Dhat Ras
Ainuatha
Kh.ed-Dajaniya
Maan
Thona ?
Charachmoba
Motha
Kh. et-Tannur
Ellebana
Thoana
Afro
Arindela
Augustopolis
Bosor
Sela
Robotha
Naar Safrai
Theman ?
Garba
Adru
Negla
Bennamarim
Sartha
Pentacomia ?
Zoara
Asuada
Phaenon
Gaia
Sodocatha
Praesidium
Toloha
Hasta
Petra, Rekem (?)
Sobora
er-Ram
En-gedi
Masada
En Boqeq
Mezad Zohar
Calamona ?
Ammatha
Jerusalem
Thamara ?
(Mezad Tamar)
Thamara, Eiseiba ?
Tekoa
Moa ?
Ariedela
Hauare ?
Mezad Aqrabbim
Ziph
Chermela
Arad
Hebron
Jettan
Tsafir
H. Mamshit (Kurnub)
Mampsis
Adora
Ad Dianam
Aila
T. Masos
Betogabris
Thala
Moahile ?
Beer-sheba,
Bersabee
Birosaba
H. Avedat
Oboda, Eboda
H. Haluza
Elusa
Gerasa ?
H. Shivta
Soubaita, Sobata
Gerara
Iarda ?
Rehoboth,
H. Rehovot
Ascalon
Birsama
Beraein
Gaza
Maiumas
H. Nizzana
Nessana
Menois
Quseima
Raphia

Section 13–3

Roman-Byzantine Period

SCALE 1:450.000
10 Km
6 M

LEGEND: Historical Source Names • Hebron
Background Names • Jericho
Lines of Communication-International
Lines of Communication-Local (Roman)

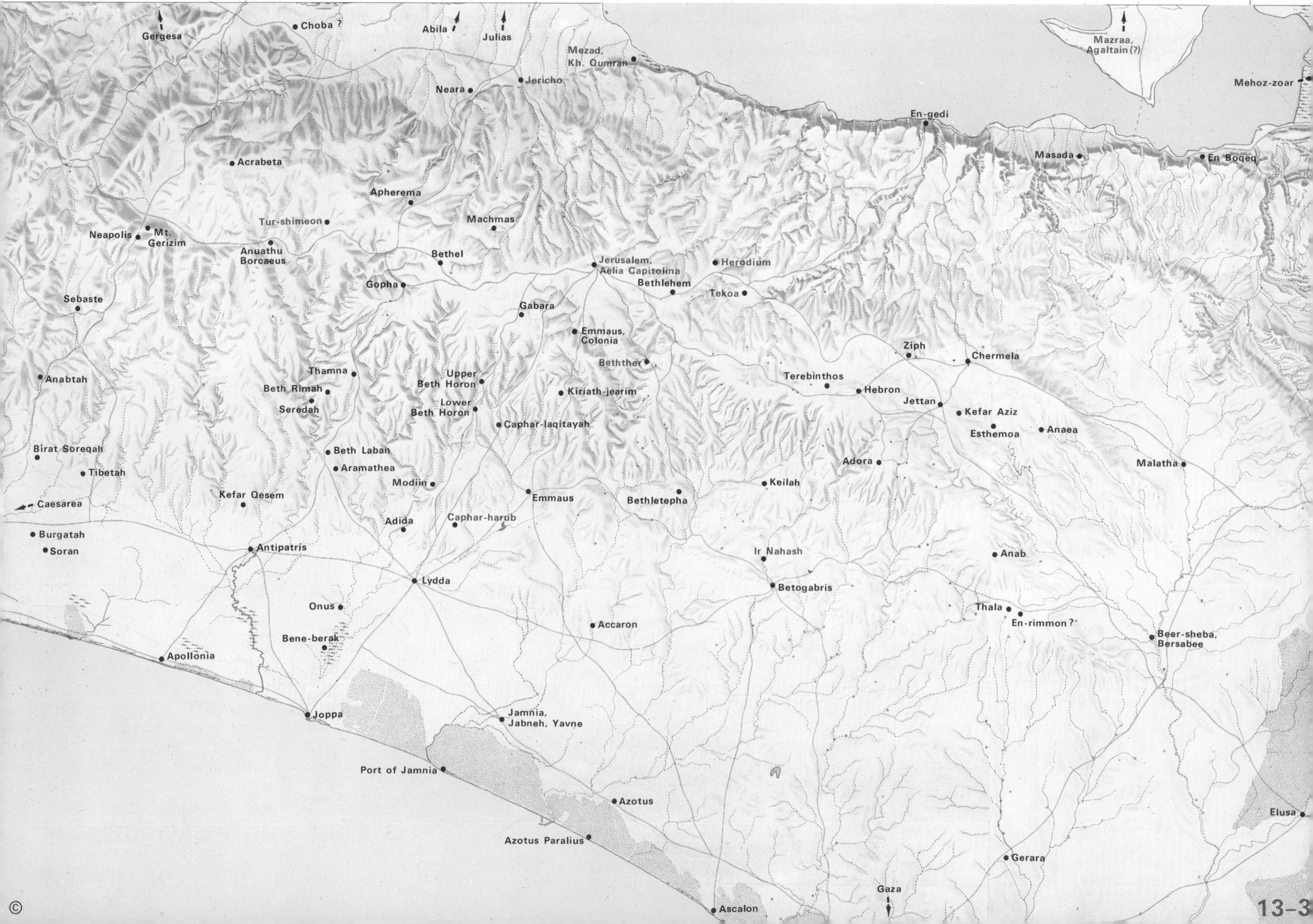

Gergesa
Choba ?
Abila
Julias
Mezad, Kh. Qumran
Jericho
Neara
Mazraa, Agaltain (?)
Mehoz-zoar
En-gedi
Masada
En Boqeq
Acrabeta
Apherema
Tur-shimeon
Machmas
Neapolis
Mt. Gerizim
Anuathu Borcaeus
Bethel
Jerusalem, Aelia Capitolina
Herodium
Bethlehem
Tekoa
Gopha
Sebaste
Gabara
Emmaus, Colonia
Bethther
Ziph
Chermela
Anabtah
Thamna
Upper Beth Horon
Beth Rimah
Seredah
Lower Beth Horon
Kiriath-jearim
Terebinthos
Hebron
Jettan
Kefar Aziz
Esthemoa
Anaea
Caphar-laqitayah
Birat Soreqah
Beth Laban
Aramathea
Tibetah
Modiin
Adora
Malatha
Keilah
Emmaus
Bethletepha
Kefar Qesem
Caesarea
Adida
Caphar-harub
Burgatah
Soran
Antipatris
Ir Nahash
Anab
Lydda
Betogabris
Onus
Thala
En-rimmon ?
Accaron
Beer-sheba, Bersabee
Bene-berak
Apollonia
Joppa
Jamnia, Jabneh, Yavne
Port of Jamnia
Azotus
Elusa
Azotus Paralius
Gerara
Gaza
Ascalon

©

Section 13-4

Roman-Byzantine Period

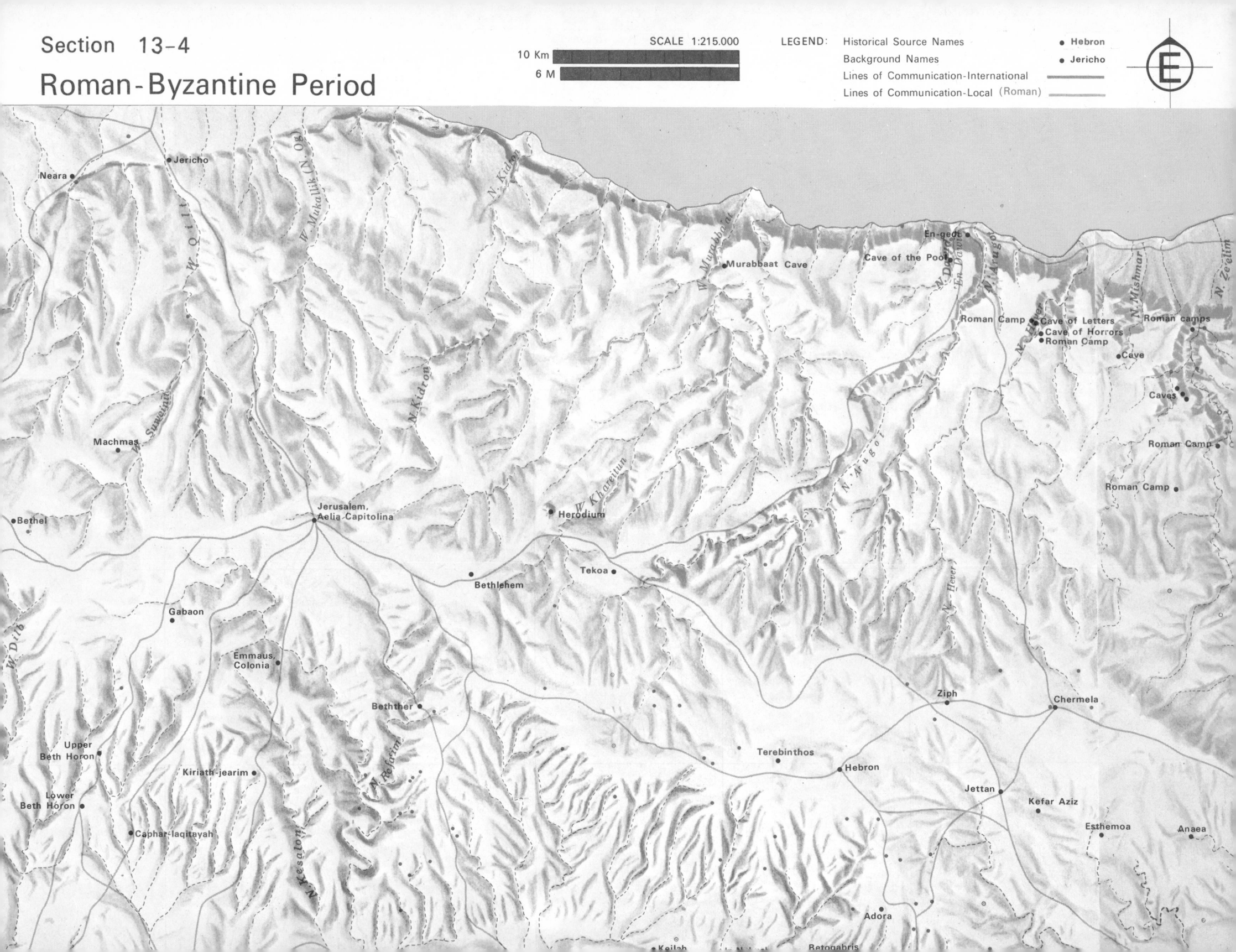

SCALE 1:215.000

10 Km

6 M

LEGEND:
- Historical Source Names • Hebron
- Background Names • Jericho
- Lines of Communication-International
- Lines of Communication-Local (Roman)

Jericho
Neara
W. Qilt
W. Mukallik (N. Og)
N. Kidron
En-gedi
Cave of the Pool
N. David
'En David
N. Arugot
Murabbaat Cave
W. Murabbaat
N. Mishmar
N. Ze'elim
Roman Camp
Cave of Letters
Cave of Horrors
Roman Camp
Roman camps
Cave
Caves
Roman Camp
Roman Camp
N. Hever
N. Kidron
W. Suweinit
Machmas
N. Arugot
W. Khareitun
Herodium
Jerusalem,
Aelia Capitolina
Bethel
Tekoa
Bethlehem
Gabaon
W. Dilb
Emmaus,
Colonia
Bethther
Ziph
Chermela
Upper
Beth Horon
Kiriath-jearim
N. Refaim
Terebinthos
Hebron
Jettan
Lower
Beth Horon
Kefar Aziz
Caphar-laqitayah
Esthemoa
Anaea
N. Kesalon
Adora
Keilah
Betogabris

Section 13-5

Roman-Byzantine Period

SCALE 1:300.000
10 Km
6 M

LEGEND: Historical Source Names — Hebron
Background Names — Jericho
Lines of Communication-International
Lines of Communication-Local (Roman)

E

Kefar Nafakh
Dabiyya
Gamala
Umm el-Qanatir
Yaarut
Camus
Ephron
Amudiyya
Qisrin
Sogane
Deir Aziz
Apheca
Ram Barag
Panias, Qisrarion,
Caesarea Philippi
ed-Danqalle, Ghadriyya
Kanaf
Hammat Gader,
Emmatha
Gadara
Kh. el-Asaliya
Ayyanosh
Hippus
Iyyon
Dabra, Dabura
Kefar Harub
Dan
Hammat Pell
Pella
Kh. er-Rafid
Julias,
Bethsaida (?)
Thella
Kh. ed-Dikke
Kefar Semah
Aricha, Beth-yerah
Philoteria
Kefar Agon
H. Shurah
Capernaum
Kh. Harrawi
Chorazin
Gesher
Heptapegon
Hammath,
Ammathus
Tiberias
Beela
Rosh Pinna
Gennesaret
Agrippina,
Cochaba ?
Cadasa
Qisyon
Jamnith
Beth Maon,
Bethmaus
Sayydatah
Kefar Yamma
Gebul ?
Kefar Neboraya
Migdal, Nunnayah,
Taricheae, Magdala
Beth-shan,
Scythopolis
Rooh
Alma
Biri
Acchabare
Sergunin
Ullama
Dalton
Zefat, Sepph
Arbel, Abila
Huqoq
H. Sarona
Adamah
Kefar Hittaya
Gush Halab,
Gischala
Safsofah
Meroth ?
Mamliah
Hapharaim ?
Kefar Shabtay
Tekoa ?,
H. Shema
Kefar Nimrah
Bet Alfa
Meron,
Meroth (?)
Parod
Lubiya
Kefar Uziel ?,
H. Ammudim
Kefar Baram
Bersabe
Kefar Hananiya
Gelbus
Mearaia
Ailabo
Mashkanah
Mt. Tabor,
Itabyrium
Sasa
Neoran
Beth Dagon
Zalmon,
Selame
Beth Netofa
Aendor
Dabaritta
Turan ?
Tubani
Araba
Rama
En Teena
Kefar Yohannah
Bethacath
En Tab ?
Nain
Kefar Aris ?, Garis ?
(Kafr Kana)
Shezor
(G)Araba, Gabara
Sulem
Baca ?
Esdraelon
Aita
Yattir
Gath Hepher
Exaloth
Rimmon
Rani ?
Mafshetah
Cana
Nazareth
Ginae
(Ca)parisima
Suhmata
Sepphoris,
Diocaesarea
Zippori
Sikhnin, Sogane
Ruma
Arbela ?
Yodefat, Jotapata
Japhia
Jokereth
Miiliya
Kefar Mandi
Janoah
Beth-haccherem
Shichin,
Asochis
Aitalo
Ginneigar
Gelil
Saab
Cochaba ?
Mahalol
Tarbenet
Simoniyah,
Simonias
Janua ?
Zenitah
Gabatha
Thaanach
Kabul, Chabulon
Apharatha ?
Tyre
Gaaton
Beth Hobaya
Kefar Tamartah
Abelim
Bethlehem
Hivria
Capercotnei, Legio,
Kefar Otnay
Hanotah
Shefaram
Beth Anath,
Beth Yanai,
Betoaenea
Pi Masoba
Kefar Yasif
Bezet
Kabrita
Ushah
Ardasqus
Kefar Sasay
Tibon
Besara
Beth shearim
Bethbeten
Achzib, Ecdippa
Cimona
Apharaea
Acco,
Ptolemais
Gedrus
13-5

Section 14 Introduction

Archaeology of Jerusalem

Map No.	Subject
14-0	Key to major archaeological remains visible today
14-1	Jerusalem in the First Temple Period (see Sections 7, 8 & 9)
14-2	Jerusalem in the Second Temple Period (see Sections 10, 11 & 12)
14-3	Jerusalem in the Byzantine Period (see Section 13)

The archaeological data have been presented symbolically, superimposed on a modern street plan of the city. For exact location of sites, however, students are referred to maps of larger scale.

Map 14-0 shows only those major archaeological remains which are visible today, together with key references which relate to the other three period maps.

Maps 14-1, 14-2 & 14-3 show the KNOWN archaeological remains of each period (depicted in BLACK and SOLID BLUE) plus the main academic 'speculations' (depicted in RED and DOTTED BLUE), which attempt to correlate these remains with the historical literary sources. Red NAMES indicate the names of places or buildings which are known from these sources, but whose exact location is uncertain.

For the sake of clarity in maps of this size, the exact configuration and relative size of the remains have been simplified graphically. Thus city walls are shown with lines of constant width although the actual thickness varies. Conjectured city walls are not interrupted by gates, although it is assumed that these existed.

Question marks indicate disagreement as to the nature or period of the remains shown.

The bibliography is for general student use. A more comprehensive bibliography covering all the data given in these maps is available separately, on request.

Names of Jerusalem

Salem
Jebus
Jerusalem
Memshath
Antiochia
Hierosolyma
Yerushalayim
el-Quds

Notes

Archaeology of Jerusalem

ABBREVIATIONS:
EAEHL — Encyclopedia of Archaeological Excavations in the Holy Land
MUSJ — Mélanges de l'Université Saint Joseph de Beyrouth
ZDPV — Zeitschrift des Deutschen Palästina-Vereins

General References

Avi-Yonah, M.
1954 *The Madeba Mosaic Map.* Jerusalem
1956 *Sepher Yerushalayim* vol. 1. (Hebrew) Jerusalem
1975 Jerusalem in the Hellenistic and Roman Periods. Vol. 7 207-49 of the *World History of the Jewish People.* Rutgers University
1976 Jerusalem. Pp. 540-647 in vol. 2 of *EAEHL*. Jerusalem

Avigad, N.
1980 *The Upper City of Jerusalem* (Hebrew) Jerusalem

Bagatti, B.
1979 Recherches sur le Site du Temple de Jérusalem (Ier-VIIe Siècle). *Studium Biblicum Franciscanum.* (French) Jerusalem

Bahat, D.
1976 *Historical Atlas of Jerusalem.* Jerusalem

Busink, T.
1970 *Der Tempel von Jerusalem, von Salmo bis Herodes.* (German) Leiden

Donner, H. and Cuppers, H.
1977 *Die Mosaikkarte von Madaba, Teil I, Tafelband.* (German) Wiesbaden

Kenyon, K.
1974 *Digging up Jerusalem.* London

Simons, J.
1952 *Jerusalem in the Old Testament.* Leiden

Tsafrir, Y.
1975 Jerusalem. *Reallexikon zur Byzantinischen Kunst.* (German) Stuttgart

Tushingham, A.
1978 *Yerushalayim — Archaeology in the Levant* 183-94. Warminster

Vincent, H.
1912 *Jérusalem Antique* vol. 1. (French) Paris

Vincent, H. and Abel, F.
1914-26 *Jérusalem Nouvelle* vols. 1-3. (French) Paris

Vincent, H. and Steve, A.
1956 *Jérusalem de L'Ancien Testament* vols. 1-3. (French) Paris

Wilkinson, J.
1978 *Jerusalem Pilgrims before the Crusades* Warminster

Yadin, Y. (Ed.)
1975 *Jerusalem Revealed — Archaeology in the Holy City 1967-1974.* Jerusalem

First Temple Period References

Avigad, N.
1954 *Ancient Monuments in the Kidron Valley.* (Hebrew) Jerusalem

Broshi, M
1974 The Expansion of Jerusalem in the Reigns of Hezekiah and Manasseh. *Israel Exploration Journal* 24.1: 20-26

Johns, C
1950 The Citadel, a Summary of Work since 1934. *Quarterly of the Department of Antiquities in Palestine* 14: 121-90

Kenyon, K.
1965 Excavations in Jerusalem, 1964. *Palestine Exploration Quarterly* 97: 18-20

Kloner, A. and Davis, D.
1978 A Burial Cave of the Late Israelite Period on the Slopes of Mt. Zion. *Qadmoniot* 11.1: 16-20. (Hebrew)

Mazar, A.
1976 Iron Age Burial Caves North of the Damascus Gate, Jerusalem. *Israel Exploration Journal* 26.1: 1-8

Shaheen, N.
1977 The Siloam End of Hezekiah's Tunnel. *Palestine Exploration Quarterly* 109.2: 107-12

Tushingham, A.
1968 The Armenian Garden. *Palestine Exploration Quarterly* 100.2: 109-11

Ussishkin, D.
1970 The Necropolis from the Kingdom of Judah at Silwan, Jerusalem. *Biblical Archaeologist* 33: 34-46

Wilkinson, J.
1978 The Pool of Siloam. *Levant* 10: 116-25

Second Temple Period References

Avigad, N.
1976 *Archaeological Discoveries in the Jewish Quarter of Jerusalem — Second Temple Period.* Jerusalem

Ben-Dov, M.
1978 Herodian Jerusalem Revisited. *Christian News from Israel* 26.3-4: 138-42

Benoit, P.
1971 L'Antonia d'Hérode le Grand et le Forum Oriental d'Aelia Capitolina. *Harvard Theological Review* 64: 135-67. (French)

Broshi, M.
1977 Along Jerusalem's Walls. *Biblical Archaeologist* 40.1: 11-17

Hamrick, E.
1977 The Third Wall of Agrippa 1. *Biblical Archaeologist* 40.1: 18-23

Kaufmann, A.
1977 A New Light upon Zion: The Plan and Precise Location of the Second Temple. *Anel* 43: 63-99

Lux, U.
1972 Vorläufiger Bericht uber die Ausgrabung unter der Erlöserkirche im Muristan in der Altstadt von Jerusalem in dem jahren 1970-1971. *ZDPV* 88: 185-201

Mazar, B.
1978 Herodian Jerusalem in the Light of the excavations of the South and Southwest of the Temple Mount. *Israel Exploration Journal* 28.1: 236-37

Pixner, B.
1976 An Essene Quarter in Jerusalem. *Studia Hierosolymitana PT 1 Collectio Major* 22: 56-286 Jerusalem
1979 Noch Einmal das Prätorium. *ZDPV* 95.1. (German)

Schick, C.
1892 'Gordon's Tomb'. *Palestine Exploration Fund Quarterly Statement* 120-24

Tsafrir, Y.
1975 The Location of the Seleucid Akra in Jerusalem. *Revue Biblique* 82.4: 501-22

Vriezen, K.
1978 Zweiter Vorläufiger Bericht uber der Erlöserkirche im Muristan in der Altstadt von Jerusalem (1972-74). *ZDPV* 94.1: 76-81

Wilson, C.
1906 *Golgotha and the Holy Sepulchre* 124-26. London

Wilkinson, J.
1975 The Streets of Jerusalem. *Levant* 7: 118-36

Byzantine Period References

Avigad, N.
1977 A Building Inscription of the Emperor Justinian and the Nea Inscription of Jerusalem: Preliminary Note. *Israel Exploration Journal* 27.2-3: 145-51

Coüasnon, C.
1974 *The Church of the Holy Sepulchre, Jerusalem.* London

Margalit, S.
1977 The Christian Quarter Road. *Hadashot Arkheologiot* 61-62: 32. (Hebrew)

Margowski, Y.
1971 Burdj Kabrit et Environs. *Revue Biblique* 78: 597-98. (French)

Milik, J.
1960-61 La Topographie de Jerusalem vers La Fin de l'Epoque Byzantine. *MUSJ* 37: 127-84 (French)

Ovadiah, A.
1970 *Corpus of the Byzantine Churches in the Holy Land.* Bonn

Pinkerfeld, J.
1960 David's Tomb: Notes of the History of the Building. *Bulletin Rabinowitz* 3: 41-43

Tobler, T.
1874 *Descriptiones Terrae Sanctae.* (Latin, German) Leipzig

Tsafrir, Y.
1977 Muqaddasi's Gates of Jerusalem: a New Identification Based on Byzantine Sources. *Israel Exploration Journal* 27.2-3: 152-61

Watson, C.
1913 Commemoratorium de Casis Dei Vel Monasteriis. *Palestine Exploration Fund Quarterly Statement* 22-23

LEGEND: °Access by special permission
*To be opened to the public in the future

Archaeology of Jerusalem

1st Temple Period

City Walls

1-1 Wall & building remains: E *slope of Ophel*
1-2 * Hezekiah's wall & building remains: *Jewish Quarter*
1-3 * Israelite tower & building remains: *Jewish Quarter*
1-4 Israelite wall remains: *Citadel of David*

Water Supply

1-5 Gihon spring & Warren's shaft: *Kidron valley*
1-6 Siloam tunnel: *Kidron valley*
1-7 Hezekiah's tunnel: *Kidron valley*
1-8 Hamra pool (Birkat el-Hamrah): *Kidron valley*

Religious Buildings

1-9 The Sacred Rock: *mosque of Omar (Dome of the Rock)*

Secular Buildings

1-10 Building remains: E *Slope of Ophel*
1-11 Building remains (Millo): *Ophel*
1-12 * Building remains: N *of Haye Olam St, Jewish Quarter*
1-13 * Building remains: W *of Jews St, Jewish Quarter*
1-14 Building remains: W *side of Armenian Quarter*
1-15 Building remains: *Citadel of David*

Tombs

1-16 Tomb of Pharaoh's Daughter & Monolithic tomb. *Silwan*
1-17 Royal tombs: *Ophel*
1-18 Tombs: *inside Dung gate*
1-19 Tombs ?: *outside Dung gate*
1-20 Tombs: *outside* W *city wall*
1-21 Tombs: *by St. Andrew's church*
1-22 Tombs: *Hinnom valley*
1-23 * Tombs: *by Birkat es-Sultan*
1-24 ° Tombs: *Ecole Biblique (Française)*
1-25 Tomb ('Gordon's/Garden'): *Nablus Rd*
1-26 ° Tombs: *White Sisters convent, Nablus Rd*
1-27 Tombs: *Nablus Rd bus station*
1-28 ° Tombs: *Greek Orthodox Praetorium*

Miscellaneous

1-29 *° Israelite remains: *church of the Redeemer*

2nd Temple Period

Walls

2-1 1st wall remains: E *slope of Ophel*
2-2 Wall remains: *near* S *Temple wall*
2-3 * Hellenistic tower (1st wall): *Jewish Quarter*
2-4 * 1st wall remains & gate tower: *Jewish Quarter*
2-5 Tower of Hippicus, wall,* towers & building remains (1st and ? 3rd walls): *Citadel of David*
2-6 1st wall remains: *under and beside* W *Turkish city wall*
2-7 *° 1st wall tower & gate: *by Protestant cemetery, Mt Zion*
2-8 *° Wall fragment (? 2nd): *church of the Redeemer*
2-9 Wall (? 2nd) & gate: *Alexandrovsky church (White Russian)*
2-10 Wall (? 2nd or 3rd) & gate: *under Damascus gate*
2-11 Triumphal arch ('Ecce Homo'): *Sisters of Sion convent*
2-12 ° Wall (? 3rd) remains: *college of Christian Brothers*
2-13 Wall (? 3rd) remains: N *of the Old City,*
by (1) Rizek's garage (St George's Rd)
by (2) American consulate
in (3) Albright institute of archaeology

Water Supply

2-14 Lower aqueduct: SW & S *of the Old City and Jewish Quarter*
2-15 Mamilla pool: *Independence park*
2-16 Amygdalon (Hezekiah's pool): *by Petra hotel, Jaffa gate*
2-17 Struthion pools: *by 'Ecce Homo' arch*
2-18 Sheep pools & building remains: *seminary of St Anne*
2-19 Birkat Sitti Maryam: *pool by St Stephen's gate*
2-20 Gihon spring, Hezekiah's tunnel, Siloam & Hamra pools

Religious Buildings (Temple)

2-21 Temple enclosure with surrounding walls, including building remains, baths, pools, conduits & streets
2-22 *° Warren's gate: *Western wall*
2-23 Wilson's arch: *Western wall*
2-24 Barclay's gate: *Western wall*
2-25 Robinson's arch: *Western wall*
2-26 Hulda gates & steps and Single gate: S *Temple wall*
2-27 The Sacred Rock: *mosque of Omar (Dome of the Rock)*
2-28 *° 'Solomon's stables': *under Temple Mt*

Secular Buildings

2-29 ° Building remains (House of Caiaphas): *Armenian cemetery*
2-30 Building remains & terraces: SE *corner of Ophel*
2-31 *Building remains: *Jewish Quarter*
2-32 *Building remains & pool: *Jewish Quarter*
2-33 Building remains: *outside* S *Turkish city wall*
2-34 Building remains & cisterns: *St Peter's church*
2-35 Building remains: *inside* S *Turkish city wall*

Tombs

2-36 Herod's family tomb: *by King David hotel*
2-37 Tombs of the Sanhedrin: *Sanhedria*
2-38 'Tomb of the Kings' (family tomb of Queen Helena of Adiabene): *Salah ed-Din St*
2-39 Tomb ('Gordon's/Garden'): *Nablus Rd*
2-40 Tombs of 'the Prophets': *Mt of Olives*
2-41 Tombs of 'Absalom', 'Zachariah' & Bene Hezir: *Kidron Valley*
2-42 Necropolis: *Silwan*
2-43 Tombs: *Hinnom valley*
2-44 Tombs: *church of the Holy Sepulchre*
2-45 Tombs: *by church of St Peter in Gallicantu*
2-46 Tombs: *Hebrew university on Mt Scopus*
2-47 Tomb of Jason: *Alfasi St, Rehavia*

Miscellaneous

2-48 Foundations, cisterns etc: SW *of Dung gate*
2-49 'Solomon's quarries': *by Damascus gate*

Byzantine Period

City Walls

3-1 Tower of David, city wall, towers & building remains: *Citadel of David*
3-2 Wall remains: E *slope of Ophel*
3-3 Wall remains: *near* S *Temple wall*
3-4 Wall remains: *under* W *Turkish city wall*
3-5 Wall & gate remains: *under Damascus gate*
3-6 Triumphal arch ('Ecce Homo' arch) & the Small Forum pavement: *Flagellation monastery, Sisters of Sion* ° *convent and Greek Orthodox Praetorium*
3-7 *° Wall, tower, gate: *by Protestant cemetery, Mt Zion*
3-8 Gate, atrium, wall, pavement & columns: *in the Alexandrovsky church (White Russian), Christian Quarter*
3-9 ° Golden gate: E *side of city wall*
3-10 Wall remains: *under* N *Turkish city wall*

Streets

3-11 Pavement: *Christian Quarter Rd*
3-12 * Pavement & wall of 'Cardo': *opposite Rambam & Hurvah synagogues, Jewish Quarter*
3-13 ° Pavement: *Armenian cemetery, Mt Zion*
3-14 Pavement: *by Western wall*
3-15 Pavement & steps: *outside Dung gate*
3-16 Stepped street: *inside* S *Turkish city wall*
3-17 Stepped streets: *by St. Peter's church*

Water Supply

3-18 Lower aqueduct: SW & S *of the Old City & Jewish Quarter*
3-19 Mamilla pool: *Independence park*
3-20 Amygdalon (Hezekiah's pool): *by Petra hotel, Jaffa gate*
3-21 Struthion pools: *by 'Ecce Homo' arch*
3-22 Probatica pool: *seminary of St Anne*
3-23 Birkat Sitti Maryam. *pool by St Stephen's gate*
3-24 Gihon spring, Hezekiah's tunnel, Siloam & Hamra pools: *Kidron valley*
3-25 ° Pool of St Abraham: *monastery of St Abraham by the church of the Holy Sepulchre*

Religious Buildings

3-26 Church of the Holy Sepulchre: *Christian Quarter*
3-27 * Foundations, walls & cistern of Nea church complex: *Jewish Quarter*
3-28 ° Church complex of Sts Menas & James: *Armenian Quarter*
3-29 ° Church of St John the Baptist: *Christian Quarter*
3-30 Probatica church: *seminary of St Anne*
3-31 Church of the Virgin Mary & tombs: *Gethsemane*
3-32 Grotto of Gethsemane
3-33 Church of Gethsemane & tombs
3-34 Church of 'St Anna' & tombs: *Mt of Olives*
3-35 Church of the Ascension: *Mt of Olives*
3-36 Church of Eleona: *Mt of Olives*
3-37 Monastery of Haceldama & tombs: *Hinnom valley*
3-38 Church of St Peter in Gallicantu
3-39 Church of St Stephen: *Ecole Biblique (Française)*
3-40 Church of St Polyeucte: N *of Damascus gate*
3-41 Church in the Small Forum: *monastery of Flagellation*
3-42 'David's tombs': *synagogue on Mt Zion*

Secular Buildings

3-43 Bath house: *by* SW *corner of Temple Mt*
3-44 Hospice: *by* S *wall of Temple Mt*
3-45 ° Building remains (House of Caiaphas): *Armenian cemetery*
3-46 * Building remains & mosaic: N *of Haye Olam St, Jewish Quarter*
3-47 * Building remains & pool: W *of Jews St, Jewish Quarter*
3-48 * Building with apse: *Syrian convent Rd, Jewish Quarter*
3-49 Building remains: *by church of St Peter in Gallicantu*
3-50 Building remains: N *of Franciscan cemetery, Mt Zion*
3-51 Building remains: *by* S *Turkish city wall*
3-52 Foundations, cisterns & street: SW *of Dung gate*

Tombs

3-53 Tombs: *on slopes of Hinnom valley*
3-54 Tombs & building remains: *by American consulate*

Inscriptions

3-55 Inscription: *Western wall*
3-56 Inscriptions: *Syrian church of St. Mark*

Section 14-0

Key to major archaeological remains visible today

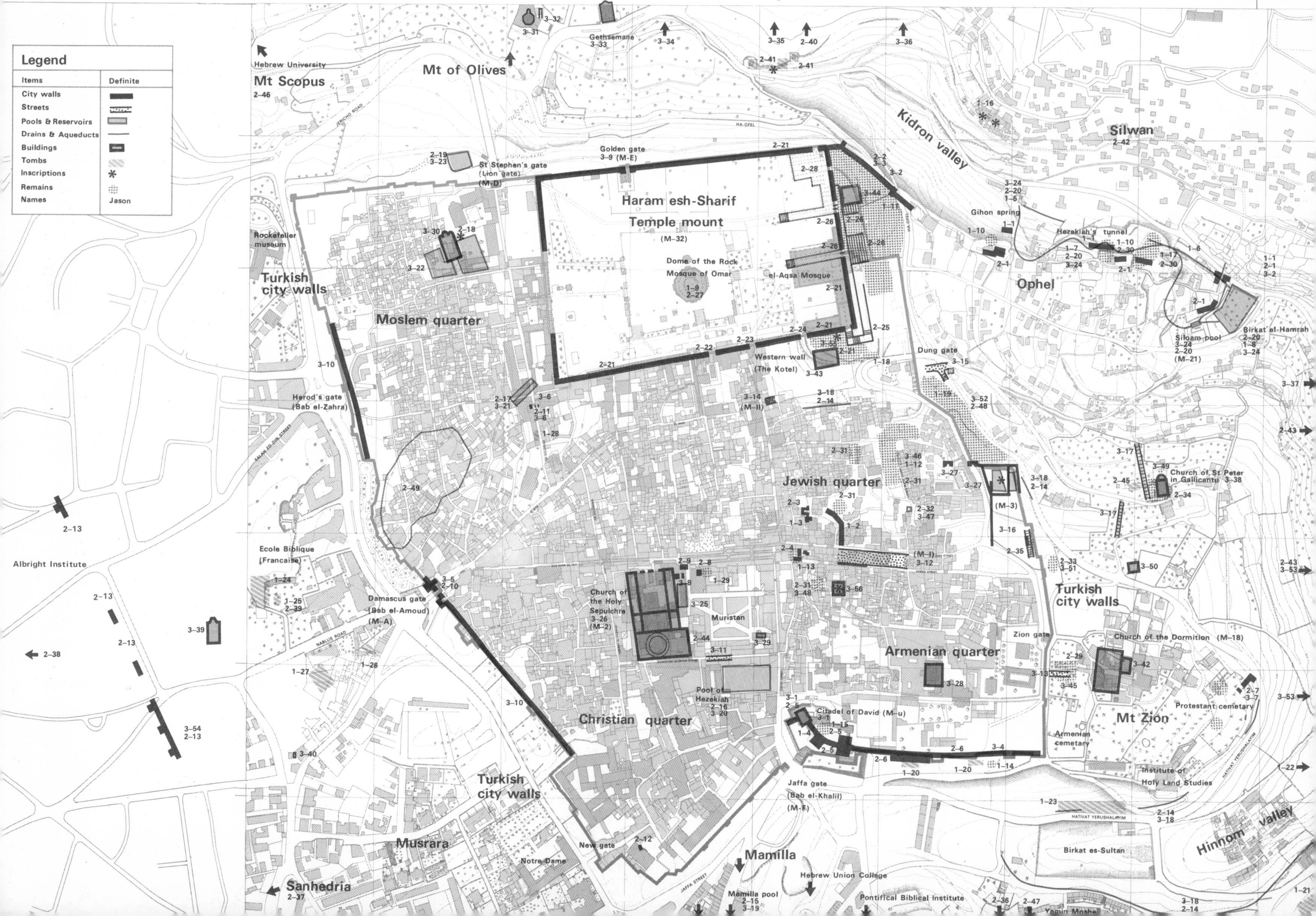

SCALE
300 Metres
300 Yards
E
Legend
Items
Definite
City walls
Streets
Pools & Reservoirs
Drains & Aqueducts
Buildings
Tombs
Inscriptions
Remains
Names
Jason
Hebrew University
Mt Scopus
Mt of Olives
Gethsemane
Kidron valley
Silwan
Golden gate
St Stephen's gate (Lion gate)
Haram esh-Sharif
Temple mount
Dome of the Rock
Mosque of Omar
el-Aqsa Mosque
Western wall (The Kotel)
Gihon spring
Hezekiah's tunnel
Ophel
Siloam pool
Birkat el-Hamrah
Dung gate
Rockefeller museum
Turkish city walls
Moslem quarter
Herod's gate (Bab el-Zahra)
Jewish quarter
Church of St Peter in Gallicantu
Ecole Biblique (Francaise)
Albright Institute
Damascus gate (Bab el-Amoud)
Church of the Holy Sepulchre
Muristan
Armenian quarter
Zion gate
Church of the Dormition
Pool of Hezekiah
Christian quarter
Citadel of David
Mt Zion
Protestant cemetary
Armenian cemetary
Institute of Holy Land Studies
Jaffa gate (Bab el-Khalil)
Musrara
Notre Dame
New gate
Mamilla
Hebrew Union College
Birkat es-Sultan
Hinnom valley
Sanhedria
Mamilla pool
Pontifical Biblical Institute
Yamin Moshe

Section 14-1

Jerusalem in the First Temple Period

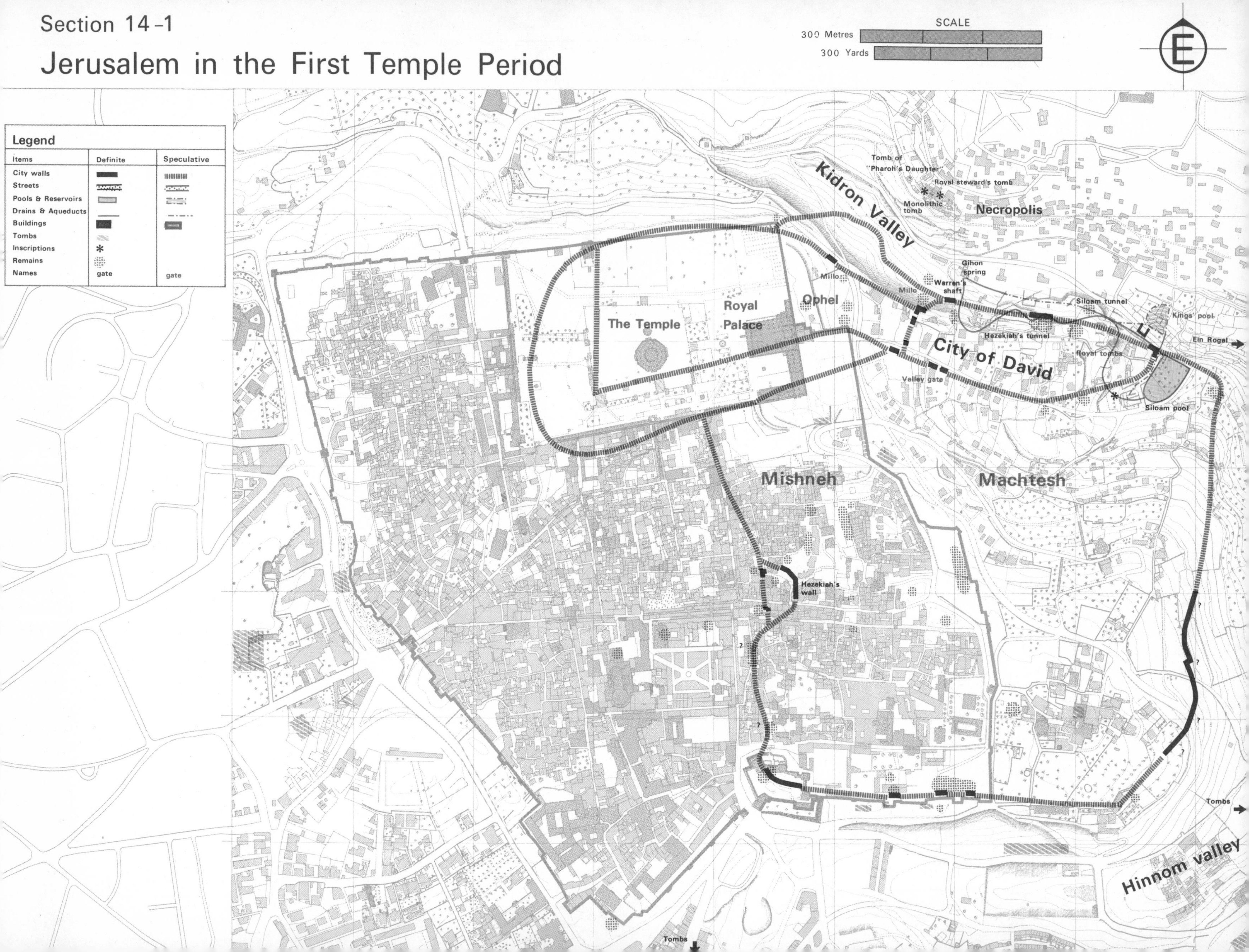
SCALE
300 Metres
300 Yards
E
Legend
Items
Definite
Speculative
City walls
Streets
Pools & Reservoirs
Drains & Aqueducts
Buildings
Tombs
Inscriptions
Remains
Names
gate
gate
Kidron Valley
Tomb of "Pharoh's Daughter"
Royal steward's tomb
Monolithic tomb
Necropolis
Gihon spring
Millo
Millo
Warren's shaft
Siloam tunnel
Kings' pool
Ophel
Royal Palace
The Temple
Hezekiah's tunnel
City of David
Ein Rogel
Royal tombs
Valley gate
Siloam pool
Mishneh
Machtesh
Hezekiah's wall
Tombs
Hinnom valley
Tombs

Section 14–2

Jerusalem in the Second Temple Period

SCALE
300 Metres
300 Yards

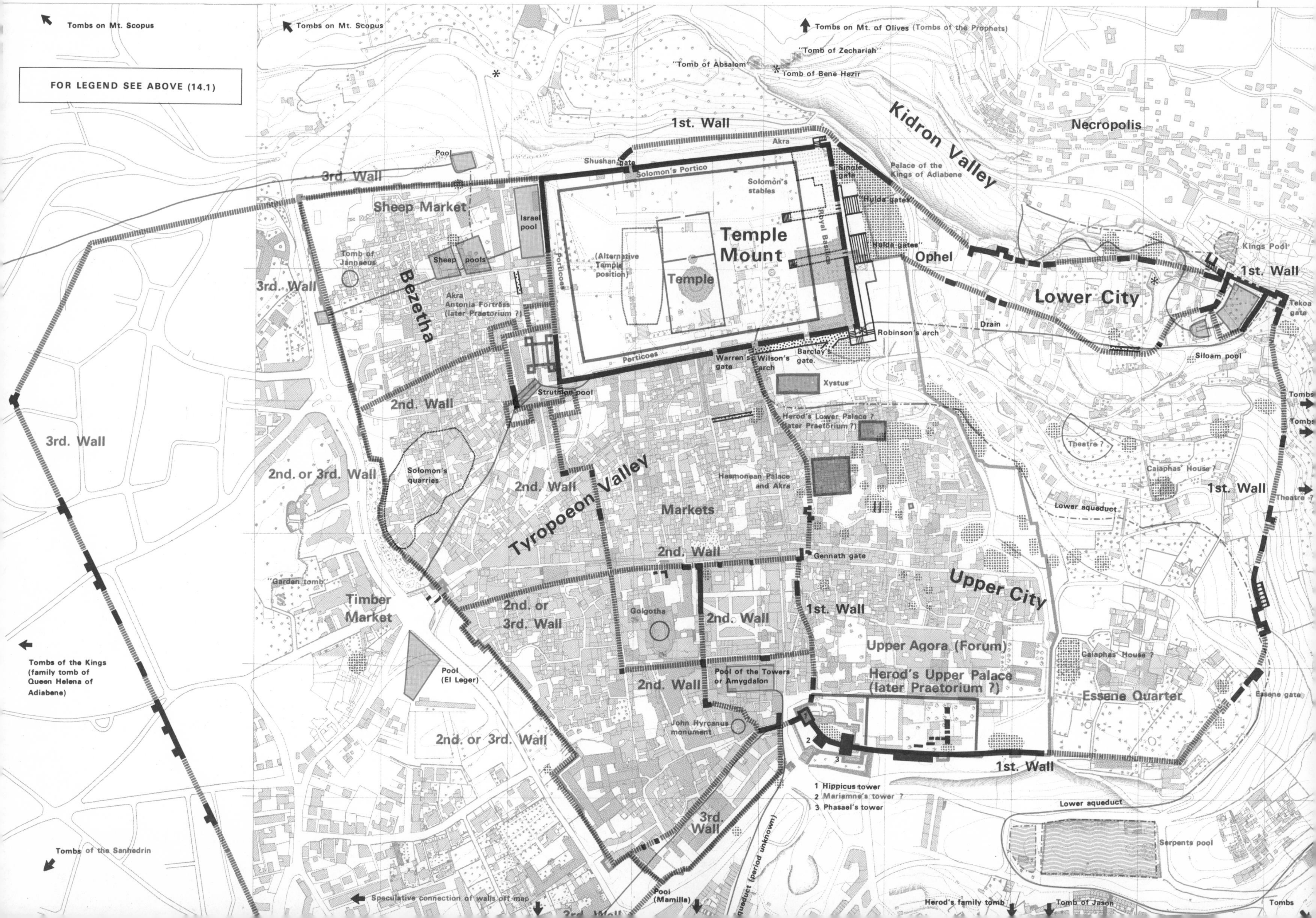

Tombs on Mt. Scopus
FOR LEGEND SEE ABOVE (14.1)
Tombs on Mt. Scopus
Tombs on Mt. of Olives (Tombs of the Prophets)
"Tomb of Zechariah"
"Tomb of Absalom"
Tomb of Bene Hezir
Kidron Valley
Necropolis
1st. Wall
Akra
Shushan gate
Solomon's Portico
Solomon's stables
Single gate
Palace of the Kings of Adiabene
"Hulda gates"
"Hulda gates"
Pool
3rd. Wall
Sheep Market
Israel pool
Temple Mount
Royal Basilica
Ophel
Kings Pool
1st. Wall
Tomb of Jannaeus
Sheep pools
Porticoes
(Alternative Temple position)
Temple
Bezetha
3rd. Wall
Akra Antonia Fortress (later Praetorium ?)
Lower City
Drain
Tekoa gate
Robinson's arch
Porticoes
Warren's gate
Wilson's arch
Barclay's gate
Siloam pool
2nd. Wall
Struthion pool
Xystus
Herod's Lower Palace ? (later Praetorium ?)
Tombs
Tombs
3rd. Wall
Theatre ?
Solomon's quarries
2nd. or 3rd. Wall
2nd. Wall
Tyropoeon Valley
Hasmonean Palace and Akra
Caiaphas' House ?
1st. Wall
Theatre
Markets
Lower aqueduct
2nd. Wall
Gennath gate
"Garden tomb"
Upper City
Timber Market
2nd. or 3rd. Wall
Golgotha
2nd. Wall
1st. Wall
Upper Agora (Forum)
Tombs of the Kings (family tomb of Queen Helena of Adiabene)
Pool (El Leger)
2nd. Wall
Pool of the Towers or Amygdalon
Herod's Upper Palace (later Praetorium ?)
Caiaphas' House ?
Essene Quarter
Essene gate
John Hyrcanus monument
2nd. or 3rd. Wall
1st. Wall
1 Hippicus tower
2 Mariamne's tower ?
3 Phasael's tower
Lower aqueduct
3rd. Wall
Serpents pool
Tombs of the Sanhedrin
Aqueduct (period unknown)
Speculative connection of walls off map
Pool (Mamilla)
Herod's family tomb
Tomb of Jason
Tombs

Section 14–3

Jerusalem in the Byzantine Period

SCALE
300 Metres
300 Yards
E
Legend
Items
Definite
Speculative
City walls
Streets
Pools & Reservoirs
Drains & Aqueducts
Buildings
Tombs
Inscriptions
Remains
Names
Church
Church
Madaba map references
(M-22)
Tomb of the Virgin
Grotto of Gethsemane
Church of the Agony (Gethsemane)
Tombs and Church of St Anna or St. Anastasia
Church of the Ascension and Eleona church on the Mt. of Olives
Chapels
Chapels
Kidron Valley
Pinnacle of the Temple (M-m)
Golden gate (M-E)
Pool
Benjamin or Eastern gate (M-D)
Chapel of St Mary
Probatica church (M-31)
Probatica pools
Street (M-III)
Temple area (deserted) (M-32)
Monastery (M-34)
Church of St. Mary Magdalene (M-30)
Small Forum
Triumphal Arch ("Ecce Homo")
Bath house
Bath house
Gate (M-C)
Grotto of Jeremiah
Church of Siloam
Drain
Street and drain
Monastery & Tombs of Haceldama
Cardo Colonnaded Street (M-II)
Cardo Colonnaded street (M-II)
Bath house (M-28)
Church of St. Sophia (Pilates house) and Byzantine Praetorium (M-24)
Decumanus
Church complex of the Nea (M-3)
Cisterns
Stepped street
Church of St. Peter (M-22)
Bath house (M-21)
Stepped street
Eudocia's palace ?(M-29)
Church of Sts. Cosmas and Damian (M-27)
Bath house
Tetrapylon (M-23)
Cardo Colonnaded street (M-I)
Cardo Colonnaded street (M-I)
Steps
Monastery (M-20)
(M-p)
Tombs
Column (M-1)
Arch (M-4)
Plazza
Neapolis or St. Stephen's gate (M-A)
Priests' house (M-6)
Byzantine Forum (M-8)
Street (M-IV)
Syrian church
Drain
Gate of the Nea (M-B)
Church of St. Stephen
Patriarch's Hospice or Smith's Market (M-7)
Church of St. John the Baptist
Iberian monastery (M-16)
House of Caiaphas (M-16)
Basilica of the Holy Zion (M-18)
Patriarch's palace (M-5)
Church of the Holy Sepulchre (Anastasis) (M-2)
Monastery of St. Sabas (M-15)
Church complex of St Menas & St James
Synagogue Coenaculum (M-19)
(M-r)
Tombs
Gate
(M-s)
Tower of David (M-v)
Monastery of St Menas
Church of St Polyeuctus
Orpheus mosaic
Gate (M-F)
Lower aqueduct
Aqueduct
Pool (Mamilla)
Monastery & Tombs (in YMCA)
Church & tombs
Diagram of Madaba map

Section 15 Introduction

Indexes

15-2 Index of Main Names
15-1 Index of Alternative Names
15-3 Index of Grid references

Index of Main Names (Main Index)

Mini-Archive Reference Number (Column 1)

Column 1 of the Main Index provides each site with a sequential identification number, known as the Mini-Archive Reference Number, to which all the Alternative Names, Grid References and slides in the Mini-Archive are cross-indexed. (including names from Student Maps 'A' and 'B')

This cross-index to the Mini-Archive provides a quick and simple guide to the USE of the slides in the Mini-Archive, as illustrations for lessons based on the Student Manual. This collection of 2500 35mm colour slides is one of the major components of the Wide Screen Project and has been selected with the Student Manual in mind. The Main Index provides the clue to its use (see below).

Main Names and Modern Names (Column 3)

Since there is no accepted STANDARD for the naming (or spelling) of sites, Pictorial Archive has developed its own system for use within the Wide Screen Project, based on the concept of ONE MAIN NAME per site, to which all the Alternative Names, Grid References and the Mini-Archive are cross-indexed.

The Main Index contains both ANCIENT and MODERN names. Many of the ancient names are BIBLICAL, taken from the REVISED STANDARD VERSION. The other (extra-Biblical) ancient names are taken from the primary sources. When the ancient name is unknown, the MODERN NAME is used, usually in the official form adopted by the appropriate Government Department of Antiquities. The MODEREN ARABIC names are given in all cases, since phonetic affinities are often important in site identification. The official MODERN HEBREW names are given in italics, where relevant. This system has been modified in certain cases to conform with current usage, as expressed in some contemporary archaeological reports and modern maps of the area.

It is impossible to be totally consistent and compromises have also been made for simplicity and convenience.

Several sites have the same Main Name and these have been distinguished in the Main Index by giving their approximate geographical location (in italics). The following abbreviations have been used:

Acco Pl.	Acco Plain	Jez. V.	Jezreel Valley
B-shan V.	Beth-shan Valley	L. J. V.	Lower Jordan Valley
C. Pl.	Coastal Plain	Jud.	Judaea
Pl. of Dor	Plain of Dor	Sam.	Samaria
L. Gal.	Lower Galilee	Sheph.	Shephelah
U. Gal.	Upper Galilee	T-J.	Transjordan
Gil.	Gilead		

Alphabetical Priorities

Many names of sites are compounded with descriptive titles* and these compound names are printed ON THE MAPS sometimes as single words and sometimes as separate words, as transliterated from the primary sources. However, in the INDEXES, all such compound names are treated ALPHABETICALLY as SINGLE words and are indexed accordingly.

No attention is paid, alphabetically, to the prefix 'el-' (and its variants) or 'ha-', when these come at the BEGINNING of the name.

* ARABIC	HEBREW	ENGLISH
Bir	Beer	Well
Beit	Beth, Bet	House
Ein	En	Spring
Jebel	Har	Mount
Kafr	Kefar, Caphar	Village
Qasr, Qalaat	Migdal, Mezad	Tower, Fort, Castle

Encyclopedia of Archaeological Excavations (Column 4)

Column 4 gives a cross-index to the Encyclopedia of Archaeological Excavations in the Holy Land (EAEHL). Since the Wide Screen Project provides a framework for the integration of Archaeology into standard Bible study, this recent publication (in 4 volumes) is an essential textbook. Many of the artifacts and architectural remains included in the Mini-Archive are described here in their proper archaeological context, with additional references to the literature. Thus the EAEHL provides a unique point of entry into this literature, especially for non-specialists to whom the subject is unfamiliar.

NOTE: Any student wishing to study ONE PARTICULAR ARCHAEOLOGICAL PERIOD, using the EAEHL, should refer to Columns 5-14 (Section 2) of the Main Index, since the EAEHL has no comparable cross-index of its own.

The same distinction between PRIMARY sites (red) and BACKGROUND sites (black), as used in the Historical Maps**, is followed in the Main Index. Thus the Main Index provides a quick visual resumé of the archaeological and historical relevance of any site listed. It also provides an effective 'caption' for the slides in the Mini-Archive, especially when used in conjunction with the 'SUMMARIES OF CONTENTS AND SOURCES' which list the appropriate primary sources for all the maps in each Section. **This is one of the most important uses of the Student Manual, in the context of the Wide Screen Project.**

**See Introduction: 'Place-Names'

Notes

Section 15-1

Index of Alternative Names

Cross reference to column one Index of Main Names

771 Abbad, Kh.
001 Abda, Kh.
651 Abda, Kh.
005 Abel (-maim)
011 Abel
007 Abela ?
004 Abil, T.
004 Abila
005 Abil el-Qamh
153 Abu Dis
472 Abu el-Ala(y)iq, T.
149 Abu esh-Shiba, Kh.
548 Abu Haw(w)am, T.
379 Abu Hureira, T.
548 Abu Huw(w)am, T.
659 Abu Musarrah, Kh.
387 Abu Shusha
623 Abu Sultan, T.
009 Abu Sus, T.
601 Abu Tabaq, Kh.
304 Accaron
014 Acchabaron
677 Acre
088 Adadah
022 Adami, T.; Adamim
297 el-Adar, Kh.
026 Adara
108 Adaroth ?; Adarus ?
422 Addar ?
023 Addasa, Kh.
405 Adida; Aditha
026 Adir
027 Adora; Adoreon
652 Adullam (H.)
475 Aelia Capitolina
321 Aendor
814 Aenon ?
452 Aesora
067 Afeq, T.
068 Afeq, T.
655 el-Affula
429 el-Afshar, T.
655 Afula
693 Agaba
035 Agalla ?
581 Agalla ?; Agal(t)ain ?
062 Agrippias
711 Agrippina ?
062 Agrippium
039 Aija
308 Aila
048 Ailamon
039 Ailon ?
666 Ain
043 el-Aine
044 Aita esh-Shaab
832 el-Aiyadiya
753 el-Ajjul, T.
036 Ajlan, Kh.
014 Akbara
677 Ake
056 el-Akhdar, T.
017 Akhziv
677 Akka; Akko
015 Akko, T.
501 Aleiyan
048 Alemeth
046 Alexandreion
083 Allonim
048 Almit, Kh.
313 Al(o)usa ?
407 Alulos; Alurus
040 Alus
845 Amathus
689 Amman
411 Ammathus
506 Amqa
372 el-Amr, T.
845 Amtah, T.
053 Anab el-Kabira, Kh.
061 Anaea
060 Anata
061 Anim, H.
215 Anin
054 Annab es-Saghira, Kh.
280 Antiochia
434 Antiochia
475 Antiochia
383 Antiochia-on-Chrysorrhoas
067 Antipatris
656 Aphairema
070 Apheca
071 Aphecu Pyrgus
656 Apherema
068 Aphik
670 Aphta ?
308 Aqaba(h)
272 el-Aqabba, T.
018 Aqraba (el-Husn)
092 Ara, Kh.
359 Araba
690 Arabath(a)
078 Arad, T.
089 Arair, Kh.
204 el-Araj
487 el-Araj
088 Arara, Kh.
833 el-Arayis, Kh.
631 Arbat(t)a
081 Arbel, H.
164 Arbela
655 Arbela ?
427 Arbita, Kh.
690 Areopolis
067 Arethusa ?
211 Aricha
079 Arimathea
334 Arjan
088 Aroer, T.
090 Aroueir
093 Arous ?
427 Arpad, H.
359 Ar(r)aba
076 Arrabuna
073 Arshaf, T.; Arsuf
719 Aruma
090 Arura
337 el-Asawir, T.
100 Ascalon
099 Asdudimmu
307 el-Ashshi, Kh.
098 Ashdod, T.
099 Ashdod-yam, H.
069 el-Asheq, Kh.
100 Ashqelon, T.
734 Ashraf, Kh.
101 Ashtarah, T.
423 Asira esh-Shamaliya
785 Askar
414 Asochis
846 Asophon
121 Asor, Mt.
100 Asqalan
121 Asur, T.
340 el-Ata, Kh.
104 Atarus
806 Athone ?
104 el-Attara
106 Attarus, Kh.
468 Attir, Kh.
817 Augustopolis ?
082 el-Auja et-Tahta, Kh.
643 Auja Hafir
432 Aurelia
001 Avdon, T.
651 Avdat, H.
005 Avel Bet Maakha, T.
111 Awanish
109 Awarta
042 el-Ayun (Kh.)
637 Ayun Musa, Kh.
039 Ayyah ?
367 Aza
058 el-Azariya
190 el-Azeima, T.
112 Azeqa, T.
115 Aznot Tavor, T.
424 Azor
098 Azotus (Hippenus)
099 Azotus Paralius
116 Azuru
539 Baala(t)h; Baale-judah
167 Baal-meon
123 Baaru
143 Bab el-Hawa/Hawwah
399 Bab el-Hawa
414 el-Badawiya, T.
064 el-Baddadin, Kh.
445 Balama, Kh.; Balamo
707 el-Balat, T.
755 el-Balata, T.
008 Balbaim
234 Banias
494 Bani Dar, Kh.
242 Bani Naim
128 Barbara; H. Barbarit
129 Barqa
130 Basca ?
223 el-Bassa
033 Basset el-Kharrar
811 Batash/el-Batashi, T.
219 Batna, Kh.
618 Bazal, H.
414 el-Bedawiya, T.
644 Bedd Faluh, Kh.
167 Beelmaus
403 Beer Oded
147 Beerotayim
148 Beeroth ?
226 Beer-sheba
227 Beer Shema, H.
226 Beer Sheva
149 Beer Sheva, H.
136 Beer Sheva, T.
120 Beer Yeroham
148 Beerzeth ?
547 el-Beida, Kh. T.
631 Beidus, Kh.
206 Beisan
306 Beit Alam, Kh.
216 Beit Annaba, Kh.
165 Beit Arif
145 Beit Arif (el-Khirba)
168 Beit Bassa
169 Beit Dajan
170 Beit Dajan
162 Beit Einun, Kh.
250 Beit er-Ras
154 Beit Ilfa, Kh.
110 Beit Illu
173 Beitin
318 Beit Itab
171 Beit Jann
323 Beit Jann, Kh.
218 Beit Jibrin
193 Beit Lahm
194 Beit Lahm
245 Beit Liqya
621 Beit Mizza, Kh.
635 Beit Nabala
645 Beit Nasib, Kh.
195 Beit Nattif
217 Beit Nuaba
158 Beit Qad
203 Beit Rima
213 Beit Sikariya, T.
189 Beit Ur el-Fauqa
188 Beit Ur et-Tahta
212 Beit Zita, Kh.
563 Beiyudat, Kh.
864 Bela
445 Belemoth
008 Belma(i)n; Belmen
167 Beon
308 Berenice
662 Berenice
232 Beror, T.; Beror Hayil
063 Berqit, Kh.
136 Bersabee
715 Bersinya
228 Berzetha; Berzetho
190 Besimoth
218 Betabris
216 Bet Anava, H.
169 Bet Dagan
509 Bet Dikhrin, H.
306 Bet Elem, H.
218 Bet Guvrin
174 Bet ha-Emeq, T.
159 Bet ha-Gaddi, H.
186 Bethagla
180 Bet ha-Kerem
215 Beth-anath
216 Beth-annabra
033 Bethany ?
058 Bethany
549 Betharam(ph)tha
113 Beth-azmaveth
155 Beth-beten
188 Beth-car ?
049 Beth-diblathaim ?
173 Bethela
162 Bethennim
218 Beth Gubrin
401 Beth Gufnin
183 Beth-haran
185 Beth Hobaia
197 Beth Maon
167 Beth-meon
144 Beth Nimrin
175 Beth Nimrin
140 Bethoma ?
141 Bethoma ?
166 Beth-on ?
637 Beth-peor
549 Beth-ramatha
250 Beth-reshah
487 Bethsaida ?
207 Bethsames
206 Beth-shean
151 Beth-shearim
780 Beth-succoth
214 Beth-sura
176 Bethther
220 Beth Ther
215 Beth Yanai ?
228 Beth-zaith ?
139 Beth-zedek ?
194 Bet Lehem
193 Bet Lehem ha-Gelilit
138 Bet Mirsham, T.
195 Bet Natif, H.
198 Bet Netofa, H
206 Bet Shean, T.
151 Bet Shearim, H.
207 Bet Shemesh, T.
211 Bet Yerah, T.
852 Bet Zeneta, H.
118 Biilin
160 el-Bina
146 el-Bir, Kh.
148 el-Bira
706 Bira, T.
133 Bir Abu Matar
329 Bir Aiyub
147 Bir Birein
706 Bir el-Gharbi, T.
688 Bir el-Hilu, Kh.
226 Bir es-Saba
137 Bir es-Safedi
225 Biria; Biriyya
669 Birket er-Ram
235 Bir Madkur
120 Bir Rekhme
826 Birtha
456 Bir Yaqub
228 Bir Zeit, Kh.
241 el-Biss, Kh.
156 el-Bitar, Kh.
135 el-Biyar, Kh.
199 el-Bleibil, T.
146 Borer, H.
229 Borin, H.
230 Bosor(a)
572 Botnah
108 Bucolon Polis
661 Budrus, Kh.
125 el-Buqeia
700 Bureiqa
232 Bureir
231 Burgeta, H.
229 Burin, Kh.
134 el-Burj
231 el-Burj, Kh.
293 el-Burj, Kh.
231 Burj el-Atut
476 Burj el-Lisana
125 el-Buqeia
230 Buseirah
491 Cabul
502 Cadasa; Cades
548 Calamon
855 Callirrhoe
495 Camus
498 Cana
169 Caparadagon
242 Capharbaricha
240 Capharnaum
249 Caphar Ruta
778 Capharsorech
192 Caphartoba ?
238 Caphethra
532 Cariatha
256 Cartha
257 Caspein
179 Cathisma
433 Cave of Horrors
433 Cave of Letters
285 Cave of the Pool
504 Cedron
531 Cela
242 Ceipharbaricha
255 Ceparaira
240 Cepharnocus
249 Ceruta ?
722 Chaal(l)is
246 Chabarsaba
491 Chabulon
535 Charachmoba
260 Chasalon
425 Chebron
253 Chermela
262 Chinneroth
261 Chisloth-tabor
264 Chorazim
384 Chorsia
266 Chous ?
482 Cimona
685 City of Salt ?
263 Coabis
711 Cochaba ?
317 Colonia
270 Conas
567 Constantia Neapolis
481 Coreae
265 Cosiba (St. George)
482 Cyamon
502 Cydasa
272 Cyprus
049 Dabaloth
274 Dabaritta; Dabburiya; Dabira
283 Dafna
279 Dallata
795 Dalmanutha
020 Damin, H.
172 ed-Damita
020 ed-Damiya, Kh.
019 ed-Damiya, T.
280 Dan, T.
813 Dawarta
551 Debir
024 ed-Deir, Kh.
523 Deir Abu Salama
780 Deir Alla, T.
539 Deir el-Azar
562 Deir el-Mus, Kh.
265 Deir el-Qilt
854 Deir Ghassana
186 Deir Hajlah
530 Deir Hanna
804 Deir Isfin, Kh.
265 Deir Mar Jiryis
578 Deir Mar Saba
448 Deir Nakhkhas
139 Deir Saad
165 Deir Tarif
049 Deleilat esh-Sherqiya, Kh.
281 ed-Denn, Kh.
565 edh-Dhahab el-Gharbiya, T.
664 edh-Dhahab esh-Sherqiya, T.
290 Dhiban
509 Dhikhrin, Kh.
602 edh-Dhurur, Kh. T.
560 Dimna, Kh.
748 Diocaesarea
734 Diocletianupolis ?
550 Diospolis
292 Dok
295 Doma ed-Deir, Kh.
293 Dor, T.
294 Dothaim
283 Dufna, Kh.
049 Duleilat, Kh.
298 Duma
027 Dura
030 ed-Dura
256 Dustri, Kh.
294 Duthan, T.
813 Duwara
543 ed-Duweir, T.
651 Eboda
001 Ebron
017 Ecdippa
078 Eder
297 Edrayim, H.
036 Egla, H.
035 Eglaim ?
581 Eglaim ?
041 Eilabun
132 Ein Bala
338 Ein el-Atan
025 Ein el-Ghadyan
163 Ein el-Gharaba
332 Ein el-Joz
002 Ein el-Qana
492 Ein el-Qudeirat
500 Ein el-Quseima
659 Ein Fara
666 Ein Fara, Kh.
330 Ein Haud
790 Ein Husb
003 Ein Ibl
326 Ein Jalud
358 Ein Jennata
324 Ein Jidi
322 Ein Jinne
178 Ein Karim
331 Ein Mahil
114 Ein Muweila
638 Ein Najl
422 Ein Qedeis
207 Ein Shams
821 Ein Tabun
025 Ein Yotvata
790 Eiseiba
301 Eitun, T.
018 Ekrebel
012 Elat
572 Elath ?
307 Eleasa
218 Eleutheropolis
040 Elon-beth-hanan ?
308 Eloth
308 El-paran
537 En-anab ?
321 En Dor, H.
324 Engaddi
069 En Gev
178 En Kerem
430 En Sheva
785 En Soker
656 Ephraim; Ephrain
194 Ephrath(ah)
656 Ephron
084 Erani, T.
328 Eremmon
474 Ericha
432 Esbus
479 Esdraelon
432 Esebonitis; Es(s)ebon
336 Eshtemoh
452 Esora
335 Esthaol
336 Esthemoa
340 Eter, T.
301 Eton, T.
261 Exaloth
665 Faghur, Kh.
662 Fahil, Kh.
227 el-Far, Kh.
814 el-Fara(h), T. (North)
672 Farata
663 el-Fardah
660 Farradiye
126 Farwa, Kh.

Section 15-1

Index of Alternative Names

Cross reference to column one Index of Main Names

667 Fasayil, Kh.
673 Fasga
561 Fassuta
678 Feinan
126 Ferweh, Kh.
070 Fiq
015 el-Fukhkhar, T.
390 el-Ful, T.
758 el-Ful, T.
583 el-Fureidis
431 el-Fureidis, Kh. (Jebel)
065 Fureir, Kh.
668 Furt, Kh.
670 Futeis, Kh.
348 Gaba (Hippeum) ?
392 Gabaon
359 Gabara
368 Gabatha
390 Gabath Saul
352 Gader
375 Gadora
473 Galgala ?
378 Galil, H.
842 Gamma, T.
440 Gamon, H.
395 Gamzo; Ganizo
375 Garada ?
768 Garada ?
385 Garizeim; Garizein
365 Gat Hefer, T.; Gath-opher
347 Gaton, H.
400 Gaulan(a)
353 Gayah
387 Gazara
348 Geba ?
379 Geder
504 Gedera
376 Gedora, H.; Gedorah
504 Gedrus
262 Gennesar(et)
333 Gephrus
381 Gerez
366 Gerisa, T.
362 Geth
368 Geva ha-Carmel
351 Gevat
373 Gevul, H
387 Gezer, T.
282 Ghadriyya
603 el-Ghanam, Kh.
085 Gharandal
086 Gharandal
471 el-Gharra, Kh.
367 Ghazza
702 Ghazza, Kh.
676 Ghor el-Feifa
061 Ghuweina el-Gharbiya, Kh.
061 Ghuweina et-Tahta, Kh.
367 el-Ghuzze
374 Gidora
181 Ginae; Ginna(y)
262 Ginnosar
398 Gittham
768 Givat Yoav
349 Gobolis
619 Goded, T.
324 Goren, T.
037 Grophina ?
397 Gush Halab/Halav
185 el-Habay, Kh.
072 el-Hadab, Kh.
258 Hadar
325 el-Hadatha; T. en-Hadda
426 Hadera
405 Hadid, T.; el-Haditha
039 Haiyan, Kh.
408 Hali, T. (East)
402 Halif, T. (Lahav)
313 Haluza, H.
411 Hamei Teverya
314 el-Hamma
410 el-Hamma, T.
010 el-Hammam, T.
411 Hammam Tabariya
314 Hammat(h) Gader
412 el-Hammi, T.
845 Hamtan
415 Hanita
414 Hannaton, T.
415 Hanuta, Kh.
599 el-Hara el-Fauqa, Kh.
079 Haramatha
080 Harat, H.
348 el-Harathiya; Kh.
016 el-Harbaj; Kh.
080 Hareish, Kh.
184 el-Harezan, Kh.
207 Har-heres
093 Haris
554 Har Loz
326 Harod (Spring)
379 Haror, T.
496 Har Qina
419 el-Harra, Kh.
789 Har Tavor
257 Hasfiyah
300 el-Hasi, T.
417 Hauran, Kh.
439 Hauronen ?
818 Hawanit, Kh.
790 Hazezon-tamar
121 Hazor
424 Hazor, T.
429 Hefer, T.
208 Hekhalim ?
274 Helenopolis
406 Hepha
431 Herodeion
432 Hesban
300 el-Hesi, T
425 Hevron
422 Hezron ?
474 Hiericho
475 Hierosolyma
196 el-Hilu, Kh. T.
537 Hini-anabi ?
414 Hinnatuna
434 Hippos
432 Hisban
299 Hit
513 Hittin
831 Hosah ?
443 Hosefa
830 Hosha, Kh.
831 Hozah ?
653 Huj, Kh.
240 Hum, T.
050 Humeima
238 Hureisa, Kh.
650 Hurshat Yaala
442 Husan
284 el-Husn
206 el-Husn, T.
436 Huwwara
435 el-Huwwara
657 Iarda ?
006 Ibillin
142 Ibn Ibraq
155 Ibtin, Kh.
221 Ibziq, Kh.
247 Id, Kh.
652 Id el-Minya, Kh.
469 Idna, Iedna
429 el-Ifshar, T.
261 Iksal
183 Iktanu, Kh.
045 Il(l)ut
437 Imaret el-Khureisha
311 Immatin
315 Imwas
216 Innaba
841 Iqrit
471 Ira, T.
439 el-Iraq
826 Iraq el-Emir/Amir
427 Irbada, Kh.
164 Irbid
081 Irbíd, Kh.
657 Irq, Kh.
207 Ir-shemesh
476 Isana
647 el-Isawiya
779 Isbeita
098 Isdud
443 Isfiya
335 Ishwa
087 Istabul, Kh.
789 Itabyrium
155 Ivtan, H.
446 Iye-abarim; Iyim ?
042 Iyyon
296 Izbet Sarta
368 Jaba
369 Jaba
350 el-Jaba
373 Jabbul
454 Jabneh
699 Jalad, Kh.
377 Jalbun
378 Jalil, Kh.
354 Jaljuliya
356 Jalud
568 el-Jamid, T. (Maqarein)
842 Jamma, T.
243 Jammala
454 Jamnia
461 Janua
483 Japha
383 Jarash
366 Jarisha, T.
467 Jarmucha
711 Jarmuth ?
347 Jathun, Kh.
363 Jatt
364 Jatt
718 Jauna
588 Jawâh, T.
387 el-Jazar(i), T.
451 Jazer
452 Jazer
451 Jazzir, Kh.
371 Jeba
351 Jebata, Kh.
121 Jebel el-Asur
431 Jebel el-Fureidis
385 Jebel et-Tur
789 Jebel et-Tur
554 Jebel Lussan
292 Jebel Quruntul
438 Jebel Rekhme
475 Jebus(ite)
374 Jedur, Kh.
375 Jedur, T.
440 el-Jemeija, Kh.
842 Jemmeh, T.
454 Jemnaan
181 Jenin
836 Jeshub
468 Jethira
489 Jettan
353 el-Ji
392 el-Jib
349 el-Jiblin
376 Jidru, Kh.
484 Jifat, Kh.
401 Jifna
355 Jilya
395 Jimzu
397 el-Jish
625 el-Jisr, T.
386 Jisr el-Majami
841 Jokereth
742 Joktheel
484 Jotapata
480 el-Jubeihat
619 el-Judeida, T.
374 Judur, Kh.
698 Jul, Kh.
549 Julias
177 el-Jumeil, Kh.
130 el-Jummeize
159 el-Jundi, Kh.
396 Junjar
457 el-Jura
360 Jurabe
382 Jureish
324 Jurn, T.
639 el-Kabbara, Kh. (Nahhalin)
490 el-Kabri
471 Kabzeel ?
259 el-Kafira, Kh.
654 Kafr Ana
508 Kafr Birim
011 el-Kafrein, Kh.
512 Kafr Harib
251 Kafr Hatta, Kh.
511 Kafr Inan
361 Kafr Kan(n)a
244 Kafr Kharib
249 Kafr Lut, Kh.
141 Kafr Malik
514 Kafr Manda
519 Kafr Qasim
249 Kafr Rut, Kh.
522 Kafr Sabt
254 Kafr Samir, Kh.
478 Kafr Sibb
237 Kafr Sumei
528 Kafr Yasif
178 Karem ?
179 Karem ?
601 Karm (el-) Atrad, Kh.
253 el-Karmil, Kh.
694 Kart(h)an ?
260 Kasla
540 Kasyun, T.
179 Kathisma
268 Kaukab
269 Kaukab
711 Kaukab el-Hawa (vicinity)
491 Kavul
361 Kefar Aris ?
241 Kefar Bish, H.
280 Kefar Dan
511 Kefar Hananya, H.
251 Kefar Hitta, H.
238 Kefar Horsha
240 Kefar Nahum
239 Kefar Otnay, H.
246 Kefar Sava
722 Kefar Shihlaim ?
775 Kefar Signa ?
778 Kefar Soreq
051 Kefar Uziel ?
255 Kefar Zecharia
259 Kefira, T.
609 Keisan, T.
535 el-Kerak
211 el-Kerak, Kh.
264 Kerraza, Kh.
260 Kesalon
433 Khabra, W. (Caves)
313 el-Khalasa
421 el-Khaldi, Kh.
425 el-Khalil
779 Khan el-Ahmar (Kh.)
033 Kharrar (Wadi/Basset)
244 Kharruba
142 el-Kheiriya
342 el-Kheleifa, T.
540 el-Khirba
589 el-Khirba, T.
257 Khisfin
339 el-Khokh, Kh.
616 Khureibet el-Waten
658 el-Khureisa, Kh.
420 el-Khusaiya, W.
402 Khuweilifa, T.
503 el-Kidish, Kh.
504 Kidron
262 Kinrot, T.
425 Kiriath-arba
539 Kiriath-baal
537 Kiriath-enab ?
286 Kiriath-sanneh
286 Kiriath-sepher
535 Kir of Moab
261 Kislot Tavor
609 Kison, T.
675 el-Kitara (W. Itm/Yutm)
683 Kobaa ?
270 Kona
264 Korazim
384 Kourci
380 Kuntilla
068 Kurdana, T.
571 Kurnub
384 Kursi
544 Kush, H.; Kh. el-Kushsha
543 Lachis
402 Lahav (T. Halif)
280 Laish
239 Lajjun
543 Lakhish, T.
815 Latatin, Kh.
553 Lauza, Kh.
547 Lavnin, H.
058 Lazarium
239 Legio
187 Lejjun
280 Leshem
546 Libb, Kh.; Libba
551 Lidebir ?
642 Lifta
545 el-Lubban
191 Lubban el-Gharbiya
550 el-Ludd
173 Luz
550 Lydda
634 Mabartha
568 Macer ?
600 Macher
599 Machmas
608 Machmish
584 Madeba
021 Madon ?
589 Madon ?
590 Madon ?
394 el-Mafjar, Kh.
795 Magadan; Magdala
606 Magdiel
119 el-Maghar
600 Mahanaim
623 Mahoz, T.
610 Mahras, W. (Caves)
167 Main
574 Main, Kh.
587 el-Main, Kh.
612 Maiyat Awad
795 Majdal
604 el-Majdala, Kh.
071 Majdal Yaba
180 Majd el-Kurum
502 el-Majnuna
558 el-Makawer
568 Maker ?
562 el-Makhbiya, Kh.
608 Makhmish
600 Makhna el-Fauqa, Kh.
558 Makhwar
271 el-Malat, T.
389 el-Malat, T.
077 Malatha
029 Maledomnei
077 Malhata, T.
008 el-Malih, Kh.
573 el-Maliha
605 Maliha, Kh.
754 el-Mallaha, Kh.
389 Malot, T.
564 Malul
570 Mamilya, Kh.
571 Mamshit, H.
573 Manach, Manahat
544 Mansura, Kh.
587 Maon, H.
568 Maqarein
646 el-Maqari, Kh.
453 el-Maqlub, T.
576 Mareal ?
577 Maresha, T.; Marisa
303 Marjama, Kh.
263 el-Marmala
466 Marmita, Kh.
589 Maron ?
590 Maron ?
591 Maroun er-Ras
166 Maryam, T.
458 Maschana ?
763 Masharfawi
438 el-Mashash, Kh.
558 el-Mashneke
580 Maskana, Kh.
438 Masos, T.
671 el-Masub, Kh.
197 Maun, T.
620 el-Mautah
239 Maximianopolis
497 Mazraat Kanaf
372 Meammer, T.
583 Mearot Telimon
446 el-Medeiyina
458 el-Medeiyina, Kh.
267 el-Medina, Kh.
586 Megiddo, T.
862 Mehoz-zoar
590 Meirun
604 el-Mejdela, Kh.
536 el-Mekhaiyet, Kh. ?
475 Memshath
515 el-Menara
642 Me Neftoah
810 Meneiya, W. (vicinity)
515 Menorim, H.
732 Merkaz Shapira
590 Meron; Meroth(?)
098 Mesogaeus
594 Mevorakh, T.
579 Mezada, H.
320 Mezad Boqeq
417 Mezad Hakhlil
685 Mezad (Hasidim)
790 Mezad Hazeva
613 Mezad Mohila
799 Mezad Tamar
614 Midya, Kh.
615 Midya, Kh. (vicinity)
071 Migdal Afeq
604 Migdal Gad, H.
605 Migdal Malha, H.
795 Migdal Nunnayah
602 Migdal-yen ?
077 el-Milh, T.
174 Mimas, T.
570 Mimlah, H.
567 el-Mina
099 Minat el-Qala; Minat Isdud
459 Minat Rubin
622 Minat Rubin
304 Miqne, T.
444 el-Mird (Kh.)
438 el-Mishash, Kh.
580 Mishkena, H.
575 Mishlat Maahaz
140 Misiliya
075 el-Misna
611 Mizpeh
252 Mizpe Yona
614 Modein
614 Moditha
317 Mozah
621 ha-Mozah, H.
594 Mubarak, T.
582 Mughar
057 el-Mukharkhash, T.
599 Mukhmas
304 el-Muqanna, Kh.
617 Murra, T.
586 el-Mutasallim, T.
455 en-Naam, T.
625 Naarah
648 Nab
627 Nabatha
391 Nabi Samwil
494 en-Nabi Yakin
252 en-Nabi Yunis
634 Nablus
517 en-Nabratein, Kh.
557 Nafaat
449 en-Nahas, Kh.
639 Nahhalin
630 Naim
666 Nain
628 en-Najila, T.
366 Napoleon, T.
094 Naqb el-Arud
631 Narbeta, T.
611 en-Nasba/en-Nasbeh, T.
633 en-Nasira
198 Natif, Kh.
007 Naur
641 Naura
632 Nawa
633 Nazerat
095 Nazle

Section 15-1

Index of Alternative Names

Cross reference to column one Index of Main Names

567 Neapolis ?
625 Neara
517 Neboraya
536 Nebo ?
647 Nebo ?
396 Negingar
630 Nein
234 Neronias
635 Nevallat, H.
517 Nevoraya, H.
567 New Gaza
315 Nicopolis
199 Nimrah
175 en-Nimra, T.
518 Nimrin
643 Nizzana
625 Noaran; Noarath
704 Nofekh
636 Nuba
206 Nysa
677 Ocina
066 Ofrat, H.
654 Onus
262 el-Oreimeh, Kh.
439 Oronaim
839 Ovadya, T.
367 Pa-Canaan
753 Palea Gaza
234 Paneas; Paneion; Panias
237 Parisima
065 Parur, T.
670 Pattish, H.
067 Pegae
662 Pella
125 Peqiin
668 Petora, H.
710 Petra
678 Phaenon
666 Phara; Pheretae
689 Philadelphia
211 Philot(h)eria
201 Phogor
671 Pi Mazzuva, H.
683 el-Qabu
502 Qadas, T.
280 el-Qadi, T.
434 Qalaat el-Husn
037 Qalaat er-Rabad
447 Qalaat Sheikh Ghazal
236 Qalqilya
317 Qalunya
495 Qamm
499 Qana
498 Qana, H./Kh.
021 Qarne Hittim; Qarn Hattin
046 Qarn Sartaba
256 Qarta, H.
532 el-Qaryatein, Kh.
013 Qaryat el-Inab
536 Qaryat el-Mekhaiyet
538 Qaryat Hajja
428 Qashish, T.
680 Qasile, T. (el-Khirba)
626 Qasr el-Buleida, Kh. (W. Zafri)
799 Qasr el-Juheiniya
310 Qasr el-Labani
613 Qasr el-Mahalla
157 Qasr el-Yahud
447 Qasr esh-Sheikh Ghazal
816 Qasr et-Tlah
597 Qasr ez-Zuweira
681 Qasrin
592 Qasr Mahrun
320 Qasr Umm Baghiq
428 el-Qassis, T.
254 Qastra, H.
682 Qasyun, Kh.
504 Qatra
270 Qaun
182 el-Qaus, T.
681 Qazrin
682 Qazyon, H.
503 Qedesh, H.
502 Qedesh, T.
531 Qeila, Kh.
482 Qeimun, T.
533 el-Qereiyat
419 Qeren Naftali
532 Qeriyyot, T.
481 Qeruhim ?
233 Qesari, H.
424 el-Qidah, T.
496 Qina
865 Qiri, T. (ha-Zorea)
539 Qiryat Yearim, T.
234 Qisarion
233 Qisariya
540 Qishyon, T.
682 Qision
683 Qoba ?; H. Qove
316 el-Qubeiba
475 el-Quds
694 el-Quneitira, Kh.
500 Quseima
541 Qusin es-Sahl
083 Qusqus Tabun
266 Quza, Kh.
690 er-Rabba
689 Rabbah; Rabbatamana
689 Rabbath-bene-ammon
286 Rabud, Kh.
107 Raddana
727 er-Radgha, T.
705 Rafah, T.
105 Rafat, Kh.
693 Rajib
697 er-Ram
696 er-Rama
702 Ramah of the Negeb ?
572 Ramat el-Khalil
079 Ramathaim
697 Ramathaim-zophim
179 Ramat Rahel
549 er-Rame, T.
701 Ramith, T.
713 Rammun
699 Ramoth ?
704 Rantiya
694 Raqqat, T.
385 er-Ras, T.
398 Ras Abu Humeid
408 Ras Ali, Kh.
113 Ras Dhukeir (Hizma)
067 Ras el-Ein
059 Ras el-Kharruba
673 Ras es-Siyaghah
851 Ras et-Tahuna
127 Ras et-Tumein
831* Rashidiya, T.
139 Rasm Abd el-Hamid
079 Rathamin
693 Regeb
016 Regev, T.
566 er-Reheil, T.
708 Rehov, T.
709 Rehovot, H.
703 er-Reina
057 Rekhesh, T.
711 Remet, T.
713 Remmon
079 Remphthis; Rentis
658 Rhesa ?
031 Ria, W.
716 er-Ribba, Kh.; H. Ribbo
727 er-Ridgha, T.
328 Rimmon (H.)
712 Rimona, H.
708 Roob
208 Rosh, T.
688 Rubute ?
709 Ruheibe, Kh.
035 Rujm el-Jilima
144 Rujm en-Numeira
719 Ruma, H.; Kh. er-Ruma
207 Rumeila, Kh.
712 Rummana
714 er-Ruwat, Kh.
510 Ruweihina, Kh.
208 er-Ruweisi, Kh. T.
722 Saaleim
721 Saba
136 es-Saba, T.
729 Sabastiya
579 es-Sabba
246 Sabiya, Kh.
770 es-Sabre
774 es-Sadaqa
747 Safad
161 Safad el-Battikh
733 Saffa
748 Saffuriya
862 es-Safi
362 es-Safi, T.
732 Safir
723 Safsaf
321 es-Safsafa, Kh.
400 Sahm el-Jaulan/Jolan
846 es-Saidiya, T.
848 Saiyal, W. (Caves)
757 Sajur
775 Sakhnin
357 es-Salam
247 Salama, Kh.
751 Salbit
475 Salem
357 es-Salem
726 Sal(e)im
727 Saleim ?
725 Salhab, Kh.
179 Salih, Kh.
726 Salim
743 es-Sallama, Kh.
843 es-Salmana
727 Salumias
744 Saluqiya
784 es-Samak, T.
521 Samakh
728 Samik, Kh.
760 Sammuniya, Kh.
728 Samoga
733 Sampho
103 es-Samra, Kh.
741 es-Samra, Kh.
336 es-Samu
577 Sandahanna, T.
726 Sanim
730 Sansanna, H.
362 Saphitha
200 es-Saqati, T.
452 es-Sar, Kh.
864 Sara(a)
750 Sarafand el-Amr
737 Sari
708 es-Sarim, T.
749 Sarjuna, Kh.
736 Sarona, H./Kh.
046 Sartaba
520 Sasa, Kh.; H. Sasay
477 es-Sawa, T.
732 es-Sawafir el-Gharbiya
206 Scythopolis
729 Sebaste
746 Sefarin
034 Seil Afra
759 Seilun, Kh./T.
739 es-Seiyada, Kh.
742 es-Sela
751 Selebi
004 Seleucia
563 Senaah ?
211 Sennabris ?
857 Sera, T.
854 Seredah
721 Shaab
751 Shaalabin; T. Shaalevim
348 Shaar ha-Amaqim
735 Shad(d)ud, T.
756 Shafa Amr
650 Shajarat el-Kalb
312 Shalaf, T.
523 Shalem, H.
727 Shalem, T.
312 esh-Shallaf, T.
152 Shallala, W.
797 Shama, Kh.
760 Shamhuna
729 Shamir
273 esh-Shammam, T.
730 esh-Shamsaniyat, Kh.
734 esh-Sharaf, Kh.
752 esh-Sharia, Kh.
857 esh-Sharia, T.
344 'Sharuhen', T.
756 Shefar Amr
793 Sheikh Abu Zarad
460 esh-Sheikh Banit, Kh.
151 esh-Sheikh Bureik
209 Sheikh esh-Shamsawi, Kh.
201 esh-Sheikh Jayil, Kh.
029 esh-Sheikh Madkur
598 esh-Sheikh Meisar, Kh.
248 esh-Sheikh Suleiman, Kh.
722 Shelah, H.
273 Shem, T.
797 Shema, H.
209 Shemesh, H.
021 Shemesh-adam/edom ?
149 esh-Shihab, Kh.
414 Shichin
537 esh-Shihab, T.
740 Shihan, T.
548 Shihor-libnath ?
760 Shim(r)on
784 Shiqmona, T.
010 Shittim
779 Shivta, H.
803 esh-Shobek
729 Shomron
200 Shoqet, T.
576 Shor, T.
767 Shufah
684 esh-Shuna
524 esh-Shuna, Kh.
764 Shura, H./Kh.
773 Shuweika (er-Ras)
771 Shuweika, Kh.
772 Shuweika, Kh.
755 Sichem
723 Sifsufa
775 Sigoph
740 Sihan, Kh.
766 Siir
775 Sikhnin
525 Silet edh-Dhahr
759 Silo
481 es-Simadi, T.
760 Simonias; Simoniyah
765 Sindiyana, W.
745 Sinn en-Nabra
205 Siris(i)ya, Kh.
853 es-Sitt Leila, Kh.
478 Siv, H.
603 Siyar el-Ghanam, Kh.
768 Skufiya
779 Sobata
771 Soccoth; Sokho, H.
193 Soraia
825 Sour
073 Sozusa
233 Strato(n)'s Tower
579 'The Stronghold'
863 Suba
779 Subeita
762 Sulam; Sulem
473 es-Sultan, T.
782 Sumaq, H.
786 Suq Mazen, Kh.
825 es-Sur
778 es-Sureik, Kh.
783 Suseya, Kh.
434 Susita, H.
783 Susiya, Kh.
150 Suweime, Kh.
485 Taba
662 Tabaqat Fahl
807 Tabariya
800 et-Tabbana, Kh.
430 et-Tabgha
809 Tabun
210 Taffuh
817 et-Tafila
192 et-Taiyiba
333 et-Taiyiba
416 et-Taiyiba
656 et-Taiyiba
808 et-Taiyiba
066 et-Taiyiba, Kh.
823 Talluza
526 Tamra
788 Tana el-Fauqa, Kh.
271 Tanninim, T.
293 Tantura
780 Taralah
794 Tarbana, Kh.; H. Tarbenet
819 Tarqumiya
559 Tatrit, Kh.
097 Tayasir
062 Te(i)da, Kh.
627 et-Teim, Kh.
487 et-Tell
022 et-Tell, Kh.
038 et-Tell, Kh.
370 et-Tell, Kh.
793 Tephon ?
796 Tephon ?
572 Terebinthos
807 Teverya
787 Thaanach
402 Thala
802 Thala
790 Thamara ?
381 eth-Thamila
800 Thamna ?
812 Thamna; Thamnatha (?)
606 Thanath(a)
801 Thebes
814 Thebez ?
796 Thekoue
402 Thella
788 Thena
806 eth-Theniya
576 Thorah, T.
272 Threx ?
812 Tibnah, Kh.
792 Tibnin
787 Tiinnik, T.
812 Timnath-heres
220 et-Tira
822 Tiran ?
800 Tivna, H.
809 Tivon
793 Tochoa ?
796 Tochoa ?
816 Tolona
576 Tora, T.
801 Tubas
214 et-Tubeiqa, Kh.
802 Tuleil
224 Tulkarm
796 et-Tuqu, Kh.
202 et-Tur
822 Turan
824 Turmus Aiya
805 Tuwane, Kh.
798 Tuwilan
860 et-Tuyur, T.
826 Tyros, Tyrus
825 Tyrus
839 el-Ubeidiya
028 Udruh
827 Ulam
015 Ummah ?
551 Umm ed-Dabar
522 Umm el-Alaq, Kh.
222 Umm el-Amad
051 Umm el-Amad, Kh.
413 Umm el-Awamid
618 Umm el-Basal, Kh.
710 Umm el-Bayyara
556 Umm el-Hanafish
032 Umm el-Umdan
328 Umm er-Ramamin, Kh.
606 Umm et-Tut, Kh.
847 Umm Hamad, T.
115 Umm Jubeil, Kh.
505 Umm Juna, Kh.
722 Umm Kalkha, Kh.
352 Umm Qeis
012 Umm Rashrash
777 Umm Sur, Kh.
593 Umm Tuba, Kh.
078 Urad, T.
262 el-Ureima, Kh.
091 el-Urma, Kh.
830 Usha, H.
702 Uza, H.
832 Uza, H.
296 Uzbat Sarta
507 el-Uzeiz, Kh.
831 Uzu
450 Valtha
424 Waqqas, Kh.
261 Xaloth
640 Yaanin, H.
454 Yabneh
460 Yabnit
465 Yafa
483 Yaffa, Yafo
176 el-Yahudi, Kh.
470 el-Yahudiya
776 Yahudiy(y)a
040 Yalu
527 Yamma, H./Kh.
835 Yamma, Kh.
464 el-Yamun
640 Yanin, Kh.
462 Yanoah
839 Yanoam
462 Yanuh
461 Yanun
463 Yanun, Kh.
465 Yapu
441 Yaquq
457 Yaqur
467 Yarmuk, Kh.; T. Yarmut
840 Yarun
838 Yasid
836 Yasuf
837 Yatir
529 Yatma
489 Yatta
468 Yattir, H.
454 Yavne
459 Yavne Yam, H.
116 Yazur
470 Yehud
475 Yerushalayim
477 Yeshua, T.
478 Yeshub
454 Yibna
351 Yifat
455 Yinam, T.
616 Yittan, H.
479 Yizreel, T.
484 Yodefat (H.)
482 Yoqneam, T.
102 ez-Zafaran, Kh.
853 Zafi, T.
362 Zafit, T.
255 Zakariya
112 Zakariya, Kh. T.
743 Zalmon (H.), Zalinon
548 Zalmonah
844 Zanoah, H.; Kh. Zanu; Zanua
855 ez-Zarat
750 Zarifin
117 Zawata
739 Zedata, H.
747 Zefat
698 Zeitun er-Rama, Kh.
850 Zeizun
750 Zerifin, H.
602 Zeror, T.
123 Zerqa Main
856 Zey, Kh.
017 ez-Zib
859 Zif, Kh.
858 Zif, T.
509 Zikrin, Kh.
748 Zippori
479 Zirin
850 Zizion
864 Zora, T.
777 Zoran, T.
863 Zova
769 ez-Zubala, Kh.
122 ez-Zuhur
365 ez-Zurraa, Kh. (Mash-had)
852 Zuweinita, Kh.
861 Zuweiza

Section 15-2

Index of Main Names

Archaeological Periods: 2-1 Chalcolithic, 2-2 Early Bronze, 2-3 Middle Bronze, 2-4 Late Bronze, 2-5 Iron I, 2-6 Iron II, 2-7 Persian, 2-8 Hellenistic, 2-9 Herodian, 2-10 Roman-Byz. | 3-1 Early Bronze | Middle & Late Bronze – Canaanite (4-1 to 4-9) | Late Bronze – Israelite Conquest (5-1 to 5-6) | Iron I – Settlement & Judges (6-1 to 6-7) | Iron II – Samuel & United Monarchy (7-1 to 7-7) | Iron II – Divided Kingdom A (8-1 to 8-8) | Iron II – Divided Kingdom B (9-1 to 9-7) | Persian (10-1, 10-2) | Hellenistic – Hellenistic & Hasmonean (11-1 to 11-13) | Herodian – Herodian (12-1 to 12-13) | Roman & Byz. – Roman & Byz. (13-1 to 13-5)

Mini Archive Reference No.	Grid Reference Israel/Palestine Grid	Main Name	Modern Name (Arabic; *Hebrew*)	Encycl. Arch. Excav. in Holy Land Page Ref. No.
001	165-272	Abdon	Kh. Abda; *T. Avdon*	
002	180-235	Abel ? (*L. Gal.*)	Ein el-Qana	
003	188-279	Abel (*U. Gal.*)	Ein Ibl	
004	231-231	Abel; Abila (*Gil.*)	T. Abil	
005	204-296	Abel-beth-maachah	Abil el-Qamh; *T. Avel Bet Maakha*	
006	168-247	Abelim	Ibillin	
007	228-142	Abel-keramim ?	Naur	
008	195-192	Abelmea	Kh. el-Malih	
009	203-197	Abel-meholah ?	T. Abu Sus	
010	214-138	Abel-shittim	T. el-Hammam	
011	210-139	Abila (*L. J. V.*)	Kh. el-Kafrein	
012	145-884	Abronah ?	Umm Rashrash; *Elat*	
013	160-134	Abu Ghosh	Abu Ghosh, Qaryat el-Inab	3
014	197-260	Acchabare	Akbara	
015	158-258	Acco; see Ptolemais	T. el-Fukhkhar; *T. Akko*	14
016	158-240	Achshaph ?	Kh. el-Harbaj; *T. Regev*	23
017	159-272	Achzib; Ecdippa	ez-Zib; *T. Akhziv*	26
018	182-170	Acrabeta	Aqraba (el-Husn)	
019	201-167	Adam	T. ed-Damiya	
020	193-239	Adamah	Kh. ed-Damiya; *H. Damin*	
021	193-245	Adamah ?	Qarn Hattin; *Qarne Hittim*	
022	193-239	Adami-nekeb	Kh. et-Tell; *T. Adami*	
023	170-139	Adasa	Kh. Ad(d)asa	
024	165-161	Addara ?	Kh. ed-Deir	
025	154-921	Ad Dianam	Ein el-Ghadyan; *Ein Yotvatah*	
026	222-068	Ader; Adir	Ader, Adir	31
027	152-101	Adoraim; Adora	Dura	
028	207-971	Adru	Udruh	
029	150-117	Adullam	Kh. esh-Sh. Madkur	
030	212-266	Aduru	ed-Dura	
031	161-157	Aenam	Wadi Ria	
032	199-199	Aenon ? (*B-shan V.*)	Umm el-Umdan	
033	203-138	Aenon (*L. J. V.*)	Basset el-Kharrar (Wadi)	
034	212-037	Afro	Seil Afra	
035	217-064	Agal(t)ain ?	Rujm el-Jilima	
036	123-108	Agla	Kh. Ajlan; *H. Egla*	
037	218-192	Agrippina ? (*Gil.*)	Qalaat er-Rabad	
038	174-147	Ai	Kh. et-Tell	36
039	175-145	Aiath; Ayyah ?	Kh. Haiyan	38
040	152-138	Aijalon	Yalu	
041	187-249	Ailabo	Eilabun	
042	212-236	Ain ?	(Kh.) el-Ayun	
043	224-042	Ainuatha	el-Aine	
044	181-278	Aita	Aita esh-Shaab	
045	174-235	Aitalo	Ilut	
046	193-167	Alexandrium; Sartaba	Qarn Sartaba	
047	196-273	Alma	Alma; *Alma*	
048	176-136	Almon; Alemeth	Kh. Almit	
049	228-116	Almon-diblathaim ?	Kh. Deleilat esh-Sherqiya	
050	180-929	Ammatha	Humeima	
051	188-246	Ammudim, H.	Kh. Umm el-Amad; *H. Ammudim*	1137
052	216-267	Amudiyya	Am(m)udiyya	
053	143-089	Anab	Kh. Anab el-Kabira	
054	145-091	Anab	Kh. Annab es-Saghira	
055	161-190	Anabtah	Anabta	
056	210-286	Anafa, T.	T. el-Akhdar; *T. Anafa*	65
057	194-228	Anaharath ?	T. el-Mukharkhash; *T. Rekhesh*	
058	174-131	Ananiah; Bethany	el-Azariya	
059	174-135	Anathoth	Ras el-Kharruba	
060	174-135	Anathoth	Anata	
061	156-084	Anim	Kh. Ghuweina et-Tahta; *H. Anim*	
062	098-105	Anthedon	Kh. Teda, Kh. Teida	
063	175-166	Anuathu Borcaeus	Kh. Berqit	
064	152-137	Apedno?	Kh. el Baddadin	
065	159-226	Apharaea	Kh. Fureir; *T. Parur*	
066	169-243	Apharatha ?	Kh. et-Taiyiba; *H. Ofrat*	
067	143-168	Aphek; Antipatris	Ras el-Ein; *T. Afeq*	70
068	160-250	Aphek (*Acco Pl.*)	T. Kurdana; *T. Afeq*	
069	210-243	Aphek (Lower) ?	Kh. el-Asheq; *En Gev*	381
070	216-242	Aphek (Upper) (*Golan*)	Fiq	466
071	146-165	Aphek, Tower (*Sharon*)	Majdal Yaba; *Migdal Afeq*	
072	155-098	Aphekah	Kh. el-Hadab	
073	131-178	Apollonia	Arsuf; *T. Arshaf*	310

Index of Main Names

Archaeological Periods: Chalcolithic 2-1; Early Bronze 2-2; Middle Bronze 2-3; Late Bronze 2-4; Iron I 2-5; Iron II 2-6; Persian 2-7; Hellenistic 2-8; Herodian 2-9; Roman-Byz. 2-10 | Early Bronze 3-1 | Middle & Late Bronze – Canaanite 4-1 to 4-9 | Late Bronze – Israelite Conquest 5-1 to 5-6 | Iron I – Settlement & Judges 6-1 to 6-7 | Iron II – Samuel & United Monarchy 7-1 to 7-7 | Iron II – Divided Kingdom A 8-1 to 8-8 | Iron II – Divided Kingdom B 9-1 to 9-7 | Persian 10-1, 10-2 | Hellenistic – Hellenistic & Hasmonean 11-1 to 11-13 | Herodian – Herodian 12-1 to 12-13 | Roman & Byz. – Roman & Byz. 13-1 to 13-5

Mini Archive Reference No.	Grid Reference Israel/Palestine Grid	Main Name	Modern Name (Arabic; *Hebrew*)	Encycl. Arch. Excav. in Holy Land Page Ref. No.
074	225-098	el-Aqraba, Kh.	Kh. el-Aqraba	
075	224-076	Ar ?	el-Misna	
076	184-213	Araba	Arrabuna	
077	152-069	Arad	T. el-Milh; *T. Malhata*	771
078	162-076	Arad	T. Urad; *T. Arad*	74
079	151-159	Aramathea; Arimathea	Rentis	
080	163-132	Arath	Kh. Hareish; *H. Harat*	
081	195-246	Arbela *(L. Gal.)*	Kh. Irbid; *H. Arbel*	1133
082	194-150	Archelais	Kh. el-Auja et-Tahta	
083	164-236	Ardasqus	Qusqus Tabun; *Allonim*	
084	129-113	el-Areini, T.	T. esh-Sh. Ahmad el-Areini; *T. Erani*	89
085	169-944	Ariedela	Gharandal	
086	212-014	Arindela	Gharandal	
087	163-097	Aristobulias	Kh. Istabul	
088	148-062	Aroer *(Negev)*	Kh. Arara; *T. Aroer*	
089	228-097	Aroer *(T-J.)*	Kh. Arair	98
090	166-161	Aruir	Arura	
091	180-172	Arumah	Kh. el-Urma	
092	157-212	Aruna	Kh. Ara	
093	163-169	Arus ?	Haris	
094	128-006	Arydda ?	Naqb el-Arud	
095	100-104	Asalea	Nazle	
096	213-263	el-Asaliya, Kh.	Kh. el-Asaliya	
097	187-194	Aser	Tayasir	
098	117-129	Ashdod; Azotus	Isdud; *T. Ashdod*	103
099	114-132	Ashdod-yam	Minat Isdud/el-Qala; *H. Ashdod-yam*	119
100	107-118	Ashkelon; Ascalon	Asqalan; *T. Ashqelon*	121
101	243-244	Ashtaroth	T. Ashtarah	
102	167-110	Asphar	Kh. ez-Zafaran	
103	195-010	Asuada ?	Kh. es-Samra	
104	165-192	Ataroth *(Sam.)*	el-Attara	
105	170-142	Ataroth *(Jud.)*	Kh. Attara (Kh. Rafat)	
106	213-109	Ataroth *(T-J.)*	Kh. Attarus	
107	169-146	Ataroth (-addar) ?	Raddana	
108	144-234	Atlit; Athlit	Atlit; *Atlit*	130
109	177-174	Awartha	Awarta	
110	161-153	Ayyalon ?	Beit Illu	
111	212-247	Ayyanosh	Awanish	
112	144-123	Azekah	Kh. T. Zakariya; *T. Azeqa*	141
113	174-137	Azmaveth	Ras Dhukeir (Hizma)	
114	085-010	Azmon ?	Ein Muweila	
115	186-237	Aznoth-tabor ?	Kh. Umm Jubeil; *T. Aznot Tavor*	
116	131-159	Azor	Yazur; *Azor*	144
117	171-183	Azzah	Zawata	
118	156-148	Baalah ?	Biilin	
119	129-138	Baalath ?	el-Maghar	
120	138-043	Baalath-beer ?	Bir Rekhme; *Beer Yeroham*	
121	177-153	Baal-hazor	T. Asur, Jebel el-Asur	
122	167-127	Baal-perazim ?	ez-Zuhur	
123	207-113	Baaras	Zerqa Main	
124	202-074	Bab edh-Dhra	Bab edh-Dhra	149
125	181-264	Baca ?	el-Buqeia; *Peqiin*	
126	180-185	Baddan	Kh. Farwa (Wadi Beidan)	
127	174-133	Bahurim ?	Ras et-Tumein	
128	110-114	Barbarit	Barbara; *H. Barbarit*	
129	121-131	Bareca	Barqa	
130	211-256	Bascama ?	el-Jummeize	
131	218-199	Baun	Baun	
132	201-210	Beela	Ein Bala	
133	128-071	Beer Matar	Bir Abu Matar; *H. (Beer) Matar*	153
134	167-136	Beeroth ?	el-Burj	
135	169-137	Beeroth ?	Kh. el-Biyar	
136	134-072	Beer-sheba *(Negev)*	T. es-Saba; *T. Beer Sheva*	160
137	128-070	Beer Zafad	Bir es-Safedi; *H. (Beer) Zafad*	153
138	141-096	Beit Mirsim, T.	T. Beit Mirsim; *T. Bet Mirsham*	171
139	139-109	Belzedek ?	Deir Saad, Rasm Abd el-Hamid	
140	177-199	Bemeselis ?	Misiliya	
141	179-155	Bemeselis ?	Kfar Malik	
142	133-160	Bene-berak	el-Kheiriya, Ibn Ibraq; *H. Bene Beraq*	184
143	134-166	Bene Beraq	Bab el-Hawa/Hawwah; *Givat ha-Radar*	185
144	200-060	Bennamarin	Rujm en-Numeira	
145	143-151	Ben Shemen	Beit Arif (el-Khirba); *Ben Shemen*	
146	143-129	Bera ?	Kh. el-Bir; *H. Borer*	

Index of Main Names

Archaeological Periods: Chalcolithic 2-1; Early Bronze 2-2; Middle Bronze 2-3; Late Bronze 2-4; Iron I 2-5; Iron II 2-6; Persian 2-7; Hellenistic 2-8; Herodian 2-9; Roman-Byz. 2-10 — Early Bronze 3-1 — Middle & Late Bronze: Canaanite 4-1 to 4-9 — Late Bronze: Israelite Conquest 5-1 to 5-6 — Iron I: Settlement & Judges 6-1 to 6-7 — Iron II: Samuel & United Monarchy 7-1 to 7-7 — Iron II: Divided Kingdom A 8-1 to 8-8 — Iron II: Divided Kingdom B 9-1 to 9-7 — Persian 10-1, 10-2 — Hellenistic: Hellenistic & Hasmonean 11-1 to 11-13 — Herodian: Herodian 12-1 to 12-13 — Roman & Byz.: Roman & Byz. 13-1 to 13-5

Mini Archive Reference No.	Grid Reference Israel/Palestine Grid	Main Name	Modern Name (Arabic; *Hebrew*)	Encycl. Arch. Excav. in Holy Land Page Ref. No.
147	099-022	Beraein	Bir Birein; *Beerotayim*	
148	170-146	Berea	el-Bira	
149	189-259	Bersabe *(L. Gal.)*	Kh. (Abu) esh-Shiba; *H. Beer Sheva*	
150	206-131	Besimoth	Kh. Suweime	
151	162-234	Besara	esh-Sh. Bureik; *H. Bet Shearim*	229
152	102-075	Besor, N. (site)	Wadi Shallala; *Nahal ha-Besor*	157
153	175-130	Betabudison	Abu Dis	
154	190-213	Bet Alfa	Kh. Beit Ilfa; *Bet Alfa*	187
155	160-241	Beten ?	Kh. Ibtin; *H. Ivtan*	
156	129-071	Beter, H.	Kh. el-Bitar; *H. Beter*	153
157	201-138	Bethabara	Qasr el-Yahud	
158	183-208	Bethacath	Beit Qad	
159	113-092	Bethagidea	Kh. el-Jundi; *H. Bet ha-Gaddi*	
160	175-259	Beth-anath ? *(L. Gal.)*	el-Bina	
161	190-289	Beth-anath ? *(U. Gal.)*	Safad el-Battikh	
162	162-107	Beth-anoth	Kh. Beit Einun	
163	197-139	Beth-arabah	Ein el-Gharaba	
164	229-218	Beth-arbel *(Gil.)*	Irbid	
165	144-155	Bethariph	Deir Tarif; *Beit Arif*	
166	175-141	Beth-aven ?	T. Maryam	
167	219-120	Beth-baal-meon	Main	
168	171-122	Beth-basi	Beit Bassa	
169	134-156	Beth-dagon *(C. Pl.)*	Beit Dajan; *Bet Dagan*	
170	185-177	Beth-dagon *(Sam.)*	Beit Dajan	
171	185-263	Beth-dagon *(U. Gal.)*	Beit jann	
172	090-092	Beth Daltha	ed-Damita	
173	172-148	Bethel	Beitin	190
174	164-263	Beth-emek	T. Mimas; *T. Bet ha-Emeq*	
175	209-145	Bethennabris	T. en-Nimra	
176	162-126	Bether *(Jud.)*	Kh. el-Yahudi	
177	235-099	Beth-gamul	Kh. el-Jumeil	
178	165-130	Beth-hacc(h)erem ?	Ein Karim; *En Kerem*	304
179	170-127	Beth-hacc(h)erem ?	Kh. Salih; *Ramat Rahel*	1000
180	173-258	Beth-hacc(h)erem	Majd el-Kurum; *Bet ha-Kerem*	
181	178-207	Beth-haggan; Ginae	Jenin	
182	193-140	Beth-hakkoz	T. el-Qaus	
183	214-136	Beth-haram	Kh. Iktanu	
184	175-126	Beth Harodon	Kh. el-Harezan	
185	169-264	Beth Hobaya	Kh. el-Habay; *Beth Hobaia*	
186	197-136	Beth-hoglah ?	Deir Hajlah	
187	232-071	Beth Horon *(Moab)*	Lejjun	
188	158-144	Beth-horon, Lower	Beit Ur et-Tahta	
189	160-143	Beth-horon, Upper	Beit Ur el-Fauqa	
190	208-132	Beth-jeshimoth	T. el-Azeima	
191	153-160	Beth Laban	Lubban el-Gharbiya	
192	153-107	Beth-leaphrah ?	et-Taiyiba	
193	168-238	Bethlehem *(L. Gal.)*	Beit Lahm; *Bet Lehem ha-Gelilit*	
194	169-123	Bethlehem *(Jud.)*	Beit Lahm; *Bet Lehem*	198
195	149-122	Bethletepha	Beit Nattif; *H. Bet Natif*	
196	197-192	Bethmaela	Kh. T. el-Hilu	
197	198-243	Bethmaus	T. Maun	
198	186-248	Beth Netofa	Kh. Natif; *H. Bet Netofa*	
199	210-146	Beth-nimrah	T. el-Bleibil	
200	141-079	Beth-pelet ?	T. es-Saqati; *T. Shoqet*	
201	215-133	Beth Peor	Kh. esh-Sh. Jayil	
202	173-131	Bethphage ?	et-Tur	
203	159-160	Beth Rimah	Beit Rima; *Beth Rima*	
204	208-255	Bethsaida ?	el-Araj	
205	151-168	Bethsarisa	Kh. Sirisiya	
206	197-212	Beth-shan; Scythopolis	T. el-Husn, Beisan; *T. Bet Shean*	207
207	147-128	Beth-shemesh *(Sheph.)*	Kh. Rumeila, Ein Shams; *T. Bet Shemesh*	248
208	181-271	Beth-shemesh ? *(U. Gal.)*	Kh. T. er-Ruweisi; *T. Rosh*	
209	199-232	Beth-shemesh ? *(L. Gal.)*	Kh. Sh. esh-Shamsawi; *H. Shemesh*	
210	154-105	Beth-tappuah	Taffuh	
211	204-235	Beth-yerah; Philoteria	Kh. el-Kerak; *T. Bet Yerah*	253
212	161-114	Beth-zaith	Kh. Beit Zita	
213	161-118	Beth-zechariah	T. Beit Sikariya	
214	159-110	Beth-zur; Beth-sura	Kh. et-Tubeiqa	263
215	165-211	Betoaenea	Anin	
216	145-145	Betoannaba	Kh. Beit Annaba, Innaba	
217	153-140	Betoannaba	Beit Nuba	
218	140-112	Betogabris; Eleutheropolis	Beit Jibrin; *Bet Guvrin*	194
219	217-154	Betonim	Kh. Batna	

Index of Main Names

Mini Archive Reference No.	Grid Reference Israel/Palestine Grid	Main Name	Modern Name (Arabic; *Hebrew*)	Encycl. Arch. Excav. in Holy Land Page Ref. No.
220	145-182	Betthar *(Sharon)*	et-Tira	
221	187-197	Bezek	Kh. Ibziq	
222	235-132	Bezer ?	Umm el-Amad	
223	163-275	Bezet	el-Bassa; *Bezet*	
224	152-190	Birat Soreqah	Tulkarm	
225	196-265	Biri	Biria; *Biriyya*	
226	130-072	Birosaba	Bir es-Saba; *Beer Sheva*	158
227	106-074	Birsama	Kh. el-Far; *H. Beer Shema*	
228	168-152	Birzaith	Kh. Bir Zeit	
229	153-203	Borim	Kh. Burin; *H. Borin*	
230	208-016	Bozrah; Bosor(a) *(Edom)*	Buseirah	
231	145-191	Burgatah	Burj el-Atut, Kh. el-Burj; *H.Burgeta*	1073
232	116-108	Buriron	Bureir; *T. Beror*	
233	140-212	Caesarea; Strato's Tower	Qisariya; *H. Qesari*	270
234	215-294	Caesarea Philippi; Panias	Banias	
235	182-978	Calamona ?	Bir Madkur	
236	146-177	Calecaelea	Qalqilya	
237	178-264	Caparasima	Kafr Sumei	
238	151-099	Caparorsa	Kh. Hureisa; *Kefar Horsha*	
239	167-220	Capercotnei; Legio	Lajjun; *H. Kefar Otnay*	
240	204-254	Capernaum	T. Hum; *Kefar Nahum*	286
241	145-113	Capharabis	Kh. el-Biss; *H. Kefar Bish*	
242	165-102	Capharbarucha	Bani Naim	
243	158-153	Caphargamala	Jammala	
244	146-146	Caphar-harub	Kharruba, Kafr Kharib	
245	156-141	Caphar-laqitavah	Beit Liqya	
246	141-177	Capharsaba	Kh. Sabiya; *Kefar Sava*	
247	167-140	Capharsalama ?	Kh. Id, Kh. Salama	
248	146-142	Caphartob	Kh. esh-Sh. Suleiman	
249	154-145	Capheruta ?	Kh. Kafr Rut/Lut; *Caphar Ruta*	
250	230-222	Capitolias	Beit er-Ras	
251	146-169	Capparetaea	Kh. Kafr Hatta; *H. Kefar Hitta*	
252	116-135	Cariathmaus	en-Nabi Yunis; *Mizpe Yona*	
253	162-092	Carmel *(Jud.)*	Kh. el-Karmil	
254	147-244	Castra Samaritanorum	Kh. Kafr Samir; *H. Qastra*	
255	144-124	Ceper Zacharia	Zakariya; *Kefar Zecharia*	
256	145-234	Certha	Kh. Dustri; *H. Qarta*	130
257	226-250	Chaspho; Caspein	Khisfin	458
258	227-298	Chedaron	Hadar	
259	160-137	Chephirah	Kh. el-Kafira; *T. Kefira*	
260	154-132	Chesalon	Kasla; *Kesalon*	
261	180-232	Chesulloth; Exaloth	Iksal; *Kislot Tavor*	
262	200-252	Chinnereth; Gennesaret	Kh. el-Ureima; *T. Kinrot*	719
263	196-163	Choba ?	el-Marmala	
264	203-257	Chorazin	Kh. Kerraza; *Korazim*	299
265	189-139	Chozba	Deir Mar Jiryis, Deir el-Qilt	
266	174-171	Chusi?	Kh. Quza	
267	232-076	City of Moab ?	Kh. el-Medina	
268	173-248	Cochaba ?	Kaukab	
269	235-249	Cochaba	Kaukab	
270	194-201	Cola	Qaun	
271	141-216	Crocodilon Polis	T. el-Malat; *T. Tanninim*	
272	190-139	Cypros; Threx (?)	T. el-Aqabba	565
273	164-230	Dabbesheth ?	T. esh-Shammam; *T. Shem*	
274	185-233	Daberath; Dabaritta	Dabburiya	
275	218-268	Dabiyya	Dabiyya, Dabbiye	464
276	212-272	Dab(u)ra	Dab(u)ra	464
277	222-996	ed-Dajaniya, Kh.	Kh. ed-Dajaniya	
278	203-228	Dalhamiya, Kh.	Kh. Dalhamiya	
279	197-269	Dalton	Dallata; *Dalton*	
280	211-294	Dan; Antiochia	T. el-Qadi; *T. Dan*	313
281	221-087	Dannaea	Kh. ed-Denn	
282	215-269	ed-Danqalle	ed-Danqal(l)e	
283	209-292	Daphne	Kh. Dufna; *Dafna*	
284	232-210	Dathema ?	el-Husn	
285	185-097	David, N. (Cave)	*N. David (Cave)*	666
286	151-093	Debir	Kh. Rabud	995
287	217-252	Deir Aziz	Deir Aziz	466
288	088-093	Deir el-Balah	Deir el-Balah	324
289	223-045	Dhat Ras	Dhat Ras	
290	224-101	Dibon (-gad)	Dhiban	330
291	208-258	ed-Dikke, Kh.	Kh. ed-Dikke	1134
292	190-142	Docus	Jebel Quruntul	

Archaeological Periods										Middle & Late Bronze	Late Bronze	Iron I	Iron II	Iron II	Iron II		Hellenistic	Herodian	Roman & Byz.
Chalcolithic	Early Bronze	Middle Bronze	Late Bronze	Iron I	Iron II	Persian	Hellenistic	Herodian	Roman-Byz.	Canaanite	Israelite Conquest	Settlement & Judges	Samuel & United Monarchy	Divided Kingdom A	Divided Kingdom B	Persian	Hellenistic & Hasmonean	Herodian	Roman & Byz.
2-1	2-2	2-3	2-4	2-5	2-6	2-7	2-8	2-9	2-10	3-1 (Early Bronze); 4-1 – 4-9	5-1 – 5-6	6-1 – 6-7	7-1 – 7-7	8-1 – 8-8	9-1 – 9-7	10-1 – 10-2	11-1 – 11-13	12-1 – 12-13	13-1 – 13-5

Section 15-2

Index of Main Names

Mini Archive Reference No.	Grid Reference Israel/Palestine Grid	Main Name	Modern Name (Arabic; *Hebrew*)	Encycl. Arch. Excav. in Holy Land Page Ref. No.
293	142-224	Dor; Dora	Kh. el-Burj, Tantura; *T. Dor*	334
294	172-202	Dothan	T. Duthan	337
295	148-093	Duma(h)	Kh. Doma ed-Deir	
296	146-167	Ebenezer ?	Izbet Sarta	
297	096-093	Edrain	Kh. el-Adar; *H. Edrayim*	
298	184-162	Eduma	Duma	
299	235-239	Eeitha	Hit	
300	124-106	Eglon ? *(C. Pl.)*	T. el-Hesi/el-Hasi; *T. Hasi*	514
301	143-099	Eglon ? *(Sheph.)*	T. Eitun; *T. Eton*	
302	162-227	Ein el-Jarba	Ein el-Jarba	355
303	182-155	Ein Samiya	Ein es-Samiya (Kh. Marjama)	357
304	136-131	Ekron; Accaron	Kh. el-Muqanna; *T. Miqne*	
305	220-245	El Al	el-Al	466
306	145-109	Elam ?	Kh. Beit Alam; *H. Bet Elem*	
307	169-144	Elasa	Kh. el-Ashashi	
308	150-882	Elath; Aila	Aqaba(h)	
309	228-136	Elealeh	el-Al	
310	216-034	Ellebana	Qasr el-Labani	
311	165-177	Elmattan	Immatin	
312	128-144	Eltekeh ?	T. esh-Shallaf; *T. Shalaf*	
313	117-056	Elusa	el-Khalasa; *H. Haluza*	359
314	212-232	Emmatha	el-Hamma; *Hammat Gader*	469
315	149-138	Emmaus; Nicopolis	Imwas	362
316	163-138	Emmaus ?	el-Qubeiba	
317	165-133	Emmaus; Colonia	Qalunya	
318	155-126	Enadab	Beit Itab	
319	101-079	En Besor	Ein esh-Shallala; *En Besor*	325
320	184-067	En Boqeq (Mezad)	Qasr Umm Baghiq; *En Boqeq (Mezad)*	365
321	186-227	En-dor	Kh. es-Safsafa; *H. En Dor*	
322	222-193	Enganna	Ein Jinne	
323	196-235	En-gannim ?	Kh. Beit Jann	
324	187-096	En-gedi	Ein Jidi, T. Jurn; *En Gedi, T. Goren*	370
325	196-232	En-haddah	el-Hadatha; *T. en-Hadda*	
326	183-217	En Harod	Ein Jalud; *En Harod*	
327	169-185	En Naqura	en-Na[illegible]ura	
328	137-086	En-rimmon	Kh. Umm er-Ramamin; *H. Rimmon*	
329	172-130	En-rogel	Bir Aiyub; *En Rogel*	
330	175-131	En-shemesh	Ein Haud	
331	183-236	En Tab ?	Ein Mahil	
332	183-237	En Teena	Ein el-Joz	
333	217-216	Ephron *(Gil.)*	et-Taiyiba	
334	219-200	Erga	Arjan	
335	151-132	Eshtaol	Ishwa; *Eshtaol*	
336	156-089	Eshtemoa	es-Samu; *Eshtemoa*	386
337	152-209	Esur; T.	T. el-Asawir; *T. Esur*	100
338	166-120	Etam (Spring)	Ein el-Atan	
339	167-121	Etam	Kh. el-Khokh	
340	138-113	Ether	Kh. el-Ata; *T. Eter*	
341	160-268	Evron	*Evron*	306
342	147-884	Ezion-geber	T. el-Kheleifa	713
343	167-198	Fahma	Fahma	
344	100-076	el-Farah (South), T.	T. el-Fara(h) (South); *T. 'Sharuhen*	1074
345	228-262	Farj	Farj	
346	195-038	Feifa	Feifa	
347	168-268	Gaaton	Kh. Jathun; *H. Gaton*	
348	160-236	Gaba ? *(L. Gal.)*	Kh. el-Harathiya; *Shaar ha-Amaqim*	
349	207-054	Gabalis	el-Jiblin	
350	157-120	Gabatha	el-Jaba	
351	170-231	Gabatha	Kh. Jebata; *Yifat, Gevat*	
352	214-229	Gadara	Umm Qeis	
353	197-973	Gaia	el-Ji	
354	145-173	Galgulis	Jaljuliya	
355	137-130	Gal(l)aa	Jilya	
356	180-164	Galod	Jalud	
357	219-256	Gamala	es-Salam	
358	159-154	Gantah	Ein Jennata	
359	182-250	(G)Araba; Gabara	Arraba	
360	207-975	Garba	Jurabe	
361	182-239	Garis ?	Kafr Kanna	1136
362	135-123	Gath; Saphitha	T. es-Safi; *T. Zafit*	1024
363	154-200	Gath (-padalla)	Jatt	
364	172-264	Gath	Jatt	
365	180-238	Gath-hepher	Kh. ez-Zurraa (Mash-had); *T. Gat Hefer*	

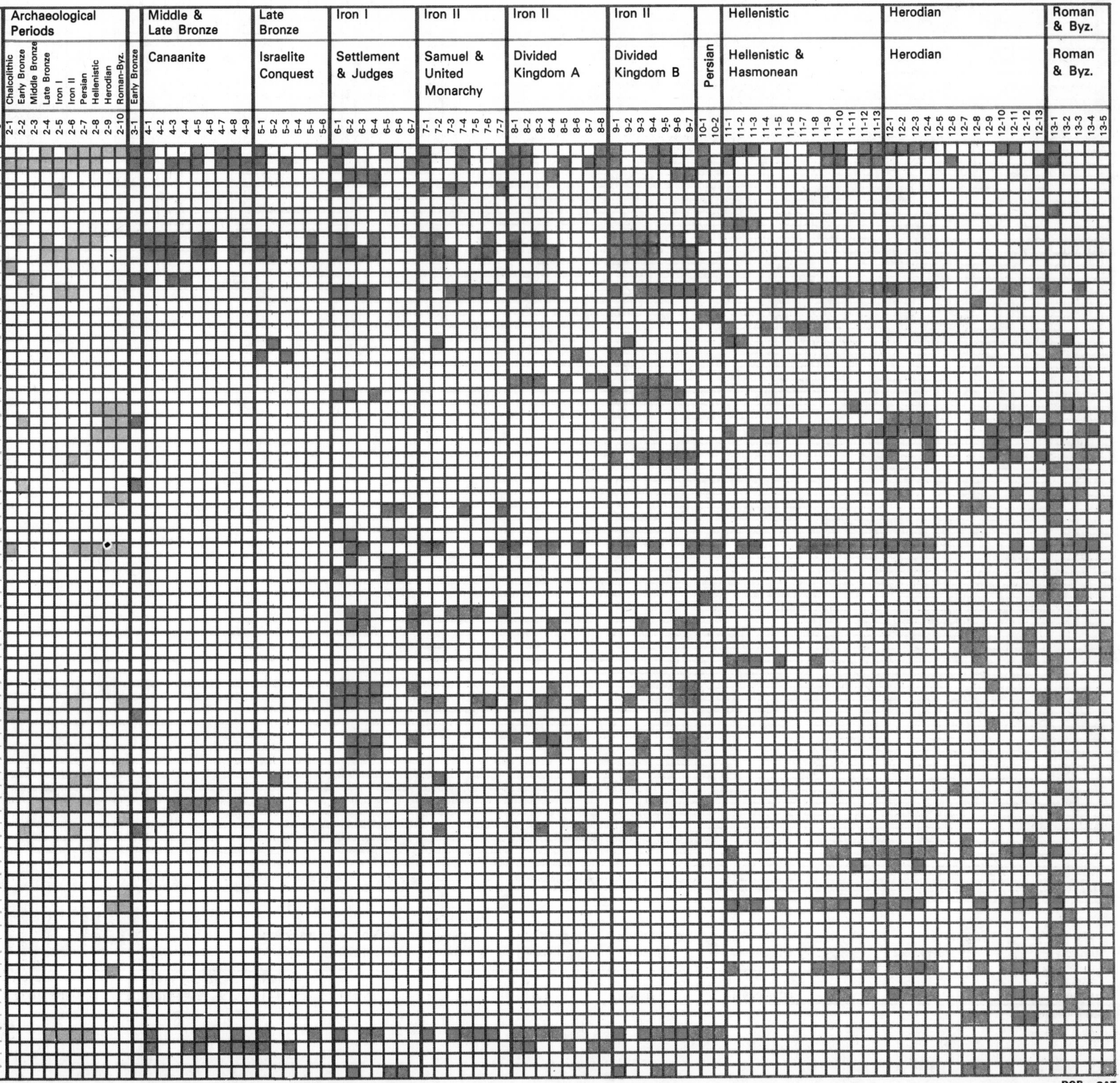

Archaeological Periods
Chalcolithic 2-1
Early Bronze 2-2
Middle Bronze 2-3
Late Bronze 2-4
Iron I 2-5
Iron II 2-6
Persian 2-7
Hellenistic 2-8
Herodian 2-9
Roman-Byz. 2-10
Early Bronze 3-1
Middle & Late Bronze
Canaanite
4-1 4-2 4-3 4-4 4-5 4-6 4-7 4-8 4-9
Late Bronze
Israelite Conquest
5-1 5-2 5-3 5-4 5-5 5-6
Iron I
Settlement & Judges
6-1 6-2 6-3 6-4 6-5 6-6 6-7
Iron II
Samuel & United Monarchy
7-1 7-2 7-3 7-4 7-5 7-6 7-7
Iron II
Divided Kingdom A
8-1 8-2 8-3 8-4 8-5 8-6 8-7 8-8
Iron II
Divided Kingdom B
9-1 9-2 9-3 9-4 9-5 9-6 9-7
Persian
10-1 10-2
Hellenistic
Hellenistic & Hasmonean
11-1 11-2 11-3 11-4 11-5 11-6 11-7 11-8 11-9 11-10 11-11 11-12 11-13
Herodian
Herodian
12-1 12-2 12-3 12-4 12-5 12-6 12-7 12-8 12-9 12-10 12-11 12-12 12-13
Roman & Byz.
Roman & Byz.
13-1 13-2 13-3 13-4 13-5

Index of Main Names

Period columns: Archaeological Periods (2-1 Chalcolithic, 2-2 Early Bronze, 2-3 Middle Bronze, 2-4 Late Bronze, 2-5 Iron I, 2-6 Iron II, 2-7 Persian, 2-8 Hellenistic, 2-9 Herodian, 2-10 Roman-Byz.); Early Bronze (3-1); Middle & Late Bronze – Canaanite (4-1 to 4-9); Late Bronze – Israelite Conquest (5-1 to 5-6); Iron I – Settlement & Judges (6-1 to 6-7); Iron II – Samuel & United Monarchy (7-1 to 7-7); Iron II – Divided Kingdom A (8-1 to 8-8); Iron II – Divided Kingdom B (9-1 to 9-7); Persian (10-1, 10-2); Hellenistic – Hellenistic & Hasmonean (11-1 to 11-13); Herodian – Herodian (12-1 to 12-13); Roman & Byz. – Roman & Byz. (13-1 to 13-5)

Mini Archive Reference No.	Grid Reference Israel/Palestine Grid	Main Name	Modern Name (Arabic; *Hebrew*)	Encycl. Arch. Excav. in Holy Land Page Ref. No.
366	132-166	Gath-rimmon ?	T. Jarisha, T. Napoleon; *T. Gerisa*	575
367	099-101	Gaza	el-Ghuzze, Ghazza; *Aza*	408
368	146-228	Geba *(Pl. of Dor)*	Jaba; *Geva ha-Carmel*	
369	171-192	Geba *(Sam.)*	Jaba	
370	174-158	Geba ? *(Jud.)*	Kh. et-Tell	
371	175-140	Geba *(Jud.)*	Jeba	
372	159-237	Geba-shemen	T. el-Amr; *T. Meammer*	23
373	198-219	Gebul ?	Jabbul; *H. Gevul*	
374	158-115	Gedor *(Jud.)*	Kh. Jedur, Kh. Judur	
375	220-160	Gedor; Gedora *(Gil.)*	T. Jedur	
376	158-247	Gedru	Kh. Jidru; *H. Gedora*	
377	189-207	Gelbus	Jalbun	
378	173-273	Gelil	Kh. Jalil; *H. Galil*	
379	112-087	Gerar; Gerara	T. Abu Hureira; *T. Haror*	
380	119-933	Gerasa ?	Kuntilla	
381	142-942	Gerasa ?	eth-Thamila; *Gerez*	
382	180-167	Gerasa *(Jud.)*	Jureish	
383	234-187	Gerasa *(Gil.)*	Jarash	417
384	210-248	Gergesa (Church 211-248)	Kursi	459
385	176-179	Gerizim (Mt.)	Jebel et-Tur (T. er-Ras)	1015
386	203-225	Gesher	Jisr el-Majami; *Gesher*	
387	142-140	Gezer; Gazara	T. Jazar(i), Abu Shusha; *T. Gezer*	428
388	207-135	el-Ghassul, T.	T. el-Ghassul	1205
389	137-140	Gibbethon	T. el-Malat; *T. Malot*	
390	172-136	Gibeah (of Saul)	T. el-Ful	444
391	167-137	Gibeath-elohim ?	Nabi Samwil	
392	167-139	Gibeon; Gabaon	el-Jib	446
393	117-081	Gilat	*Gilat*	
394	193-143	Gilgal ?	Kh. el-Mafjar	754
395	145-148	Gimzo	Jimzu	
396	174-229	Ginneigar	Junjar; *Ginneigar*	
397	191-270	Gischala	el-Jish; *Gush Halav*	1135
398	140-145	Gittaim, Gath	Ras Abu Humeid	
399	132-164	Givatayim	*Givatayim*	451
400	238-243	Golan	Sahm el-Jaulan/Jolan	
401	170-152	Gophna	Jifna	
402	137-087	Goshen ?	T. Khuweilifa; *T. Halif (Lahav)*	
403	124-973	Gubba	*Beer Oded*	
404	129-958	Gypsaria ?	(Wadi Jerafi)	
405	145-152	Hadid; Adida	el-Haditha; *T. Hadid*	
406	149-248	Haifa	Haifa; *Haifa*	
407	160-109	Halhul	Halhul	
408	164-241	Hali	Kh. Ras Ali; *T. Hali (East)*	
409	226-213	Ham	Ham	
410	197-197	Hammath *(B-shan V.)*	T. el-Hamma	
411	201-241	Hammath, Ammathus	Hammam Tabariya; *Hamei Teverya*	1178
412	208-208	Hammat(h) Pella	T. el-Hammi	
413	164-281	Hammon	Umm el-Awamid	
414	174-243	Hannathon; Asochis	T. el-Badawiya; *T. Hannaton*	
415	166-276	Hanotah	Kh. Hanuta; *Hanita*	308
416	192-223	Hapharaim	et-Taiyiba	
417	144-117	Harim ?	Kh. Hauran; *Mezad Hakhlil*	
418	138-043	Har Rahama	Jebel Rekhme; *Har Rahama*	1219
419	202-277	Harrawi, Kh.	Kh. Harrawi, Kh. el-Harra; *Qeren Naftali*	
420	187-019	Hasta ?	Wadi el-Khusaiya	
421	172-896	Hauare ?	Kh. el-Khaldi	
422	100-999	Hazar-addar ? (Spring)	Ein Qedeis (Fort 103-000)	
423	175-184	Hazeroth ?	Asira esh-Shamaliya	
424	203-269	Hazor	T. el-Qidah, Kh. Waqqas; *T. Hazor*	474
425	159-103	Hebron	er-Rumeida (el-Khalil); *Hevron*	
426	142-204	Hedera	*Hedera*	496
427	189-236	Heleph ?	Kh. Irbada, Kh. Arbita; *H. Arpad*	
428	160-232	Helkath ?	T. el-Qassis; *T. Qashish*	
429	141-197	Hepher ?	T. el-Ifshar/el-Afshar; *T. Hefer*	
430	201-253	Heptapegon	et-Tabgha; *En Sheva*	497
431	173-119	Herodium	Kh. el-Fureidis (Jebel)	502
432	226-134	Heshbon; Esbus	Hisban, Hesban	510
433	181-093	Hever, N. (Caves)	Wadi Khabra; *Nahal Hever*	670
434	212-242	Hippus	Qalaat el-Husn; *H. Susita*	521
435	167-236	Hivria	el-Huwwara	
436	174-173	Hivria	Huwwara	
437	104-017	Hor, Mt. ?	Imaret el-Khureisha	
438	146-069	Hormah ?	Kh. el-Mishash (Mashash); *T. Masos*	816

Section 15-2

Index of Main Names

Mini Archive Reference No.	Grid Reference Israel/Palestine Grid	Main Name	Modern Name (Arabic; *Hebrew*)	Encycl. Arch. Excav. in Holy Land Page Ref. No.
439	211-055	Horonaim ?	el-Iraq	
440	175-252	Huk(k)ok ?	Kh. el-Jemeija; *H. Gamon*	
441	195-254	Huqoq	Yaquq; *Huqoq*	
442	162-124	Hushah ?	Husan	
443	156-236	Husifah	Isfiya	524
444	184-125	Hyrcania	el-Mird (Kh.)	882
445	177-205	Ibleam	Kh. Balama	
446	223-041	Ije-abarim ?	el-Medeiyina	
447	189-195	In Medio	Qasr esh-Sh. Ghazal	
448	142-113	Ir Nahash *(Sheph.)*	Deir Nakhkhas	
449	191-010	Ir Nahash *(Arabah)*	Kh. en-Nahas	
450	223-107	Iskandar, Kh.	Kh. Iskandar	531
451	219-156	Ja(a)zer ?	Kh. Jazzir	
452	228-150	Ja(a)zer ?	Kh. es-Sar	
453	214-201	Jabesh-gilead	T. el-Maqlub	
454	126-141	Jabneel; Jamnia *(C. Pl.)*	Yibna; *Yavne*	
455	198-235	Jabneel *(L. Gal.)*	T. en-Naam; *T. Yinam*	
456	177-179	Jacob's Well	Bir Yaqub	
457	107-119	Jagur	el-Jura	
458	236-110	Jahaz(ah) ?	Kh. el-Medeiyina	
459	121-147	Jamnia, Port	Minat Rubin; *H. Yavne Yam*	1216
460	198-266	Jamnith	Kh. esh-Sh. Banit	
461	183-172	Jano *(Sam.)*	Yanun	
462	173-265	Janoah *(U. Gal.)*	Yanuh	
463	184-173	Janoah *(Sam.)*	Kh. Yanun	
464	171-210	Janua ? *(Jez. V.)*	el-Yamun	
465	176-232	Japhia	Yafa	541
466	151-130	Jarimuth ?	Kh. Marmita	
467	147-124	Jarmuth	Kh. Yarmuk; *T. Yarmut*	544
468	151-084	Jattir	Kh. Attir; *H. Yattir*	
469	147-107	Jedna	Idna	
470	139-159	Jehud	el-Yahudiya; *Yehud*	
471	148-071	(Je)Kabzeel ?	Kh. el-Gharra; *T. Ira*	
472	191-139	Jericho (Palaces)	T. Abu el-Ala(y)iq	565
473	192-142	Jericho	T. es-Sultan	550
474	193-140	Jericho	Ericha	
475	172-131	Jerusalem	el-Quds; *Yerushalayim*	579
476	174-156	Jeshanah	Burj el-Lisana	
477	149-076	Jeshua ?	T. es-Sawa; *T. Yeshua*	
478	152-194	Jeshub	Kafr Sibb; *H. Siv*	
479	181-218	Jezreel; Esdraelon	Zirin; *T. Yizreel*	
480	231-159	Jogbehah	el-Jubeihat	
481	196-170	Jokmeam ?	T. es-Simadi	
482	160-230	Jokneam	T. Qeimun; *T. Yoqneam*	
483	126-162	Joppa	Yaffa; *Yafo*	532
484	176-248	Jotbah; Jotapata	Kh. Jifat; *H. Yodefat*	
485	139-878	Jotbathah ?	Taba	
486	230-259	el-Jukhadar, T.	T. el-Jukhadar	457
487	209-257	Julias; Bethsaida (?)	et-Tell, el-Araj	
488	233-011	Jurf ed-Darawish	Jurf ed-Darawish	
489	158-095	Juttah	Yatta	
490	164-268	Kabrita	el-Kabri	
491	170-252	Kabul; Chabulon	Kabul; *Kavul*	
492	096-006	Kadesh-barnea	Ein el-Qudeirat	697
493	219-274	Kafr Nafakh	Kafr Nafakh	
494	164-100	Kain	Kh. Bani Dar, en-Nabi Yakin	
495	218-221	Kamon ?	Qamm	
496	170-070	Kana ?	Qina; *Har Qina*	
497	214-253	Kanaf	Mazraat Kanaf	
498	178-247	Kanah; Cana *(L. Gal.)*	Kh. Qana; *H. Qana*	
499	178-290	Kanah *(U. Gal.)*	Qana	
500	089-007	Karka(a) ?	Ein el-Quseima; *Quseima*	
501	233-104	Kedemoth ?	Aleiyan	
502	200-279	Kedesh, Cadasa *(U. Gal.)*	T. Qadas, el-Majnuna; *T. Qedesh*	406
503	202-237	Kedesh *(L. Gal.)*	Kh. el-Kidish; *H. Qedesh*	
504	129-136	Kedron; Gedrus	Qatra; *Gedera*	
505	203-233	Kefar Agon	Kh. Umm Juna	
506	166-264	Kefar Amiqo	Amqa	
507	157-093	Kefar Aziz	Kh. el-Uzeiz	
508	189-272	Kefar Baram	Kafr Birim; *Kefar Baram*	705
509	136-119	Kefar Dikhriya	Kh. Zikrin; *H. Bet Dikhrin*	
510	203-294	Kefar Giladi	Kh. Ruweihina; *Kefar Giladi*	708
511	189-258	Kefar Hananiya	Kafr Inan; *H. Kefar Hananya*	

Archaeological Periods: Chalcolithic 2-1, Early Bronze 2-2, Middle Bronze 2-3, Late Bronze 2-4, Iron I 2-5, Iron II 2-6, Persian 2-7, Hellenistic 2-8, Herodian 2-9, Roman-Byz. 2-10 | Early Bronze 3-1 | Middle & Late Bronze – Canaanite 4-1 – 4-9 | Late Bronze – Israelite Conquest 5-1 – 5-6 | Iron I – Settlement & Judges 6-1 – 6-7 | Iron II – Samuel & United Monarchy 7-1 – 7-7 | Iron II – Divided Kingdom A 8-1 – 8-8 | Iron II – Divided Kingdom B 9-1 – 9-7 | Persian 10-1 – 10-2 | Hellenistic – Hellenistic & Hasmonean 11-1 – 11-13 | Herodian – Herodian 12-1 – 12-13 | Roman & Byz. – Roman & Byz. 13-1 – 13-5

Index of Main Names

Archaeological Periods: Chalcolithic (2-1), Early Bronze (2-2), Middle Bronze (2-3), Late Bronze (2-4), Iron I (2-5), Iron II (2-6), Persian (2-7), Hellenistic (2-8), Herodian (2-9), Roman-Byz. (2-10); Early Bronze (3-1); Middle & Late Bronze – Canaanite (4-1 – 4-9); Late Bronze – Israelite Conquest (5-1 – 5-6); Iron I – Settlement & Judges (6-1 – 6-7); Iron II – Samuel & United Monarchy (7-1 – 7-7); Iron II – Divided Kingdom A (8-1 – 8-8); Iron II – Divided Kingdom B (9-1 – 9-7); Persian (10-1 – 10-2); Hellenistic – Hellenistic & Hasmonean (11-1 – 11-13); Herodian – Herodian (12-1 – 12-13); Roman & Byz. – Roman & Byz. (13-1 – 13-5)

Mini Archive Reference No.	Grid Reference Israel/Palestine Grid	Main Name	Modern Name (Arabic; *Hebrew*)	Encycl. Arch. Excav. in Holy Land Page Ref. No.
512	212-240	Kefar Harub	Kafr Harib	
513	192-245	Kefar Hittaya	Hittin	
514	174-246	Kefar Mandi	Kafr Manda	
515	201-240	Kefar Menori	el-Menara; *H. Menorim*	
516	143-194	Kefar Monash	*Kefar Monash*	
517	197-267	Kefar Neboraya	Kh. en-Nabratein; *H. Nevoraya*	710
518	190-245	Kefar Nimrah	Nimrin	
519	148-169	Kefar Qesem	Kafr Qasim	
520	162-242	Kefar Sasay	Kh. Sasa; *H. Sasay*	
521	205-234	Kefar Semah ?	Samakh	
522	191-238	Kefar Shabtay	Kafr Sabt, Kh. Umm el-Alaq	
523	146-150	Kefar Shalem	Deir Abu Salama; *H. Shalem*	
524	145-215	Kefar Shuni	Kh. esh-Shuna	
525	167-191	Kefar Silah	Silet edh-Dhahr	
526	169-250	Kefar Tamartah	Tamra	
527	198-233	Kefar Yamma	Kh. Yamma; *H. Yamma*	
528	165-262	Kefar Yasif	Kafr Yasif	
529	175-168	Kefar Yatma	Yatma	
530	184-252	Kefar Yohannah	Deir Hanna	
531	150-113	Keilah	Kh. Qeila	
532	161-083	Kerioth ?	Kh. el-Qaryatein; *T. Qeriyyot*	
533	215-105	Kerioth	el-Qereiyat	
534	192-032	Khanazir	Khanazir	
535	217-066	Kir-hareseth	el-Kerak	
536	220-128	Kiriathaim ?	Qaryat el-Mekhaiyet	
537	241-233	Kiriath-anab ?	T. esh-Shihab	
538	162-179	Kiriath Haggah	Qaryat Hajja	
539	159-135	Kiriath-jearim	Deir el-Azar; *T. Qiryat Yearim*	
540	187-229	Kishion ?	el-Khirba (T. Kasyun); *T. Qishyon*	
541	167-182	Kozoh	Qusin es-Sahl	
542	094-954	Kuntilet Ajrud	Kuntilet Ajrud	
543	135-108	Lachish	T. ed-Duweir; *T. Lakhish*	735
544	202-233	Lakkum ?	Kh. el-Kushsha, Kh. Mansura; *H. Kush*	
545	173-164	Lebonah	el-Lubban	
546	222-112	Lemba; Libba	Kh. Libb	
547	145-116	Libnah ?	Kh. T. el-Beida; *H. Lavnin*	
548	152-245	Libnath ?	T. Abu Hawa[illegible]/Huwam	9
549	211-137	Livias; Julias	T. er-Rame	
550	140-151	Lod; Lydda; Diospolis	el-Ludd; *Lod*	753
551	207-219	Lo-debar ?	Umm ed-Dabar	
552	190-242	Lubiya	Lubiya	
553	175-178	Luza	Kh. Lauza	
554	114-989	Lysa ?	Jebel Lussan	
555	220-956	Maan	Maan	
556	232-137	Maanith	Umm el-Hanafish	
557	234-246	Maapha	Nafaat	
558	209-108	Machaerus	el-Mukawer, el-Mashneke	
559	143-084	Madmannah	Kh. Tatrit	
560	217-077	Madmen ?	Kh. Dimna	
561	179-272	Mafshetah	Fassuta	
562	145-116	Magbish ?	Kh. el-Makhbiya, Kh. Deir el-Mus	
563	194-152	Magdalsenna	Kh. Beiyudat	
564	172-233	Mahalol	Malul	
565	214-177	Mahanaim ?	T. edh-Dhahab el-Garbi	
566	228-177	Mahanaim ?	T. er-Reheil	
567	096-104	Maiumas	el-Mina	
568	232-237	Maked; Macer ?	T. el-Jamid (Maqarein)	
569	198-170	el-Makhruq, Kh.	(Kh.) el-Makhruq	766
570	191-251	Mamliah	Kh. Mamilya; *H. Mimlah*	
571	156-048	Mampsis	Kurnub; *H. Mamshit*	722
572	160-107	Mamre ?, Terebinthos	Ramat el-Khalil	776
573	167-129	Manahath	el-Maliha; *Manahat*	
574	162-090	Maon *(Jud.)*	Kh. Main	779
575	131-102	el-Maqhaz, Kh.	Kh. el-Maqhaz; *Mishlat Maahaz*	
576	166-228	Maralah ?	T. Tora; *T. Shor*	
577	140-111	Mareshah; Marisa	T. Sandahanna; *T. Maresha*	782
578	181-123	Mar Saba	Mar Saba (Deir)	
579	183-080	Masada; 'The Stronghold'	es-Sabba; *H. Mezada*	793
580	188-243	Mashkanah	Kh. Maskana; *H. Mishkena*	
581	201-078	Mazraa	Mazraa	
582	188-255	Mearaia	Mughar	
583	147-223	Mearath Telimon	el-Fureidis; *Mearot Telimon*	
584	225-124	Medeba	Madeba	819

Section 15-2
Index of Main Names

Mini Archive Reference No.	Grid Reference Israel/Palestine Grid	Main Name	Modern Name (Arabic; *Hebrew*)	Encycl. Arch. Excav. in Holy Land Page Ref. No.
585	145-236	Megadim; T.	*T. Megadim*	823
586	167-221	Megiddo	T. el-Mutasallim; *T. Megiddo*	830
587	093-082	Menois *(C. Pl.)*	Kh. el-Main; *H. Maon*	
588	239-140	Mephaath ?	T. Jawah	
589	190-275	Merom ?	T. el-Khirba	
590	191-265	Merom; Meroth ?	Meirun; *Meron*	856
591	191-278	Meroth ?	Maroun er-Ras	
592	174-202	Merrus	Qasr Mahrun	
593	172-126	Metopa	Kh. Umm Tuba	
594	143-215	Mevorach, T.	T. Mubarak; *T. Mevorakh*	866
595	163-038	Mezad Aqrabbim	*Mezad Aqrabbim*	
596	120-146	Mezad Hashavyahu	*Mezad Hashavyahu*	862
597	183-062	Mezad Zohar	Qasr ez-Zuweira; *Mezad Zohar*	
598	154-205	Mezer	Kh. esh. Sh. Meisar; *Mezer*	864
599	176-142	Michmash; Machmas	Mukhmas, Kh. el-Hara el-Fauqa	309
600	175-176	Michmethath	Kh. Makhna el-Fauqa	
601	188-127	Middin ?	Kh. Karm Atrad/Abu Tabaq	269
602	147-203	Migdal ?	Kh. T. edh-Dhurur; *T. Zeror*	1223
603	171-123	Migdal Eder	Kh. Siyar el-Ghanam	884
604	140-105	Migdal-gad ?	Kh. el-Majdala; *H. Migdal Gad*	
605	144-231	Migdal Malhah	Kh. Maliha; *H. Migdal Malha*	
606	090-096	Migdal Thauath(a)	Kh. Umm et-Tut	
607	169-274	Milliya	Milliya	
608	131-174	Mikhal, T.	Makhmish; *T. Mikhal*	768
609	164-253	Mishal ?	T. Keisan; *T. Kison*	711
610	181-088	Mishmar, N. (Caves)	Wadi Mahras; *Nahal Mishmar*	683
611	170-143	Mizpah	T. en-Nasba	912
612	166-995	Moa?	Maiyat Awad (Moa)	
613	141-004	Moahile ?	Qasr el-Mahalla; *Mezad Mohila*	
614	150-148	Modiin; Modein	el-Arbain, Ras Midya	
615	149-148	Modiin/Modein (Tombs)	Kh. Midya (vicinity); *Modiin*	
616	142-074	Moladah ?	Khureibet el-Waten; *H. Yittan*	
617	117-136	Mor, T.	T. Murra; *T. Mor*	889
618	140-114	Morasthi	Kh. Umm el-Basal; *H. Bazal*	
619	141-115	Moresheth-gat(h) ?	T. el-Judeida; *T. Goded*	694
620	216-055	Motha	el-Mautah	
621	165-134	Mozah	Kh. Beit Mizza; *H. ha-Mozah*	
622	231-044	Muhai	Minat Rubin	
623	125-147	Muhhazi; Mahoz ?	T. Abu Sultan; *T. Mahoz*	1113
624	185-110	el-Murabbaat, W. (Caves)	Wadi el-Murabbaat	691
625	190-144	Naaran; Naarah	T. el-Jisr	891
626	204-076	Naar Safrai	Kh. Qasr el-Buleida (Wadi Zafri)	
627	223-123	Nadabath	Kh. et-Teim	
628	127-101	Nagila, T.	T. en-Najila; *T. Nagila*	894
629	159-267	Nahariyya	*Nahariyya*	908
630	183-226	Nain	Nein	
631	153-206	Narbatah; Arbatta	Kh. Beidus; *T. Narbeta*	
632	248-255	Naveh	Nawa	
633	178-234	Nazareth	en-Nasira; *Nazerat*	919
634	175-180	Neapolis *(Sam.)*	Nablus	
635	146-154	Neballat	Beit Nabala; *H. Nevallat*	
636	153-112	Nebo ? *(Sheph.)*	Nuba	
637	220-131	Nebo ?	Kh. Ayun Musa	924
638	201-992	Negla	Ein Najl	
639	160-121	Nehelam	Kh. el-Kabbara (Nahhalin)	
640	171-255	Neiel	Kh. Yanin; *H. Yaanin*	
641	187-224	Neoran	Naura	
642	168-133	Nephtoah, Waters	Lifta; *Me Neftoah*	
643	095-031	Nessana	Auja Hafir; *Nizzana*	927
644	171-119	Netopha(h) ?	Kh. Bedd Faluh	
645	151-110	Nezib	Kh. Beit Nasib	
646	186-123	Nibshan ?	Kh. el-Maqari	269
647	173-134	Nob? *(Jud.)*	el-Isawiya	
648	224-248	Nob *(Golan)*	Nab	
649	201-059	Numeira	Numeira	
650	200-232	Oak in Zaanannim ?	Shajarat el-Kalb; *Hurshat Yaala*	
651	128-022	Oboda/Eboda	Kh. Abda; *H. Avdat*	345
652	150-118	Odollam	Kh. Id el-Minya; *H. Adullam*	
653	114-102	Oga	Kh. Huj	
654	137-159	Ono	Kafr Ana; *Ono*	
655	177-223	Ophrah ? *(Jez. V.)*	el-Affula, *Afula*	32
656	178-151	Ophrah; Apherema *(Jud.)*	et-Taiyiba	
657	108-086	Orda	Kh. Irq	

Index of Main Names

Archaeological Periods: 2-1 Chalcolithic, 2-2 Early Bronze, 2-3 Middle Bronze, 2-4 Late Bronze, 2-5 Iron I, 2-6 Iron II, 2-7 Persian, 2-8 Hellenistic, 2-9 Herodian, 2-10 Roman-Byz. | 3-1 Early Bronze | Middle & Late Bronze – Canaanite: 4-1 – 4-9 | Late Bronze – Israelite Conquest: 5-1 – 5-6 | Iron I – Settlement & Judges: 6-1 – 6-7 | Iron II – Samuel & United Monarchy: 7-1 – 7-7 | Iron II – Divided Kingdom A: 8-1 – 8-8 | Iron II – Divided Kingdom B: 9-1 – 9-7 | Persian: 10-1 – 10-2 | Hellenistic – Hellenistic & Hasmonean: 11-1 – 11-13 | Herodian – Herodian: 12-1 – 12-13 | Roman & Byz. – Roman & Byz.: 13-1 – 13-5

Mini Archive Reference No.	Grid Reference Israel/Palestine Grid	Main Name	Modern Name (Arabic; *Hebrew*)	Encycl. Arch. Excav. in Holy Land Page Ref. No.
658	162-095	Or(h)esa ?	Kh. el-Khureisa	
659	177-137	Parah	Kh. Abu Musarrah (Ein Fara)	
660	190-259	Parod	Farradiye; *Parod*	
661	149-152	Patros	Kh. Budrus	
662	207-206	Pehel; Pella	Kh. Fahil, Tabaqat Fahl	939
663	200-958	Pentacomia ?	el-Fardah	
664	215-177	Penuel	T. ed-Dhahab esh-Sherqiya	
665	164-119	Peor	Kh. Faghur	
666	179-138	Pharathon	Kh. Ein Fara	
667	191-159	Phasaelis	Kh. Fasayil	
668	132-110	Phathura	Kh. Furt; *H. Petora*	
669	221-293	Phiale, Lake	Birket er-Ram	
670	114-081	Photis	Kh. Futeis; *H. Pattish*	
671	164-276	Pi Masoba	Kh. el-Masub; *H. Pi Mazzuva*	
672	165-177	Pirathon	Farata	
673	218-130	Pisgah; Fasga	Ras es-Siyaghah	923
674	135-185	Poleg, T.	Wadi Faliq (vicinity); *T. Poleg*	959
675	162-884	Praesidium	el-Kitara (Wadi Itm/Yutm)	
676	192-039	Praesidium	Ghor el-Feifa	
677	157-258	Ptolemais; see Acco	Acre, Akka; *Akko*	14
678	197-004	Punon	Feinan	
679	239-028	Qalaat el-Hasa	Qalaat el-Hasa	
680	130-167	Qasila, T.	T. Qasile (el-Khirba); *T. Qasila*	963
681	216-266	Qisrin	Qasrin; *Qazrin*	460
682	199-272	Qisyon	Kh. Qasyun; *H. Qazyon*	
683	161-126	Qobi	el-Qabu; *H. Qove*	
684	129-167	Qudadi, T.	esh-Shuna, T. Qudadi; *T. Qudadi*	720
685	193-127	Qumran, Kh.; City of Salt ?	Kh. Qumran	978
686	227-281	Quneitra	Quneitra	
687	144-167	Rabba, W. (site)	Wadi Rabba; *Wadi Rabba*	994
688	149-137	Rabbah; Rubute?	Kh. Bir el-Hilu	
689	238-151	Rabbath-ammon; Philadel.	Amman	987
690	220-075	Rabbath-moab	er-Rabba	
691	234-262	Rafid	Rafid	
692	209-262	er-Rafid, Kh.	Kh. er-Rafid	467
693	215-182	Ragaba	Rajib	
694	199-245	Rakkath	Kh. el-Quneitira; *T. Raqqat*	
695	190-887	er-Ram *(T-J.)*	er-Ram	996
696	184-260	Rama *(L. Gal.)*	er-Rama	
697	172-140	Rama(h) *(Jud.)*	er-Ram	
698	187-259	Ramah *(L. Gal.)*	Kh. Zeitun er-Rama, Kh. Jul	
699	223-169	Ramath-mizpeh ?	Kh. Jalad	
700	214-237	Ram Baraq	Bureiqa	
701	244-210	Ramoth-gilead	T. Ramith	
702	165-068	Ramoth of the Negeb ?	Kh. Ghazza; *H. Uza*	
703	179-236	Rani ?	er-Reina	
704	142-161	Rantia	Rantiya; *Nofekh*	
705	077-079	Raphia	T. Rafah	
706	166-256	Rehob ? *(Acco Pl.)*	T. Bir el-Gharbi; *T. Bira*	24
707	177-280	Rehob ? *(U. Gal.)*	T. el-Balat	
708	197-207	Rehob *(B-shan V.)*	T. es-Sarim; *T. Rehov*	
709	108-048	Rehoboth	Kh. Ruheibe; *H. Rehovot*	
710	192-971	Rekem ?; Petra	Umm el-Bayyara	943
711	199-221	Remeth ; Jarmuth?	Kaukab el-Hawa (vicinity); *T. Remet*	
712	179-243	Rimmon *(L. Gal.)*	Rummana; *H. Rimona*	
713	178-148	Rimmon *(Jud.)*	Rammun	
714	205-038	Robotha	Kh. er-Ruwat	
715	223-215	Rogelim ?	Bersinya	
716	148-118	Roobo	Kh. er-Ribba; *H. Ribbo*	
717	160-277	Rosh ha-Niqra	Ras en-Naqura: vicinity; *Rosh ha-Niqra*	1023
718	200-264	Rosh Pinna	Jauna; *Rosh Pinna*	
719	177-243	Rumah	Kh. er-Ruma; *H. Ruma*	
720	086-089	er-Ruqeish, T.	T. er-Ruqeish	
721	173-255	Saab	Shaab	
722	132-113	Saalis	Kh. Umm Kalkha; *H. Shelah*	
723	192-268	Safsofah	Safsaf; *Sifsufa*	
724	181-133	St. Euthymious'	Khan el-Ahmar (Kh.)	
725	185-195	Salaba	Kh. Salhab	
726	181-179	Salem; Salim (?) *(Sam.)*	Salim	
727	199-200	Salim ? *(B-shan V.)*	T. er-Radgha/er-Ridgha; *T. Shalem*	
728	231-133	Samaga	Kh. Samik	
729	168-187	Samaria; Sebaste	Sabastiya; *Shomron*	1032
730	140-083	Sansannah	Kh. esh-Shamsanivat; *H. Sansanna*	

Section 15-2

Index of Main Names

Archaeological Periods: Chalcolithic (2-1), Early Bronze (2-2), Middle Bronze (2-3), Late Bronze (2-4), Iron I (2-5), Iron II (2-6), Persian (2-7), Hellenistic (2-8), Herodian (2-9), Roman-Byz. (2-10)

Early Bronze (3-1) | Middle & Late Bronze – Canaanite (4-1 – 4-9) | Late Bronze – Israelite Conquest (5-1 – 5-6) | Iron I – Settlement & Judges (6-1 – 6-7) | Iron II – Samuel & United Monarchy (7-1 – 7-7) | Iron II – Divided Kingdom A (8-1 – 8-8) | Iron II – Divided Kingdom B (9-1 – 9-7) | Persian (10-1 – 10-2) | Hellenistic – Hellenistic & Hasmonean (11-1 – 11-13) | Herodian – Herodian (12-1 – 12-13) | Roman & Byz. – Roman & Byz. (13-1 – 13-5)

Mini Archive Reference No.	Grid Reference Israel/Palestine Grid	Main Name	Modern Name (Arabic; *Hebrew*)	Encycl. Arch. Excav. in Holy Land Page Ref. No.
731	173-195	Sanur	Sanur	
732	122-123	Sapheir	es-Sawafir el-Gharbiya; *Merkaz Shapira*	
733	155-146	Sappho	Saffa	
734	106-114	Sarafia	Kh. esh-Sharaf (Kh. Ashraf)	
735	172-229	Sarid	T. Shadud; *T. Shaddud*	
736	194-235	Sarona, H.	Kh. Sarona; *H. Sarona*	
737	202-029	Sartha	Sari	
738	187-270	Sasa	Sasa; *Sasa*	
739	198-237	Sayydatah	Kh. es-Seiyada; *H. Zedata*	
740	105-095	Seana	Kh. Sihan; *T. Shihan*	
741	187-125	Secacah ?	Kh. es-Samra	269
742	205-020	Sela	es-Sela	
743	185-254	Selame	Kh. es-Sallama; *H. Zalmon*	
744	222-267	Seleucia ? *(Golan)*	Saluqiya	
745	203-236	Sennabris ?	Sinn en-Nabra	
746	160-185	Sepher	Sefarin	
747	196-263	Sepph	Safad; *Zefat*	
748	176-239	Sepphoris; Diocaesarea	Saffuriya; *Zippori*	1051
749	197-239	Sergunin	Kh. Sarjuna	
750	136-151	Serifin	Sarafand el-Amr; *H. Zerifin*	
751	148-141	Shaalbim	Salbit; *T. Shaalevim*	1070
752	145-124	Shaaraim ?	Kh. esh-Sharia	
753	093-097	Sharuhen ?	T. el-Ajjul	52
754	158-265	Shave(i) Ziyyon	Kh. el-Mallaha; *Shave Ziyyon*	311
755	176-179	Shechem	T. el-Balata	1083
756	166-245	Shefaram	Shafa Amr; *Shefaram*	
757	182-260	Shezor	Sajur	
758	132-136	Shikkeron	T. el-Ful	
759	177-162	Shiloh	Kh. Seilun	1098
760	170-234	Shimron; Simonias	Kh. Sammuniya; *T. Shimron*	
761	207-224	esh-Shuna, T.	T. esh-Shuna	656
762	181-223	Shunem	Sulam	
763	213-251	Shuqayyif	Shuqayyif, Masharfawi	
764	204-264	Shurah, H.	Kh. Shura; *H. Shura*	
765	150-218	Sindenon	Wadi Sindiyana	
766	163-110	Sior	Siir	
767	157-186	Siphtan ?	Shufah	
768	214-245	Skoufiye	Skufiya	
769	126-091	Sobila	Kh. ez-Zubala	
770	189-968	Sobora	es-Sabre	
771	147-121	Soc(h)oh *(Sheph.)*	Kh. Abbad (Kh. Shuweika); *H. Sokho*	
772	150-090	Soc(h)oh *(Jud.)*	Kh. Shuweika	
773	153-194	Soc(h)oh *(Sharon)*	Shuweika (er-Ras)	
774	197-952	Sodocartha	es-Sadaqa	
775	177-252	Sogane *(L. Gal.)*	Sakhnin	
776	216-260	Sogane *(Golan)*	Yahudiya	
777	143-190	Soran	Kh. Umm Sur; *T. Zoran*	
778	145-131	Sorech	Kh. es-Sureik; *Kefar Soreq*	
779	114-032	Soubaita	Isbeita, Subeita; *H. Shivta*	1116
780	208-178	Succoth	T. Deir Alla	321
781	178-267	Suhmata	Suhmata	312
782	154-230	Summaqa, Kh.	Kh. Summaqa; *H. Sumaq*	1136
783	159-090	Suseya/Susiya, Kh.	Kh. Suseya/Susiya	1124
784	146-247	Sycaminum	T. es-Samak; *T. Shiqmona*	1101
785	177-180	Sychar	Askar	
786	090-091	Sycomazon	Kh. Suq Mazen	
787	170-214	Taanach	T. Tiinnik	1138
788	185-175	Taanath-shiloh	Kh. Tana el-Fauqa	
789	186-232	Tabor, Mt.; Itabyrium	Jebel et-Tur; *Har Tavor*	
790	173-024	Tamar	Ein Husb; *Mezad Hazeva*	
791	217-042	et-Tannur, Kh.	Kh. et-Tannur	1152
792	188-288	Taphnith	Tibnin	
793	172-168	Tappuah	Sh. Abu Zarad	
794	173-226	Tarbenet	Kh. Tarbana; *H. Tarbenet*	
795	198-247	Taricheae; Magdala	Majdal	
796	170-115	Tekoa *(Jud.)*	Kh. et-Tuqu	
797	191-264	Tekoa ? *(U. Gal.)*	Kh. Shama; *H. Shema*	1094
798	197-971	Teman ?	Tuwilan	
799	173-048	Thamara ?	Qasr el-Juheiniya; *Mezad Tamar*	1148
800	154-122	Thamnatha ?	Kh. et-Tabbana; *H. Tivna*	
801	185-192	Thebez	Tubas	
802	208-272	Thella	Tuleil	
803	204-993	Theman ?	esh-Shobek	

Section 15-2

Index of Main Names

Mini Archive Reference No.	Grid Reference Israel/Palestine Grid	Main Name	Modern Name (Arabic; *Hebrew*)	Encycl. Arch. Excav. in Holy Land Page Ref. No.
804	145-184	Theraspis	Kh. Deir Isfin	
805	219-018	Thoana	Kh. Tuwane	
806	219-064	Thona ?	eth-Theniya	
807	201-242	Tiberias	Tabariya; *Teverya*	1171
808	151-185	Tibetah	et-Taiyiba	
809	162-236	Tibon	Tabun; *Tivon*	
810	145-910	Timnah *(Arabah)*	Wadi Meneiya	1184
811	141-132	Timnah *(Sheph.)*	T. el-Batashi; *T. Batash*	1204
812	160-157	Timnath-serah; Thamna	Kh. Tibnah	
813	176-178	Tirathana ?	Dawarta, Duwara	
814	182-188	Tirzah; Aenon (?)	T. el-Fara(h) (North)	395
815	166-141	To Ennaton	Kh. Latatin	
816	189-026	Toloha	Qasr et-Tlah	
817	208-027	Tophel ?	et-Tafila	
818	171-138	To Tetarton	Kh. Hawanit	
819	151-109	Tricomias	Tarqumiya	
820	161-035	Tsafir	*Tsafir*	
821	185-218	Tubani	Ein Tabun	
822	185-242	Turan?	Turan	
823	177-186	Tur Lozah	Talluza	
824	177-160	Tur Shimeon	Turmus Aiya	
825	168-297	Tyre *(Phoenicia)*	es-Sur, Sour	
826	221-147	Tyre of Tobiah; Tyrus	Iraq el-Emir	527
827	197-230	Ullama	Ulam	
828	219-250	Umm el-Qanatir	Umm el-Qanatir	1137
829	172-117	Umm Qatafa Cave	Umm Qatafa Cave	658
830	163-244	Ushah	Kh. Hosha; *H. Usha*	
831	170-293	Usu	T. Rashidiya	
832	164-257	Uza, H.	Kh. el-Aiyadiya; *H. Uza*	
833	220-240	Yaarut	Kh. el-Arayis	
834	236-139	Yaduda	Yaduda	
835	153-197	Yaham	Kh. Yamma; *Yaham*	
836	172-168	Yashub ?	Yasuf	
837	181-284	Yattir	Yatir	
838	176-189	Yazith	Yasid	
839	202-232	Yenoam	el-Ubeidiya; *T. Ovadya*	
840	189-276	Yiron	Yarun	
841	176-275	Yoqereth	Iqrit	408
842	097-088	Yurza ?	T. Jamma; *T. Gamma*	545
843	188-021	Zalmonah ?	es-Salmana	
844	150-125	Zanoah	Kh. Zanu; *H. Zanoah*	
845	208-182	Zaphon ?; Amathus	T. Amtah	
846	204-186	Zaphon; Zarethan ?	T. es-Saidiya	1028
847	205-172	Zarethan ?	T. Umm Hamad	
848	179-085	Zeelim N. (Caves)	Wadi Saiyal; *Nahal Zeelim*	673
849	155-199	Zeitah	Zeita	
850	238-236	Zeizin	Zeizun	
851	170-146	Zemaraim ?	Ras et-Tahuna	
852	170-269	Zenitah	Kh. Zuweinita; *H. Bet Zeneta*	
853	150-215	Zephath	Kh. es-Sitt Leila; *T. Zafi*	
854	159-161	Zeredah	Deir Ghassana	
855	203-111	Zereth-shahar?	ez-Zarat	
856	217-166	Zia	Kh. Zey	
857	119-088	Ziklag ?	T. esh-Sharia; *T. Sera*	1059
858	162-098	Ziph	T. Zif	
859	163-098	Ziph	Kh. Zif	
860	124-118	Zippor, T.	T. et-Tuyur; *T. Zippor*	1111
861	240-123	Ziza	Zuweiza	
862	194-049	Zoar(a)	es-Safi	
863	162-132	Zobah ?	Suba; *Zova*	
864	148-131	Zorah	Sara; *T. Zora*	
865	160-227	ha-Zorea (T. Qiri)	T. Qiri; *ha-Zorea (T. Qiri)*	

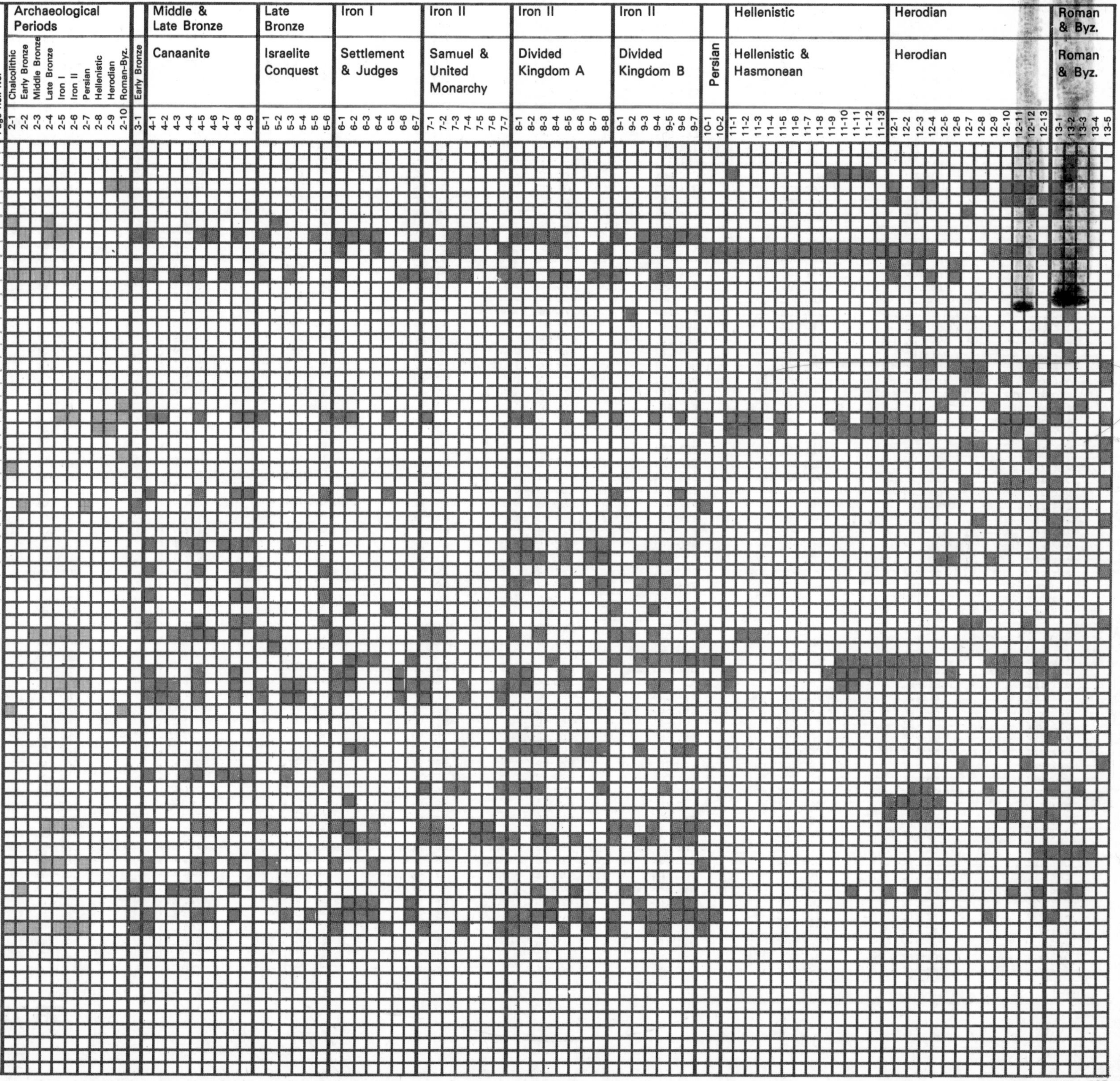

Archaeological Periods
Chalcolithic 2-1
Early Bronze 2-2
Middle Bronze 2-3
Late Bronze 2-4
Iron I 2-5
Iron II 2-6
Persian 2-7
Hellenistic 2-8
Herodian 2-9
Roman-Byz. 2-10
Early Bronze 3-1
Middle & Late Bronze
Canaanite
4-1 4-2 4-3 4-4 4-5 4-6 4-7 4-8 4-9
Late Bronze
Israelite Conquest
5-1 5-2 5-3 5-4 5-5 5-6
Iron I
Settlement & Judges
6-1 6-2 6-3 6-4 6-5 6-6 6-7
Iron II
Samuel & United Monarchy
7-1 7-2 7-3 7-4 7-5 7-6 7-7
Iron II
Divided Kingdom A
8-1 8-2 8-3 8-4 8-5 8-6 8-7 8-8
Iron II
Divided Kingdom B
9-1 9-2 9-3 9-4 9-5 9-6 9-7
Persian
10-1 10-2
Hellenistic
Hellenistic & Hasmonean
11-1 11-2 11-3 11-4 11-5 11-6 11-7 11-8 11-9 11-10 11-11 11-12 11-13
Herodian
Herodian
12-1 12-2 12-3 12-4 12-5 12-6 12-7 12-8 12-9 12-10 12-11 12-12 12-13
Roman & Byz.
Roman & Byz.
13-1 13-2 13-3 13-4 13-5

Section 15-3

Index of Grid References

Cross reference to column one Index of Main Names

705 077-079	116 131-159	778 145-131	636 153-112	253 162-092	825 168-297	414 174-243	018 182-170	449 191-010	718 200-264	314 212-232	290 224-101
114 085-010	608 131-174	216 145-145	217 153-140	658 162-095	194 169-123	514 174-246	814 182-188	472 191-139	502 200-279	042 212-236	648 224-248
720 086-089	073 131-178	395 145-148	191 153-160	858 162-098	135 169-137	184 175-126	361 182-239	667 191-159	663 200-958	512 212-240	074 225-098
288 088-093	668 132-110	405 145-152	773 153-194	162 162-107	307 169-144	153 175-130	359 182-250	522 191-238	649 201-059	434 212-242	584 225-124
500 089-007	722 132-113	354 145-173	835 153-197	442 162-124	107 169-146	330 175-131	757 182-260	570 191-251	581 201-078	111 212-247	432 226-134
786 090-091	758 132-136	220 145-182	229 153-203	176 162-126	327 169-185	371 175-140	235 182-978	797 191-264	157 201-138	030 212-266	409 226-213
172 090-092	399 132-164	804 145-184	631 153-206	863 162-132	066 169-243	166 175-141	597 183-062	590 191-265	019 201-167	276 212-272	257 226-250
606 090-096	366 132-166	231 145-191	210 154-105	538 162-179	526 169-250	039 175-145	579 183-080	397 191-270	132 201-210	106 213-109	686 227-281
587 093-082	142 133-160	524 145-215	800 154-122	302 162-227	185 169-264	063 175-166	461 183-172	591 191-278	515 201-240	763 213-251	258 227-298
753 093-097	136 134-072	256 145-234	260 154-132	151 162-234	607 169-274	529 175-168	158 183-208	534 192-032	411 201-241	096 213-263	089 228-097
542 094-954	169 134-156	585 145-236	249 154-145	809 162-236	085 169-944	600 175-176	326 183-217	676 192-039	807 201-242	183 214-136	049 228-116
643 095-031	143 134-166	012 145-884	363 154-200	520 162-242	496 170-070	553 175-178	630 183-226	473 192-142	430 201-253	010 214-138	309 228-136
492 096-006	543 135-108	810 145-910	598 154-205	675 162-884	796 170-115	634 175-180	331 183-236	416 192-223	638 201-992	565 214-177	007 228-142
297 096-093	364 135-123	438 146-096	782 154-230	595 163-038	179 170-127	423 175-184	332 183-237	513 192-245	737 202-029	453 214-201	452 228-150
567 096-104	674 135-185	248 146-142	025 154-921	087 163-097	023 170-139	440 175-252	320 184-067	723 192-268	124 202-074	352 214-229	566 228-177
842 097-088	509 136-119	244 146-146	072 155-098	859 163-098	105 170-142	160 175-259	444 184-125	710 192-971	839 202-232	700 214-237	345 228-262
062 098-105	304 136-131	523 146-150	318 155-126	766 163-110	611 170-143	048 176-136	298 184-162	685 193-127	544 202-233	768 214-245	164 229-218
147 099-022	750 136-151	635 146-154	733 155-146	080 163-132	148 170-146	599 176-142	463 184-173	182 193-140	503 202-237	497 214-253	250 230-222
367 099-101	327 137-086	071 146-165	849 155-199	316 163-138	851 170-146	813 176-178	076 184-213	474 193-140	419 202-277	533 215-105	486 230-259
344 100-076	402 137-087	296 146-167	571 156-048	093 163-169	401 170-152	385 176-179	530 184-252	394 193-143	855 203-111	201 215-133	622 231-044
095 100-104	355 137-130	251 146-169	061 156-084	830 163-244	787 170-214	755 176-179	696 184-260	046 193-167	033 203-138	664 215-177	728 231-133
152 102-075	389 137-140	236 146-177	336 156-089	223 163-275	351 170-231	838 176-189	285 185-097	020 193-239	009 203-197	693 215-182	480 231-159
422 103-000	654 137-159	368 146-228	245 156-141	494 164-100	760 170-234	465 176-232	624 185-110	022 193-239	386 203-225	282 215-269	004 231-231
437 104-017	120 138-043	784 146-247	118 156-148	665 164-119	491 170-252	748 176-239	788 185-175	021 193-245	278 203-228	234 215-294	187 232-071
740 105-095	418 138-043	469 147-107	443 156-236	273 164-230	873 170-269	484 176-248	170 185-177	862 194-049	505 203-233	310 216-034	267 232-076
227 106-074	340 138-113	771 147-121	507 157-093	083 164-236	831 170-293	841 176-275	801 185-192	082 194-150	745 203-236	620 216-055	556 232-137
734 106-114	139 139-109	467 147-124	350 157-120	408 164-241	644 171-119	659 177-137	725 185-195	563 194-152	264 203-257	070 216-242	284 232-210
100 107-118	470 139-159	198 147-128	767 157-186	609 164-253	168 171-122	121 177-153	821 185-218	270 194-201	424 203-269	776 216-260	568 232-237
457 107-119	485 139-878	602 147-203	092 157-212	832 164-257	603 171-123	824 177-160	274 185-233	057 194-228	510 203-294	681 216-266	488 233-011
709 108-048	730 140-083	583 147-223	677 157-258	174 164-263	818 171-138	759 177-162	822 185-242	736 194-235	626 204-076	052 216-267	501 233-104
657 108-086	604 140-105	254 147-244	489 158-095	490 164-268	117 171-183	109 177-174	743 185-254	103 195-010	846 204-186	791 217-042	383 234-187
128 110-114	577 140-111	342 147-884	374 158-115	671 164-276	369 171-192	456 177-179	171 185-263	346 195-038	211 204-235	035 217-064	557 234-246
379 112-087	218 140-112	088 148-062	188 158-144	413 164-281	464 171-210	785 177-180	646 186-123	008 195-192	240 204-254	535 217-066	691 234-262
159 113-092	618 140-114	471 148-071	243 158-153	702 165-068	640 171-255	823 177-186	321 186-227	081 195-246	764 204-264	560 217-077	177 235-099
779 114-032	398 140-145	295 148-093	016 158-240	242 165-102	829 172-117	140 177-199	789 186-232	441 195-254	005 204-296	219 217-154	222 235-132
670 114-081	550 140-151	716 148-118	376 158-247	178 165-130	593 172-126	445 177-205	115 186-237	263 196-163	803 204-993	856 217-166	299 235-239
653 114-102	233 140-212	864 148-131	015 158-258	317 165-133	329 172-130	655 177-223	198 186-248	481 196-170	742 205-020	333 217-216	269 235-249
099 114-132	613 141-004	751 148-141	754 158-265	621 165-134	475 172-131	719 177-243	420 187-019	325 196-232	714 205-038	287 217-252	458 236-110
554 114-989	200 141-079	519 148-169	783 159-090	024 165-161	390 172-136	775 177-252	324 187-096	323 196-235	847 205-172	673 218-130	834 236-139
232 116-108	138 141-096	477 149-076	425 159-103	311 165-177	697 172-140	707 177-280	741 187-125	747 196-263	521 205-234	037 218-192	689 238-151
252 116-135	619 141-115	195 149-122	214 159-110	672 165-177	173 172-148	713 178-148	097 187-194	225 196-265	150 206-131	131 218-199	850 238-236
313 117-056	811 141-132	688 149-137	539 159-135	104 165-192	793 172-168	656 178-151	221 187-197	047 196-273	349 207-054	495 218-221	400 238-243
393 117-081	246 141-177	315 149-138	358 159-154	215 165-211	836 172-168	181 178-207	641 187-224	678 197-004	123 207-113	275 218-268	649 239-028
098 117-129	429 141-197	615 149-148	203 159-160	528 165-262	294 172-202	633 178-234	540 187-229	186 197-136	388 207-135	805 219-018	588 239-140
617 117-136	271 141-216	661 149-152	854 159-161	001 165-272	735 172-229	498 178-247	041 187-249	163 197-139	662 207-206	806 219-064	861 240-123
857 119-088	616 142-074	406 149-248	065 159-226	338 166-120	564 172-233	237 178-264	698 187-259	196 197-192	551 207-219	167 219-120	537 241-233
380 119-933	448 142-113	772 150-090	372 159-237	815 166-141	364 172-264	781 178-267	738 187-270	410 197-197	761 207-224	451 219-156	101 243-244
596 120-146	387 142-140	531 150-113	629 159-267	090 166-161	421 172-896	499 178-290	843 188-021	708 197-207	028 207-971	334 219-200	701 244-210
129 121-131	704 142-161	029 150-117	017 159-272	576 166-228	790 173-024	848 179-085	601 188-127	206 197-212	360 207-975	828 219-250	632 248-255
459 121-147	426 142-204	652 150-118	572 160-107	756 166-245	799 173-048	666 179-138	580 188-243	827 197-230	230 208-016	357 219-256	[redacted]
732 122-123	293 142-224	844 150-125	407 160-109	706 166-256	431 173-119	141 179-155	051 188-246	749 197-239	817 208-027	493 219-274	
036 123-108	381 142-942	614 150-148	639 160-121	506 166-264	202 173-131	703 179-236	582 188-255	014 197-260	190 208-132	690 220-075	
300 124-106	559 143-084	853 150-215	013 160-134	415 166-276	647 173-134	712 179-243	003 188-279	517 197-267	780 208-178	536 220-128	
860 124-118	053 143-089	765 150-218	259 160-137	612 166-995	545 173-164	561 179-272	792 188-288	279 197-269	845 208-182	637 220-131	
403 124-973	301 143-099	308 150-882	189 160-143	102 167-110	731 173-195	356 180-164	816 189-026	774 197-952	412 208-208	375 220-160	
623 125-147	146 143-129	468 151-084	812 160-157	339 167-121	794 173-226	382 180-167	265 189-139	798 197-971	204 208-255	833 220-240	
769 126-091	145 143-151	286 151-093	746 160-185	122 167-127	268 173-248	091 180-172	447 189-195	353 197-973	291 208-258	305 220-245	
454 126-141	067 143-168	238 151-099	865 160-227	573 167-129	721 173-255	126 180-185	377 189-207	569 198-170	802 208-272	555 220-956	
483 126-162	777 143-190	819 151-109	482 160-230	134 167-136	180 173-258	261 180-232	427 189-236	373 198-219	558 209-108	281 221-087	
628 127-101	516 143-195	645 151-110	428 160-232	391 167-137	462 173-265	002 180-235	511 189-258	527 198-233	175 209-145	826 221-147	
094 128-006	594 143-215	466 151-130	348 160-236	392 167-139	378 173-273	365 180-238	149 189-259	455 198-235	487 209-257	669 221-293	
651 128-022	417 144-177	335 151-132	155 160-241	247 167-140	058 174-131	050 180-929	508 189-272	739 198-237	692 209-262	026 222-068	
137 128-070	112 144-123	079 151-159	068 160-250	541 167-182	127 174-133	610 181-088	840 189-276	137 198-243	283 209-292	546 222-112	
133 128-071	255 144-124	205 151-168	341 160-266	525 167-191	059 174-135	433 181-093	770 189-968	795 198-247	011 210-139	322 222-193	
312 128-144	165 144-155	808 151-185	820 161-035	343 167-198	060 174-135	578 181-123	272 190-139	460 198-266	199 210-146	744 222-267	
156 129-071	687 144-167	077 152-069	532 161-083	239 167-220	113 174-137	724 181-133	292 190-142	032 199-199	069 210-243	277 222-996	
084 129-113	605 144-231	027 152-101	212 161-114	586 167-221	038 174-147	726 181-179	625 190-144	727 199-200	384 210-248	446 223-041	
504 129-136	108 144-234	064 152-137	213 161-118	435 167-236	476 174-156	479 181-218	154 190-213	711 199-221	056 210-286	289 223-045	
119 129-138	054 145-091	040 152-138	683 161-126	642 168-133	370 174-158	762 181-223	552 190-242	209 199-232	439 211-055	450 223-107	
684 129-167	306 145-109	224 152-190	110 161-153	228 168-152	266 174-171	125 181-264	518 190-245	694 199-245	549 211-137	627 223-123	
404 129-958	241 145-113	478 152-194	031 161-157	729 168-187	436 174-173	208 181-271	660 190-259	682 199-272	130 211-256	699 223-169	
226 130-072	547 145-116	337 152-209	055 161-190	193 168-238	592 174-202	044 181-278	589 190-275	144 200-060	280 211-294	715 223-215	
680 130-167	562 145-116	548 152-245	078 162-076	006 168-247	396 174-229	837 181-284	161 190-289	650 200-232	086 212-014	043 224-042	
575 131-102	752 145-124	192 153-107	574 162-090	347 168-268	045 174-235	303 182-155	695 190-887	262 200-252	034 212-037	075 224-076	